NATIONAL GEOGRAPHIC
TRAVELER
Australia

D0051557

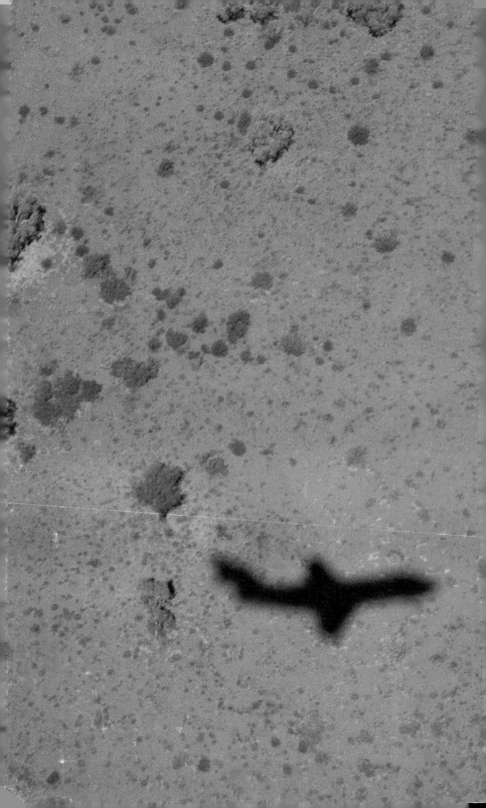

NATIONAL GEOGRAPHIC

TRAVELER
Australia

Roff Martin Smith

Contents

How to use this guide 6–7 About the author 8
The regions 73–354 Travelwise 355–87
Index 388–97 Credits 398–99

Page 1: Aboriginal bark
painting
Pages 2–3: The Red Centre
near Alice Springs
Left: Beach shacks near
Melbourne

How to use this guide

See back flap for keys to text and map symbols.

The *National Geographic Traveler* brings you the best of Australia in text, pictures, and maps. Divided into three main sections, the guide begins with an overview of history and culture. Following are nine regional chapters with featured sites selected by the author for their particular interest. Each chapter opens with its own contents list.

The regions and sites within the regions are arranged geographically. Some regions are further divided into smaller areas. A map introduces each region, highlighting the featured sites. Walks and drives, plotted on their own maps, suggest routes for discovering an area. Features and sidebars give intriguing detail on history, culture, and contemporary life.

The final section, Travelwise, lists essential information for the traveler—pre-trip planning, getting around, communications, money matters, and emergencies—plus a selection of hotels, restaurants, shops, and activities.

To the best of our knowledge, all information is accurate as of the press date. However, it's always advisable to call ahead when possible.

Floors We have used the Australian convention when referring to the floors of a building. Hence, in this book ground floor refers to the first floor, the first floor refers to the second, and so on.
Metric measurements In this book metric equivalents are given in parentheses after imperial measurements.

130

Color coding
Each region is color coded for easy reference. Find the region you want on the map on the front flap, and look for the color flash at the top of the pages of the relevant chapter. Information in **Travelwise** is also color coded to each region.

Taronga Park Zoo
⬛ 75 E3
✉ Bradleys Head Road, Mosman
☎ (02) 9978 4786
🕐 Closed some Mon.
💲 $$$
⛴ Ferry from Circular Quay

Visitor information
Practical information for most sites is given in the side column (see key to symbols on back flap). The map reference gives the page number of the map and grid reference. Other details are address, telephone number, days closed, entrance charge in a range from $ (under $4) to $$$$$ (over $25), and nearest train station for sites in Sydney. Other sites have information in italics and parentheses in the text.

TRAVELWISE

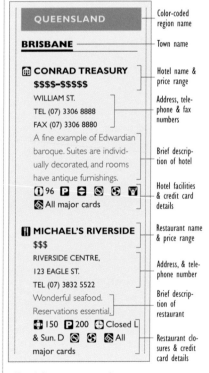

QUEENSLAND — Color-coded region name

BRISBANE — Town name

🏨 **CONRAD TREASURY**
$$$$–$$$$$ — Hotel name & price range

WILLIAM ST. — Address, telephone & fax numbers
TEL (07) 3306 8888
FAX (07) 3306 8880

A fine example of Edwardian baroque. Suites are individually decorated, and rooms have antique furnishings. — Brief description of hotel

🛈 96 🅿 🔄 🕿 ☎ 🎾 — Hotel facilities & credit card details
🚫 All major cards

🍴 **MICHAEL'S RIVERSIDE** — Restaurant name & price range
$$$

RIVERSIDE CENTRE, 123 EAGLE ST. — Address, & telephone number
TEL (07) 3832 5522

Wonderful seafood. Reservations essential. — Brief description of restaurant

🍴 150 🅿 200 🕐 Closed L & Sun. D 🔄 🕿 🚫 All major cards — Restaurant closures & credit card details

Hotel & restaurant prices
An explanation of the price bands used in entries is given in the Hotels & Restaurants section (beginning on p. 367).

REGIONAL MAPS

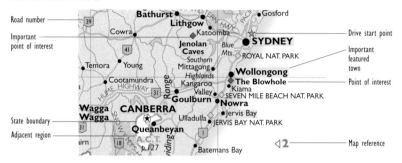

Road number

Important point of interest

State boundary

Adjacent region

Drive start point

Important featured town

Point of interest

Map reference

- A locator map accompanies each regional map and shows the location of that region in the country.
- Adjacent regions are shown, each with a page reference.

WALKING TOURS

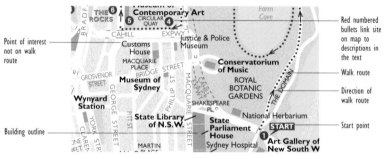

Point of interest not on walk route

Building outline

Red numbered bullets link site on map to descriptions in the text

Walk route

Direction of walk route

Start point

- An information box gives the starting and ending points, time and length of walk, and places not to be missed along the route.
- Where two walks are marked on the map, the second route is shown in orange.

DRIVING TOURS

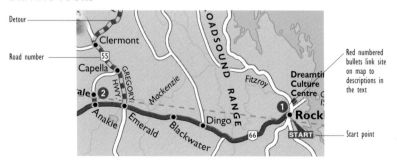

Detour

Road number

Red numbered bullets link site on map to descriptions in the text

Start point

- An information box provides details including starting and finishing points, time and length of drive, places not to be missed along the route, and tips on terrain.

NATIONAL GEOGRAPHIC

TRAVELER

Australia

About the author

Originally a New England Yankee, Roff Smith has lived most of his adult life in Australia, since arriving down under as a 23-year-old geology graduate in 1982. After quickly deciding that writing and travel were more enjoyable pursuits than cracking rocks, he began work as a journalist for the *Sydney Morning Herald* and later as a feature writer for Melbourne's *Sunday Age*. He joined *Time Magazine* in 1993, and as an award-winning senior writer he covered stories around Australia and as far afield as New Guinea, French Polynesia, and Antarctica.

In 1996, to try to get a feel for the country he had lived in so long but never came to know, Roff set off alone into the Australian Outback on a 10,000-mile bicycle trek. Over the next nine months he stayed at remote sheep and cattle stations, old pearling ports, mining towns, Aboriginal communities, quiet rain forest villages, occasional big cities, and many solitary desert campsites, some 100 miles from the nearest dwelling. The story of his journey appeared as a three-part series in NATIONAL GEOGRAPHIC, and is described in more detail in *Cold Beer and Crocodiles: A Bicycle Journey into Australia,* published in 2000 by National Geographic Adventure Press. In 1999 his book *Australia: Journey Through a Timeless Land* was published by NATIONAL GEOGRAPHIC. Roff now lives in South Australia, where he freelances for a number of international magazines and publications, including NATIONAL GEOGRAPHIC.

History
& culture

**A northwest Aborigine
dances at a corroboree.**

Australia today

AUSTRALIA HAS INTRIGUED THE REST OF THE WORLD FOR MORE THAN TWO centuries, with its fantastic marsupials, noisy and colorful birds, and the incredibly vast sweeps of outback landscape. It is home to one of the world's oldest human cultures. Aborigines came here by rafts and little boats from Asian archipelagos more than 50,000 years ago. It was a period known to them as the Dreamtime, and the magical events of that time are celebrated with an elaborate cycle of songs, and enshrined in rock paintings and engravings found in thousands of rock shelters and caves throughout the country.

Australia is a geological marvel as well, famous for the haunting monolith of Uluru, the tropical wetlands of Kakadu, and of course the magnificent Great Barrier Reef. It is the world's smallest continent and its largest island, a 2.9-million-square-mile (7.5 million-sq-km) landmass that went walkabout 65 million years ago to peaceful isolation in the South Pacific. Some of the world's most ancient landscapes are found here, dating back more than 3.5 billion years. Living examples of the world's earliest life-forms, stromatolites, can still be found on the rocks along the shore of Hamelin Bay, in Western Australia. Primitive cycad palms are found nestled in gorges in the heart of the outback. In 1994 a living specimen of Wollemi pine—an ancient species of tree dated to the age of dinosaurs and previously known only through fossils— was found in a dense forest close to Sydney.

Fascination has drawn visitors here as tourists for more than 160 years. Charles Darwin remarked on Sydney's high real estate prices when he passed through in 1836. English novelist Anthony Trollope was enamored with the high Victorian architecture in the gold rush town of Ballarat. Mark Twain marveled at Tasmania's paradoxical beauty and its violent, sordid history. The millions of visitors who come through the turnstiles here today come to experience Australia's sunny beach-loving lifestyle: Sydney's Opera House and Bondi Beach, Melbourne's bustling restaurant scene, the theme parks along Queensland's Gold Coast, and Adelaide's festivals and wine country of the Barossa Valley.

Thankfully Australia is far more accessible now than it was in the days of steamers and the Qantas Empire flying boats that made the journey from London to Sydney's Rose Bay in "just" five days. But it is still a marathon journey: about a 15-hour flight non-stop from Los Angeles and 24 hours from London. Jet-lagged travelers step off the plane in another time, another day, and in another season. The stars are strange and new, the Australian bush has a bracing, spicy tang, and even in the city a traveler can wake to the raucous screeches of cockatoos. Thankfully, in a world grown small, Australia is still tinged with the romance of distance.

THE REAL AUSTRALIA

In my wild erratic fancy visions come to me of
*   Clancy;*
Gone a-droving 'down the Cooper' where the
*   western drovers go;*
As the stock are slowly swinging, Clancy rides
*   behind them singing;*
For the drover's life has pleasures that the towns-
*   folk never know.*
—From *Clancy of the Overflow* by Andrew Barton "Banjo" Patterson

Ask any Australian where the real Australia is, and chances are he or she will point you toward a broad immensity of dust and sky, while sketching a verbal portrait of a sun-bronzed stockman with a tattered Akubra hat nudging a mob of sheep along a gum-shaded lane. It's a lovely, picturesque fancy, but it just isn't so. The truth of the matter is that the real Australia is a sprawl of terra-cotta roofs in the suburbs. Typical Australians work in offices, pushing bureaucratic pens, and they did even in 1891 when Banjo Patterson wrote his much-loved bush classic, *Clancy of the Overflow.*

Ninety percent of Aussies live in cities or towns on the coast, usually within a 30-minute

Great surfing waves roll onto many of Australia's beaches such as Sydney's Bondi.

drive of the nearest beach. This is one of the most suburbanized societies on Earth. Aussie children grow up between the surf-lifesaving flags, walking sidewalks bright with Lebanese, Chinese, Italian, Greek, and Vietnamese shops, and dodging city traffic. They aspire to a brick veneer home in a comfortable suburb, ideally one with a quarter-acre (0.1 ha) backyard, a Hills Hoist (an ingenious Australian clothesline), and a barbecue. Although real estate is expensive—hideously so in Sydney—more than 70 percent of Australians are paying off home mortgages. They have the highest rate of home ownership in the world, and they like to keep their places spruced up. One of the most popular programs on Australian TV is *Burke's Backyard*, a cheerfully middle class do-it-yourself show full of gardening tips, home care advice, remodeling ideas, and interviews with celebrities in their gardens.

Cities tend to sprawl outward (rather than upward in high-rise tenements) because

Australians all want that suburban quarter-acre plot. Sydney's metropolitan sprawl spreads almost as wide as Los Angeles's. There are tough neighborhoods, but few slums. Sydney's Redfern is about the closest thing Australia has to the South Bronx. By and large this is a safe country, with a murder rate of 1.9 in 100,000 population—about half that of Switzerland.

Australians tend to be loyal to their home cities, generally spending their lives and careers close to the neighborhood where they

The lights of Sydney's glittering skyline reflect in the waters of its famous harbor.

grew up. Although shopping malls, American fast-food chains, and supermarkets are making huge inroads, a lot of shopping in country towns and inner cities is still done the old-fashioned way: People walk along a main street and dip into the butcher's, the baker's, the fishmonger's, and the greengrocer's shop. Or they visit a bustling market, where vendors

shout and thrifty shoppers come near closing time to haggle over prices.

This is an easygoing, generally permissive society, with a belief that everybody ought to have a "fair go" at leading life the way they see fit. Despite the presence of more than 160 different nationalities, everyone gets along pretty well down here. Sydney has a higher percentage of gay people than San Francisco, and its Gay and Lesbian Mardi Gras is the single biggest fete in Australia, attracting crowds of over 500,000—gay and straight—from around the country and overseas.

Surveys show that three-quarters of Australians believe in God, but on a typical Sunday morning only 22 percent will be in church. Most will be sleeping late, or nursing their second espresso while they peruse a weekend newspaper, or they will be gearing up to play (or watch) some kind of sport. This is a nation of weekend warriors. Flick on the TV news Saturday or Sunday evening and you'll see a litany of horse-race results, footy or cricket highlights, and sporting news from overseas, often followed by reports of the helicopter rescue of a hiker from the bottom of a gorge, or a Jet Ski collision, or a fisherman swept off a rock by a "freak" wave of the sort that claimed another life at that very spot the previous week.

Weekends and vacations are the only times most Australians ever actually visit the "bush," the Australian term for countrified landscapes. Even then they are mighty particular where they go. Kakadu, Uluru, the Great Barrier Reef, the Flinders Ranges, and the Snowy Mountains (for skiing) are favorites. Or maybe day trips to the Dandenong Ranges, if one lives in Melbourne, or the Blue Mountains, near Sydney.

Adventurous young Aussies usually head for Europe when they want to do some wandering, but a few go to the gold mines or the remote iron-ore ports on Australia's northwest coast. They earn big money for a couple of years and then get back to their hometowns. Adventurous retirees sometimes haul their caravans on a several-month loop around the

Massive trucks known as road trains, such as this one hauling iron ore, are the lifelines of the outback.

continent. But by and large, Australians are content to let the bush remain a comfortably distant place, something from the pages of Henry Lawson or Banjo Patterson (see p. 54). (see p. 54) Go to a suburban footy match on a rainy winter's day in Melbourne, and a lot of the crowd will be wearing Driza-bones, the traditional stockman's oilskin. In the parking lot will be gleaming, fully-equipped Range Rovers with four-wheel-drive, kangaroo (bull) bars, and cellular phones. It's not that Australians don't love their bush; they treasure it deeply. But they prefer to live in the city or suburbs.

THE OUTBACK & ITS STATIONS

When you talk to graziers in the Outback, and hear their descriptions of the bushfires, floods, and droughts that ravage their properties in a seemingly endless cycle, it's easy to understand why most Australians prefer the comfort of suburbia. The Outback landscape is often windswept and hauntingly barren. The loneliness is palpable. The nearest town might be 250 miles (400 km) away. The work is tough, dirty, and can be hazardous: Wild bulls, rolling tractors, and dirt-bike accidents during livestock musters (Aussie for "round-ups") help make farming the most dangerous occupation in Australia. The workdays are long, frequently stretching from dawn to dusk and beyond. Then an evening poring over the ledgers and often seeing red ink.

On the other hand, once you've felt the camaraderie and buzz of a woolshed at shearing time, with a team of shearers toiling like demons, family and friends pitching in as roustabouts and sorters while the smallest kids play on the wool bales, it's hard to imagine wanting anything else. The shed seems like the center of the world. Imagine being a farmer bouncing across a dusty vastness in a Land Rover with the "windmill man," inspecting the water holes on a million-acre cattle station somewhere out on the Great Sandy Desert. Nobody could seem any freer.

The Australian economy needs its 147,000 farmers, relying on them to the tune of about 20 billion Australian dollars (10 billion U.S. dollars) a year. Australia is the world's largest exporter of beef and veal, having a national herd of 25 million or so cattle. It is also a major producer of wheat. But wool is king.

Since the first merinos were introduced in 1795, Australia has built up a flock of between 120 million and 160 million sheep—the number fluctuates depending on droughts and commodity prices—and supplies about 70 percent of the wool used by the world's clothing industry. The Golden Fleece of legend seems a little less remarkable when you consider some of the ultrafine fleeces produced on specialist farms in Victoria and Tasmania. These can literally be worth more than their weight in gold and are used by top-name fashion houses for lightweight suits. Sheep that grow wool this fine (about 15 microns) are cosseted creatures that wear little coats to protect them from burrs and aren't shorn so much as given a haircut.

The rest of the nation's flock is clipped in the spring by roving teams of contract shearers. This is brutally tough and competitive work. Because shearers are paid per fleece, both money and pride rest on getting the

highest total possible in a day. A top hand (a "gun shearer" in outback parlance) will regularly shear more than 150 a day, and some do many more. Back in the 1890s, when shearers used crude iron scissorlike shears, Big Jackie Howe used to draw crowds to watch him clip 250 a day. In 1892, at Alice Downs Station in outback Queensland, he sheared a record 321 ewes in a union-prescribed working day of seven hours and forty minutes. This record has never been beaten, at least with hand-

Bouncing in the thermals of a hot outback afternoon, a grazier inspects his property from the air.

powered shears. Modern electric combs have changed things a bit. The world record is held by a New Zealander named Alan MacDonald, who sheared 805 lambs in nine hours in 1990.

Anyone who has read or watched *The Thorn Birds* (1979) knows that Australian ranches, called stations, can be vast. The

Right: A stockman nudges a mob of cattle through the scrub in a timeless scene straight out of a Banjo Patterson poem.

Below: Branding the stock is hot, hard, dusty work. Up to a dozen ringers (cowboys) work at Belgium-size Anna Creek Cattle Station.

world's largest is Anna Creek Cattle Station, owned by the long-established Kidman family, in the South Australian outback. At 7.7 million acres (about 12,030 square miles, 31,000 sq km) it is about the size of Connecticut and Massachusetts combined. The world's biggest sheep property, Commonwealth Hill, also in South Australia, covers just over 4,000 square miles (10,360 sq km) and runs 70,000 sheep. In the vastness of the Outback, particularly up in the Northern Territory or Western Australia's rugged Kimberley region, a million-acre spread is nothing unusual.

Sometimes the scale can be a little hard for visitors to comprehend. A cattleman who ran 465,000 acres (188,325 ha) in the Great Sandy Desert tells the story of how his immigrant father returned to the island off the coast of Yugoslavia where he had come from, and told relatives how, back in Australia, his son had a ranch bigger than their entire island. His brother simply shook his head and replied

very solemnly and sadly "We never thought you would come back and lie to us." But in Europe it doesn't take 50 acres (20.25 ha) to support one cow; out in the Great Sandy Desert, it does.

Station life is unique. A trip to town can mean a day-long trek in a four-wheel-drive, or a gut-churning plane ride bouncing over the thermals rising from the hot Outback scrub. Supplies come by road train, monster-size triple-trailer trucks that can be 165 feet (50 m) long and weigh 170 tons. Cattle are mustered by helicopter. Services come by air. Out here there are flying priests, taking the sacrament to stations and outlying Aboriginal communities. The Royal Flying Doctor Service, a unique Australian institution established by Presbyterian minister Rev. John Flynn in 1928, provides medical care. Station children between the ages of six and eleven attend another unique Outback institution: the School of the Air. They receive their lessons by

radio and send in their homework by mail. A couple of times a year they go into town to meet their teachers and classmates. Older kids go to boarding school.

ABORIGINES & EUROPEANS

About 300,000 Aborigines lived in Australia in 1788, when the First Fleet arrived from England and began the uneven contest for control of the continent. Actually, at first it wasn't such a one-way game. Although the soldiers had rifles, they were also starving in this strange new land, and the unwilling convict-settlers were demoralized by being so far from home. The Aborigines were home, and feasting on native foods that had sustained them for thousands of generations.

Two years after the fleet arrived, an Aboriginal leader named Pemulwuy united some of the local tribes and launched a highly effective guerrilla campaign against the invaders. Over the next 12 years he became such a

thorn in the side of the colonial authorities that large rewards were posted for his capture. A convict who grabbed him could get a pardon and passage back to England. Pemulwuy was killed in 1802, his head pickled and sent to England. Pemulwuy's son continued the resistance movement for a few more years, until the fragile alliance of tribes broke up.

Because there were so many different, widely scattered tribes—divided by about 400 languages—Aborigines had difficulty putting up a united front against the invaders. The latter soon gained the upper hand, using rifles against spears. The most appalling instances were in Tasmania, where farmers simply shot Aborigines on sight. In the 1830s the few who survived were rounded up and shipped off to Flinders Island in Bass Strait.

As settlers with their sheep and cattle pushed deeper into the continent, taking up huge swaths of land, Aborigines were pushed off to ever more remote pockets. Tribes that

had nothing in common found themselves scratching a living together on hardscrabble terrain many days' journey from their ancestral grounds. Ancient traditions and cultures built over 50,000 years crumbled and vanished.

Some Aborigines received food from church missions, others worked on the stations for the new property owners. Although raising animals and riding horses had never been part of their culture, Aborigines quickly became superb stockmen and riders. Just as Aboriginal guides enabled the early explorers to cross the deserts, so Aboriginal stockmen made it possible for the early stations to prosper. They were generally paid in food and tobacco. By the 1930s, the authorities had settled on a program of assimilation to bring half-caste Aborigines into society. One well-intentioned, but breathtakingly cruel, policy was to rob Aboriginal mothers of their babies and foster them out to white parents in the hope that perhaps the next generation would forget its Aboriginality. Incredibly, this practice went on until the 1960s. It left a ghastly legacy of broken families and heartbreak, but Aboriginal culture refused to disappear.

The 1960s were a time of radical change all over the world, including even the remotest stretches of the Outback. There were sit-ins, a prominent strike by Aborigine stockmen at the Wave Hill Cattle Station in the Northern Territory, and freedom buses traversing the Queensland Outback. Aborigines and their supporters set up a tent embassy outside Parliament House in Canberra. A constitutional referendum in 1967 gave Aborigines full Australian citizenship and voting rights. An Aboriginal flag was designed that same year. It comprised a red-and-black field with a yellow circle in the center, and has come to symbolize the struggle for land rights.

A quarter of a century passed before the next big step was taken in the recognition of Aboriginal rights. In 1992 the Australian High Court issued a landmark ruling that the continent had not, in fact, been *terra nullus* (or no-man's-land) when Captain Cook claimed it in 1770, and that the indigenous people had exercised a form of legal title and

Some Aborigines retain their ancestral skills and social structures.

had been wrongfully dispossessed. It became known as the Mabo Ruling, after Torres Straits islander Eddie Mabo, who brought the suit against the government, and it meant that Aborigines who could prove continuous contact with their land could claim vacant Crown land.

Later, in 1996, a further landmark High Court ruling, known as the Wik Decision, established that native title could coexist with mining and pastoral leases. The ruling sparked an uproar: Farmers and miners demanded legislation that would protect their rights and investments, and Aborigines insisted that the government obey the rulings of its own High Court. The debate continues, but everyone in Australia realizes that it is no longer possible to ignore the past. The Mabo and Wik rulings have forever changed the relationship between Aborigines and the people who have arrived since 1788, and put the matter of reconciliation near the top of the political agenda.

Politics and High Court rulings notwithstanding, it is still tough to be an Aborigine in Australia. Two centuries of "civilization" have been a steep downhill slide for Australia's indigenous people. The mortality and morbidity figures of Aborigines are shocking. Their infant mortality rate is triple that of non-Aboriginal Australians, and, as a killing diet of booze, drug abuse, and fast food takes its toll, their life expectancy is shorter by 15 years. Aborigines suffer from alcoholism, tuberculosis, heart disease, hepatitis, and diabetes at far higher rates than the rest of the population. Their unemployment rate is more than 50 percent and they are 16 times more likely than the rest of the Australian population to be in prison.

Statistics do not tell the whole story, though. Some Aboriginal communities have maintained deep cultural strengths, preserving their heritage with their vibrant arts and music, and matchless knowledge of the environment, and with elders who maintain strict discipline. Many of the strongest communities are to be found in remote places, out of sight of visitors who often end up with an unfair view of Aboriginal culture. Increasingly, however, these communities are cautiously opening the doors, to allow outsiders a glimpse of their ancient culture and to try to build bridges of understanding between the races. ■

Food & drink

THIRTY YEARS AGO THE PHRASE "AUSTRALIAN CUISINE" RATED WITH "HOLY War" as one of the English language's great oxymorons. Aussie tucker conjured up visions of Vegemite sandwiches, gristly meat pies, and a stodgy dinner of lamb chops, three watery vegetables, and a bowl of ice cream for dessert. Pizza was regarded as ethnic fare.

Then came the great melting pot decades of the 1970s and '80s, when immigrants from virtually every country could be found rubbing elbows in jostling city markets. Australians became curious about the herbs, spices, and exotic foods their new neighbors were cooking and found clever ways of adapting them to local fare. Out of this cultural stew a unique cuisine evolved—a blend of Asian and Mediterranean styles, and complemented by some of the world's best wines. These days Australia's top chefs enjoy celebrity status, and the vibrant restaurant and café scene is one of the highlights of a visit down under.

Asia is the dominating influence in this new Australian cuisine, although Australians are doing much more than merely aping Asian styles. With its large Mediterranean population and burgeoning vineyards, Australia has a strong wine culture—something Asia doesn't have. "Consequently we use Asian spices and ingredients in nontraditional ways that really surprise Asian visitors when they come here," says Neil Perry, one of Australia's most famous chefs and owner of Sydney's Rockpool restaurant. "It is very much an Australian style."

It helps, too, that Australia has some of the world's best produce: Sydney's rock oysters, handcrafted cheeses from King Island, olive oil from the Adelaide Hills, venison from Tasmania, corn-fed chickens from Kangaroo Island, scallops and abalone from Coffin Bay, for example. Australia is a horn of plenty, and it is also largely unpolluted.

In recent years Australia's unique native fare—kangaroo, for instance—has been appearing more frequently on the menu. Once disdained by white Australians as the "bush tucker" that older rural Australians remember eating in the grimmest days of the Depression, kangaroo is now celebrated as a lean and delicate-tasting alternative to beef or lamb at the barbecue. It frequently appears on trendy city menus as well. Although it could be a long time before the Aboriginal delicacies of goanna, Bogong moths, or witchety grubs make regular appearances on the carte du jour, other native foods such as quandong berries, wild bush tomatoes, and wattle seeds are popular enough to be found in supermarkets. They sit beside cardamom, wasabe paste, lemon grass, and tabouli. Australians are settling into their own uniqueness. Anyone for smoked emu prosciutto?

Australia's restaurant scene is incredibly diverse, from Singaporean-style food stands to Japanese sushi bars to elegant French restaurants to Lebanese takeouts. There are more than 160 nationalities in Australia and when you walk down some of the crowded "eat streets" you get a sense that every one of them has brought a thriving ethnic cuisine.

Melbourne, Adelaide, and Sydney in particular are famous for their eateries. Lygon Street in Melbourne has Italian restaurants, cafés, and gelaterias, and the inner suburb Richmond is crammed with Greek restaurants and little hole-in-the-wall Vietnamese eateries. Adelaide has Australia's highest concentration of restaurants, with polyglot Gouger Street alone counting more than 40. Sydney is famed for its seafood, with elegant restaurants at The Rocks and around the harbor, but also has its jumble of Asian, Indian, Italian, Greek, and Lebanese eateries and coffeehouses in inner suburbs such as Newtown, Glebe, and Paddington.

Even the sandwich shops are getting in on the act, serving foccacia sandwiches, Greek salads, and venison meat pies. And what of the traditional Aussie barbecue, with its burned lamb chops, sausages, and potato salad? It is still alive and well and very popular, but now it is just one of hundreds of possibilities. ∎

Picnics, here at the Adelaide Opera in the park, are as popular as barbecues in outdoor-minded Australia.

The land

AUSTRALIA IS SERIOUSLY BIG. AT JUST UNDER 3 MILLION SQUARE MILES (7.8 million sq km) it is roughly the same size as the continental United States, but it has only 18 million people in it—barely enough to populate metropolitan Los Angeles. It sits in its own sector of the globe, with the Pacific Ocean on one side and the Indian Ocean on the other. Perhaps all the blue around it on maps makes visitors think it is smaller than it is. Certainly many are stunned to learn that Sydney is about 1,500 miles (2,400 km) from Cairns. Or that Western Australia alone is the size of India. Or that individual ranches in the outback are as big as small European countries.

CLIMATE & TERRAIN

There's a reason for the low head count. With the exception of the fertile crescent along the eastern coast, and a green pocket in the south-western corner, most of this continent is arid and inhospitable scrub, if not outright desert. The ragged northern coasts are fringed with brackish mangrove swamps, inhabited by crocodiles, and lashed by tropical cyclones.

Australia is the driest inhabited continent. The tropical north has a wet-dry climate, with winters that are sunny and dry followed by torrid summers, punctuated by monsoon rains and occasional cyclones. Bone-dry central Australia gets scorching heat in the summer and sharp cold winter nights. Most

of Australia's rain falls along the east coast, where the mountains are flanked with rain forests, or in Tasmania which receives its weather from the Roaring Forties latitudes. Perth and Adelaide enjoy a sunny Mediterranean climate. Australia does get snow—dustings have been recorded even in southern Queensland—but only the Snowy Mountains in New South Wales, the Victorian Alps, and the highlands in Tasmania receive regular snowfalls. It is sun that draws most visitors, and the majority enjoy it near the sea. Australia has more than 7,000 named beaches on nearly 37,000 miles (59,533 km) of coastline, and it also has the 1,300-mile-long (2,092 km) Great Barrier Reef.

HOW THE LAND WAS MADE

Sometime around 65 million years ago Australia broke away from the vast supercontinent called Gondwanaland and began a slow migration to its isolation in the southern Indian and Pacific Oceans. It was an ancient land even then. Some formations along the northwest coast are among the oldest on the planet—well over three billion years old. One series of 3.4-billion-year-old rocks, found near the remote town of Marble Bar, contains stromatolites, primitive blue-green algae believed to be the oldest known form of life on the planet. Tracks in the red sandstones of the Kalbarri National Park, not far off the North West Coastal Highway in Western Australia, appear to mark the first recorded instance of creatures—nightmarish amphibious scorpions 6 feet long (2 m) and aquatic centipedes even longer—stepping onto land about 420 million years ago. A fossil found nearby, of a 6-inch-long (152 mm) cockroach-like animal named *Kalbarria*, is the oldest of its kind by far, and could prove to be the ancestor of all insects.

Because the landscape is so ancient, wind and rain have had millions of years to erode once towering mountains to nubs. Australia is the flattest continent. The most significant mountain range is the Great Dividing Range, which forms a spine along the eastern coastline from Victoria's Grampian Ranges to the rain forest-clad mountains in far northern Queensland. The range contains the highest point on the continent, Mount Kosciuszko (7,317 feet, 2,230 m) in New South Wales. West of these mountains, flatness reigns virtually all the way across the continent to the Indian Ocean. Notable exceptions are the Flinders Ranges in South Australia, the craggy mountains of Western Australia's rugged northwest, and those world famous stony protrusions known as Uluru and Kata Tjuta (a.k.a. Ayers Rock and the Olgas respectively). Although there are occasional fits of seismic activity, most notably an earthquake measuring 5.9 on the Richter scale near the New South Wales town of Newcastle in 1989, the continent is one of the world's most stable landmasses. Geologically speaking, Australia is a finished product.

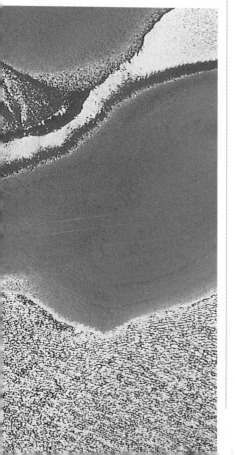

Roads like motocross tracks and remote beaches make adventure tourism Cape York Peninsula's biggest draw. This party was rescued just in time from the rising tide.

The largest and the only navigable river on the continent is the Murray–Darling, which stretches 1,650 miles (2,655 km) from the Victorian mountains to the coast of South Australia, through four states. It drains one-seventh of the continent's surface, and nourishes the best of its farmland. Although the outback is harsh and dry, it lies atop the Great Artesian Basin, a huge water source that helps support Australia's millions of sheep and cattle.

MINERAL WEALTH

Fickle geology may have left Australia alone in one of the globe's most isolated corners, and left much of it uninhabitable, but it has more than compensated for these inconveniences by making this land a virtual treasure trove of precious metals, coal, natural gas, diamonds, uranium, and opals.

The fabulous gold rushes in Victoria during the 1850s were the richest Australian strikes in history and changed the face of the country forever. Lured by gold, tens of thousands of prospectors flocked to Australia from all over the world. Some found vast fortunes; most didn't, but stayed on anyway establishing families, farms, businesses, and towns. Victoria's gold rushes were followed by rich strikes in Western Australia and Queensland. To this day Australia is one of the world's richest sources of gold, producing more than 200 tons (203 tonnes) a year. Much of the gold comes from huge open-cut mines in Western Australia, northern Queensland, and the Northern Territory's remote Tanami Desert. The Super Pit Mine, near the historic Western Australian town of Kalgoorlie, is one of the world's largest mines, producing more than 800,000 ounces (22,676 kg) of gold each year. There are plans to boost that total to over a million. Tours of the mine are available.

In 1883, at Broken Hill in far western New South Wales, a cowboy stumbled on the world's biggest known lode of silver-lead-zinc, a single chunk of rock containing more than 280 million tons (284 million tonnes) of incredibly rich ore. It spawned Australia's greatest mining companies and is still being mined to this day. The rollicking old mining town, with its gracious two-story pubs and grand Victorian and Italianate architecture, is popular with tourists, artists, and, increasingly, film crews shooting commercials and movies in its clear desert light. Tours of two underground mines are available, and for claustrophobics who don't wish to go below, there is an excellent mock-up of a mine in town.

Mount Isa, in northwestern Queensland, is another rich deposit of silver, lead, zinc, and copper and has been mined since 1923. Visitors here also have the opportunity to go underground. Untapped as yet is another fabulously rich deposit, known as the Century Zinc deposit. It was discovered about 200 miles (320 km) northwest of Mount Isa.

South Australia made its early fortunes in copper, with rich diggings at Kapunda, Burra, and around the Yorke Peninsula. More recently, the giant Olympic Dam Mine in the state's desert outback has been found to have such enormous reserves of copper and uranium that mining could continue for hundreds of years. Again, tourists have the opportunity to inspect this mine, if they care to take the detour off the Stuart Highway on the drive from Adelaide to Alice Springs.

Coober Pedy, which is on the Stuart Highway and about eight hours drive north of Adelaide (528 miles, 850 km), accounts for almost 85 percent of the world's opals. Roadside shops sell opals, tours of the diggings can be arranged, and, if you have the time and the inclination to do some digging yourself, a miner's permit is readily obtained.

Western Australia is perhaps the world's richest mineralized zone, with vast reserves of gold, nickel, and mineral sands. The iron-rich Pilbara makes Australia one of the largest exporters of iron ore. The Argyle Diamond Mine in the state's remote Kimberley region is the biggest in the world. It produces more than 35 million carats a year, more than one-third of the planet's total production, including almost all of its ultrarare pink diamonds, which can fetch a cool million dollars a carat in the trading rooms in Antwerp. Tours of this remote, highly security-conscious operation can be arranged in the town of Kununurra, about 120 miles (192 km) north of the mine.

The Walls of China, a range of wind-sculpted dunes, are a dramatic feature in Mungo National Park, New South Wales.

The seabed off the Western Australian coast is the habitat for countless numbers of pearl-bearing oysters. The historic pearling port of Broome, now a popular resort, is the hub of a modern pearling industry worth 164 million Australian dollars (82 million dollars) a year. Beneath the turquoise waters of the Timor Sea, off Australia's remote north-west coast, are sandstone formations containing billions, possibly trillions, of cubic feet of natural gas.

The craggy mountain ranges of Western Australia's isolated Pilbara region, about 1,000 miles (1,600 km) north of Perth, contain some of the world's largest iron mines, at Mount Newman, Tom Price, and Paraburdoo. They turn out 120 million tons of high-grade iron ore each year. The ore is loaded into the world's longest freight trains, up to a mile (1.6 km) in length, and are hauled almost 300 miles (480 km) to the wharves at Port Hedland and Karratha. As with almost all

of Australia's great mining projects, these operations can be visited although they are too remote for tourists on a time budget.

New South Wales and Queensland have vast seams of coal, not only of high quality but also conveniently close to the coast, helping make Australia the world's largest exporter of seaborne coal.

Beneath the storm-tossed waters of the southern coast of Victoria lurks the billion-plus-barrel Bass Strait oil field. There are zinc, gold,

An open-cut gold mine near Meekatharra on the Great Northern Highway, in Western Australia's remote Outback

tin, and copper deposits in Tasmania. Some of the world's richest deposits of bauxite (for making aluminum) lie near Weipa on the Gulf of Carpentaria side of Queensland's Cape York Peninsula, only a few miles away from where the first Dutch ship made landfall and whose captain dismissed the continent as barren. ■

History of Australia

THE FIRST AUSTRALIANS ARRIVED AT LEAST 50,000 YEARS AGO—SOME SAY AS far back as 120,000 years—coming south from Asia in one of prehistory's great migrations. They came on foot and in small boats, making a series of short hops that would be impossible today. The world was much cooler then. An ice age had locked away a lot of the world's water in mile-thick ice sheets on the Northern Hemisphere, so the sea level was as much as 400 feet (122 m) lower than it is today. It was possible to walk across the Torres Strait from New Guinea to Australia, and the Indonesian island of Timor was only about 60 miles (96 km) from what was Australia's northern coast.

Nobody knows why these people came. Restlessness or famine may have driven them; perhaps they were pushed out by stronger tribes to the north. They simply appeared on the scene and began to spread across the continent. Over thousands of years several more migrations occurred, the last one about 5,000 years ago. At least two types of people made the journey: a very heavily framed people anthropologists call "Robust," and a slender race called "Gracile." Today's Aborigines are descendants of the Gracile people.

They scattered themselves widely around the unpeopled continent, which in those days contained such bizarre creatures as giant kangaroos up to 10 feet (3 m) tall, and rhinoceros-size wombats. Archaeologists have found 40,000-year-old campsites near Melbourne's Tullamarine Airport, stone tools dating from 45,000 years ago in the Nepean Valley outside Sydney, and skeletal remains 35,000 years old in a cave as far south as Hobart. (In those days it was possible to walk from today's mainland Australia to Tasmania without getting your feet wet.) At Lake Mungo National Park in far western New South Wales, anthropologists discovered the cremated remains of a woman 35,000 years old, the world's earliest known cremation. Much of what we know about these early Australians comes from stone tools, campsite remains, and rock art. Some of these sacred sites, burial grounds, and rock-art galleries are off-limits to non-Aborigines, but there are many thousands of rock art murals, particularly in Kakadu and the Cape York Peninsula in the north, that are open to tourists, often with the benefit of an Aboriginal guide.

About 8,000 years ago, the earth began to warm. As the ice sheets melted, sea levels began to rise, and the broad plains where many generations of Aborigines had camped and hunted became shallow seas—the Gulf of Carpentaria, Torres Strait, and Bass Strait.

Vast galleries of rock art in Kakadu National Park in the Northern Territory and remote locations in the rugged Kimberley appear to tell the story of those days. Desert scenes give way to coastal ones filled with

trees. Dancing figures yield to people brandishing spears. Perhaps these scenes represent conflict as lowlanders were pushed by the rising waters onto their high-ground neighbors' territory. When the water stopped rising and Australia assumed its present shape, the Aborigines were locked away on their island, hardly to be disturbed until a hot summer day in 1788 when a fleet of 11 English ships—now known as the First Fleet—sailed into Botany Bay. The first recorded words spoken by an Aboriginal to a white man were "*Warra Warra!*" or "Go away!"

EARLY NAVIGATORS

Australia's "discovery" by Capt. James Cook in 1770, its stolidly British-to-the-bootstraps past, and the Union Jack on the flag make it easy to overlook the fact that the English were relative latecomers when it came to exploring the antipodes. Others were here first, although they left behind only scattered artifacts, shipwrecks, and place-names.

Look at a modern map of Australia and you can read which Europeans unveiled the continent. Tasmania, Western Australia's Cape Leeuwin, and Queensland's Groote Island are all Dutch names from the 17th century, when the continent was known as New Holland. The Northern Territory's Bonaparte Archipelago and South Australia's Fleurieu Peninsula were christened by the French. Western Australia's Houtman Abrolhos Islands, the site of early shipwrecks, is a corruption of the Portuguese phrase for "keep your eyes open." Torres Strait, which separates the tip of Queensland's Cape York from Papua New Guinea, is named for the Spaniard Luis Torres, who sailed this

Rock paintings at Obiri Rock in Arnhemland. Oral tradition and rock art record Australia's Aboriginal history.

PACIFIC OCEAN

SULAWESI
Macassar
JAVA INDONESIA
NEW GUINEA
Torres Strait
GROOTE EYLANDT CAPE YORK PEN.
Darwin Gulf of Carpentaria
BONAPARTE ARCHIPELAGO
Cooktown
GREAT BARRIER REEF
INDIAN OCEAN
Broome
AUSTRALIA
Shark Bay Carnarvon
Brisbane
HOUTMAN ABROLHOS IS.
Geraldton
Perth
CAPE LEEUWIN
Great Australian Bight
Adelaide
Blue Mts. Sydney
Botany Bay
Melbourne

**William Dampier
(1652–1715)**

TASMANIA

0   1000 kilometers
0   500 miles

**Abel Tasman
(1603–c.1659)**

narrow stretch of sea in 1607 and somehow missed sighting the continent.

That is the story of this continent's earliest European history; a 3-million-square-mile (7.8 million sq km) landmass in the emptiest quarter of the South Pacific found and charted by a series of accidents, chance landings, missed opportunities, and coincidences.

THE GREAT SOUTH LAND

People have wondered about Australia for centuries. The ancient Greek geographer Ptolemy speculated about the existence of a great southern land, believing the weight of such a continent was necessary to balance the globe. Early Arab merchants may have pulled into

Australian waters in the 13th century when they were spreading the word of Islam through Indonesia. Chinese and Malay ships may also have come here around the same time, fishing for *trepang,* or sea slugs, a delicacy in the markets of Canton. Fishermen from Macassar, on the Indonesian island of Sulawesi, are known to have come here since the early 16th century, catching boatloads of trepang, which they boiled then smoked on shore while waiting for the southerly winds that would carry them back home.

Although no records exist to prove it, the Portuguese could well have been the first Europeans to visit Australia, sometime in the late 15th or early 16th century. By 1516 the

"Duyfken"	1606	Dutch
Torres	1607	Spanish
"Eendracht"	1616	Dutch
"Batavia"	1629	Dutch
Tasman	1642	Dutch
Dampier	1699	British
Cook	1768-71	British

FIJI ISLANDS

James Cook (1728–1779)

NEW ZEALAND

The routes of European traders and explorers around Australia

Portuguese had established a stronghold on the island of Timor, less than 300 miles (480 km) from the Australian coastline. From there they traded throughout the Indonesian archipelago, buying pepper, nutmeg, and sandalwood, and spreading the Catholic faith. It seems inconceivable that fortune-seeking Portuguese sea captains did not venture south. They would have known the legends of the Great South Land and heard tales from the Macassar fishermen who had been there. If their curiosity did not bring them, the fickle weather must have done so. For three months

a year—generally from January through March—the monsoons blow strongly from the north. Sooner or later a Timor-bound ship would have been blown off course to within sight of the Australian coast, which was only a couple of days' sail away. Tantalizing clues include a 15th-century-style brass cannon found near Broome, on the northwest coast of Australia, and the Dieppe Maps.

These charts are believed to have been copied from Portuguese sources in 1536 and suggest that the Portuguese were acquainted with Australia's eastern seaboard. It remains a matter of debate whether the lines on the map were based on exploration, or were a lucky coincidence for a cartographer who sketched in the mythical Great South Land. The original map and notes were destroyed when a great earthquake struck Lisbon in 1755.

The honor of the first undisputed European sighting of the continent goes to the Dutch. In 1606 Willem Jansz sailed the *Duyfken* (meaning "Dove") from Java, entered the Gulf of Carpentaria, and landed on the western shore of the Cape York Peninsula. Like all the employees of the Dutch East India Company, Jansz was on the prowl for profits. Hoping for a Xanadu of ivory and silks and spices, he found instead shimmering, heat-warped horizons, a parched coast, and "wild, cruel black savages." He left unimpressed, having lost several of his men to the Aborigines. His experience pretty much set the pattern for the Dutch contact with Australia: brief landings and hurried departures.

Mostly they came by accident. The directors of the Dutch East India Company, a dour lot known as the Herren XVII, disapproved of idle exploration. They wanted a clear potential for profit before committing company funds or ships. From early reports, at least, that seemed to rule out the Great South Land, or New Holland as the Dutch had taken to calling it. Nonetheless, this same brusque efficiency was ultimately responsible for their mapping much of the western two-thirds of the coast.

Company navigators had discovered that the quickest way to reach Java was to sail into the Roaring Forties, south of Africa, ride the strong west winds of those latitudes across the Indian Ocean, and then, at the critical moment, to turn north and sail to Indonesia. But sailors don't call these latitudes "roaring" for nothing. Storms and powerful westerlies often drove ships too far, too fast, and onto the west Australian coast.

The first of these was Dirk Hartog's ship, the *Eendracht*, which in 1616 landed near Shark Bay, about halfway up the coast. Hartog nailed a pewter plate to a tree to mark the occasion. (The plate was taken as a souvenir by another Dutch seaman, Willem de Vlamingh, who landed in 1697. He, in turn, left a plate of his own that was taken a century later by an errant French explorer.)

Plenty of others followed suit. In 1627 one captain badly overshot his cue to head for Java and found himself sailing near the cliffs flanking the Great Australian Bight, more than 1,000 miles (1,600 km) off course.

Two years later another ship, the *Batavia*, was wrecked off the Houtman Abrolhos Islands, near present-day Geraldton, Western Australia. While its captain, François Pelseart, took a few men in an open boat to Java to summon aid, the crew he left behind mutinied and murdered 125 of their shipmates and passengers. They planned to seize any rescue ship and embark on careers as pirates. Instead, Pelseart returned in force, rounded them up, and meted out savage justice in an orgy of torture, mutilations, and hangings. Two of the younger mutineers were spared hanging, but were abandoned as castaways, earning them the dubious distinction of being Australia's first convict exiles. Their fate is unknown.

The directors of the Dutch East India Company decided to give New Holland another chance, although the only things reported by their captains were cliffs, desolate coasts, and the smoke of Aborigines' campfires. In 1642 they sent Abel Tasman to sail around the continent. He sailed the wild coastline of Tasmania (which he christened Van Diemen's Land, after the Dutch East Indies governor-general, Anthony Van Diemen), discovered the coast of New Zealand, and went on to the Fiji Islands. Tasman's voyage may rank among the great sea adventures of all time, but the Herren XVII were unimpressed. They wanted spices, bustling markets, gold, or at least a few willing souls to save. In 1644 they sent Tasman

Captain Cook planted the British flag on Possession Island, northern Queensland, in 1770, and claimed the territory for Britain.

back again, but when he returned with more tales of waves crashing on cliffs, scrubby forests, and savages, they had had enough. For the next century Australia was largely left alone by the Dutch, undisturbed except for the occasional East Indies-bound ship that was driven by storms onto the west coast.

English buccaneer and explorer William Dampier arrived in 1688 and again in 1699, with the notion of using New Holland as a staging-post-cum-watering-hole for English ships in the Pacific. He landed on the cheerless, treeless, sun-blasted coast of northwest Australia, and like the Dutch before him, went away shaking his head.

VOYAGE OF THE *ENDEAVOUR*

In 1768 the British Admiralty and the Royal Society decided to send an expedition to Tahiti to record the transit of Venus across the face of the sun. As the transit would occur on the morning of June 3, 1769, and wouldn't happen again for another 105 years, this was a once-in-a-lifetime opportunity. A distinguished 41-year-old Royal Navy lieutenant named James Cook was selected to captain the ship, a 368-ton (374-tonne) barque called *Endeavour*. Cook had been at sea since he was 18, at first on a North Sea collier and later in the Royal Navy. He was a proud, stern man with a strong sense of duty and an equally strong sense of fair play, who had advanced through the ranks on merit alone. Leading the scientific party was 25-year-old Joseph Banks—soon to be Sir Joseph Banks—an extremely wealthy young

man, educated at Harrow, Eton, and Oxford, and already on his way to becoming the pre-eminent botanist in England. Onto this crowded ship he brought his Swedish colleague Daniel Solander, artists Sydney Parkinson and Alexander Buchan, and four assistants. The ship sailed out of Plymouth on August 25, 1768, bound for the southern tip of South America and then across the Pacific. They were to record the transit of Venus, explore the South Pacific, and investigate the fabled great southern continent. In size and scope the *Endeavour*'s expedition was the 18th-century equivalent of a moon shot.

After wrapping up their astronomical business in Tahiti, the expedition spent six months charting the coast of New Zealand. From there they turned toward the unknown east coast of New Holland. On April 28, 1770,

they sighted land that is not far from the present-day border of New South Wales and Victoria. After sailing up the coast they turned into a large bay and dropped anchor. Here they encountered so many new species of plants, ferns, herbs, shrubs, and trees never before seen by European eyes that Cook decided to name the place Botany Bay. They also found rich black soils, lush meadows, and rushing creeks that looked as if they could power a mill very nicely. The *Endeavour* con-

A reconstruction of the First Fleet lies in Sydney Harbour during the fireworks for Australia's Bicentennial celebrations.

tinued up the coast of Australia, running aground on the Great Barrier Reef, but filling in the blank parts of the map. After repairing the *Endeavour* near present-day Cooktown, Cook claimed the eastern half of the continent in the name of George III and called it New South Wales.

CONVICT COLONY

Despite all Captain Cook's efforts, Australia might still have been left alone, had it not been for events taking place on the other side of the planet. The 13 American Colonies declared their independence on July 4, 1776, which meant that England could no longer ship convicts to Georgia, Virginia, and the Carolinas. A backlog of prisoners built up at the rate of about a thousand a year. In 1779 Sir Joseph Banks, having been there with

Cook, suggested that the Crown consider sending the prison riffraff to colonize Botany Bay. The idea drew a skeptical response. Dispatching shiploads of felons half way around the world to New South Wales seemed an expensive way to clean out prisons. But French ambitions in the Pacific provided the government in London with a good reason to act. With America gone, England had to focus on its colonies to the east. The age-old enemy France was busily widening its sphere, establishing ports in Madagascar, combing the Indian Ocean, and sailing along the coast of Australia. A British colony in Botany Bay could be a useful foothold. The timing was impeccable: Shortly after the First Fleet landed at Botany Bay, two French ships, captained by the Comte de la Perouse, just happened to drop by.

**"Natives Fishing in a Bark Canoe"
by T.R. Browne (1819)**

THE FIRST FLEET

What in America was a fine piece of rhetoric to inscribe at the base of the Statue of Liberty was harsh fact down under: This nation was literally settled by huddled masses yearning to breathe free. Who wouldn't be yearning to breathe free after spending eight months chained in a stinking hold of a ship as it bounced from Tenerife to Rio de Janeiro to Capetown, and then on to an otherworldly place called Botany Bay? But along with the relief at taking that first breath of fresh air and blinking in the dazzling Australian sunshine, came the terror of the unknown and the grim certainty that life here was going to be rough.

On January 18, 1788, a flotilla of 11 ships, known as the First Fleet, arrived in Botany Bay. It carried 778 convicts—men, women, and children as young as nine, and 250 soldiers and colonial administrators under the command of Capt. Arthur Phillip, who became the first governor of New South Wales.

A quick look around was enough to tell the newcomers that they had no chance of estab-

lishing a settlement at Botany Bay. Cook had visited in autumn, when rains had freshened the place up, but this was summer and Botany Bay was anything but green and lush. The creeks were dry, the bay was exposed, and rich meadows described by Cook were just scrub shimmering in blinding white heat. The fleet sailed 12 miles (19 km) north along the coast, between two sandstone heads that Cook had sighted but not entered. In it they discovered "the finest harbour in the world in which a thousand ships of the line may ride with the most perfect security," as Phillip put it to Lord Sydney, for whom he named the new settlement. The date was January 26, known now as Australia Day. Phillip then dispatched a ship to claim Norfolk Island, establishing an English presence and penal colony there.

Times were tough. Looking around Sydney now, with the gleaming yachts in the harbor, the cluster of red-tiled roofs and ornamental palms along the waterfront, the bridge, and the Opera House, it is hard to fathom how tough. The little colony was racked with hunger and scurvy. The soil was thin, the seed wheat had gone moldy at sea, the livestock wandered off or died. Many of the prisoners were products

"South Brisbane from the North Shore, Moreton Bay, Australia 1868" by Thomas Baines (1820–75). More than 40 years after its founding, Brisbane was still just a village.

of London's slums and knew nothing of farming. Others were too old, ill, or weakened by the voyage to perform much work. A ship had to be sent to Capetown, the nearest port, for emergency supplies. The Aborigines made their feelings known by spearing Phillip in the shoulder, an act that stunned the governor, who had apparently never thought that he and the other colonists were trespassing.

As time passed and no supplies arrived from England, more and more convicts were shifted to Norfolk Island, where the soil was better and more fish could be caught. In 1791, the Second Fleet arrived and the struggling Sydney Town began to gain its feet.

Who were the convicts? Novels such as *For the Term of His Natural Life* by Marcus Clarke (1874), an Australian classic, often portray early convicts as innocent victims who were wrongly convicted, political prisoners, or starving wretches who had stolen a cabbage to feed their children. Most, in fact, were petty criminals who had committed the kinds of crimes that might draw jail time today—or

juvenile hall. Theft was the most common charge and most of the convicts were from the English slums—not Ireland, although the Irish Rebellion of 1798 provided a few genuine political prisoners.

About half drew sentences of seven years, although given the distance and cost of returning to England, transportation to Australia generally meant a life term. Skilled, lucky, wealthy, or well-behaved prisoners earned their ticket-of-leave early and were granted farms, or were able to set up small businesses. This was, after all, meant to be an attempt to establish a colony as well as a prison camp. Others did hard time. Very, very hard time. Floggings, leg irons, and soul-breaking work regimes were routine. Punishments were meted out with breathtaking severity—sometimes up to 300 lashes at a time, enough to leave backbones and shoulder blades exposed. Medical treatment was a dousing with a bucket of saltwater. Hard cases were sent to Norfolk Island, Van Diemen's Land (Tasmania), or Moreton Bay (Brisbane), where conditions were horrific. Weighted down with irons so tight the flesh was rubbed off their bones, working 16-hour days in the rain on short rations, and infested with lice and disease, convicts were known to commit murder, simply so they could be hanged and released from misery.

Escape was fairly easy in Australia. The trouble was, there was no place to go. Some convicts headed toward the Blue Mountains, in the misguided belief that China was only a few days' hike beyond the horizon. For the most part, those who managed to get away then starved to death, died of exposure, or fell to Aboriginals' spears. Some resorted to cannibalism, killing and eating their fellow absconders. Others talked their way onto Nantucket whalers that passed this way, although that was rarely a good bargain. Some Yankee whaling captains were even more brutal than the prison guards.

One woman, Mary Bryant, led a party of escapers north along the coast in a boat. They reached Indonesia before they were recaptured and taken back to England for retrial. Her heroism touched a chord in England. She and her group were pardoned, and she returned to her native Cornwall.

With the exception of South Australia, all of Australia's states were founded on convict labor. Transportation ended in 1868; in all, about 160,000 were sent to Australia. For generations afterward, convict blood was a stain on the family tree. These days it is a point of pride. Having an ancestor on the First Fleet—either convict or guard—has the cachet of being a *Mayflower* descendant in Boston.

SETTLEMENT

Bengal rum was the currency of early Sydney, which by the early 1800s had the reputation of being one of the roughest ports anywhere on the Pacific. Most of the moneymaking enterprises in the colony were controlled by a military mafia known as the Rum Corps, named for the monopoly they held on that vital commodity. Alcoholism was rampant. Many officials were corrupt or incompetent or both, conducting business in a rummy fog. Convicts were effectively slaves, working for an elite group of profiteers and landowners, who kept them pliant with rum or the cat-o'-nine-tails.

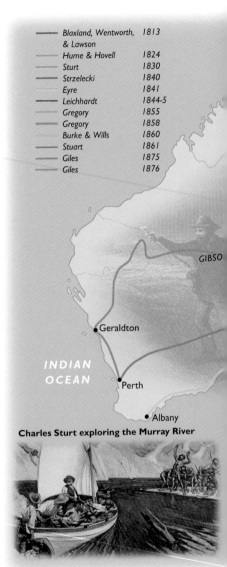

Blaxland, Wentworth, & Lawson	1813
Hume & Hovell	1824
Sturt	1830
Strzelecki	1840
Eyre	1841
Leichhardt	1844-5
Gregory	1855
Gregory	1858
Burke & Wills	1860
Stuart	1861
Giles	1875
Giles	1876

GIBSO

Geraldton

INDIAN OCEAN

Perth

Albany

Charles Sturt exploring the Murray River

In all, New South Wales did not have the kind of atmosphere that would induce decent men and women to migrate there, which was what this embryonic society needed to transform itself from a bawdy penal colony to a prosperous settlement. It needed a governor who knew how to run a tight ship, but the man selected was Capt. William Bligh, whose crew on the *Bounty* had so famously mutinied. He was dispatched to Sydney with a brief to clean up the place. Captain Bligh wasn't the

Edward John Eyre
(1815–1901)

Augustus Charles Gregory (1819–1905)

lash-crazed disciplinarian of popular legend. He was simply an old-school naval officer who needed a better press agent. He arrived in Sydney sympathetic to the little guys, and sided with them against the Rum Corps. But the Rum Corps were army men and well entrenched. He was navy and a newcomer. On January 26, 1808, the 20th anniversary of the founding of the colony, Bligh suffered the second mutiny of his career. For the next two years, New South Wales was run by the army.

The routes of Australia's inland explorers slowly filled in the center of the map.

Then a new governor arrived—a reform-minded Scot named Lachlan Macquarie. He broke the power of the Rum Corps and established the first banks, and the colony's own currency. He promoted expeditions across the Blue Mountains and began a series of public works and town planning projects for the fledgling colony. He even offered a name for

Burke and Wills and their party leaving Royal Park Melbourne in 1860, an engraving by William Strutt (circa 1880). They crossed the continent but died on the return journey.

the place, telling his masters in London of his plans to explore "the coasts of the Continent of Australia which I hope will be the name given to this country in the future."

INLAND EXPLORERS

In the early 19th century, mapmakers could sketch at least a rough outline of Australia. Matthew Flinders and George Bass had proved in 1799 that Tasmania was an island, not a long Florida-like peninsula, and between 1801 and 1803 they circumnavigated the continent. But what lay inside this 3-million-square-mile (7.8 million sq km) mass was anybody's guess.

Although settlements had been established at Sydney and in Van Diemen's Land, nobody had ventured inland, other than a handful of escaped convicts. There were hopes of an inland sea and hints of mineral wealth. One escaped convict stumbled upon a coal outcrop north of Sydney, and by the mid-1790s the colony was already exporting small cargoes of coal to India. The first major barrier was a range called the Blue Mountains, steep hills

about 3,000 feet (984 m) high just west of Sydney. Today this is a vacation area less than two hours from the city—some people commute from the hills—but two centuries ago those mountains were formidable, forest-cloaked obstacles to progress. Several attempts were made to breach them before Gregory Blaxland, William Wentworth, and William Lawson finally succeeded in 1813.

After a route was opened up through the mountains, settlers soon followed, spilling out into the flat, open grazing land beyond. In 1815 the town of Bathurst was founded 130 miles (209 km) west of Sydney, and exploration started in earnest. In 1824 explorers Hamilton Hume and William Hovell probed the Snowy Mountains to the south, and chanced upon the Murray River near present-day Albury-Wodonga. The sight of the river flowing west, seemingly into the middle of the continent, rekindled dreams of an inland sea and a fertile heartland. Those hopes were dashed in 1830 when Charles Sturt followed the river more than a 1,000 miles (1,600 km) through the outback to its bitter end, a large brackish lake on South Australia's coastline. In 1840 a Polish count, Paul Edmund de Strzelecki, climbed the continent's highest mountain, the 7,310-foot (2,228 m) peak he named for Polish freedom fighter Gen. Tadeusz Kosciuszko.

The desert center

These expeditions sketched in the southeastern corner of the continent, but vast empty reaches still awaited explorers. Edward Eyre was the first of these, crossing the continent east to west through the Nullarbor Plain in 1841. This 800-mile-wide (1,287-km) stretch of scabby earth was a brutal introduction to Australia's interior. Eyre and one of his Aborigine guides, Wylie, survived. They stumbled into Albany, Western Australia, after four months. Less fortunate was Ludwig Leichhardt, a Prussian-born immigrant, who, after crossing 3,000 miles (4,800 km) of Outback between Brisbane and what is now Darwin, vanished without a trace while attempting to cross Australia's Red Centre in 1848. In 1855 Augustus Gregory successfully crossed from the Victoria River country in the Northern Territory, around the Gulf of Carpentaria and south to Brisbane. Three years later he and his brother Francis trekked across Queensland to try to find out what had happened to Leichhardt. The German's fate remained a mystery, but the brothers found a passage through the glaring salt lakes and on to Adelaide.

Burke and Wills

Australia's most famous and elaborate inland expedition left Melbourne on a midwinter's day in 1860. Robert O'Hara Burke and William John Wills led the expedition, and the government financed it lavishly in the hope that it would discover rich pastoral lands to the north. The goal was the Gulf of Carpentaria, more than 2,500 miles (4,000 km) away. At a spot called Cooper Creek in the South Australian outback, the party divided. Four of the group remained as a sort of base camp, while Burke and Wills and two associates, John King and Charles Grey, pressed on, traveling light and fast and impatient for glory.

They reached the gulf in February—in the peak of summer heat, when the temperatures may soar to more than 120°F (50°C), and the monsoon rains had soaked the crocodile-infested wetlands. Their progress on the final push to the coast was slow.

They began retracing their footsteps immediately, but the clock was running down. Grey died and the three survivors pressed on, weak and dazed, through the desert, traveling by moonlight, eventually throwing away most of their supplies in a frantic bid to get back to base camp. Burke, Wills, and King arrived seven hours too late. They found a message carved into a giant coolabah tree instructing them to dig for a cache of supplies their colleagues had left on the off chance they returned. They discovered the supplies but lacked the strength to push on to Melbourne. The expedition's two celebrated leaders perished. King was nursed back to health by passing Aborigines. The famous "Dig Tree" still stands and can be seen by adventurous four-wheel-drive expeditions traveling on the Strzelecki Track.

At around the same time, a tough Scot named John McDouall Stuart, their rival, was trying to complete his own crossing of the continent. He had traveled north from Adelaide bound for near where Darwin is today, but disease, hostile Aborigines, and unbearable heat had held him back. He finally succeeded in reaching the Arafura Sea on July 24, 1862. They had performed the first south-to-north trek, but Stuart managed the more difficult (and to the explorer involved, more important) feat of returning. Even so, he barely survived, staggering back blind and hardly able to stand. His journey marked the apex of inland exploration and resolved the matter of an inland lake for all time: There was none. It also established a route that would be followed fairly closely in 1872 by the telegraph line, and later the Stuart Highway, the trucking lifeline between Adelaide and Darwin.

Expeditions struggled through the Western Australian deserts in the 1870s. Ernest Giles explored the Great Victorian Desert in 1875 and the Gibson Desert the following year, the latter named for his partner, Alfred Gibson, who died on the journey. Giles's two expeditions were the last gasps of Australia's heroic age of exploration. By the 1880s most of the interior had been explored, although some

isolated pockets still remained untouched for another 50 years. As recently as the 1980s clans of desert Aborigines were still leading a traditional lifestyle, as they had for 50,000 years.

GOLD

Gold was the single biggest force in Australia's transformation from a clutter of struggling settlements on the rim of the world into one of Britain's most prosperous colonies. The first real gold rush began in May 1851 after a prospector named Edward Hargraves found gold at Ophir, near Bathurst, New South Wales, and bragged about it. Almost overnight a tent city of more than a thousand diggers sprang up in the mud, and thousands more fortune seekers from around Australia quit their jobs and raced for the diggings. The human stampede was so big that employers in Melbourne, alarmed at the sudden loss of workers, and envious at New South Wales's sudden prosperity, offered a reward for any-

body who succeeded in finding gold close to their city.

They didn't have long to wait. Within weeks gold was discovered at Clunes, and then came the fabulous finds around Ballarat. Gold seemed to be everywhere in Victoria. Before the end of the year, people made enormously rich finds at Castlemaine and Bendigo, and 20,000 prospectors were scouring the hills looking for more. Word quickly spread overseas, and soon Chinese, English, Irish, and

"Australian Gold Diggings," circa 1855, by Edwin Stocqueler (1829–circa 1880), in the National Library of Australia, Canberra

Americans were pouring into Australia at a rate of 90,000 a year.

Eureka Stockade

Anybody could do it. For the first time in Australia's history, the common man had a shot at serious wealth. There were no big mining companies, just small operators. To try to keep control of events, the authorities imposed a stiff tax of 30 shillings a month ($7.50, a sizeable sum at that time) on prospectors, whether they were successful or not. Resentment at this tax smoldered in the camps and finally boiled over in November 1854 in an uprising at Eureka Stockade, a hastily built fort near the Irish diggings just east of Ballarat. This was the closest thing Australia ever had to outright civil war.

Prospectors were already simmering over the murder of one of their number, because the authorities had discharged the hotelkeeper who they believed was responsible. The volatile mix of gold diggers included German and Italian revolutionaries, Irish Republicans, and hot-tempered Americans. At a rally they burned their licenses, proclaimed their defiance of the law, and set up a barricade. They raised a flag—a white Southern Cross on a blue field (notably without the Union Jack). The government responded savagely and on December 3 crushed the rebellion. The 10-minute fight left 6 soldiers and as many as 30 miners dead. A number of miners were arrested and charged with high treason. Melbourne juries, however, refused to convict. In the political fallout after the Eureka Stockade fight, miners won many of the rights they had campaigned for: the abolition of the hated licenses and the right to vote and run for office. The following year their leader, Peter Lalor, who had lost an arm in the battle, was elected to Parliament.

To this day the Eureka Stockade flag remains a symbol of defiance to overbearing authority, and a spacious new museum dedicated to the uprising and the early life of Ballarat stands on the site of the battle. The prodigious wealth pouring in from the gold diggings quickly transformed muddy shanty-towns into elegant cities, with gardens, wide streets, mansions, and grand public buildings. Victoria's gold rushes were the biggest, but the 1860s and '70s brought finds in New South Wales, at Forbes and Young. Queensland had the white quartz reefs of Gympie, then the rich beds of Charters Towers, Palmer River, and Cape York. Prospectors went on to Pine Creek in the Northern Territory, and by the 1880s, Halls Creek in the Kimberley, the remote northwest. Prospectors scrambled for the Pilbara, then the Murchison field and Western Australia's Southern Cross. The last of the huge gold strikes was at Coolgardie and Kalgoorlie in the 1890s. Most of the sites are marked, and the towns' ornate goldfield-style architecture, which characterized the optimism and wealth, are monuments to these early days.

FEDERATION

On New Year's Day 1901, a crowd gathered in Sydney's Centennial Park to witness the birth of a nation: the Commonwealth of Australia. Until then the continent had been a patchwork of colonies, each of which stubbornly set its own time zone, issued its own postage stamps, and imposed confiscatory customs duties on goods crossing its borders. There was little cooperation, only competition. Colonies could not even agree on which railway gauge to use, a "mental paralysis" that dumbfounded the humorist Mark Twain when he swung through this part of the world in 1895.

After years of painstaking diplomacy, with the help of compromises and nudged along by a particularly destructive drought and recession, the colonies agreed to federate in 1901. The new constitution, thrashed out in a second-floor suite in Melbourne's Windsor Hotel, was not exactly a radical piece of legislation. Queen Victoria and her successors would remain head of state, the Crown's local representative would still be a regally appointed governor-general, and Britain's parliamentary style of government would prevail. In fact, the British parliament could still override any legislation passed in the Australian parliament, and for legal matters the final court of appeal would be the Privy Council in London. In essence, Mother England's six Australian colonies had simply agreed to cease their sibling rivalry. Edmund Barton, a Sydney lawyer, became the first prime minister. He put aside whatever native New South Wales parochialism he may have harbored and moved to rival Melbourne, which was to be the capital until a neutral city could be agreed upon. The six states (the present states, less the Northern Territory, which was a part of New South Wales) remained powerful, but shared a

These young Australians waded into history and a hail of bullets at Gallipoli, Turkey, on April 25, 1915—remembered as Anzac Day.

vision: Australia would be stable, white, prosperous, white, protected by trade tariffs and social welfare legislation—and white. One of the first laws they passed was to restrict Asian immigration, the beginning of the infamous White Australia policy that lasted until the late 1960s. As Australia's second prime minister, Alfred Deakin, put it in a remarkably candid moment: "It is not the bad qualities but the good qualities of these alien races that make them dangerous to us. It is their inexhaustible energy, their power of applying themselves to new tasks, their endurance, and their low standard of living that make them such competitors." And so would-be migrants from Asia had to take a literacy test, in any European language the immigration officer cared to name. Gaelic was a favorite. Not surprisingly, few passed.

Because nobody could agree on which city should be the capital, the fledgling government decided to create one from scratch. In 1909 they settled on a bit of pastureland on the Monaro Tablelands, about 200 miles (320 km) southwest of Sydney. Two years later the New South Wales government ceded the 9,650-square-mile (25,000 sq km) parcel of land to the federal government. Chicago architect Walter Burley-Griffin was selected to design the city; it would be called Canberra, from an Aboriginal word meaning either "meeting place" or "women's breasts," depending on who is doing the telling.

GALLIPOLI

After a good deal of bureaucratic haggling and compromise, Australia achieved nationhood by a stroke of the royal pen. There had been no death-or-glory freedom fighters, no midnight rides by a Paul Revere or a Bunker Hill battle to forge a unifying national myth in blood. But Australia didn't have long to wait. In August 1914 Britain went to war with Germany, which meant that Australia, as part of the British Empire, was at war also. In a frenzy of patriotism, more than 20,000 Aussies enlisted in the first two months, eager for bold overseas adventure. They got it at 4:30 a.m. on April 25, 1915, on a cliff-lined coast in Turkey, near a town called Gallipoli. Winston Churchill, who was then First Lord of the Admiralty, had decided to open a new front by taking the Dardanelles, and ordered a multinational force of English, French, Australian, New Zealand, Indian, and Gurkha troops to attack from the sea. The Turks knew what was coming and were ready to direct withering fire onto the beaches. For the next eight months the allied troops clung onto the exposed beachhead.

Both sides saw desperate fighting and horrific carnage. Although Australians had fought for Britain in the Sudan campaign and in the Boer War, this was the first time they had fought as Australians. Australia's national myths were born at Gallipoli, out of courage, mateship, and the understated heroics of men such as Simpson, who with his donkey braved the deadly open ground to retrieve those who had been wounded (until he himself was killed by a sniper). In all, 8,587 men from the Australian and New Zealand Army Corps (ANZAC) were killed. The French, English, Indians, and especially the Turks suffered far greater losses at Gallipoli, something Australians often overlook in their patriotic fervor on Anzac Day (April 25). Actually they also tend to overlook Australia's much greater losses in France, at the Somme (23,000) and Ypres (38,000).

WORLD WAR II

World War II marked a turning point in Australia's view of the world. "Without inhibitions of any kind, I make it quite clear that Australia looks to America, free of any pangs as to our traditional links or kinship with the United Kingdom," said John Curtin, Australia's prime minister, after Singapore fell to the Japanese in February 1942. Japanese planes began bombing Darwin that same month, and Broome in March.

Australia was faced with the very real possibility of a Japanese invasion. For the United States, Australia offered a last-chance Pacific foothold near Asia. Three months later a combined United States and Australian naval force stopped the Japanese fleet in the Battle of the Coral Sea. Australian slouch-hatted infantry soldiers then had to fight a brutal guerrilla war in the Papua New Guinea Highlands to save Australia's colonial outpost at Port Moresby. Its fall would have given the Japanese a springboard into mainland Australia.

Although the Japanese came within 30 miles (48 km) of the town, the Australians fought a gritty hand-to-hand, yard-by-yard campaign, and pushed them back to the island's north coast. They were assisted by Papua New Guinea inhabitants, who became known as the Fuzzy Wuzzy Angels. In Thailand, thousands of Australian prisoners of war died of abuse, starvation, and disease, while being forced to build the infamous Burma Railway (the railroad of the film *Bridge Over the River Kwai*). Others were saved by the unflagging efforts of "Weary" Dunlop, their fellow prisoner and an army surgeon who became a symbol of Australia's unflinching yet soft-spoken style of heroism.

NEW AUSTRALIANS

After the war Australia went through enormous changes. When the government launched one of the greatest migration programs of the 20th century, more than two million immigrants poured into the country. According to the census of 1947, about 98 percent of Australians were Anglo-Saxon. Now "New Australians" were coming in from all over war-ravaged Europe—Italy, Germany, Yugoslavia, Greece, and the Baltic countries. As long as they were white, the government would underwrite the cost of their passage. A berth on one of the liners that brought these immigrants down under could be had for as

"Populate or Perish" became the catchphrase in Australia in the 1950s and '60s, when more than two million New Australians arrived at the steamship terminals such as this one in Sydney.

S. ROPPOLO. GIUSEP
252. HAWTHORNE.
PADERE. HABFIELD.
SIDINE.
AUSTRALIA.

little as ten English pounds ($40 at the prevailing exchange rate).

The newcomers settled in with surprisingly little friction. For one thing, plenty of jobs could be had all around in those prosperous postwar years so nobody felt cheated. Factories were sprouting up, steel mills and coal mines were busy, and the government was spending big money on major public works such as the Snowy Mountains Hydroelectric Scheme, an enormous project. There were also thousands of new suburban houses to build for this booming population. The country positively oozed good health and high spirits. Bronzed Aussie tennis players won at Wimbledon, and their swimmers were the finest in the world. When the Olympics came to Melbourne in 1956, the home team walked off with 35 medals—an unheard-of success for such a small population.

The age was also an artless one. Australians wince today when they see old newsreel footage, and hear the narrator's cheerfully jingoistic, sexist, and racist observations. Blokes were blokes, and the women stayed home. Aborigines were not citizens and could not vote until 1967. For all the influx of other peoples after the war, Australia remained culturally a stodgy pocket of the British Empire.

TIME FOR CHANGE

It wasn't all sunny isolation. Always obliging to its allies, Canberra signed up for the Korean War and conflicts in Malaya and Borneo. It let Britain use a patch of South Australian desert to test atomic bombs and allowed the United States to set up spy-satellite monitoring posts around the continent. In 1962 Australia followed the U.S. into Vietnam. But as the body bags came back—Australia lost about 500 lives in Vietnam—a vocal antiwar movement sprang up. In Australia, as elsewhere, the late sixties blossomed into a time of liberalization, questioning, and protest. Australia

Surf rescue started as a service to safeguard swimmers, but it quickly became a sport with its own competitions and carnivals in this sports-mad country.

was changing rapidly. A charismatic, bushy-browed giant named Gough Whitlam emerged to lead the Australian Labor Party to victory in 1972 with the slogan, "It's time." The time brought health-care reforms, free college education, the formal end of the White Australia policy, widespread new social pro-grams, and increased support for the arts. Like Camelot of the U.S., the Australian ver-sion lasted about three years and ended abruptly in November 1975, although with considerably less brutality. Whitlam's adminis-tration could not pass through parliament the spending legislation necessary to keep the government running. On November 11, the governor-general, Sir John Kerr, exercised a rarely used and highly controversial preroga-

tive: He sacked the Whitlam government and declared a general election. Conspiracy theorists have dined out on it ever since. Was it a coup d'état? Was the CIA involved? What really happened? The only thing beyond dispute is that four weeks later Whitlam lost the election in a landslide, and Malcolm Fraser, an equally physically towering but very conservative sheep grazier from Victoria, became Australia's next prime minister.

PACIFIC RIM & REPUBLIC

Alarm clocks rang all over Australia at four o'clock one morning in September 1983, and a sleepy nation got out of bed to watch live TV coverage of a yacht race on the other side of the world. Australians held their collective breath while their yacht, *Australia II,* knifed through the waters of Narragansett Bay in Rhode Island. An American yacht was bobbing somewhere astern. A horn blared. The race was over. Australia had won the America's Cup.

Back in Sydney people were dancing in the streets, free beer flowed in the pubs, and Bob Hawke, the new Labor prime minister, crowed on national TV that any boss who didn't give his workers this historic day off was "a bum." For Australians this was more than a great sporting triumph. It was a catharsis, dispelling lingering doubts about whether their remote country, with its tiny, fiercely blue-collar population and convict roots, could make it in the glamour leagues. For many it seemed to kick start the roaring eighties. A confident, outward-looking Australia strode onto the world stage as a player in its own right, not as England's wild colonial cousin.

It was the time of the global bull market, and Australia dealt itself in with alacrity. The dollar was floated on the world exchange, trade barriers were lowered, and foreign banks were allowed to set up shop in Australia. Meanwhile Australians headed overseas, buy-ing 20th Century Fox, the London *Times,* and the national telephone company in Chile. *Crocodile Dundee,* Fosters lager, and "tossing another shrimp on the barbie" became part of the world's vernacular.

The clock could not be turned back. In 1988, as the country started its third century since colonization, Australians began to ask themselves questions about who they were

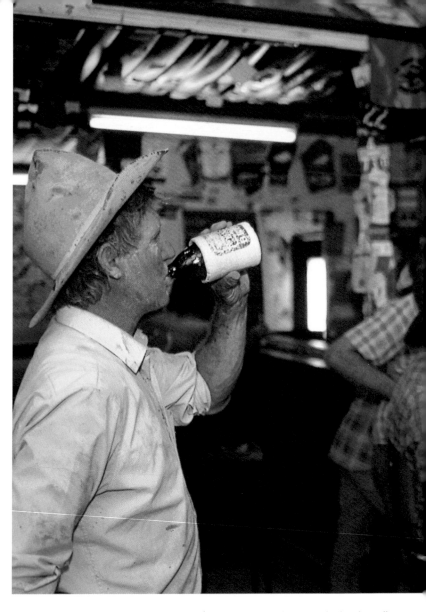

and where they belonged in the world. After 200 years of being distracted by links to Europe, they suddenly realized they had box seats where it seemed the economic action was going to be in the 21st century—Asia. They began to think of themselves in Asian terms, rather than as a far-flung corner of England. Asian countries were already Australia's biggest trading partners—about 61 percent of Australia's exports now head north and west—but by the early 1990s the focus became diplomatic and cultural as well. Asian immigration was stepped up. It was an Australian initiative that helped create APEC, the 18-nation forum for Asian-Pacific Economic Cooperation that is to remove regional trade barriers by 2020. Out in the broad, sunny suburbs of the cities, formerly xenophobic Australia has become almost glee-fully multicultural.

Over the past decade, Australians have done other soul-searching as well, such as

confronting ugly truths about the plight of the Aborigines (see p. 19).

Republic?

As the nation drifts toward Asia—literally, as well as figuratively, with plate tectonics nudging the continent at the rate of 2 inches (50 mm) a year—Australians are starting to question why they still have the Union Jack on their flag and the English monarch on their currency. Why not become a republic? The idea would have

"Tinnies" or "stubbies" of beer quench the Outback thirst at the far flung William Creek hotel, near Oodnadatta.

been discussed only on the radical fringe a decade ago, but is now a mainstream topic of conversation. New Australians no longer swear allegiance to the Queen, and her portrait has been removed from many public offices. Still, most Australians voted to retain the Queen in a referendum held in November 1999. ∎

The arts

ANYONE WHO STILL THINKS THAT AUSTRALIANS ARE SIMPLY SPORTS-MAD Philistines should look at a few figures. In 1986 a touring display of 19th-century Australian art attracted more than 550,000 visitors—more than the total number of spectators at all the season's Test cricket matches and the Aussie Rules football grand final combined. Or they could listen to the squabbling over which painting should really have won the Archibald Prize. This is Australia's most prestigious art award, given to the best portrait painted within the previous year.

LITERATURE

Aborigines were by far the earliest storytellers on the continent, having the rich heritage of Dreamtime tales to draw upon. Their oral tradition was handed down through stories told around campfires. The first Aborigine to have work published was David Unaipon, whose book, *Native Legends,* came out in 1929. Since then several translations of Dreamtime legends have been published, such as Joe Nangan's *Dreaming: Aboriginal Legends of the Northwest,* and a variety of children's books illustrated by Aboriginal artists. One good source of Aboriginal literature, both modern and ancient, is Magabala Books, an Aboriginal publishing house based in Broome on the remote northwest coast of Western Australia. *Stories from the Fitzroy River Drovers* is an Aborigine's perspective on life on the remote Kimberley stations. Some of the best books about Aborigines are Thomas Kenneally's *Chant of Jimmie Blacksmith* (1972), Bruce Chatwin's offbeat *Songlines,* and David Malouf's *Remembering Babylon.*

White Australia's literature began when explorers such as Edward Eyre, Charles Sturt, and Ernest Giles kept journals of their expeditions. Some are still available in bookshops (look under Australiana), and make a nice read if you're crossing the country on the Indian-Pacific Railway or traveling up to Alice Springs on the Ghan. It wasn't until the latter part of the 19th century that Australians felt ready to tackle their bizarre landscapes and convict heritage in literature. Marcus Clarke's *For the Term of His Natural Life* (published in 1874) is probably the first Australian classic. His protagonist, Rufus Dawes, is a wealthy young gentleman wrongfully convicted of murder and sentenced to transportation to Australia. He endures the penal colonies at Port Arthur and Macquarie Harbour, but he makes good in the end, retrieving name and fortune. Gold rushes and bushrangers provided material for Rolf Boldrewood's *Robbery Under Arms* (1888), another Australian classic.

In the 1890s Australia's strongest national myths were forged by a handful of journalists and poets writing for the *Bulletin* magazine. Probably the best known of these—to foreigners—is the balladeer and humorist Andrew Barton Patterson, who borrowed his pen name "Banjo" from a racehorse his family owned. His bush ballads and yarns of swagmen, shearers, outlaws, and squatters celebrated a freedom that Australians, and the rest of the world, still like to imagine exists just over the horizon. He is best known for *The Man from Snowy River, Clancy of the Overflow,* and the lyrics of Australia's unofficial national anthem, "Waltzing Matilda." Henry Lawson, a dour and much less folksy contemporary of Patterson's, is arguably Australia's finest short-story writer. While he could be as ironically humorous as Banjo, his social commentary goes much deeper. *The Drover's Wife,* about a woman sitting up all night to protect her young children against a snake that has crawled into a crack in the wall of their bush shack, is a haunting story of strength, struggle, and aching loneliness. Lawson died an almost penniless alcoholic in 1922 but was accorded a state funeral.

Arthur Hoey Davis, writing in the 1890s under the name of Steele Rudd, created two of Australia's best loved characters, Dad and Dave, in *On Our Selection.* These two wide-eyed bumpkins went on to greater glory in a radio serial and in novels, plays, and films.

Aboriginal rock group Yothu Yindi's lead singer, Mandawuy Yunupingu, was named Australian of the Year in 1993.

Later, coupled with C.J. Dennis's poem about a city-bred larrikin (mischievous young chap), *The Sentimental Bloke,* they reinforced the already popular image of the good-hearted Aussie battler.

Australia's Outback landscapes began to find their way into novels in the 1920s, helped along by a brilliant visitor, English novelist

Poet, essayist, war correspondent, and songwriter, Andrew Barton "Banjo" Patterson (1864–1941)

D.H. Lawrence, who published *Kangaroo* in 1923. Fifteen years later came Xavier Herbert's sweeping epic *Capricornia,* with its vivid descriptions of life in the tropical landscapes of Australia's far north. Nobel Prize winner Patrick White used the Outback as a backdrop for such major works as *Voss* (1957), a novel about a mad explorer trying to cross a desert, supposedly based on the life of Ludwig Leichhardt.

If you are looking for something evocative but a trifle easier to read, try Nevil Shute's 1950 classic *A Town Like Alice* or Colleen McCullough's *The Thorn Birds* (1979).

Among the nonfiction, Robert Hughes's *The Fatal Shore* (1987) is a gripping and deeply thought-out history of Australia's years as a convict colony. *The Great Australian Loneliness* (1937) by Queensland-born

adventuress Ernestine Hill brings the frontier to life with charm and warmth, even if her prose tends to be flowery and dated. She spent five years traveling the Outback by camel, pearling lugger, biplane, railway, and truck in the mid-1930s. In the rugged Kimberley, Mary Durack chronicled three generations of her family history in the 1959 Outback classic *Kings in Grass Castles* and its 1983 sequel, *Sons in the Saddle.* In 1981, 87-year-old A.B. Facey stepped seemingly out of nowhere with an autobiography that began when he went to work at the age of eight on a farm in the Outback and followed his adventures through Gallipoli and his life in Western Australia. *A Fortunate Life* went on to sell more than 600,000 copies—a blockbuster in the tiny Australian market.

Over the past 55 years Australians have shifted their literary gaze to the cities and suburbs where they live, rather than to an Outback that few of them really know. Ruth Park's *Harp in the South* (1948) and *A Poor Man's Orange* (1949) are set in the inner Sydney slums and have never been out of print. Helen Garner's novel *Monkey Grip* is about sex and drugs in the inner Melbourne suburb of Carlton during the 1970s. Multiculturalism has become another big theme in modern Australian literature, sparking a major literary scandal in the early 1990s when a young author who went by the name of Helen Demidenko won the prestigious Miles Franklin Literary Award for her novel *The Hand that Signed the Paper.* The novel's unusual and disturbing perspective on the Holocaust, seen through the eyes of a camp guard, relied heavily on the author's exploration of painful aspects of her Ukrainian ancestry for its acceptability. When it turned out that Helen Demidenko was in fact Helen Darville, an imaginative descendant of English immigrants, Australia's hoodwinked literary establishment was turned on its ear.

THEATER & DANCE
How remarkable that since 1974, when the Sydney Opera House was completed, people have used the words "Sydney" and "opera" together without a second thought. For most of its history, Australia was dismissed as a cultural wasteland by the rest of the world and by Australians themselves. The term for

this sense of something lacking was "the cultural cringe."

The cringe was partly a hangover from colonial days when sophistication was considered an inverse ratio of distance from Europe. Certainly Sydney is about as far as you can go from London's West End theaters or the gilt of the Paris Opéra. Australians who aspired to careers in theater and opera were obliged to head overseas. Opera singers Dame Nellie Melba and much later, Joan Sutherland, did just that. So did pianist Percy Grainger, best known for his 1908 composition "In an English Country Garden." "Sing 'em muck," Dame Nellie is reported to have told a performer heading down under, "that's all they understand."

If that was ever the case, it isn't any more. Australia not only has a world famous opera house, it also has something to put in it. The Australian Opera Company, the Australian Ballet, and the Sydney Dance Company—New South Wales's first professional ballet troupe, founded in 1971—are all based at the Sydney Opera House.

Across the bay from the Opera House, the Aboriginal Islander Dance Theatre has performances of traditional and modern Aboriginal dances. Melbourne competes with Sydney to be the theater capital of Australia, and Adelaide's Festival Centre is said to have even better acoustics than Sydney's Opera House. Adelaide's biennial Festival is huge.

The National Institute for Dramatic Arts (NIDA) was formed as a training ground for actors, directors, and set designers and has launched Mel Gibson and other international stars. In Melbourne's inner suburb of Carlton, experimental theaters La Mama and the Pram Factory give fledgling playwrights an opportunity to have their works performed. Among their alumni is David Williamson (1942–), Australia's most successful playwright. His credits include *Don's Party*, *The Club*, and the screenplay for the 1981 film *Gallipoli*. He lives in Sydney.

MUSIC

Australia's mainstream musical tastes tend to revolve around American-style light rock, with the play lists on the major radio stations pretty much following the standard blend of Top 40 hits and baby boomers' golden oldies that you can find from Portland, Maine, to San Diego, California. Government efforts to stem this cultural tide by requiring stations to include at least 20 percent of local product in their programs, for example, have come to little because much of the local sound is indistinguishable from that produced in the United States or Europe.

The didgeridoo, a ceremonial Aboriginal musical instrument from Arnhemland, has a deep throbbing note.

Rock stars

Australia has contributed enormously to the global talent pool, from Johnny O'Keefe in the 1950s ("Real Wild Child") to superstar rock groups such as INXS, AC-DC, Silverchair, Men at Work, the Little River Band, the Bee Gees, Black Sorrows, and Midnight Oil. The 1990s Aboriginal rock group Yothu Yindi is a refreshingly original band, using a blend of ancient Aboriginal rhythms and instruments. It has a very powerful, compelling sound that has done a considerable amount to popularize land rights causes.

Country

The musical traditions of Scots and Irish pioneers had a big influence in Australia, just as they did in the development of bluegrass and country music in America's Appalachia. Although strongly influenced by American Country-and-Western stars in the early years—Aussie performers adopted stage names like Tex—Australians included a healthy dose of Outback humor and bush themes, and created a distinctively local variety of country music. Tamworth, a country town of some 40,000 about 200 miles (320 km) northwest of Sydney on the New England Highway, serves as a sort of Australian Nashville, with recording studios and a ten-day country music festival held every January, at which the Golden Guitar award is given to the year's top performer.

Probably the best known Australian country star is Slim Dusty, who recorded his perennial classic, "The Pub with No Beer," back in the 1950s. It is still a big seller. And Slim Dusty himself has handily out-sold every rock band to hit these shores, including the Beatles, even if country music tends to be overlooked by the big city radio stations. That is starting to change. Country music is making inroads in the cities around Australia, partly because of the success of American superstar Garth Brooks, but perhaps more because of the appeal of homegrown stars such as Lee Kernaghan and James Blundell. Blundell's "Way Out West" perceptively captures the mood of the tough, restless young man who heads out to the Outback to find a new life.

Jazz & classical

Australia has world-class jazz musicians such as trumpeters James Morrison and Bob Barnard, pianist Graeme Bell, and all-around Don Burrows. Barry Tuckwell, one of the world's leading virtuosos on the French horn, is an Australian, and Australia's composers include Richard Meale, Peter Sculthorpe, Nigel Butterley, and Anne Boyd. The Australian Broadcasting Corporation maintains six symphony orchestras around the country.

CINEMA

Australia got off to a quick start in the film industry. A cinema opened on Pitt Street, Sydney, in 1896, only a year after the Lumière brothers opened the world's first cinema in Paris. Four years later, in Melbourne, a Salvation Army officer named Joseph Perry produced *Soldiers of the Cross,* which film

historians regard as the world's first genuine movie in the sense that it relied on a plot, not just visuals. It premiered at the Melbourne Town Hall in 1901 and was shown in the United States the following year. In 1906 the world's first feature film, *The Story of the Kelly Gang,* was also produced in Melbourne. Although it lasted only 40 minutes, short by today's standards, it was considerably longer and more involved than the typical ten-minute offerings of the age.

Australia had a thriving film industry throughout the silent film era, and more than 250 movies were produced here. Perhaps the most popular was an adaptation of C.J. Dennis's poem, *The Sentimental Bloke,* in 1919. Hollywood outshone the Australian film industry in the 1930s and helped to establish the American cultural hegemony in movies, pop music, and TV that Australia has never been able to shake.

Cinematic high points during World War II included Charles Chauvel's *Forty Thousand Horsemen,* about the charge of the Australian Light Horse at Beersheba in 1917, and the 1942 documentary *Kokoda Frontline,* which captured the toughness of the New Guinea campaign. *Kokoda Campaign* won an Oscar for cameraman Damien Parer. It wasn't until 1968, and the establishment of the Australian Film Institute to promote Australian cinema, that local filmmaking began a renaissance that continues to this day. The 1970s saw an emphasis on introspective productions, such as Peter Weir's *Picnic at Hanging Rock* and *My Brilliant Career,* which launched the international career of actress Judy Davis. In the 1980s Australian filmmaking became more commercial, with *Gallipoli, Breaker Morant, The Man from Snowy River* movies, and *Mad Max* and its sequels. In 1986 Paul Hogan's *Crocodile Dundee* became Australia's first international blockbuster, and it remains the most profitable Australian film ever made.

Over the past few years, Australian filmmakers have relied on Australia's unique brand of offbeat humor, with quirky films such as *Strictly Ballroom, Priscilla, Queen of the Desert,*

The 2,679-seat concert hall is the heart of the Sydney Opera House. Controversy raged over architect Jørn Utzon's design.

The balconied streets of Ballarat, Victoria, epitomize classic Australian town architecture.

Muriel's Wedding, The Castle, and *Babe.* In 1996 *Shine,* about the troubled pianist David Helfgott, earned Geoffrey Rush the Oscar for best actor. He has plenty of big name compatriots: Mel Gibson, Nicole Kidman, Greta Scacchi, directors Gillian Armstrong (*Little Women*), Bruce Beresford (*Driving Miss Daisy*), and Peter Weir (*Witness* and *Green Card*). Also in 1996, the cameraman John Seale won an Oscar for his work on *The English Patient.*

TELEVISION

The first TV viewing in Australia was an image of Brisbane's old convict-built windmill, broadcast to Ipswich, Queensland, in 1934. This was just an experiment—regular television broadcasting did not begin until 1956. Color TV reached Australia only in 1974.

From the start, American fare dominated Australian television, with early line-ups including *Lassie, Father Knows Best,* and *Hopalong Cassidy.* So it remains today, although traveling Americans will find that the "latest" episodes of their favorite shows

are actually about a year behind those back home. Australian television producers have also tended to borrow heavily from successful American themes. Late-night shows have hosts who shamelessly style themselves after David Letterman or Jay Leno, and medical dramas bear a striking resemblance to *ER* or *Chicago Hope.* The Australian versions of *60 Minutes* and *Wheel of Fortune* are straightforward adaptations.

For years Australians were vaguely embarrassed by their own locally conceived television, which seemed amateurish in comparison with slick American productions. No longer. Smartly produced Australian shows are gaining ground, and although American fare still takes up most of the broadcasting hours, more and more of the top-rated shows are homegrown. Variety shows, crime dramas—notably *Blue Heelers* and *Water Rats*—and current events top the charts.

In 2000, Outback Queensland provided the setting for the widely watched U.S. "game" show *Survivor,* in which teams of contestants pitted themselves against the elements.

Magazine shows are another mainstay. Australians may have borrowed the concept from Americans, but they have improved upon it considerably. *Burke's Backyard,* a folksy gardening and home care show, has been a long-running favorite, but there are many other magazine shows about travel, money, health, and sex.

Australians are pretty frank and don't shirk from candidly discussing the mechanics of sex on magazine shows, or showing bare breasts, or salting dialogue with a modest number of expletives. The episode of *Ellen* that turned America on its ear when the title character acknowledged she was gay, drew a yawn here. All of that was explored back in the early 1970s with a racy Sydney soap opera called *Number 96,* which had an openly gay character. (*Number 96* also featured full-frontal nudity, something American TV is still unlikely to show.)

That said, Australian TV is not one big bawdy cavalcade. A few years ago Channel Nine ran a show called *Australia's Naughtiest Home Videos*—or rather, they started to do so. When the network's proprietor, billionaire Kerry Packer, got a glimpse of what was appearing on his TV screen, he called the producers and in unbroadcastable language ordered them to take it off the air immediately. Suddenly a rerun of *Cheers* appeared, and the next morning switchboards at talk-back radio stations around the nation lit up with calls congratulating Mr. Packer and asking him to be Australia's next prime minister.

TV channels

Australia has three major commercial networks—Seven, Nine, and Ten—and they command the lion's share of the audience. Next in line comes the government-owned Australian Broadcasting Corporation, affectionately known as "Aunty" in TV's early days but now watched regularly by only about 15 percent of Australians. It has a lock on the "quality" end of news and current affairs shows, as well as some of the best locally produced dramas. Foreign fare on ABC tends to come from Britain. Last in the ratings stakes comes SBS. This station is devoted almost exclusively to foreign language broadcasts and arty movies, and has an audience share of about 4 percent.

Its evening news is superb, covering all parts of the globe. There are also two cable networks, and smaller networks in rural centers. Outback Australia has the Aboriginal-run Imparja Network, which shows a mix of popular American, Australian, and British shows.

ART & ARCHITECTURE

This is a young nation. A 19th-century building rates as "old" here, and 18th-century structures are almost unknown. The oldest building in Australia is Elizabeth Farm, a brick farmhouse built for the MacArthur family in Parramatta, west of Sydney, in 1793. (The MacArthur family was responsible for the early development of Australia's wool industry.) The house, with its simple lines and wide veranda, is open to visitors *(Tel (02) 9635 9488).*

A convicted forger named Francis Greenway laid the foundations of Australia's architecture. He arrived in New South Wales in 1814 and was appointed civil architect two years later by Lachlan Macquarie, the high-minded governor who was already embarking on an ambitious public works program. Over the next six years, Greenway designed 40 buildings—including the Hyde Park Barracks, St. James Church, and the courthouse in Windsor—often using the honey-colored sandstones from the nearby Hawkesbury Valley. Although his classic Georgian lines were crisp and harmonious, Greenway himself was argumentative and hot tempered; he was dismissed by Governor Brisbane in 1822. (A footnote to history: Greenway's portrait appeared until recently on Australia's ten dollar note, giving him the distinction of being the only forger honored on a nation's currency.)

For the most part Australia's civil architecture through the 19th century simply borrowed Europe's neo-Gothic, Renaissance, and classical styles. The University of Sydney was patterned on Oxford. Melbourne and the goldfield towns of Ballarat and Bendigo used the grand, ornate styles of Victorian England to display their wealth in the mid-19th century.

Domestic buildings, on the other hand, began to reflect their unique surroundings—after all, Australians had to live in them. In tropical Queensland, settlers elevated their homes and opened them up to allow cooling air to circulate. Verandas appeared all over

**"Rainbow Serpent Dreaming" (1989) by
Ginger Tjakamarra & Wingie Napaltjarri**

Australia. So did the classic two- or three-story Aussie pub, with its double-decked veranda and lacy ornamental ironwork. Row houses, embellished with similar ironwork, mushroomed in the inner cities. Out in the suburbs, the bungalow came into its own in the 1920s.

Around this time Australian civil architects began experimenting with their own style. The Sydney Harbour Bridge, completed in 1932, was the country's first quintessentially Australian landmark. It was to have been the world's longest single-arch bridge, but by the time it opened, New York's Bayonne Bridge had beaten it by 2 feet (0.6 m). Sitting opposite its southern pylons, over on Bennelong Point, is that other great Australian architectural marvel, the Sydney Opera House, designed by Danish architect Jørn Utzon in 1955. Other striking structures are Sydney's Australia Square tower and the MLC Centre, both by Austrian-born Harry Seidler. The principal designer for the Olympic Games site was Phillip Cox, designer of Darling Harbour, the Sydney Football Stadium, and the Yulara Resort near Uluru (Ayers Rock).

PAINTERS

Australia's first European artists did not know what to make of the prehistoric landscapes that spread before them, so they did what came naturally to 19th-century European minds: They rendered Arcadia, with noble savages and gum tree-lined lanes that look suspiciously like those in English villages.

In the late 1880s, Australian artists began to confront their country's harsh open spaces and blinding sun. A group of Melbourne artists, influenced by French plein-air painters and the Japanese aesthetic movement, took their easels out of their studios and into the dazzling sunshine. They often went to nearby villages such as Box Hill and Heidelberg, now part of suburbia. There they painted Australian bush scenes as they really are, working in the open air and refusing to succumb either to Australia's 100°F (38°C) summer heat, or to the Old World notion that landscapes must be lush to be beautiful. They embraced sunburned scrub with nationalist zeal. They became known as the Heidelberg school—after the village in the Yarra valley, not the German city—although they painted in other areas as well. Tom Roberts, Arthur Streeton, Charles Condor, and Frederick McCubbin were among the school's biggest names. Their works, which can be found in most of the major art galleries around the country, are some of Australia's masterpieces. Tom Roberts's "Shearing the Rams," which he painted in 1890 at a shearing shed in Brocklesby, New South Wales, is an Australian icon. Equally iconic is Charles Condor's "A Holiday at Mentone," a beach scene at a resort town (now suburb) south of Melbourne that captured Australia's heat probably better than any previous painting.

Landscapes and the bush have continued to be major themes in Australian art. Some of the biggest names are Sidney Nolan (who made a classic series of portraits of the bushranger Ned Kelly), Arthur Boyd, Clifton Pugh, Lloyd Rees, and Fred Williams. Albert

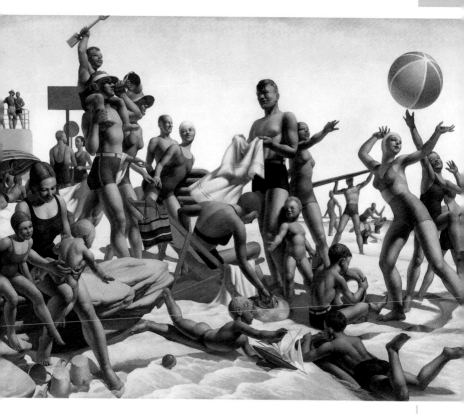

"Australian Beach Pattern" (1940) by Charles Meere hangs in the Art Gallery of New South Wales, in Sydney.

Namatjira, an Aboriginal watercolorist who died in poverty in 1959, had one of the surest eyes in capturing the harsh light of the central Australian deserts.

The National Gallery in Canberra houses Australia's largest art collection. Although the building was opened in 1982, the national collection had been started in 1968. In the early days there was a great deal of controversy about some of the spectacular purchases—most notably the million-dollar sum paid for American artist Jackson Pollock's "Blue Poles." Lately, Australian artists have been nudging their way into the seven-figure bracket. Rupert Bunny, a landscape artist in 1920s Melbourne, made the grade in 1988 when his "Nuit de Canicule" brought 1.25 million Australian dollars (800,000 dollars) at auction. You won't see it hanging anywhere, however. It was des-

troyed in a fire. To date, the record for an Australian painting is the 1.9 million Australian dollars (1 million dollars) paid in 1996 for Eugene von Guerard's 1856 landscape "View of Geelong."

Who is Australia's best known modern artist? That depends. The cognoscenti in Sydney's art circles will almost invariably point to the late Brett Whiteley, who died of a heroin overdose in 1992. Down in The Rocks area of Sydney, however, a large gallery sells the splashy works of the very much alive Ken Done, both originals and reproduced on scarves, table placemats, and sweatshirts. Decried as kitsch by Australia's so-called "serious" art world, Done is regarded as a living treasure in Japan where he has been accorded rare honors. Displays of his work there attract the same size of crowd as rock stars do. ■

Flora & fauna

WHEN AUSTRALIA SEPARATED FROM THE SUPERCONTINENT OF GOND-wanaland 65 million years ago, it took a continent's worth of ancient flora and fauna with it. Undisturbed by outside influences for millions of years, this wildlife evolved along unique lines and became the strangest assortment of creatures on the planet. Only Australia has monotremes (egg-laying mammals)—the platypus and echidna. It also has prehistoric landscapes with termite mounds 50 feet tall (15 m), boab trees, and ancient cycad palms, a species that dates back to the time of the dinosaurs.

Most of the mammals here are marsupials, a primitive family of animals that vanished long ago from most other parts of the world. A female gives birth to an embryo that continues its development in a separate pouch on the mother's belly (or back, depending on the species). As the offspring grows older and larger it can climb in and out of the pouch, riding piggyback on its mother. Kangaroos are best known for this, and you may see surprisingly large joeys—slang for baby kangaroos—bundling themselves into their mother's pouches for a fast bound across the plains. There are 150 species of marsupials, in a variety of sizes, from tiny kangaroo mice to powerful western gray kangaroos that can be well over 6 feet (1.8 m) tall. Koalas and wombats are also marsupials. They have an equally wide variety of foods. Kangaroos and koalas are vegetarians, but the Tasmanian devil, for instance, is very much a carnivore, as was the now presumed extinct Tasmanian tiger.

Because we live in such a small high-tech world these days, where satellites can plot your position within a few feet anywhere on the globe, it's comforting to know that all the backyard discoveries have not yet been made. In 1994 a ranger rappelled into a narrow 2,000-foot-deep (609 m) gorge in Wollemi National Park, less than 100 miles (160 km) from downtown Sydney, and discovered an ancient species of pine tree thought to have been extinct for 170 million years. Until that moment it was known only through fossils. (Its location and identity has been kept secret in case you were thinking of paying it a visit.)

Only a month later came the discovery of a unique stand of Huon pines, which appears to be more than 10,000 years old, on the jungly flanks of Tasmania's Mount Read. The pines, all male, have apparently been cloning themselves all that time, their bent branches touching the Earth and giving rise to new trees that carry on the DNA line. Although no individual is more than 1,100 years old, the DNA—identical to that of 10,000-year-old fossilized pollen found nearby—makes this stand a contender for the world's oldest living organism.

The deep, dripping forests of Tasmania give rise to periodic—but unconfirmed—sightings of the thylacine, a striped, wolf-size, carnivorous marsupial known as the Tasmanian tiger, believed to have been extinct since the 1930s. While this mystery captures the public's imagination, rangers in the central deserts have recently found several supposedly extinct mouse-size marsupials with far less fanfare.

If you travel in the Outback up north you'll see "wanted" posters tacked up on roadhouses and pubs—for the night parrot. Thought to have been extinct for more than a century, a dead specimen was found by a roadside in Queensland a decade ago. Although large rewards have been posted for (living) proof of another night parrot, the shy bird has proved elusive. The rewards have gone unclaimed.

KANGAROOS & KOALAS

It is easy to see kangaroos. Although 17 species of mammal are thought to have become extinct since the First Fleet arrived, 'roos are believed to be more numerous now than they were 200 years ago. Their population is estimated to be 50 million, or about three times the number of Australians. This is because graziers have made water so much more plentiful out on the plains. Farmers regard

A palm tree shoots up toward the light in a gap between the rocks in Purnululu (Bungle Bungle) National Park.

A red kangaroo in Outback New South Wales. A big male can stand 6 feet (1.8 m) tall and weigh up to 145 pounds (66 kg). They are grazers, competing with sheep and cattle for feed.

kangaroos as pests, and the government permits a cull of around three million yearly. Many are shot for food (see p. 22). If you want to see them, just take a drive at dusk, out in the grazing country west of the coastal ranges. Carry collision insurance, though, because kangaroos have a habit of appearing suddenly by the roadside, where they blend in splendidly. They look left, look right, and then hop out anyway.

Finding koalas in the wild isn't that easy, so zoos or game parks will be your best option. Most Australians have never seen a koala in the wild. Koalas can eat only the leaves of certain gum trees, and the best habitat for these has been swallowed by expanding suburbs. Estimates of koala numbers vary from 40,000 to 500,000. It is a far cry from what they were in the 1920s, when more than three million were shot for their pelts, known as "Adelaide chinchilla." They were protected in 1927.

Koalas these days are also plagued by chlamydia infections, blamed partly on stress, causing infertility and blindness. Although tree-planting and koala relocation programs are underway, suburban spread continues.

Kangaroo Island, off South Australia, gives probably your best chance of seeing one in the wild. Look in the forks of blue gums or manna gums—two of their favorite tree species—along the riverbanks. Or take evening walks on Victoria's Phillip Island; bushy fringe suburbs in Melbourne, Brisbane, or Sydney; or parklands along the coast. Or go to zoos or game parks, such as Cleland outside Adelaide, Healesville near Melbourne, or Eastern Creek Wildlife Park near Sydney. Private game parks used to let visitors cuddle the tubby little creatures, but many discourage that now, because it stresses the animals. As former Australian tourism minister John Brown said, "It stinks, it scratches you, and it's covered with fleas." His point was that they are wild animals, not beanie babies. (They are not bears either, but simply koalas.)

You are unlikely to see Australia's other special creatures—wombats, Tasmanian devils, echidnas, and platypuses—outside a zoo or game park. It is not that they are so endangered or rare, but they are shy, nocturnal creatures, and keep to themselves in forests and scrub, or quiet little streams.

A flock of budgerigars (*Melopsittacus undulatus*) at a water hole near Alice Springs. Many pet birds are Australian in origin: Parrots and cockatoos are often to be seen in huge flocks.

BIRDS

What you will see and hear a lot of in Australia are birds. More than 750 species, having a fantastic array of colors, shapes, and sounds live here. Many are found nowhere else. Galahs, brolgas, jabirus, and parrots, bright as rainbows, flit through the bush, and in the summer it's nothing unusual to see a large gum tree virtually white with sulfur-crested cockatoos, cackling and screeching in the branches. When you consider that bird fanciers overseas pay thousands of dollars for a pair of these cockatoos, you realize how special this place is—and how great the potential for smuggling and poaching, which are major problems.

The Aussie birds best known outside the country are the kookaburra and the emu, which is paired with the kangaroo on Australia's national coat of arms. The hooting laughter of a kookaburra is the sound effect Hollywood uses to evoke monkeys in the jungle. Emus, which can grow to 130 pounds (59 kg) and 6 feet (1.8 m) tall, strut the Outback and are a haunting sight when silhouetted against a dying orange sun. Like the other half of the coat of arms, they are also finding their way onto the dinner plates of the discerning, but the smoked emu prosciutto served in trendy city bistros will have been farmed, not shot in the wild.

KILLERS

Australia is also home to some of the world's least cuddly creatures: deadly snakes, poisonous spiders, venomous sea life, saltwater crocodiles, and the great white shark. All can kill, although fatalities are rare, newsworthy events. The taipan, the world's most toxic land snake, lives in the remote deserts of northern Australia and carries enough neurotoxin to kill 100,000 mice. The brown snake, death adder, and tiger snake also rate among the world's deadliest and are more common, but you are unlikely to see them. As a rule snakes are shy. Treat any that you see as potentially poisonous, though, and give them a wide berth. Most snakebite victims are bitten while attempting to kill the snake. When it comes to mortal combat, snakes are probably better at it than you. If you happen to be one of the 300 or so people who get bitten each year, stay calm, wrap the wound snugly, and head for

the nearest hospital. Don't wash the bite; doctors will need a sample of the venom.

Most of the deadly critters inhabit remote pockets of bush far from city lights, but Australia's most poisonous spider—the funnel web—lives in Sydney's suburbs. A relative of the trap-door spider, it lurks in rocks and cracks in brick, sometimes around swimming pools, and springs on its prey. Funnel webs are found across southeast Australia, but the most toxic varieties are near Sydney. The redback, cousin to the black widow, is found throughout the country. Antivenoms are available for both.

Ironically, the most dangerous spider in Australia is arguably the mild-mannered huntsman, but not because of its bite. It is because this large tarantula has been known on occasion to find its way into car vents, or under windsheild visors, and tumble into motorists' laps at inopportune times, scaring them into crashes.

GIANT LIZARDS
Australia has a good selection of lizards, about 400 species ranging from harmless little skinks that scamper around backyards to the peren-tie, a monitor lizard that can grow to a powerfully built 7 feet (over 2 m) long. Second only to their cousin the Komodo dragon in size, perenties are found in the central deserts and should be left alone. They are astoundingly fast, have large, strong, and razor-sharp claws, and if spooked will scamper up the highest thing they see. Out here on the plains, that's likely to be you or your mate. Another large monitor lizard, the goanna, is a much prized delicacy among desert Aborigines. For sheer comic-nightmare quality, the frill-necked lizard is hard to top. Looking like an animated gargoyle, it scampers across the desert on its hind legs with a wide frill of leathery skin extended to frighten other frill-necked lizards.

IN THE WATER
Northern Australia, north of the Tropic of Capricorn, has some of Australia's loveliest beaches and most inviting turquoise waters. Summers are crushingly hot and muggy, so it is deeply tempting to take a dip, and deeply

First catch your goanna! Chasing a tasty meal in the Outback

disappointing to see signs forbidding swimming from November through March. There are several very good reasons. Sea wasps, which are a highly toxic box jellyfish with nearly invisible tentacles up to 10 feet (3 m) long, killed about 60 swimmers in the last century. (Diehard surfers usually wear nylon stockings to help protect them from stings.)

A children's python rears up, in threatening posture, ready to attack, but snakes usually avoid conflict with humans.

Bluebottles, another variety of jellyfish, are painful, but not deadly, nuisances. Stonefish lurk in tidal pools and their spines can kill if stepped upon. The shy little blue-ringed octopus, which is actually brown until it gets upset, is found all around Australia. It has a gentle nibble, but its toxin causes respiratory failure within 12 hours. Given all that, the hotel pool starts to look pretty good.

Farther out along the Queensland coast lies the Great Barrier Reef, at 1,300 miles (2,092 km) long the world's largest living thing. Made of around 300 species of hard reef coral polyps, it grows as successive generations build on their predecessors. Around it live 1,500 species of tropical fish, 4,000 species of shellfish, and 400 species of sponge. There are giant clams, tortoises, whales, black marlins,

For the adventurous ecotourist: diving in a protective cage in waters patrolled by the great white shark off the southern coast of Australia

and dugongs (relatives of the manatee). Exploring it is an otherworldly experience.

The largest shark ever caught with rod and reel, a 2,664-pound (1,208-kg) white pointer, was taken in the waters off Ceduna, South Australia, in 1959. An even larger one was caught more recently near Albany, Western Australia, but was disallowed for record purposes because whale meat was used as bait. Steven Spielberg got his live shark footage for *Jaws* near Port Lincoln, South Australia. This is frightening stuff, but actually these magnificent creatures have been victims of bad press. Honeybees kill three times as many Australians as sharks do. There have been only about 550 known shark attacks in Australia since European settlement, according to the shark-attack file at Sydney's Taronga Park Zoo. Of these about 200 were fatal, a very small number considering the millions of Australians who swim in the ocean every weekend. The last fatal shark attack in Sydney Harbour was in 1937. The only man eating shark you're likely to see on the beaches down under will be a sun-bronzed Aussie devouring fish and chips made from school and gummy sharks. If the rod-and-reel record for a shark is ever broken, it won't be in Ceduna. South Australia put sharks on its protected species list in 1997. A quarter of a century after Spielberg scared a generation out of the water, ecotourists flock to places like Port Lincoln for opportunities to dive, in protective cages, with these amazing animals.

Crocodiles are the other monsters in Australian waters. At the Shire Offices, in the northern Queensland town of Normanton, is a plaster cast of possibly the world's largest crocodile—28 feet 4 inches (8.6 m) long, with the build of a modest-size dinosaur. It was shot in 1957 in the Norman River, which flows past this rough Outback town into the Gulf of Carpentaria. Saltwater crocodiles inhabit the estuaries, rivers, and mangrove swamps along the coast of tropical Australia, but they sometimes appear in pools up to 60 miles (96 km) inland. They are extremely dangerous and sly, using a high degree of skill to stalk prey. Prey includes anything up to and including pack-horses and cattle. Sometimes people fall victim to their appetites. It is extremely unwise to swim in these rivers and estuaries. Some

Saltwater crocodiles flourish in the slow-moving rivers and mangrove swamps of Queensland and the Northern Territory. They may travel up to 60 miles inland as well as out to sea.

victims, sadly, didn't know any better, because tourists had taken the Beware of Crocodile signs as souvenirs. To thwart that, copies of the signs are available for sale.

Freshwater crocodiles are also found in the tropics. They are smaller and shy, although on rare occasions they, too, have been known to attack people. They have slightly different snouts than saltwater ones, although this can be rather a fine distinction to try to make if you are swimming in a pond and see a "log" puttering along the bank.

TREES, SHRUBS, & FLOWERS

Laymen tend to divide Australian trees into two broad categories: those that are eucalyptuses, and those that are not. After you have asked a dozen locals to identify scores of different trees and learned that nearly all were some form of eucalyptus—blue gum, manna gum, red gum, snow gum, ghost gum, and so on—it is no surprise that there are about 600 different species of gum. They range from stunted mallee gums to towering giants like the karri trees in southwestern Australia, which at over 300 feet (91 m) tall are the world's tallest hardwoods. The coolabah tree, under which the jolly swagman camps in the song "Waltzing Matilda," is another form of gum tree. Gums are found everywhere, from harsh Outback desert to the snowfields in the mountains.

Australia has trees other than eucalyptuses, notably acacias, commonly known as wattle trees. There are more than 660 species of these flowering trees. One variety, known as mulga, is the dominant tree species in large parts of the Outback. Another, golden wattle, has become Australia's floral emblem, inspiring the green and gold livery of its sports teams from cricket to the Olympics. They are called wattles because the early settlers used the supple branches to build daub-and-wattle cottages, resembling ones they used to make back in England. Banksias, which were named for botanist Joseph Banks, are widely found and have orange, red, or yellow flowers. Casuarinas, or shea-oaks, are nearly as widespread and varied as eucalyptuses, ranging from the desert oaks of central Australia to river shea-oaks growing along the banks of the Murray River.

The Huon pine is an ancient and extremely slow-growing species found these days only in Tasmania. Its beautiful, dense, honey-colored wood was used to fashion cabinetry and rot-resistant boats until people woke up to the fact that it could take a thousand years to replace a big Huon pine.

New South Wales's floral emblem is the waratah tree, famed for its flaming red flowers. Up in the floodplains of the remote Kimberley are bizarre boab trees, which look as though they've been planted upside down. Although they do not grow exceptionally tall—60 feet (18 m) is a high one—their bulbous trunks can grow more than 80 feet (24 m) in circumference. The hollowed shell of one near Derby, Western Australia was used as a jail.

Much of Australia's interior is covered with low grasses and shrubs. Spinifex is ubiquitous north of the Tropic of Capricorn. From a distance these spiny shrubs look downy, but they were the torment of early desert explorers. Their needlelike leaves are easily capable of penetrating blue jeans and scratching your skin. Snakes and lizards love them.

Cattle flourish on the Mitchell grass that covers vast areas of the tropics. During the rainy season, these grasses can grow up to 30 feet (9 m) in a month. In the south, silvery-green saltbush covers much of the open country and supports most of the cattle and sheep in this arid landscape. Thousands of species of wildflowers grow in Australia, and many are found nowhere else on Earth. Western Australia is particularly rich, with more than 7,000 varieties (see pp. 220–223).

ALIEN INVADERS

Australia's native flora and fauna had the continent to themselves for millions of years, during which they adapted to the changing moods of the land. Then all the rules changed. Suddenly they were competing against sheep, cattle, wheat, barley, blackberry vines, carp, cats, and foxes. The new culture had very different ideas from the Aborigines about using the land. The fine balance was changed forever.

Rabbits have been one of the worst of the alien villains. In 1859 Thomas Austin, a grazier in Victoria, had a dozen rabbits brought out from England to provide a bit of sporting pleasure for him and his guests. Once the rabbits were turned loose in the scrub they bred like, well, rabbits, and soon their numbers were far beyond any amount of gentlemanly shot gunning. By 1865 hunters had already shot more than 20,000 rabbits, but there were thousands more in the bush. By the 1930s rabbit numbers had exploded to an estimated one billion. Their destructive nibbling had stripped bare large areas and endangered many native species of grass and wildflowers that were unused to this intense grazing. Shooting, poison, bulldozing their burrows—nothing seemed to work until in the 1950s scientists let loose the myxomatosis virus, which is lethal to rabbits but doesn't infect humans or native Australian species. Rabbit numbers plummeted, but the problem never went away. Over the years the population built up again. Some rabbits had developed immunity to myxomatosis. By the early 1990s, there were an estimated 350 million rabbits hopping around the bush. Scientists released a new disease, rabbit calicivirus, in 1996 which has wiped out 98 percent of rabbits in parts of the Outback, but seems to have left other populations untouched.

Rabbits may be the most destructive of the introduced species, but they are far from alone. In the past two centuries settlers have let loose an army of plants, fish, reptiles, and mammals that have wreaked havoc on the Australian environment. Some, such as foxes, rabbits, and trout, were introduced by English settlers for sport. Others, such as the American cane toad, were brought in to control pests—in this case insects that ravaged sugarcane—only to became noxious pests themselves.

The domestic cat is believed to be responsible for endangering many species of native birds and smaller mammals. Some city councils have passed ordinances requiring cats to be neutered and locked up at night, but cat owners are vocal lobbyists. The worst offenders are feral cats—descendants of pets gone wild.

Pigs, horses, and donkeys also run wild in the bush. So do camels, which were brought to Australia for the Burke and Wills expedition in 1860 and later to carry supplies to crews building the railroads and telegraph lines across the deserts. When trains and roads made the camels obsolete, they were simply slapped on the rump and chased into the bush where they have prospered ever since. ■

Sydney is Australia's oldest, largest, wealthiest, and most cosmopolitan city, with its internationally famous bridge, Opera House, and exuberantly glitzy skyline showcased around one of the most beautiful harbors in the world.

Sydney

Sydney Harbour Bridge

Sydney

FLYING INTO SYDNEY HAS TO BE THE FINEST INTRODUCTION TO AUSTRALIA imaginable. Look out your window and it's all there: the dramatic city skyline, the deep blue of the harbor spread into scores of inlets and bays, and a sprawl of terra-cotta roofs stretching to the horizon. And then you see it: the graceful ironwork of the Harbour Bridge, a perfect miniature from this height, and beside it, the white tiles of the Opera House shimmering like a pearl. You've definitely arrived. This is Australia. And it's just as they said it would be.

From 1,000 feet, anyway. After you land and begin to make your way through the tangle of grubby and crowded urban streets, craning your neck to look for landmarks such as the 960-foot (293 m) Centrepoint Sydney Tower, you realize that this city can be a little deceptive as well. Some Australians—chiefly staid Victorians from arch-rival Melbourne, who tend to draw morals from this sort of thing— will say you've learned your first lesson about the shallowness of Sydney's flashy money and California-style glamour.

A Sydneysider, on the other hand, will simply give you directions down to Circular Quay. The view is like a visual mantra—just sitting on an ornamental bench by the Opera House brings back the magic, as you watch the sunlight sparkle on one of the world's great harbors, the ferries coming and going, and the spread of million-dollar bungalows along the North Shore. No matter how many times you've been there before, when you go down to the quay on a sunny afternoon it's like seeing it for the first time all over again. Even the convicts supposedly cheered on their first glimpse of the harbor when the First Fleet sailed in through the Heads in 1788.

Sydney's secret is this dazzling waterfront, with its ornamental palms, gleaming yachts in quiet coves, and 70 beaches. Walk along any of them and you feel like whistling something bold and adventurous. If somebody hasn't made you a vice president, they will any day now. It's this infectious waterborne confidence that lures Australia's smartest and most artistically gifted, the very rich and those who want to be. Their scramble for waterfront footage has bumped real-estate prices to absurd levels, and the shock waves can be felt in the western suburbs, where much of the population lives. A house out there can still cost $A250,000 ($160,000), but a comparable one along the harbor could range well into eight figures. So most of Sydney's 3.7 million residents reluctantly live away from the water, then crowd the beaches, the Manly ferry, Darling Harbour, and Circular Quay on the weekends.

Area of map detail

Sun worshiper on the beach at Bondi

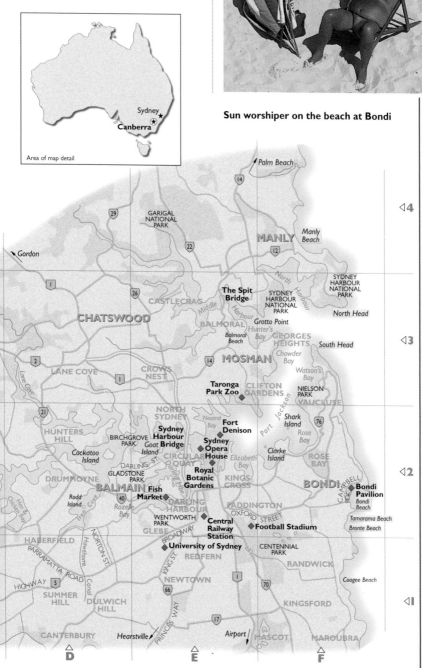

Palm Beach

14

GARIGAL NATIONAL PARK

29

MANLY

Manly Beach

22

12

Gordon

1

26

CASTLECRAG

The Spit Bridge

SYDNEY HARBOUR NATIONAL PARK

North Harbour

SYDNEY HARBOUR NATIONAL PARK

North Head

CHATSWOOD

Middle Harbour

BALMORAL

Grotto Point

Hunter's Bay

Balmoral Beach

GEORGES HEIGHTS

South Head

2

LANE COVE

CROWS NEST

MOSMAN

Chowder Bay

Watson's Bay

1

14

Lane Cove

21

NORTH SYDNEY

Taronga Park Zoo

CLIFTON GARDENS

NIELSON PARK

VAUCLUSE

HUNTERS HILL

BIRCHGROVE PARK

Sydney Harbour Bridge

Goat Island

Neutral Bay

Fort Denison

Port Jackson

Shark Island

76

Rose Bay

Cockatoo Island

DARLING ST.

CIRCULAR QUAY

Sydney Opera House

Elizabeth Bay

Clarke Island

ROSE BAY

DRUMMOYNE

GLADSTONE PARK

Royal Botanic Gardens

KINGS CROSS

BALMAIN

Fish Market

40

DARLING HARBOUR

BONDI

CAMPBELL

Bondi Pavilion

Bondi Beach

Rodd Island

Rozelle Bay

Iron Cove

PADDINGTON

OXFORD STREET

Tamarama Beach

HABERFIELD

WENTWORTH PARK

GLEBE

BROADWAY

Central Railway Station

Football Stadium

Bronte Beach

PARRAMATTA ROAD

NORTON ST.

University of Sydney

CENTENNIAL PARK

Hawthorne Canal

KING ST.

REDFERN

RANDWICK

HIGHWAY

5

NEWTOWN

66

1

70

Coogee Beach

SUMMER HILL

DULWICH HILL

PRINCES WAY

KINGSFORD

CANTERBURY

Heartsville

17

Airport

MASCOT

MAROUBRA

D

E

F

4

3

2

1

Sydney
🏔 75 E2
Visitor information
✉ 106 George St.,
The Rocks
☎ (02) 9255 1788

CITY DISTRICTS

Sydney sprawls. Despite its relatively small population, it covers almost as large an area as Los Angeles and seven times larger than Paris. It has more than 400 suburbs, the farthest being about 60 miles (96 km) from Sydney's Central Business District, or CBD.

The historic section of the city is known as **The Rocks,** a beautifully restored warren of alleyways and old stone buildings tucked away under the southern approach to the Harbour Bridge.

Pitt Street and George Street are the city's two main thoroughfares. They both begin at **Circular Quay** and stretch through the heart of downtown, lined with glittering skyscrapers, department stores, and gritty old shops that have somehow managed to survive the scramble for building land. This juxtaposition of styles, old and new, gives Sydney flair. For the past ten years **North Sydney,** across the harbor, has been sprouting modernistic skyscrapers, and it now looks like a downtown annex.

Residential suburbs in the North Shore and Sydney's ritzy east, such as **Point Piper, Double Bay,** and **Vaucluse,** rank among the priciest real estate in Australia, with harborfront mansions running into many millions of dollars—the record is 25 million Australian dollars (16 million U.S. dollars) for a mansion on Point Piper. Farther east is **Bondi Beach,** the most famous of the chain of surfing beaches fronting the Pacific Ocean close to the city.

The inner east section has Kings Cross, Paddington, and Darlinghurst. **Kings Cross** is Sydney's red-light district. Oxford Street is the main artery of trendy **Paddington** and **Darlinghurst,** with their brash nightlife and stylish row houses. This is Sydney's gay

center, where the Gay and Lesbian Mardi Gras draws half a million spectators, gay and straight, from Australia and around the world.

To the west is **Darling Harbour,** a pleasant walk from most places in the downtown part of the city. Or you can ride the monorail that runs along Pitt and Market Streets. Farther out are the inner west suburbs of **Glebe** and **Balmain,** old working-class docklands that have become fashionable. Also at this end of town is the raffishly chic **Newtown,** which was formerly a tough slum. Neighboring **Redfern** is still tough.

Farther west are **Homebush Bay**—site of the Olympics in 2000—and **Parramatta,** Australia's second oldest city. You can reach these by ferry from Circular

Quay, a better option than struggling through miles of stop-start traffic on the Parramatta Road, with its aggressive motorists, garish advertising, and tacky used car lots.

Sydney is multicultural, home to more than 200 nationalities. In the past 20 years it has become a strongly Asian city, though you might be disappointed by Chinatown, which is just a token two streets on the Darling Harbour side of the city. To see Sydney's Asian community at its most vibrant, go west to suburbs like **Cabramatta,** with its busy food stands, Asian apothecaries, sidewalks cluttered with signs in Chinese, Vietnamese, and Cambodian, cramped restaurants, and everywhere a fragrance of scorched spices and cooking oil.

For all the urban sprawl and tangle of streets, getting about Sydney is fairly easy. Central Railway Station and Circular Quay are the main transportation hubs, with regular trains, buses, and ferries reaching all parts of the city, into the nearby Blue Mountains, and down the Illawarra Coast. There are water taxis on the harbor, and a monorail links Darling Harbour with the CBD.

There are nice walks to be had downtown, notably in Hyde Park and the Botanic Gardens. This is not a bicycle-friendly city, but there are spectacularly scenic bicycle lanes over the Harbour Bridge. The safe exception for riders is leafy Centennial Park, near Paddington, where there is a riding track and jogging path through the gardens and past ornamental ponds. ■

The towers of Sydney's CBD, seen from The Domain, stand above the harbor.

Sydney Harbour

Manly

⛰ 75 F4

Visitor information

✉ South Steyne St.

☎ (02) 9977 1088

Manly ferry

✉ Circular Quay

🕐 30 minutes

💲 $

Fort Denison tours

✉ Circular Quay

☎ (02) 9206 1166

🕐 90-minute tours
noon & 2 p.m.
Mon.–Fri., & 10 a.m.
on weekends

💲 $

TO GET TO KNOW SYDNEY YOU NEED TO KNOW THE harbor (its real name is Port Jackson), and the best way to introduce yourself is to go down to Circular Quay and take a ferry. Any ferry will do, but the legendary ferry to Manly is the pick of the bunch. Take the slower-moving old-style ferry, rather than the speedy hydrofoil, and sit up on the bow and savor the sea air on the half-hour trip. The ferry cuts its way east from the quay, around the Opera House and the Botanic Gardens, past Sydney's leafy and most glamorous harborside suburbs, and out toward the magnificent sandstone promontories—the Heads—that guard the entrance to the harbor. Manly itself is a breezy seaside suburb on a spit of land between the north shore of the Harbour and the open ocean, with a line of Norfolk pines along its esplanade and the sun-splashed Manly Corso humming with life. It is a much more family oriented place than Sydney's other famous beach, Bondi. The return trip on the ferry is, if anything, even more majestic as you pass Fort Denison and draw up to the city skyline, Opera House, and Harbour Bridge.

of local shellfish. **Neutral Bay** *(Map 75 E2)*, was where ships of various nationalities docked. The city's earliest attempts at agriculture were at Farm Cove *(Map p. 83)*, now the **Royal Botanic Gardens.**

Water travel is a way of life in this harbor city. There are ferries from Circular Quay to the Olympic grounds at **Homebush Bay** *(Map 74 C2, see pp. 98–99)*, **Taronga Park Zoo** *(Map 75 E3, see p. 100)*, **Watson Bay** *(Map 75 F3)*—where you can sprawl in a manicured park eating some of Sydney's best fish and chips—and **Darling Harbour** *(see pp. 92–93)* precinct. The Hunter's Hill Ferry gives a nice tour of the hidden northwest arms of the harbor. All of the western ferry rides give a spectacular photo opportunity of the Opera House and Botanic Gardens, framed by the Sydney Harbour Bridge, as you return to the quay.

Tours operate to some of the harbor's islands. **Fort Denison** *(Map 75 E2)* was originally a place where poorly behaved convicts were sent to reconsider their conduct—sharks and strong currents proving efficient guards. Tours are also available to **Goat Island,** an old quarantine station and shipyard *(Map 75 E2, tours from Harbourmaster's Steps, west side of Circular Quay, on weekends at 10:25 a.m. and 1:25 p.m.).*

Landlubbers who get queasy even at the thought of being on a ship can take some excellent harbor walks, including the mile-long **Hermitage Walking Track** *(start from Nielson Park)* around the exclusive suburb of Vaucluse and Rose Bay.

A longer hike can be had on the **Manly Scenic Walkway,** which goes 6 miles (9.6 km) from Manly Cove to the Spit Bridge *(brochures and maps from the Sydney or Manly visitor centers, see p. 76 and p. 78).*

HARBOR TOURS

The harbor has tour boats as well as ferries leaving from Circular Quay—anything from a reproduction of Captain Bligh's *Bounty* to Mississippi-style paddle wheelers. There are also dinner cruises and floating restaurants. ■

View of Sydney Harbour from a ferry returning from Manly

If you are lucky enough to be in town on Boxing Day—the day after Christmas—you can see Sydney's harbor in full flower, as the world's fastest blue-water racing yachts swirl for position ahead of the start of the Sydney–Hobart Yacht Race.

The harbor is much more than a showcase for yachts and expensive real estate. Despite astronomical land prices, a surprising amount of the coast here is still forested. From the colony's earliest days, the military held much of the land, and it was never developed.

The harbor spills into countless bays and coves, whose names tell their story. **Chowder Bay** *(Map 75 F3)*, on the north shore, was where 19th-century Yankee whalers tied up and made their chowder out

THE BRIDGE

Sydney Harbour Bridge is instantly recognizable. This iconic structure is one of Australia's architectural and engineering wonders, and for 30 years it was the tallest structure in Sydney. Designed by Dorman Long and Co. of England to the specifications of its Chief Engineer J.J.C. Bradfield, the bridge was started in 1923 and completed during the Depression in 1932.

The bridge has a span of 1,650 feet (503 m) and the top of the arch is 439 feet (134 m) above the water. Originally designed to carry 6,000 cars an hour, it now tops 15,000 at peak times, in eight lanes. It also carries two railroad lines, a pedestrian walkway, and a bicycle track.

Hinges at the base support the full weight of the bridge and also allow for expansion.

Ventilation shafts for the Harbour Tunnel

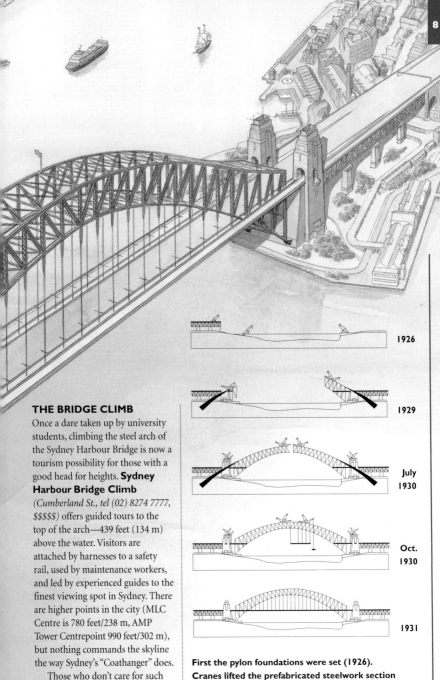

THE BRIDGE CLIMB

Once a dare taken up by university students, climbing the steel arch of the Sydney Harbour Bridge is now a tourism possibility for those with a good head for heights. **Sydney Harbour Bridge Climb** *(Cumberland St., tel (02) 8274 7777, $$$$$)* offers guided tours to the top of the arch—439 feet (134 m) above the water. Visitors are attached by harnesses to a safety rail, used by maintenance workers, and led by experienced guides to the finest viewing spot in Sydney. There are higher points in the city (MLC Centre is 780 feet/238 m, AMP Tower Centrepoint 990 feet/302 m), but nothing commands the skyline the way Sydney's "Coathanger" does.

Those who don't care for such drama can walk across the bridge on the pedestrian walkway, or go to the top of the South Pylon which, at 290 feet (88 m) above the water, gives nearly as spectacular a view. ■

1926

1929

July 1930

Oct. 1930

1931

First the pylon foundations were set (1926). Cranes lifted the prefabricated steelwork section by section, moving forward onto each new section as they built (1929). Cables sunk deep into the ground held the weight. When the arch was complete (1930), roadway sections were lifted into place and the cables removed.

SYDNEY HARBOUR BRIDGE WALK

Sydney Harbour Bridge walk

This can be anything from a brisk hour-long walk to an all-day excursion. It can even be satisfactorily jogged because it crosses only one busy street. The distance is something over 4 miles (7 km).

Start your walk at the Art Gallery of New South Wales. The steps leading up to the massive Corinthian columns of the entrance are a favorite meeting place.

Start at the **Art Gallery of New South Wales** ❶ *(Art Gallery Rd., The Domain, tel (02) 9225 1744, www.artgallery.nsw.gov.au)* in the leafy park known as The Domain. (You can take either the Explorer Bus or the free bus, No. 666, from Wynyard station on George Street to get there.) This beautiful, colonnaded, sandstone building dates from 1885 and is inscribed with mood-setting names of great Italian artists of the Renaissance, none of whom are actually represented inside. Instead the gallery has a collection of Australian masterpieces and one of the nation's most comprehensive collections of Aboriginal and Torres Strait Islander art.

From the gallery steps, follow the narrow road down through the botanic gardens and toward **Mrs. Macquarie's Point** ❷. This fig-shaded promontory was named in honor of Governor Macquarie's wife, Elizabeth, when the gardens were laid out in 1816. Supposedly she used to sit out here to watch the harbor and wait for the next ship to arrive from England. The **Royal Botanic Gardens** are

⚠ Also see area map 75 E2
▶ Art Gallery of NSW
↔ 4 miles (7 km)
⏱ 1 hour–1 day
▶ North end of Bridge

NOT TO BE MISSED
- Mrs. Macquarie's Point
- Circular Quay
- The Rocks
- Sydney Harbour Bridge

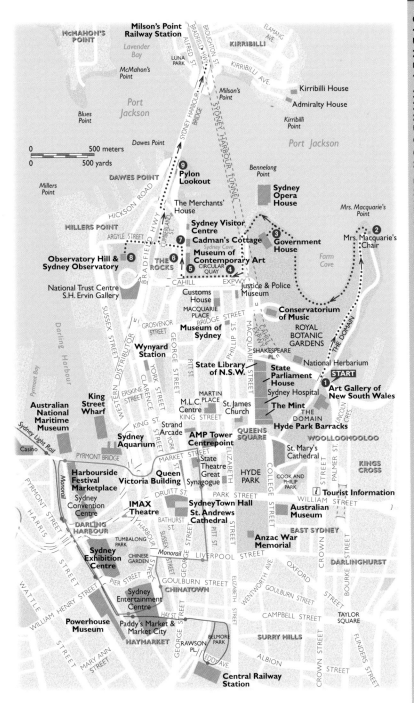

McMAHON'S POINT

Milson's Point Railway Station

Lavender Bay

KIRRIBILLI

ELAMANG AVE.

KIRRIBILLI AVE.

LUNA PARK

ALFRED ST.

BROUGHTON ST.

McMahon's Point

Milson's Point

Kirribilli House

Admiralty House

Port Jackson

Blues Point

Kirribilli Point

Dawes Point

Port Jackson

Millers Point

Bennelong Point

0   500 meters
0   500 yards

DAWES POINT

HICKSON ROAD

9 Pylon Lookout

Mrs. Macquarie's Point

Sydney Opera House

MILLERS POINT

The Merchants' House

Sydney Visitor Centre

7 Cadman's Cottage

Sydney Cove

3 Government House

2 Mrs. Macquarie's Chair

ARGYLE STREET

CUMBERLAND ST.

Museum of Contemporary Art

Farm Cove

Observatory Hill & Sydney Observatory

8

THE ROCKS

6

5

CIRCULAR QUAY

4

BRADFIELD HWY

CAHILL EXPWY

National Trust Centre S.H. Ervin Gallery

Customs House

Justice & Police Museum

Conservatorium of Music

MACQUARIE PLACE

BRIDGE STREET

PITT ST.

MACQUARIE ST.

THE DOMAIN

ROYAL BOTANIC GARDENS

GROSVENOR STREET

Museum of Sydney

CAHILL EXPWY

SUSSEX STREET

Darling Harbour

WESTERN DISTRIBUTOR

ERSKINE ST.

CLARENCE STREET

YORK STREET

GEORGE STREET

Wynyard Station

PHILLIP ST.

SHAKESPEARE PL.

National Herbarium

State Library of N.S.W.

START

1 Art Gallery of New South Wales

Australian National Maritime Museum

King Street Wharf

KING ST.

MARTIN PLACE

M.L.C. Centre

St. James Church

KING STREET

State Parliament House

Sydney Hospital

The Mint

LINCOLN CRES.

PALMER ST.

Casino

Sydney Light Rail

PYRMONT BRIDGE

Strand Arcade

AMP Tower Centrepoint

QUEENS SQUARE

THE DOMAIN

Hyde Park Barracks

HARRIS STREET

PYRMONT STREET

Monorail

Harbourside Festival Marketplace

Sydney Convention Centre

Sydney Aquarium

MARKET STREET

State Theatre

Great Synagogue

ELIZABETH STREET

HYDE PARK

COLLEGE STREET

St. Mary's Cathedral

COOK AND PHILIP PARK

WOOLLOOMOOLOO

WILLIAM STREET

KINGS CROSS

i Tourist Information

DARLING HARBOUR

Queen Victoria Building

DRUITT ST.

PARK STREET

Australian Museum

EAST SYDNEY

IMAX Theatre

BATHURST STREET

Sydney Town Hall

St. Andrews Cathedral

PITT ST.

WENTWORTH AVE.

OXFORD STREET

DARLINGHURST

TUMBALONG PARK

Sydney Exhibition Centre

CHINESE GARDEN

Monorail

LIVERPOOL STREET

Anzac War Memorial

GOULBURN STREET

BOURKE STREET

CROWN STREET

WATTLE STREET

PIER STREET

GOULBURN STREET

CHINATOWN

ELIZABETH STREET

CAMPBELL STREET

TAYLOR SQUARE

Sydney Entertainment Centre

HAY ST.

Powerhouse Museum

Paddy's Market & Market City

HAYMARKET

RAWSON PL.

BELMORE PARK

GEORGE STREET

EDDY AVE.

SURRY HILLS

ALBION STREET

FLINDERS STREET

WILLIAM HENRY STREET

MARY ANN STREET

Central Railway Station

a wonderful place for a picnic. In addition to the ornamental trees, duck ponds, sweeping lawns, and flower beds, the gardens have a glassed-in pyramid housing a collection of tropical plants and ferns.

From Mrs. Macquarie's chair you can look straight across Farm Cove to the Opera House. The path hugs the waterfront, but you can take a side trip to **Government House** ❸ *(Tel (02) 9931 5222, house closed Mon.–Thurs.),* whose grounds lie within the botanic gardens. This massive two-story home in Gothic Revival style was built in 1843 for the governor of New South Wales, but the republican-minded Labor government gave it to the people in 1996. You can wander freely in the gardens or take a tour of the house, with its Australian masterpieces on the walls, ornate drawing and dining rooms, and stenciled ceilings.

The shoreline path curves around to the **Sydney Opera House** (see pp. 86–87), and from there it follows another inlet (Sydney Cove) a couple of hundred yards to **Circular Quay** ❹. This stretch of footpath honors Australia's literary greats, with commemorative plaques set into the paving.

Circular Quay is the point of arrival for thousands of office workers who come daily to the city by ferry. It also attracts visitors taking sightseeing cruises and tour buses, or simply strolling the waterfront. It is probably the liveliest place for people-watching in all of Australia, with its blend of stockbrokers and secretaries and street sweepers, tourists speaking almost any language imaginable, derelicts, peddlars, hippies, and rural Australians taking a look at "the big smoke." You usually see a gaggle of jugglers, puppeteers, and street musicians, whose talents range from brilliant to embarrassingly awful. Just beyond the quay is the **Museum of Contemporary Art** ❺ *(George St., tel (02) 9241 5892, $$),* in a restored art deco building with a fashionable outdoor café.

The area known as **The Rocks** ❻ lies between George Street and the approach road to the bridge. This is Sydney's historic district, a warren of narrow streets and old stone buildings that have been lovingly restored. It is a far cry from the way the place looked in Sydney's Dickensian days, when these alleyways were the most squalid and dangerous in

Australia. Here lurked pickpockets, razor gangs, and hard-case thugs. An outbreak of bubonic plague around the turn of the century forced the authorities to step in and demolish some of the rat-infested structures. More were torn down in the 1920s to make way for the approach to the Harbour Bridge. By the 1970s, the government was ready to raze what was left of Sydney's oldest structures and replace them with office blocks. Only a hard-fought campaign by left-wing unions saved the historic quarter. Militant construction workers placed the first of their famous "green bans" on the proposed redevelopment, thereby stopping work. It was a tactic they were to use throughout the 1970s to save numerous heritage buildings around Sydney.

These days The Rocks is one of Sydney's treasured tourist precincts. It has boutiques, art dealers, cafés, an upscale hotel, and pubs such as the Hero of Waterloo, Sydney's oldest, built in 1844. **Cadman's Cottage** ❼, the

oldest house in Sydney (built in 1816), is at 110 George Street *(Tel (02) 9247 5033)*. Just along the street, at No. 106, the Sydney visitor center is in the Sailor's Home, built in 1864 to provide respectable lodgings for sailors. Upstairs, you can see a sailor's cubicle fitted out as it would have been in the 19th century.

From George Street you can take a short side trip along Argyle Street and then up **Observatory Hill** ⑧. It is a steep climb, but well worth it for the spectacular—and different—view of the Harbour Bridge, across to North Sydney and down to The Rocks below. Otherwise wind your way through the lanes up to the steps for the Sydney Harbour Bridge walkway on Cumberland Street.

The walk across the bridge to the North Shore is about three-quarters of a mile long (1.2 km), and every step seems to put both Sydney and the bridge's graceful ironwork in a new perspective. A museum inside the massive South Pylon tells the story of the building of

Circular Quay is the heart of the city, where ferries set out for waterside suburbs and where ocean liners such as the *QE II* still berth at the passenger terminal.

the bridge, and gives a grand view of the sky-line and harbor if you climb to the **Pylon Lookout** ⑨ at the top. For a really stupen-dous view, ambitious visitors might like to attempt the Bridge Climb, right over the top of the arch itself (see p. 81).

The walk ends on the north side of the bridge, and the two options for getting back to the city are both beautifully simple. The Milson's Point train station is only a stone's throw from the northern end of the bridge walkway, and from there you can catch a train back across the bridge to Wynyard station. Or you can go the scenic way and walk a couple of hundred yards down to the Luna Park or Milson's Point ferry landing, and cut across the harbor back to Circular Quay. ∎

Sydney Opera House

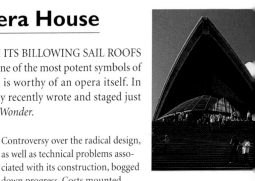

SYDNEY'S OPERA HOUSE, WITH ITS BILLOWING SAIL ROOFS and breathtaking harbor setting, is one of the most potent symbols of Australia. The story of its creation is worthy of an opera itself. In fact, the Australian Opera Company recently wrote and staged just such a piece, aptly titled *The Eighth Wonder*.

The saga started in 1955 with a contest to design an opera house for the site of the old tram terminus on Bennelong Point. After looking over 233 entries, the judges selected an innovative design by a Danish architect named Jørn Utzon. His vision for the building, which was to cost around 7 million Australian dollars (3.5 million U.S. dollars), resembled sails on the harbor. Perfect for a breezy, yachtie-style city like Sydney. (Utzon later said he had actually been inspired by a sequence of orange segments.)

Construction began in 1959, and the trouble started almost immediately.

Controversy over the radical design, as well as technical problems associated with its construction, bogged down progress. Costs mounted, adding fuel to the controversy. By 1966 Utzon had had enough. He

The Monumental Steps give the Opera House a grand entrance.

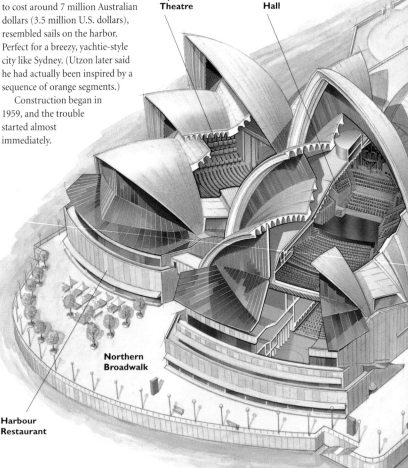

Opera Theatre

Concert Hall

Northern Broadwalk

Harbour Restaurant

Opera House

✉ Bennelong Point

☎ (02) 9250 7111, reservations (02) 9250 7777; e-mail: bookings@soh.nsw.gov.au

💲 Tours: $$

Monumental Steps

withdrew from the project and returned to Denmark, bitter about what he saw as heavy-handed interference in his work.

For its part, the New South Wales government seemed glad to see Utzon go, turning the project over to a team of local architects. Costs continued to spiral. The state funded it with Opera House lotteries. Even so, by the time Queen Elizabeth II opened the building in 1973, Sydney's new landmark had cost more than ten times the origi-

nal estimate, and it was ten years behind schedule. Its first production, appropriately enough, was Prokofiev's *War and Peace.* Happily, more than 30 years after Utzon left Australia, the architect and the New South Wales government reached a rapprochement. Utzon, now in his eighties, was hired to refurbish the interior and fulfill some of his original vision.

Inside are the 1,547-seat **Opera Theatre,** the 2,679-seat **Concert Hall,** two smaller theaters, a cinema, an exhibition hall, and a bistro restaurant. The second flock of sails, the "baby" opera house beside the main complex, contains the **Bennelong restaurant,** one of the finest in Sydney (see p. 368). Take a tour to see the complex. ∎

Bennelong Restaurant

Playhouse

Western Broadwalk

The 2,679-seat Concert Hall stages operas, here Monteverdi's *The Coronation of Poppaea,* as well as concerts.

The Sydney Youth Orchestra performs in one of the large northern foyers.

Downtown Sydney

SYDNEY IS AN INTERNATIONAL CITY. ONCE AWAY FROM ITS dazzling waterfront, its concrete-and-glass canyons and traffic-clogged streets resemble those of cities the world over. Cranes on the skyline and construction pits between buildings speak of change. Nevertheless, a stroll through Sydney takes you shopping and sight-seeing your way around a uniquely Australian downtown.

Australian Museum

www.austmus.gov.au

✉ 6 College St. (opposite Hyde Park)

☎ (02) 9360 6000

$ $

A stained-glass window in Sydney Town Hall commemorates Captain Cook's 1770 landing at Botany Bay.

A good place to start is the almost ludicrously ornate Victorian-era **Sydney Town Hall** *(Tel 1300 651301)* on the corner of George and Druitt Streets *(Map p. 83).* Built of golden sandstone in 1874, it has an elaborate concert hall. Next to it is **St. Andrews Cathedral** *(Tel (02) 9265 1661),* about the same age but simpler in style. This is the oldest cathedral in Australia, and at lunchtime on Thursdays you can hear free recitals on the powerful pipe organ. The subway station of Town Hall lies beneath these two buildings.

Across Druitt Street is the beautiful **Queen Victoria Building,** which was built in 1898 for the city's fruit and vegetable markets. This extravagant three-story sandstone building occupies a full city block and was carefully restored in the early 1980s, after having fallen into serious disrepair. The sculptured exterior is impressive, but the interior is even more opulent, with mosaics, stained-glass windows, and the elaborate one-ton Royal Clock, which is suspended from a central glass dome. During the Christmas season, a huge tree is set up on the ground floor and rises past the mezzanine levels. Carolers gather around it and create a cozy Yuletide atmosphere. The QVB, as it is known, houses more than 200 upscale boutiques and cafés, and has some of the best shopping in Sydney. The cellar holds an inexpensive and varied food court. For something a bit more ostentatious,

go across George Street, and in the **Strand Arcade** beneath the Hilton Hotel you'll find the exuberantly Victorian Marble Bar.

The Queen Victoria Building stretches an entire city block along George Street. At the end of the building, turn right on Market Street. Two blocks will take you past the ornate **State Theatre** *(49 Market St., tel 13 61 00)* with its gilt decor and on to the **AMP Tower Centrepoint** *(100 Market St., tel (02) 8223 3806, $$),* on the corner of Pitt Street. Opened in 1981, the 960-foot-high (293 m) tower with its gold minaret is the highest structure in the Southern Hemisphere. It's not exactly heritage Sydney, but few visitors pass up an opportunity to go to the observatory or two revolving restaurants, and get sweeping views that stretch as far as the Blue Mountains (see pp. 104–105).

Farther down Market Street is **Hyde Park,** with flower beds, fountains, and the **Anzac War Memorial.** This is Sydney's central park. Australia's first cricket match was played here in 1803, and on sunny days the park fills up with office workers having lunch. The art deco Anzac War Memorial, at the southern end of the park, was built in 1934 to commemorate the dead of World War I. A worthwhile detour here is the **Australian Museum,** on the southeast corner of Hyde Park. This massive sandstone structure houses the nation's largest natural history collection, as

well as displays of Aboriginal and Papua New Guinean artifacts.

Otherwise head to **Hyde Park Barracks** on the northern end of the Queens Square, which was home to 800 convicts in Sydney's bad old days, when they were marched out in chains each morning, little more than slaves, to work on public projects or for one of the free settlers. After transportation to New South Wales ceased in 1848, the barracks became an immigration office and later a court building. The convict-architect Francis Greenway (see p. 61) designed this three-story structure in 1819 in a Grecian style. Today it is a museum on Sydney's early days and social history. Australians can check genealogical records on a computer to see if they have any convicts in their ancestral woodpiles.

Next door to the Hyde Park Barracks is **The Mint** *(10 Macquarie St., tel (02) 9232 3488, $)* which started out in 1814 as the Rum Hospital. After gold was dis-covered in the colonies, it became the Royal Mint, stamping out gold coins from 1854 until 1927. Today it is a museum devoted to gold in Australia.

Just beyond the mint is New South Wales's **State Parliament House** *(Macquarie St., tel (02) 9230 2111)*. The public gallery is open when parliament is sitting, and tours are available when it is not. The **State Library of New South Wales** is next on Macquarie Street's sandstone row. Some of Australia's historic records are here, including the ships' logs of Captains Cook and Bligh. The entryway floor has a mosaic of Capt. Abel Tasman's 17th-century chart of Australian waters.

Continue past the **Museum of Sydney** *(37 Philip St., tel (02) 9251 5988)* and the Greenway-designed **Conservatorium of Music** *(Tel (02) 9351 1263)*, which has free lunchtime recitals on Wednesdays, to Circular Quay. ■

The Queen Victoria Building on George Street, built as a fruit and vegetable market, was restored in the early 1980s and now contains upscale boutiques and cafés.

Hyde Park Barracks
✉ Queens Sq.
☎ (02) 9223 8922
💲 $

State Library of New South Wales
✉ Macquarie St.
☎ (02) 9273 1414

Cricket

Cricket is virtually a way of life for Australians in the summer. People play it in every park, on the beaches, and even in offices, where workers playfully bat at crumpled bits of paper with rolled up magazines around the water cooler. It murmurs in the background, on radio or TV, whenever the Australian national team is playing against a visiting country. Airline pilots have been known to make inflight announcements when a vital wicket falls or a batsman makes his "century"—a landmark score of a hundred runs in a single innings (or at-bat).

This fascination with what appears to be one of the world's slowest games bemuses and puzzles most visitors—unless they come from South Africa, England, India, Pakistan, Sri Lanka, New Zealand, or the Caribbean. After all, this is a game that, in its "test match" version, takes five days to play, generally under a broiling sun, and more often than not results in a draw. All this time nobody ever seems to be doing much, except one bloke who keeps running across the field to hurl the ball at another well-padded bloke who slashes at it with a paddle-shaped bat. Maybe he'll hit it and run. Maybe he won't. Hours pass this way. "Baseball on Valium," is how some visiting Americans have dismissed it. Or croquet on speed. But that is to miss all its drama and strategy.

The place to see a big-league cricket match in Sydney is the Sydney Cricket Ground (SCG), near Centennial Park in eastern Sydney. The ground holds a little over 40,000 spectators. The nicest seating is in the elegant Members' Pavilion, built in 1886, but since this haven of politeness is open only to members and their guests you will probably have to make do with one of the regular stands. (You could always put your name on the 20-year waiting list for a membership and come back another time.) The most atmospheric seating used to be the notorious Hill, a grassy patch opposite the Members' Pavilion, where shirtless, sun-bronzed, tattooed spectators drank, brawled, and lazed away the scorching Australian afternoons, offering wittily obscene comments on the fielders. These days the Hill

Shane Warne bowls one of his tricky spun balls in an England-Australia Test Match. Opposite: Matches under floodlights scandalized the purists when first introduced but proved popular with spectators.

is gone, replaced with soulless but more comfortable seating.

There are two varieties of cricket: the old-style, five-day-long test matches and the newer—and to traditionalists, more vulgar—one-day cricket. The faster one-day cricket is becoming the game's money-spinner these days, and a big international match will have the most rousing atmosphere. If you want to get just a glimpse of the game, try going along to the Sydney Cricket Ground for a Sheffield Shield match—played between the states—late in the afternoon, when you can often get in for free to see the last hour's play.

The rules are a little hard to explain, but if you ask an Aussie in the stands, he or she will undoubtedly be only too happy to give you a play-by-play rundown. Discerning Americans will be able to see the origins of baseball in cricket. The game is played with a wide, flat bat made out of willow, and a red ball, slightly

larger and heavier than a baseball, with a single line of stitches around the middle. The playing area is an oval, generally much larger than a ballpark in the U.S. Each side has 11 players, and one team fields while the other bats.

Unlike baseball, however, cricket has two batsmen up at once, although only one at a time faces the pitcher (called a bowler here). The batsman's job is to use his bat to defend a wooden frame behind him, called "the stumps" or "wicket," upon which two pieces of wood, the bales, are balanced. If the bowler can get a ball past him and dislodge those bales, the batsman is out. To use cricket terminology, he's lost his wicket.

Bowlers hurl the ball stiff armed, making it bounce at the batter's feet. They use all manner of tricks to take a wicket, craftily putting spin on the ball so it bounces weirdly off the seam or simply relying on brute power and intimidation, racing in and hurling it at 100 miles an hour so that it rears up in the batsman's face. This can be a dangerous game. Strategically placed fielders wait with cupped hands to catch a nicked ball. As with baseball, anything caught on the fly is out. The fielder behind the wicket (the wicket keeper) wears

mitts, but nobody else does. It's a game for players with lightning reflexes and tough, callused hands, who don't mind the odd broken finger or three.

For their part, batsmen have to try to hit the ball and score runs. The duel between batsman and bowler can go on for hours. A ball hit to the boundary is worth four runs. One hit over the fence, home-run style, is worth six. Otherwise the batsmen scamper back and forth between the stumps. Eventually somebody loses their wicket and a new batsman comes in. When a team loses ten wickets its innings ends and the fielding side comes in to bat. In a test match each side gets two innings.

Although professional cricket players are anything but choir boys—the beer drinking record of 56 cans on the flight from Sydney to London is held by a former Australian batsman—there are no American-style tantrums or umpire bullying displays on the field. The pride of nations rests on the decorum of their cricketers. Even outrageous umpiring decisions are accepted with tensely gritted teeth. Another note to globetrotting American sports buffs: If the ball is hit into the stands, you must give it back. ∎

Darling Harbour

Darling Harbour
🅰 75 E2
Visitor information
www.darlingharbour.com
☎ (02) 9286 0111
🚝 Monorail from
Market St. or Pitt
St., Sydney Explorer
bus or ferry from
Circular Quay

**Powerhouse
Museum**
www.phm.gov.au
✉ 500 Harris St.
☎ (02) 9217 0111
💲 $

DARLING HARBOUR IS ONE OF SYDNEY'S REDEVELOPMENT successes. What was once an eyesore of dilapidated wharves is now a humming tourism and leisure precinct on the waterfront in the city's inner west. It started in the mid-1980s with bull-market cash, vision, optimism, and some very heavy politicking, particularly in regard to the monorail that provides the public transportation link from Darling Harbour to the city. It opened in 1988, amid the fanfare of Australia's bicentennial, and the area has not looked back since. Skyscrapers have sprouted nearby, as have a convention-center-scale hotel and a glittering new casino, and businesses have shifted to the area. But Darling Harbour was designed for family-oriented entertainment—and it delivers. This is a great place to bring kids.

The area's two biggest family attractions are the Powerhouse Museum and the Sydney Aquarium. Both are world class. The **Powerhouse Museum** is in an old electricity generating station

The plasma ball is one of the popular hands-on exhibits at the spectacular Powerhouse Museum in Darling Harbour.

that used to power Sydney's tramway system—hence the name. Nominally a museum of applied industry (and it does have superb exhibits of working steam engines), it exuberantly exceeds its brief, offering imaginatively displayed collections on the history of Australian rock music, costume jewelry, trains, and more. Airplanes hang from the ceiling, a cinema is in art deco style, and the top-floor restaurant has brilliantly colored murals by Australian pop artist Ken Done. The emphasis in the

museum is hands-on fun and interactive displays, which is why it makes a particularly nice place to bring kids. On the first Saturday of each month, it's free.

Darling Harbour's other blockbuster attraction is the **Sydney Aquarium** (the ferry stops here). Its transparent underwater tunnels allow visitors to stroll among the sharks, eels, and stingrays of its immensely popular "Open Ocean" exhibit. This is one of three oceanariums moored in the harbor in front of the aquarium building. Another is devoted to the ecosystem in the harbor itself, and the third—also hugely popular—to seals and sea lions. Inside the main building are coral displays, a Great Barrier Reef exhibit, and saltwater crocodiles. The aquarium's popularity is also its main drawback: The place can get very crowded on weekends. Nearby is the restored 1938 steam ferry, the S.S. *Steyne*. Star City, Sydney's glitzy casino-hotel complex, sprawls on the northeastern flank of Darling Harbour.

AROUND THE HARBOR
The aquarium is a good place to begin a looping walk around Darling Harbour. Start by walking across the **Pyrmont Bridge,** built

in 1902 as the world's first electrically operated swing bridge to accommodate tall-masted ships. It is used only by pedestrians and the monorail today.

When you get across, the **Australian National Maritime Museum** is on the right. As an island nation, much of Australia's heritage is tied in with the sea, and the museum tells the story, from the Aboriginal canoes to the convict ships to the liners of the 20th century. The broader story of Australia and the sea is also covered, from the age of exploration, to surfing culture and the immigrants who have come by sea, both legally and illegally. A World War II destroyer, a Soviet sub, and a Vietnamese refugee boat are moored in the harbor in front.

On the left as you step off the Pyrmont Bridge is the enormous, tinted glass-and-steel **Harbourside Festival Marketplace.** This tourist shopping mall has a multistory food court, which devel-

opers hoped would make it the focal point for the Darling Harbour project. In fact, it is probably the least interesting feature of the precinct, but if you don't mind the lack of atmosphere, it is a convenient place to have lunch when you are here.

A stroll along the harborside, past the **Sydney Exhibition Centre,** will bring you to the **Chinese Garden** *(Harbour Rd., tel (02) 9281 6863, $)* at the southern end of the Darling Harbour complex. Landscaped by architects from Guangdong, the walled enclave has a Lake of Brightness and Courtyard of Welcoming Fragrance, and it is stunningly effective at shutting out all the hustle and bustle of the city. Chinese tea and cakes are available.

Get revved up again at the eight-story **IMAX Theatre** nestled in the freeway interchange nearby. Follow the waterfront back to Pyrmont Bridge, or catch the monorail as it slithers along the city streets. ∎

Sydney's monorail links Darling Harbour with the Central Business District.

Sydney Aquarium
- ✉ Darling Harbour
- ☎ (02) 9262 2300
- 💲 $$$

Australian National Maritime Museum
www.anmm.gov.au
- ✉ Darling Harbour
- ☎ (02) 9298 3777
- 💲 $$

IMAX Theatre
- ✉ Southern Promenade, Darling Harbour
- ☎ (02) 9281 3300

Bohemian Sydney

PINNING DOWN THE BOHEMIAN QUARTER IN SYDNEY IS no easy task. In a city known the world over for its breezy, beachy indolence, bohemia (in shorts, thongs, and Bollé sunglasses) seems to be everywhere. Paddington and Darlinghurst, though, in the inner east, make a pretty strong claim with their blend of seediness and sophistication. Oxford Street, the main thoroughfare, is a cavalcade of retro cafés, bookshops, nightclubs, strip joints, galleries dealing in ultracool kitsch, sex shops, and black leather. It starts at the southeastern end of Hyde Park and winds on to Centennial Park. This spread-out strip has no particular social focus, although on Saturday mornings the bustling Paddington Village Bazaar comes close. One of the architectural features of Sydney's inner east is the elegantly restored Victorian-era row houses, their balconies trimmed with wrought iron that used to be known as "Paddington lace."

Oxford Street
Bus 380 or 382 from Circular Quay run the length of Oxford St.

Paddington Village Bazaar
Corner Oxford & Newcombe Sts.

Kings Cross
Bus 324, 325, or 327 from Circular Quay. Train station on Darlinghurst Rd.

Opposite: The Gay and Lesbian Mardi Gras is one of the biggest events on Sydney's calendar. The highlight is the spectacular parade down Oxford Street.

Darlinghurst is a sort of trendy Little Italy, with its self-consciously cool sidewalk cafés. Stanley Street, which runs due east off Hyde Park, is the social scene here, and it is a good spot to linger over an espresso and the Sunday newspaper, soaking up ambience and sunshine. **Kings Cross,** a few blocks farther north, is Sydney's red-light district—a weird blend of prostitution, crime, strip joints, nightclubs, fast food, and hard drugs, with a smattering of expensive restaurants and international hotels thrown in to confuse. The Cross, as it is known, was a popular R&R hangout for troops on leave during the Vietnam War and it still attracts a lot of them, along with curious tourists, runaways, derelicts, college students on a big night out, and bachelor parties (called Bucks' nights here). The El Alamein Fountain in Fitzroy Gardens is the area's focal point.

Just east, **Elizabeth Bay** rubs shoulders with the Cross, but it is decidedly quieter and infinitely more fashionable. This was Sydney's fashionable bohemian quarter in the 1920s, and, with its stylish period apartment blocks, it is still popular with writers, entertainers, and journalists.

The peninsular suburbs of **Glebe** and **Balmain,** in Sydney's inner west, used to be rough working-class neighborhoods for dockyard workers, but they have now been discovered and their houses carefully restored. Balmain is rich in Victorian-era waterfront pubs, while Glebe is a jumble of interesting hole-in-the-wall eateries, cafés, and bistros. *(Balmain is accessible by ferry from Circular Quay, or bus 442 from the Queen Victoria Building. To get to Glebe, take bus 431 or 434 along George St. and up Glebe Point Rd.)*

Newtown *(take the Liverpool-City rail line)* is a funky melting pot of students, gays and lesbians, intellectuals, and artists, perched on the edge of Sydney University. Twenty years ago it was regarded as a grungy slum. Now it is fashionably chic, although it still has a strong underground feel to it. King Street, the main thoroughfare, has trendy cafés, ethnic restaurants, and secondhand bookshops. The hot, sweaty, and smoky pubs here are the focus of Sydney's dwindling live band scene. ■

Beaches

THERE ARE MORE THAN 70 NAMED BEACHES AROUND Sydney, some of them on the harbor, others fringing the ocean. The closest ocean beach to downtown Sydney is Bondi Beach, which has become synonymous around the world with Aussie surf culture. On weekends this golden crescent of sand, located 5 miles (8 km) west of Sydney, becomes a coconut oil-scented kaleidoscope of thousands of beach towels, bronzed swimmers, surfers, and sunbathers.

As a suburb, **Bondi** (pronounced Bond-EYE) calls to mind a fading seaside resort. Despite decades of decline, it still offers a great sunny, salty, breezy day out, but is only a shadow of its former self. Bondi's glory days would have been in the 1920s and '30s, judging by the art deco Bondi Hotel, the jumble of 1920s apartment blocks overlook-

ing the beach, and the gaudy Spanish-style Bondi Pavilion, which was built as deluxe changing rooms in 1928. In the 1990s the town spent a lot of money to spruce up tired facades, landscape the foreshore, and improve Campbell Street —a traffic-clogged thoroughfare of ice cream parlors, surf shops, and in-line skate rentals. Christmas on

Bondi Beach is a Sydney tradition, but drunken hooliganism has tainted it. Alcohol has now been banned on the beach in a bid to regain the family atmosphere.

South of Bondi is **Tamarama Beach,** known as Glamarama because it is where Sydney's beautiful people hang out. A mile or so farther south are **Bronte** and **Coogee Beaches,** both very family oriented. **Manly Beach,** north of the Harbour, is probably Sydney's second best-known cres-

cent of sand. Manly (see p. 78) occupies a narrow spit of land that ends in the dramatic sandstone cliffs at the entrance to the harbor. All these beaches are "outer beaches" facing the open Pacific.

The inner harbor has dozens of lovely beaches. One of the prettiest is **Balmoral,** on Hunters Bay. It has a genteel, Edwardian atmosphere, with palm trees and an old bandstand at the Bather's Pavilion, now an extremely classy restaurant known for its champagne breakfasts. ■

Right: Surf Carnival at Bondi Beach. After rescuing hundreds of thoughtless tourists during the 2000 Olympics, many of whom were well outside the safety flags, Sydney's lifesavers have had enough: They can now fine persistant errant swimmers $A220 for going out of bounds.

Surf lifesavers

Nothing evokes Sydney better than images of hard-blue sky, golden sand, and the bronzed figures of its legendary surf lifesavers in their distinctive yellow and red caps. The world's first surf lifesaving club was formed at the Bondi Pavilion in 1906. A bronze sculpture of a surf lifesaver stands in front of the pavilion to mark the fact. The club was formed in response to a rising number of drownings, when more people began to pursue the new craze called bodysurfing. Few knew anything about riptides or surf conditions then, because until around 1900 the authorities discouraged daylight swimming as an affront to public decency.

Surf lifesaving clubs quickly sprang up all around Australia. There are now 260 of them, with 73,000 volunteer members, who rescue about 11,000 swimmers each year. Surf lifesaving has become a sport in its own right, with colorful surf carnivals.

Bondi's lifesavers, who guard Australia's busiest and most famous beach, have plucked more than 400,000 people out of the surf since 1906. To make sure you don't add to that tally, swim between the yellow-and-red lifesaving flags. If you do get caught in a riptide, do not try to fight it. Swim to the side to try to get out of it and raise your hand to attract a lifesaver. ■

Olympics 2000

When Australia's much-loved 400-meter sprinting champion Cathy Freeman lit the Olympic flame in Sydney's new Olympic Stadium on September 21, 2000, it marked the beginning not only of a fabulous ten-day sporting spectacular, watched by billions around the world, but a sort of grand "coming out" party by Australia.

Australia is one of only five nations with a perfect record of attendance at the modern Olympic Games. They weren't going to bother with the first one in 1896—it seemed a bit far to go—but a 22-year-old Melburnian named Edwin Flack happened to be in London at the time, working for an accounting firm. He took a couple of weeks off work, went to Athens, and won the 800 and 1,500 meters. Australians have competed in every Olympics since, taking home a prodigious number of medals for such a thinly populated country. Melbourne hosted the 1956 Olympics, the first time the games have been held in the Southern Hemisphere. In 2000 it was Sydney's turn....

Well aware that the eyes of the world would be on their far-flung nation, Australia had spent seven anxious years and more than 5 billion Australian dollars (U.S.$2.5 billion) preparing for this fortnight in the sun. But stage-fright butterflies quickly turned to delight as the world's athletes, commentators, and officials marvelled that these had been the best-run and most successful Olympics in history, with many observers remarking (only half jokingly) that the games ought to remain in Sydney permanently. More than 10,000 athletes from 200 countries competed in 28 sports, and millions of spectators were housed and transported round the city without a hitch.

Cathy Freeman lit the Olympic torch at the start of the most successful games ever.

If it was a high water mark for the Olympic movement, it was also a seminal moment for Australia, creating a deep sense of family-like unity and pride among its 18 million inhabitants. Thousands volunteered to help out in Sydney, neighbors all across the country held Olympics parties on their streets to cheer their local heroes. A strong and positive sense of national identity had been revived, and applications for citizenship flooded the Department of Immigration. This deep pride and confidence remained after the flame was extinguished, and so, of course, did Sydney's transformed Homebush Bay—the main venue for the games. Thousands of trees were planted on what had been a dreary industrial site, leafy streets were laid out (and named after earlier Australian Olympic heroes), and restaurants, hotels, and shops were constructed. A new ferry terminal and a special railway spur were built. At the heart of the site is the spectacular 110,000-seat Stadium Australia, which served as the main venue for 15 sports, as well as the memorable opening and closing ceremonies. It now hosts football and rugby matches.

The Homebush Bay Visitor Centre *(Tel (02) 9735 4800)* has maps and brochures of the area. Other major sports facilities at Homebush include the Athletic Centre and the Tennis Centre. The Sydney Showground, to the north of the complex, is the venue for the annual Easter Show, one of the biggest events on Sydney's calendar.

The Sydney International Aquatic Centre *(Tel (02) 9752 3666, entrance $, additional fees apply for using the facilities)*, just off Olympic Boulevard, is a state-of-the-art swimming complex with competion and leisure pools, as well as sauna, gymnasiums, cafés, and gardens. ■

Above and below: Sydney's opening and closing ceremonies presented Australia as a good humored nation that was confident of itself and a vibrant part of the modern world.

Zoos & wildlife parks

YOU MIGHT GET LUCKY AND COME UPON A POSSUM ONE evening in Sydney's Centennial Park or spot a lizard or two in the Royal Botanic Gardens, but if you want a good look at native fauna while in Sydney, you should go to one of the zoos or wildlife parks. There are several options.

Taronga Park Zoo

🗺 75 E3

✉ Bradleys Head Rd., Mosman

☎ (02) 9978 4786

💲 $$$

⛴ Ferry from Circular Quay

Taronga Park Zoo is the easiest to reach from Sydney and has the most spectacular setting. It sits on a leafy hill in Mosman, overlooking Sydney Harbour, just a 15-minute ferry trip from Circular Quay. Combination zoo-ferry tickets are available at the ferry landing.

The zoo has a world-class collection of wildlife, and the spacious enclosures resemble natural habitats. Nocturnal houses and low-light enclosures reduce the stress on

Taronga Park Zoo has one of the loveliest settings in Sydney Harbour and offers encounters with everything from koalas to giraffes.

night-loving animals, while allowing visitors to observe them. The gorilla rain forest and the chimpanzee park are always popular, but for visitors from outside Australia the enclosures where kangaroos, wombats, and other indigenous creatures are on display are the must sees. The koala one features a walkway that winds up to the creatures in the treetops.

Three major wildlife parks in Sydney's far western outskirts give closer, and perhaps more touristy, encounters with Australian fauna. The largest is the **Australian Wildlife Park,** in the suburb of Eastern Creek (25 miles/40 km out of Sydney on the Western Highway). Its roll call of Australian fauna includes koalas, crocodiles, and aviaries filled with rain-forest birds. You can also watch a demonstration of sheep shearing in the Outback Woolshed. This wildlife park is part of a large complex called **Australia's Wonderland** *(Wallgrove Rd., Eastern Creek, tel (02) 9830 9100, $$$).*

Featherdale Wildlife Park *(217 Kildare Rd., Doonside, tel (02) 9622 1644, $$)* and **Koala Park** *(84 Castle Hill Rd., West Pennant Hills, tel (02) 9484 3141, $$)* both have native fauna and educational exhibits. These places used to allow visitors to cuddle a koala, but in recent years the practice has been discouraged because it seemed to be distressing the animals.

If you don't mind going farther afield, there is a superb zoo at the Outback town of **Dubbo** *(Visitor information, Macquarie St., tel (02) 6884 1422),* 275 miles (442 km) to the west of Sydney. The 750-acre (304 ha) **Western Plains Zoo** *(Obley Rd., tel (02) 6882 5888, $$)* has helped to conserve and breed some endangered wildlife, such as cheetahs and Mongolian horses. The zoo is divided according to the various continents, with moats separating animals and visitors. ■

New South Wales is a cavalcade of almost everything Australia has to offer, from subtropical rain forests to high alpine grasslands to dusty frontier Outback, with its glamorous capital, Sydney, sitting like a pearl on its coast.

New South Wales

Snow gum in Kosciuszko National Park

New South Wales

NEW SOUTH WALES IS KNOWN AS THE PREMIER STATE, OSTENSIBLY BECAUSE it was Australia's first colony but also because it tops the rest of Australia in just about everything these days, at least in the minds of the proudly parochial New South Welsh. Sydney is here, for one thing, and Sydney is the financial and arts capital of Australia, as well as its biggest population center. Australia's tallest buildings, most expensive properties, and richest people are here.

But the state is much more than Sydney and its suburban crawl. It has spectacular and diverse landscapes, from winter snowfields on the country's highest mountain (the 7,310-foot/2,228-m Mount Kosciuszko), to sultry banana plantations on the north coast, and the dusty reaches of the Outback to the west.

The mighty Murray River forms its southern boundary and nourishes the country's agricultural heartland: Wool, fruit, grains, meat, and vegetables all come from here. One of the world's richest sources of silver, lead, and zinc lies beneath the scaly wastelands around Broken Hill, and Broken Hill itself is one of the grand old Australian mining towns, with elegant two-story pubs and a history of brawling. Now it's also an Outback art colony, attracting both painters and filmmakers with its clear fragile light.

New South Wales is where most visitors first touch down in Australia, and for those on a time budget this is the place to concentrate their efforts. There is a piece of almost everything in Australia here—rain forests, dusty Outback landscapes, mountains, beaches— and all within easy reach of Sydney. Almost everything, because the must-see Great Barrier Reef, Kakadu, and Uluru are elsewhere. For those, you have to go to other states. But New South Wales does have three of Australia's World Heritage sites—an improbable trio of the Central Eastern Rainforests, the dusty lake beds of Willandra National Park (where Aborigines have lived for 40,000 years), and Lord Howe Island, 430 miles (692 km) off the central coast. New South Wales also has Tamworth, Australia's country music capital.

About an hour's drive north of Sydney on the Pacific Highway will bring you to the Hunter Valley, Australia's oldest winemaking region and a popular weekend retreat.

Cessnock, the main town in the valley, is surrounded by more than 50 wineries with ample opportunities to visit and taste. If you follow the New England Highway on through the valley you'll come to Scone, home to some of Australia's finest racehorse studs and glamorous polo tournaments. Farther north on the Pacific Highway are the World Heritage rain forests of Dorrigo National Park. ∎

The Three Sisters near Katoomba

Area of map detail

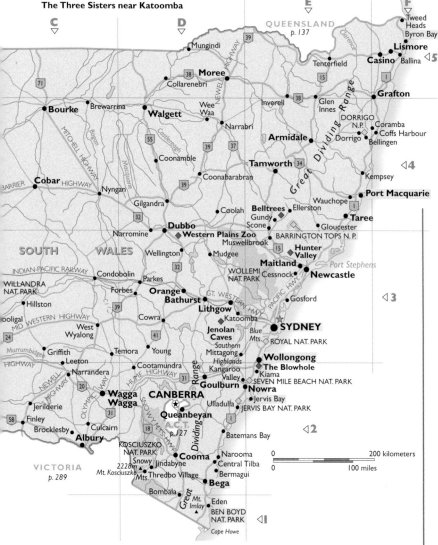

C

D

E
p. 137

F

QUEENSLAND

Tweed
Heads
Byron Bay

Mungindi

49

Tenterfield

Lismore

Casino   Ballina

5

38   **Moree**

Collarenebri

15

Bourke   Brewarrina

Wee
Waa

Inverell

38

Glen
Innes

Grafton

Walgett

Narrabri

DORRIGO
N.P.

Coramba

Coffs Harbour

55

Coonamble

39   37

Armidale

Dorrigo

Bellingen

Tamworth   34

Kempsey

4

Cobar HIGHWAY   Nyngan

Coonabarabran

39

Port Macquarie

Gilgandra

Wauchope

1

BARRIER

32

Narromine

Dubbo   **Western Plains Zoo**

Cɵolah

Belltrees Ellerston

Gundy
Scone

Gloucester

Taree

SOUTH   WALES

Wellington

Mudgee

Muswellbrook

BARRINGTON TOPS N. P.

15

**Hunter
Valley**

Port Stephens

INDIAN-PACIFIC RAILWAY

Condobolin

Parkes

WOLLEMI
NAT. PARK

Cessnock

Maitland

Newcastle

WILLANDRA
NAT. PARK

Forbes

Orange

Hillston

32

Bathurst

GT. WESTERN HWY

Gosford

3

oligal

Cowra

Lithgow

39

West
Wyalong

Katoomba

SYDNEY

MID WESTERN HIGHWAY

Murrumbidgee

Griffith

Temora

Young

**Jenolan
Caves**

Blue
Mts.

ROYAL NAT. PARK

HIGHWAY

Leeton

Cootamundra

Southern
Highlands

Mittagong

Wollongong
The Blowhole

Narrandera

Kangaroo
Valley

Kiama

20

**Wagga
Wagga**

Goulburn

SEVEN MILE BEACH NAT. PARK

Nowra

Jerilderie

CANBERRA

Ulladulla

Jervis Bay

JERVIS BAY NAT. PARK

58

Finley

31

Queanbeyan

A.C.T.
p.127

1

2

Brocklesby

Culcairn

18

Batemans Bay

Albury

KOSCIUSZKO
NAT. PARK

Cooma

Narooma

VICTORIA
p. 289

Snowy
2228m

Jindabyne

Central Tilba

Mt. Kosciuszko

Thredbo Village

Bermagui

Bombala

Bega

Mt.
Imlay

Eden
BEN BOYD
NAT. PARK

1

Cape Howe

0   200 kilometers

0   100 miles

Blue Mountains

FROM A DISTANCE THE BLUE MOUNTAINS RESEMBLE AN old oil painting, with hazy blue hues that seem a trifle overdone. The blue haze is actually a fine mist of eucalyptus oil given off by dense forests. The droplets refract the sunlight, tinting the air and giving the horizon a painted-on effect. Although the Blue Mountains are only just over 3,000 feet high (984 m), they proved an impenetrable barrier for the first settlers. It was not until 1813 that a trio of explorers—Lawson, Blaxland, and Wentworth—found a way through and opened up the wide, flat grazing country on the other side. In 1868 the railroad was built, opening up the mountains themselves. Suddenly it was possible for well-heeled Sydneysiders to escape the coastal heat and take the air in the mountains. By 1900 Katoomba, Wentworth Falls, and Mount Victoria had become fashionable resorts, with high-toned restaurants and shops, and graceful Victorian hotels to cater to those who didn't have the money to build a mountain retreat themselves. The high point was reached in the 1920s, with guesthouses catering to families, while the art deco Hydro Majestic in Medlow Bath drew society's high rollers.

Blue Mountains
🅜 103 E3
Visitor information
✉ Great Western Hwy., Glenbrook
☎ 1-300 653 408

Katoomba
🅜 103 D3
Visitor information
✉ Echo Point
☎ (02) 4739 6266

Opposite: A guitarist tests the stability of Hanging Rock above the hazy blueness of the Jamison Valley.

A New Englander may find something nookish that reminds him or her of home about these leafy old resort towns, with their antiques shops, cafés, and homemade fudge. The mountains have hiking trails and tourist marvels like the Scenic Railway, which plunges into a gorge in what is said to be the world's steepest railway. It even snows here, a little, in winter. In June the region has a Yuletide Festival, with crackling fires, roast beef and Yorkshire pudding dinners, and hot spiced wine. Afternoon tea at the **Lilianfels Blue Mountains Hotel** (see p. 369), in Katoomba, is a year-round tradition.

Katoomba is the main town in the Blue Mountains. It perches on the rim of the Jamison Valley, with spectacular outlooks over the wilderness below. This is the best place to base yourself if you decided against driving through the snarl of traffic in Sydney's western suburbs and took the train. Katoomba has hotels, inns, and B&Bs. Almost everything is within walking distance of the station, and local buses serve the area as well. In fact, if you are short on time, the Blue Mountains can be a longish, but by no means unreasonable day trip from Sydney. Bring a sweater because it will be cooler here than in Sydney.

A six-story **IMAX theater** (Tel (02) 4782 8928) is within a stone's throw of the station. It offers a stunning introduction to the ecology of the area—particularly the 1994 discovery of a stand of Wollemi pines, a species of tree thought to have been extinct for 60 million years. (Don't bother asking directions to the rare pines. Their location is kept a strict secret.)

A 20-minute walk down Katoomba Street takes you past antiques shops, galleries, and the sumptuous art deco **Paragon Café,** established in 1916 and famous since the 1920s for its fine handmade chocolates and confectionery. Then you come to **Echo Point.** The view here is simply

stunning. Off to the left are the **Three Sisters,** a rock formation of honey-colored sandstone nubs. They take their name from an Aboriginal Dreamtime legend. One version tells of a tribal leader who turned his daughters to stone rather than risk their being carried away by raiding enemies. Unfortunately, he was killed in battle and could not reverse his spell.

Easy clifftop paths are marked along the edge of the valley. Or you can take the **Giant Staircase—**a steep set of steps cut into the rock—1,000 feet (303 m) down to the valley floor. From here you can take day hikes to popular features like the **Ruined Castle** rock formation, or take longer treks as far as **Jenolan Caves,** 26 miles (42 km) away (see p. 108). Or you can hike along the valley floor to **Orphan Rock** and then take the **Scenic Railway** back up to Katoomba *(Tel (02) 4782 2699)*. Nearby is the **Scenic Skyway** *(Tel (02) 4782 2699)*, a cable car that gives spectacular views of the valley.

Leura, smaller and prettier than Katoomba, lies about 2 miles (3.2 km) to the east. It has a quaint village atmosphere that evokes its 1920s origins. There are great cafés, art galleries, and antiques galleries. Scenic hiking paths lead to Leura Cascades, Bridal Veil Falls, and Gordon Falls. You can also hike along the clifftops to Katoomba.

Five miles (8 km) northwest of Katoomba is the old spa town of **Medlow Bath.** Because the eucalyptus-laden air was believed to have therapeutic powers, early 20th-century hoteliers hoped guests would come to take the waters as well. The **Hydro Majestic Hotel** *(Tel (02) 4788 1002)* here still has its eye-catching art deco facade but has faded since its heyday. Even so, its dining room offers one of the best views of the valley. ∎

Bush fires

January 1994 saw Sydney's exclusive north shore suburbs go up in flames as a huge bush fire, fanned by hot winds, veered out of control toward the heart of the city. Dozens of homes were razed, the sky was bleary with smoke, and terrifying hundred-foot tongues of flame licked the sky. Even to Australians, long used to stories of bush fires, this one seemed hard to believe, for these weren't images from some dusty Outback town, but rather of Sydney's nicest and leafiest neighborhoods.

The journals of Australia's early explorers were filled with references to bush fires and a land shrouded by smoke. Many of the fires they encountered were caused by summer lightning strikes in the tinder-dry grass, but others were deliberately set by Aborigines, who used fire as a management tool to clear scrub, drive game, and help their ancient land to renew itself.

While scorched earth and the blackened ribs of a eucalypt forest may not be pretty to look at, such periodic wiping out and starting over is vital for the health of the Australian bush. Many of its species, such as banksias, grass trees, and cycads are known as "fire climax" plants—those whose seeds are matured and released only by the intense heat of a bush fire. The eucalypt even provides the tinder for its own eventual demise by continually shedding its crisp, paperlike bark. When fire comes, as it inevitably must, it sweeps away the forests' old, mature growth, allowing space for the next generation to sprout.

While this may be part of the natural order, it can have devastating human consequences, and not even the nation's most cosmopolitan neighborhoods are immune, as the residents of Sydney were reminded in 1994. They were hardly the first. In 1939 vast bush fires roared out of control throughout South Australia, Victoria, and New South Wales. And on Ash Wednesday in 1983, South Australians suffered one of the country's most devastating bush fires, as the Adelaide Hills went up in flames, with wildfires claiming dozens of lives and scores of fashionable homes.

Australians have had to learn to live with fire. Each day's fire danger is usually given with the weather report on the evening news. Homeowners prepare for the summer fire season by cutting away the bushy undergrowth from around their houses, clearing dead leaves and twigs from their guttering, and making sure their garden hoses are in good working order. Many join the volunteer fire brigade—known as the Country Fire Service (C.F.S.)—and devote weekends to training and practice. Town councils, working alongside the C.F.S. and meteorology bureau, often arrange controlled burn-offs to clean out the drying scrub, particularly if the winter has been rainy and the undergrowth has sprouted up thick and tall. Beyond that, it is a matter of waiting and hoping. The highest risk comes on hot, windy days, late in summer, when the bush is just so many square miles of crisp, dry tinder waiting for a spark. And that can literally be all it takes —a spark, or a carelessly discarded cigarette to start a raging fire of biblical proportions.

And there are few things more terrifying than an Australian bush fire, with its

roaring walls of flame. Fueled by the flammable natural oils in the leaves and wood of the eucalypti, which make each tree a potential torch, bush fires race from treetop to treetop, like chain lightning, sweeping down a hillside faster than a man can run, or a horse can gallop—sometimes too fast even for a fleeing vehicle to evade. There is a random quality to the destruction that Americans who live in the tornado belt of the Midwest would recognize: A car and its occupants can be incinerated, while the one stranded immediately behind is untouched; one house can be razed, but its neighbor doesn't even get its gardens singed.

If the destructive power of its fires is awesome, the bushland's capacity for renewal seems nothing short of miraculous. Even with the blackened earth still warm and the air fragrant with eucalypt smoke there are signs of life, dashes of green amid the ashes from the fire-resistant shrubs that survived the blaze. Within weeks, grasses are sprouting and the first shoots of the next generation of trees are peeking through. ■

Above: Orange spears of *Xanthorroea* are the first signs of new life after a bush fire. **Below:** Bush fires of 1994, fanned by strong winds, resulted in a state of emergency being declared across New South Wales.

Jenolan Caves

Jenolan Caves

103 D3

(02) 6359 3311

$$–$$$

Turnoff to the caves is marked 18 miles (28 km) W of Katoomba toward Lithgow on the Great Western Highway

THE JENOLAN CAVES ARE A SERIES OF 300 LIMESTONE caverns in the hillsides about 50 miles (80 km) by road southwest from Katoomba. Back in the 1920s, this was the prime honeymoon spot for adventurous young Australians, who had to drive their jalopies over hairpin roads to get here. The walls of the old Jenolan Caves House Hotel, at the caves' entrance, are lined with faded black-and-white photos of picnickers and men in straw boaters rowing lady friends on subterranean lakes. Somehow the place has managed to retain a sense of that fresh innocence: It's touristy, but delightful too.

A million years in the making, the Grand Column is a popular attraction at Jenolan Caves.

The caves are on the edge of Kanagra-Boyd National Park. In the 1830s they were a hideout for the bushranger James McKeown, an escaped convict who preyed on the coaches traveling through the

mountains. After his capture the caves became tourist attractions, but some of the farther reaches remain unexplored. Nine caves are open to the public, and the caverns and features have grandiose names such as **Temple of Baal, Sword of Michael,** and **Minaret.** Tours run every half hour, and the caves are graded in difficulty by how many steps they have. A "difficult" cave may have as many as 1,300, an easy one perhaps 300.

Public transportation does not go to Jenolan Caves, but some of the organized tours of the Blue Mountains include the caves. This twisting drive through steep and dense forests is not for the faint-hearted, but the mountainside precipices give sweeping views over the pastoral country west of the ranges.

If you are fit and well equipped, you can walk from Katoomba to the Jenolan Caves on the old **Six Foot Track.** Originally cleared as a bridle path in 1884, the track begins at the Explorer's Tree just off the Great Western Highway *(west of Katoomba railway station, information at Echo Point visitor center, tel (02) 4739 6299)* and stretches 26 miles (42 km) across some rugged and beautiful wilderness. You can do the hike in two days, and there are campsites and rustic cabins en route, near Binda Flats. ∎

Tamworth

TAMWORTH IS AUSTRALIA'S COUNTRY MUSIC CAPITAL, A sort of antipodean Nashville. In case you didn't know this already, a 40-foot (12 m) Golden Guitar will clue you in as you drive into town. If you had the radio on in the 250-mile (400 km) drive north from Sydney (on the Pacific and New England Highways), you'll have figured out that country music is big in Australia. Pull into the Tamworth Country Centre beside the giant guitar, and meet some stars—at least in effigy: Chad Morgan, Slim Dusty, and Tex Morton, to name a few.

Tamworth

103 E4

Visitor information

✉ Corner of Peel & Murray Sts.

☎ (02) 6755 4300

This love affair with country music started in 1965 when local radio station 2TM began its nightly Hoedown program and staged live shows at the Tamworth Town Hall. These shows attracted some of Australia's top country artists and drew large crowds from around the grazing districts. In 1973 the inaugural Country Music Awards began and quickly snowballed into the annual **Australasian Country Music Festival.** For ten days every January more than 30,000 country music fans, musicians, impresarios, talent scouts, agents, and bush poets all descend on Tamworth. Book well in advance if you plan to stay. The festival reaches its climax on the Australia Day weekend (January 26), when the Australasian country music awards

—the Golden Guitars—are presented. Each year a new name is added to the **Roll of Renown,** near the Radio Centre. The Hoedown program that started it all back in 1965 is still thriving, broadcast all night, every night.

The **Hands of Fame Cornerstone** on Kable Avenue has the concrete prints of more than 150 guitar-picking hands of country music stars. The **Winners Walkway** has bronze plaques set in the pavement, commemorating Golden Guitar winners since 1973. A heritage walk around town passes some fine old buildings (map from the visitor center). Out of festival time, you may not hear much country music as you go, but a couple of recording studios can be visited (ask at the visitor center). ■

Australia's country music capital, Tamworth holds the world record for most line dancers. More than 6,000 boot scooters performed simultaneously on its streets for the record book in January 1999.

Hunter Valley

Cessnock

🗺 103 E3

Visitor information

✉ Aberdare Rd.

☎ (02) 4990 4477

Singleton

Visitor information

✉ 57 George St.

☎ 1-800 449 888
(toll free)

One of Australia's best known wine regions, the Hunter Valley is carpeted by 9,500 acres (3,848 ha) of vines.

THE HUNTER VALLEY IS AN ODD MIX OF COAL-MINING towns, racehorse country, and some of Australia's best known and oldest wineries. The first vines were planted here around 1830, and today there are more than 50 wineries in the valley. The region is only a three-hour drive from Sydney, so it has become a popular day out or weekend getaway for city wine buffs and others.

The old coal-mining town of **Cessnock** on Route 82 is the gateway to the **Lower Hunter Valley.** The Cessnock Visitor Information Centre is a good source of tourism brochures and maps to help you find the various wineries. Some of the labels on the maps will be familiar to wine enthusiasts from overseas—Rosemount Estate and Lindemans, for example—but others will be mysteries worth exploring. The local magazine *Wine Hunter* is a useful guide, filled with information on the various wineries, and tasting notes. Copies of the magazine can be found at the visitor center. You might also find information in the weekend magazines of both the *Australian* and the *Sydney Morning Herald* newspapers. They run regu-

lar wine columns by well-regarded wine writers who rate new releases, discuss good buys, and cover wine-making news and personalities.

The heart of the winemaking region is around **Pokolbin,** about 6 miles (9.6 km) northwest of Cessnock on McDonalds Road. Dozens of wineries, such as Linde-mans and Tyrells, are concentrated within a few minutes drive of each other. Almost all give free tastings. Some wineries have barbecue facilities, picnic sites, and wine-making museums; others such as McWilliams, Tyrells, and Hunter Estate, give tours. A great time to visit the area is February, when the **Hunter Valley Vintage Festival** is in full swing. If you want to stay in the valley, make reservations well ahead.

Although the wineries in the Lower Valley are well known, the scenery is rather flat and uninspir-ing. The **Upper Hunter Valley,** 50 miles (80 km) farther north, has only half a dozen or so wineries but the scenery is better, and it is far less crowded on weekends.

The very scenic pastoral country around **Scone** *(Visitor information, tel (02) 6545 1526)* is home to some of Australia's finest racehorse studs and wealthiest grazing families. You can tour some of the stud farms *(ask at the visitor center),* including the **Segenhoe Stud** (famous in the horseracing world). Mid-May is the best time to visit during **Scone Horse Week.** About 10 miles (16 km) northeast of Scone is Gundy polo ground, where Australia's richest come to play. You can get a taste of this style of living at **Belltrees Station** *(Tel (02) 6546 1156),* which was the family estate of author Patrick White. Guests stay in the farm house or the mountain retreat, in the cool of the Great Dividing Range. To the east of Belltrees is the **Barrington Tops National Park,** part of a World Heritage area (see p. 120). ■

Tasting the wine as it matures is part of the art of the winemaker.

GETTING TO THE HUNTER VALLEY

The New England Highway is the main access route for the Hunter Valley, although back roads enthusiasts may want to try the Old Puthy Road, a tortu-ous byway that winds more than 100 miles (160 km) through the dense forests of the Great Dividing Range between Windsor, in Sydney's outer west, and Singleton. ■

Along the south coast

DROPPING SOUTH DOWN THE COAST MEANS TAKING IT easy and escaping the rush of city life. The coast south of Sydney doesn't have the diverse scenery of the northbound Pacific Highway but neither does it have its frantic pace. The Princes Highway rolls south through gentle farm country and placid little seaside towns.

The first interesting stop is **Royal National Park** (*Visitor information, Farwell Ave., Audley, tel (02) 9542 0648*), about 25 miles (40 km) south of Sydney. It was established in 1879, making it the second oldest national park in the world (behind Yellowstone in the U.S., founded in 1872). The park is immensely popular with Sydney bushwalkers and cross-country running clubs, but surprisingly few foreigners visit. That's a pity, because the park has some of New South Wales's finest cliff walks and wildflower displays, and bird-watchers can find as many as 200 species. Much of the park was burned in the disastrous bush fires of January 1994, but already the bush is growing back strongly. Some excellent and easily accessible trails start at the railway stations of the small towns along the Princes Highway—**Engadine, Loftus, Heathcote, Otford,** and **Waterfall**—which is something to consider if you want to see the park as a day trip on public transportation from Sydney. You can also rent canoes at the Audley boat shed (*Tel (02) 9545 4967*), if you want to float the Hacking River.

Thirty miles (48 km) south from Audley on the Princes Highway is **Wollongong,** the third largest city in New South Wales, with a copper smelter, engineering plants, steelworks, and coal mines. Like Newcastle on the Pacific Highway, it suffers from its smokestack image—after all, the copper smelter's stack is a skyscraper at 650 feet (198 m) high—but it has good

surf beaches and a pleasant feel. The harbor is particularly nice, with a fishing fleet, lighthouse, and seafood restaurants.

Kiama, 20 miles (32 km) farther, is a breezy seaside town. In 1797 the explorer George Bass heard a "tremendous noise" coming from the cliffs above the bay here, and you hear the same noise today. It occurs when a big surf crashes through a rocky fissure known as the **Blowhole** and erupts as geysers up to 200 feet (61 m) tall. The sound and sight are awesome (and floodlit by night), but do not get too close; the waves can be deadly. Just west of town a steep road leads up to the **Mount Saddleback Lookout,** which gives sweeping views along the coast, from Royal National Park down to Jervis Bay. **Jamberoo** is a pretty and historic village, 5 miles (8 km) inland.

Five miles (8 km) south of Kiama you can take the turnoff to the spectacular **Seven Mile Beach.** In 1933, aviator Charles Kingsford Smith took off from here on his pioneering flight across the Tasman Sea to New Zealand. This road hugs the coast for 16 miles (26 km) more and joins the Princes Highway at Nowra. Just north of Nowra, a scenic detour on Route 79 goes about 15 miles (24 km) north to the **Kangaroo Valley.** This rustic valley, with the Kangaroo and Shoalhaven Rivers and sandstone cliffs, is popular with picnickers.

Jervis Bay, 20 miles (32 km) south from Nowra, is a seaside town annexed to the federal

Wollongong
🅰 103 E3
Visitor information
✉ 93 Crown St.
☎ (02) 4227 5545 or 1-800 240 737 (toll free)

Kiama
🅰 103 E2
Visitor information
✉ Blowhole Point Rd.
☎ (02) 4232 3322

Jervis Bay National Park
🅰 103 D2
Visitor information
☎ (02) 4443 0977
🕐 Open weekends p.m.

The beach at Kiama on the Illawarra Coast, south of Sydney. Appropriately enough, the name Illawarra comes from an Aboriginal phrase meaning "pleasant place overlooking the sea."

Bega

⚠ 103 D2

Visitor information

✉ 91 Gipps St.

☎ (02) 6492 2045

Eden

⚠ 103 D1

Visitor information

✉ Princes Hwy.

☎ (02) 6496 1953

government to give Canberra its own port. **Jervis Bay National Park,** on the southeast arm of the bay, has rugged cliffs, white sand beaches, and fine surf.

The Princes Highway rolls on south. **Bermagui,** off the highway south of Tilba, has been popular with big-game anglers since Zane Grey, author of Westerns and a great marlin angler, began coming here in the 1930s. Big-game fishing tournaments are held here, and operators run fishing trips. Catches include black marlin and yellow-fin tuna.

Farther south the Princes Highway arcs inland to **Bega.** This cheesemaking town sits near the turnoff for the Snowy Mountains Highway. Come here in winter and you can surf in the morning and ski in the afternoon, if you make good time up the 100 miles (160 km) to the New South Wales snowfields.

Stay on the Princes Highway and you'll come to the aptly named town of **Eden.** This is an old

whaling port—Australia's first, established in 1818—on an unspoiled stretch of forested coast. Whaling remained the town's major industry until the 1920s. The fascinating **Killer Whale Museum** (*94 Imlay St., tel (02) 6496 2094*) tells the story of those days, including the adventure of a Jonah-like whaler who was swallowed by a whale and regurgitated 15 hours later—still alive. Humpback and killer whales have returned to these waters and can be seen along the coast in spring.

Nearby **Ben Boyd National Park** (*contact National Parks & Wildlife Service, tel (02) 6495 5000*) contains some magnificent expanses of temperate rain forest. A 2-mile (3.2 km) trail up **Mount Imlay** rewards hikers with fine views of the wilderness coastline. The highway bends inland beyond here and continues into the forests of Victoria's Gippsland, and on south to Melbourne. ∎

Snowy Mountains

THE SNOWY MOUNTAINS, A HIGH COUNTRY WILDERNESS, straddle the border between New South Wales and Victoria. They are the highest mountains in the Great Dividing Range, an ancient spine that runs along Australia's eastern coast from northern Queensland south to the Grampian Ranges in central Victoria. The Snowy Mountains are modest by world standards—the loftiest is Mount Kosciuszko, 7,310 feet (2,228 m) high—and are not really very snowy, but because of their vast area they have larger snowfields in the winter season than Switzerland. Australians are quick to point this out.

National Parks & Wildlife Service headquarters
- ✉ Kosciuszko Rd., 10 miles north of Jindabyne
- ☎ (02) 6456 2102
- 💲 $ per car

Cooma
- ⧄ 103 D2

Visitor information
- ✉ 119 Sharp St.
- ☎ (02) 6450 1742 or 1-800 636 525 (toll free)

On the New South Wales side of the mountains is the huge **Kosciuszko National Park,** more than 1.5 million acres (650,000 ha) of peaks, glacial lakes, high country meadows full of wildflowers, and deep forests. **Mount Kosciuszko** is here. It was climbed by the Polish explorer Paul Edmund de Strzelecki in 1840, and he named it in honor of the Polish freedom fighter Gen. Tadeusz Kosciuszko.

Cooma, about 250 miles (400 km) southwest of Sydney, is a good base for visiting the Snowy Mountains. Cooma was the construction headquarters for the Snowy Mountains Hydroelectric Scheme, one of Australia's great continent-taming public works projects. It started in 1949 and was a major source of employment for the flood of European refugees who came to Australia after World War II. Although many of their nations had been at war only a few years earlier, there was remarkably little strife among the workers, who were already beginning to see themselves as Australian. More than 100,000 people worked on the hugely complicated project, which included 16 major dams, seven power stations and a vast engineering marvel of tunnels, lakes, and pipelines. When all of these were finished, in 1974, the Tumut, Snowy, and Upper Murrumbidgee Rivers were provid-ing 4 million kilowatts of electricity. The hydroelectric authority's **Snowy Information Centre** *(Monaro Hwy., tel (02) 6450 5600)* has films and displays about how the power scheme works.

The new resort town of **Jindabyne** is 40 miles (64 km) farther south. It was built along a lake that formed when the Snowy River was dammed in the early 1960s. The original 140-year-old town of Jindabyne lies under the waters of the lake. The **Snowy Region Visitor Centre** *(Tel (02) 6456 2444)* in Jindabyne has maps and guides to the flora and fauna of Kosciuszko National Park.

For most visitors, spring and summer are more relaxed seasons in which to visit the Snowy Mountains. Hiking is fine—either day trips or extended walks—in the high country, the wildflowers are spectacular, and trout anglers have a big choice of crystal-clear lakes and mountain streams. Many ski lifts operate in the summer months, giving relatively easy access to the high country. The summit of Mount Kosciuszko is accessible via Kosciuszko Road from Jindabyne to Charlotte Pass, or you can take the Crackenback Chairlift *($$ return)* from Thredbo village to one of the high ridges, and from there do an 8-mile (12.9 km) walk to the summit and back. ∎

Snow sports

As the name of the mountains implies, the exciting thing about them for Australians is that they have snow. Between mid-June and early October visitors enjoy a thriving ski and (even more thriving) après-ski season here. Foreign skiers should temper their expectations though. While the Snowy Mountains (along with the Victorian high country) do provide the best skiing in Australia, skiers from North America and Europe are likely to find the ski slopes rather gentle and the snow wet and slushy. Still, the crowds come so if you want to ski among the snow gum trees—a surreal sensation—make a reservation for lodging well in advance. Thredbo, 20 miles (32 km) southwest of Jindabyne, has the longest runs in Australia—almost 2 miles (3 km) with more than 2,200 feet (670 m) of vertical drop. Perisher Valley, Charlotte Pass, and Smiggin Holes are the other main downhill resort areas, all on Kosciuszko Road in the south-center of the park. Cross-country skiing and snowshoeing have been growing in popularity in recent years, and they are good ways to escape the biggest crowds and explore Australia's snowy wilderness independently. But be careful, particularly if you venture off the groomed tracks. These mountains may be relatively low and the downhill skiing may seem fairly tame, but the weather up here is sudden, unpredictable, and savage. ■

New South Wales Ski Association

✉ P.O. Box 733, Glebe, NSW

☎ (02) 9552 2701

Snow gums grow around the ski resort of Charlotte Pass, though it is recorded as the coldest place in Australia at minus 10°F (minus 23°C). The road here beyond Perisher is closed in winter; skiers have to arrive on snowmobiles.

Broken Hill

IF YOU WANT A TASTE OF LIFE IN THE OUTBACK, THIS IS THE best place to come. Broken Hill, also known as the Silver City, is one of Australia's oldest Outback mining towns. For more than a century this town, about 750 miles (1,200 km) west of Sydney, has prospered from an ore body more than 5 miles (8 km) long, containing the world's richest known reserves of silver, lead, and zinc.

Broken Hill

102 A4

Visitor information

Corner of Blende & Bromide Sts.

(08) 8087 6077

So much wealth has given Broken Hill a grandeur you don't normally see in mining towns. **Argent Street,** the city's main thoroughfare, is lined with gracious two- and three-story hotels trimmed with iron lace. The town is filled with grand architecture such as the stylish brass-trimmed art deco building of the **Pasminco Broken Hill Mine** (*off Eyre St.*), and the hugely ornate **Trades Hall building** (*Sulphide St.*), built in 1898, with its pressed-iron ceilings and elaborate meeting hall. The massive Italianate **Town Hall,** built in 1891, is on Argent Street. Scores of other buildings of similar vintage exist around the town.

It all started in September 1883 when a boundary riding cowboy named Charles Rasp came upon a huge boomerang-shaped ore body on a craggy rise known as the Broken Hill. Rasp had bought a how-to-prospect guide and, thinking the ore body was tin, he and some partners pegged it out. Only later did they learn that the 280 million-ton mass was galena-sphalerite ore, unimaginably rich in silver, lead, and zinc. It was the grandest mother lode ever found—before or since—and it went on to spawn Australia's biggest mining houses: B.H.P., C.R.A., and North Broken Hill. The boomtown that sprang up grew to 35,000 by 1915, with 61 pubs, hotels, and sly grog shops. It drew prospectors, miners, con men, prostitutes, and gamblers from all over the world, and it became a honeypot for union radicals, including activists from the Industrial Workers of the World—the famous Wobblies—who had been chased out of Chicago.

These days "The Hill" is a considerably tamer town of about 20,000, and unlike most Outback mining towns, this one is easy to visit. Trains and buses have regular schedules, and daily flights arrive from Sydney, Melbourne, and Adelaide. The highways to the town are good, even if the drive is a little tedious. Don't come here expecting cosmopolitan dining, sophisticated nightlife, or luxury resorts—this is a working mining town. The line of hotels along Argent Street gives you something more interesting—the atmosphere of a real Outback hotel (the bathroom'll be down the hall).

Unlike other mining towns, Broken Hill has a flourishing arts community. Some of Australia's best loved Outback artists live here, including Pro Hart (a former miner), Jack Absolom, John Pickup, and Hugh Schultz, and their presence has attracted scores more. Painters come like moths, lured by the desert light. There are murals on the walls, artwork in the pubs, and 14 art galleries around town.

Filmmakers also discovered the area's beautiful light and average of 320 sunny days a year. *Priscilla, Queen of the Desert* and *Mad Max II* were both filmed here, as have been videos for INXS and other rock groups. BMW, Pepsi, and Levi's have all shot commercials in the area.

But mining still rules. A huge slag heap looms over the city, and streets have names such as Oxide, Sulphide, and Chloride. Broken Hill is where Australia's mining empires were born, and where militant miners wrote the most bruising chapters of trade union history.

You can put on a hard hat and miner's lamp and take an excellent tour of the **Delprats Mine** *(Tel (08) 8088 1604, $$$)* on the south side of town. The tour, which is led by retired miners, lasts about two hours and takes you some 450 feet (137 m) down into the disused mine. (By comparison, the working mine—off limits to tourists—is now down to a mile deep.) You can also tour **Day Dream Mine,** one of Broken Hill's oldest (1881), which is about 20 miles (32 km) north of town off the Silverton road *(book 1-hour tours at the visitor center, sturdy shoes essential).* Those who get claustrophobic at the idea of cramped and narrow tunnels can visit **White's Mineral Art Gallery & Mining Museum.** This complex has a walk-in reconstruction of a mine, in addition to a history of Broken Hill *(1 mile/ 1.6 km, northwest via Galena St.).*

Twelve miles (19 km) north of Broken Hill is the ghost town of **Silverton,** where many commercials and movies, such as *Mad Max II,* have been filmed. As a result, when you pull into town it looks eerily familiar. The quaint old **Silverton Hotel** has often been renamed for movies and miniseries and its walls are lined with stills and memorabilia.

Perhaps the most haunting place to visit, however, is the **Living Desert Sculptures**—a windswept hilltop just 4 miles (6.4 km) out of town, decorated with the enormous stone works of 14 sculptors from Australia and around the world *(take Kaolin St. out of town northwest, then follow signposts).* Go there at sunset. It is magic. ■

The old Silverton Hotel, a classic Outback pub

Silverton
102 A4

PACIFIC HIGHWAY DRIVE

Pacific Highway drive

For deskbound Sydneysiders, the Pacific Highway is the road to adventure and sunshine, like an Australian Route 66. It meanders north along the coast toward the warmth of tropical Queensland, pausing at popular New South Wales getaways such as Port Macquarie, Coffs Harbour, and Byron Bay. There is a little of everything along here—World Heritage rain forest, empty beaches, tacky seaside holiday towns, garish tourist marvels, odd pockets of suburbia, hippie communes, and quiet farming villages.

Like the real Route 66—not the one of myth—the Pacific Highway can be narrow, heavily trafficked, tedious, potholed, and in some places downright dangerous. You may have to contend with the white-line fever of truckers making the run to Brisbane, eager families hurrying north to theme park holidays at Sea World or Movie Land on Queensland's Gold Coast, and convoys of retirees towing their campers north to softer, sunnier pastures in the tropics. Forget the sweeping interstates back home: This is road travel the old-fashioned way.

Directions are simple: Cross Sydney Harbour Bridge and keep driving north on Route 1 to the Queensland border more than 500 miles (800 km) away. **Newcastle** ❶ *(Visitor information, 92 Scott St., tel (02) 4974 2999)* is the first big town you come to, about 100 miles (160 km) out of Sydney. It is one of Australia's major industrial centers, home to the giant B.H.P. steelworks, and the shipping port for the nearby Hunter Valley coalfields. Locals grind their teeth at the usual depiction of their town as a smoky rust belt—and rightly so. While there are plenty of smokestacks on the perimeter, Newcastle itself is a surprisingly breezy and pleasant surfing town, with wide leafy streets and good beaches. Turn off the highway here onto Route 15, the New England Highway, if you want to visit the **Hunter Valley wineries** ❷ or explore the scenic horse country around Scone (see pp. 110–111).

The highway tends to run a few miles inland because the coast here has so many inlets and necks. Most of the interesting sights require a side trip. One of the most

Snow gums, their unearthly trunks glinting in the sunlight, are a feature of Barrington Tops National Park.

🗺 Also see area map 103 E3

▶ Sydney

↔ 520 miles (837 km)

🕐 2–3 days

▶ Byron Bay

NOT TO BE MISSED

- Barrington Tops National Park
- Bellingen
- Dorrigo National Park
- Byron Bay

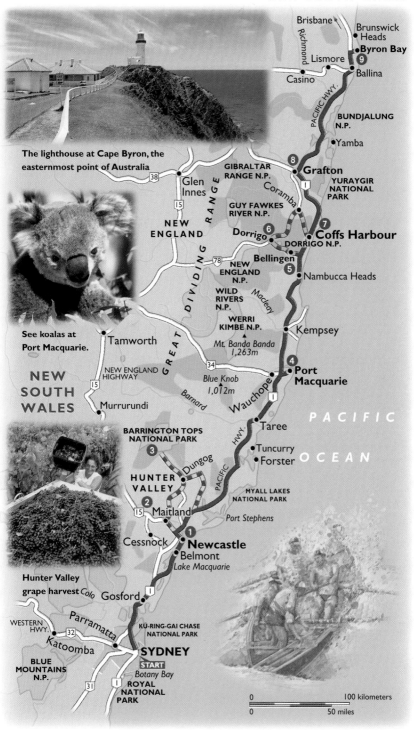

The lighthouse at Cape Byron, the easternmost point of Australia

See koalas at Port Macquarie.

NEW SOUTH WALES

Hunter Valley grape harvest

Brisbane
Brunswick Heads
Byron Bay **9**
Lismore
Richmond
Casino
Ballina

PACIFIC HWY.

BUNDJALUNG N.P.

Yamba

GIBRALTAR RANGE N.P.
Glen Innes
38
15
Coramba
8 Grafton
YURAYGIR NATIONAL PARK
1

NEW ENGLAND

GUY FAWKES RIVER N.P.

GREAT DIVIDING RANGE

Dorrigo **6**
7 Coffs Harbour
DORRIGO N.P.
78
NEW ENGLAND N.P.
Bellingen
5
Nambucca Heads

WILD RIVERS N.P.
Macleay

WERRI KIMBE N.P.
Mt. Banda Banda 1,263m
Kempsey

Tamworth

NEW ENGLAND HIGHWAY
34
Blue Knob 1,012m
4 Port Macquarie
Wauchope
1

Barnard
15
Murrurundi

PACIFIC
OCEAN

Taree
Tuncurry
Forster

BARRINGTON TOPS NATIONAL PARK
3
Dungog

PACIFIC HWY.

MYALL LAKES NATIONAL PARK

HUNTER VALLEY
2
15 Maitland

Port Stephens

Cessnock
1
Newcastle
Belmont
Lake Macquarie

Colo
Gosford
1

Parramatta

KU-RING-GAI CHASE NATIONAL PARK

WESTERN HWY.
32
Katoomba

BLUE MOUNTAINS N.P.
31

SYDNEY
START
Botany Bay
ROYAL NATIONAL PARK

0   100 kilometers
0   50 miles

worthwhile is to **Barrington Tops National Park** ❸, part of the Central Eastern Rainforests World Heritage Area *(Tel (02) 4983 1031, turn north off the New England Hwy. at Maitland to Dungog).* The drive takes you through temperate rain forests and up onto mile-high windswept plateaus dotted with snow gums and covered with alpine bogs. This back road is not paved for much of its length, so do not attempt it in a conventional vehicle after heavy rains.

Back on the coast, you have a reasonable chance of seeing wild koalas in the bush around Lemon Tree Passage, near Port Stephens. Farther north is the **Koala Hospital** *(off Lord St.),* in the tourist and retiree town of **Port Macquarie** ❹ *(Visitor information, Clarence Street, tel 1-800 025 935, toll free).* The hospital is run by the Koala Preservation Society of New South Wales on the grounds of a historic homestead. About 200 sick and injured koalas are brought here

each year for convalescence. You can visit them daily.

Ninety miles (145 km) north of Port Macquarie is the turnoff for **Bellingen** ❺ *(Visitor information, tel (02) 6655 5711),* 7 miles (11 km) off the highway via Route 78. This laid-back and picturesque village is tucked in the rain forest at the foot of a 1,000-foot-high (305 m) escarpment. Once a major timber town, it has long been a refuge for writers, craftspeople, and artists fleeing city life, and it is chock-full of galleries. Many of Bellingen's old buildings have been classified by the Australian National Trust. There's a jazz festival each August and a market in Bellingen Park on the third Saturday of every month.

The surrounding countryside is dotted with organic farms and communes. Australia doesn't have a lot of chocolate-box scenery, but there is some here. If you can spare the time, cross the Bellingen River, on the edge of town, and drive 10 miles (16 km) or so upstream through farm

The Cape Byron lighthouse, built in 1901 at the end of Byron Bay, protects the easternmost point of land in Australia.

country to a picnic area by the river called the Promised Land. It is spellbinding.

Equally spellbinding, although tougher on the nerves, is the drive 20 miles (32 km) up the escarpment on Route 78, from Bellingen to **Dorrigo** ❻ *(Visitor information, 36 Hickory St., tel (02) 6657 2486).* Lookouts along the way give views of the Pacific Ocean. On top of the plateau are the World Heritage rain forests of **Dorrigo National Park.** This is one of the best thought-out parks in the nation, with a rain-forest information center *(Tel (02) 6657 2309),* a skyline boardwalk through the rain-forest canopy, and paths through the gloom on the forest floor. To get back to the Pacific Highway you can either return through Bellingen, or follow a gravel road to Coramba and then to Coffs Harbour.

By the time you reach **Coffs Harbour** ❼ *(Visitor information, Marcia St., tel (02) 6652 1522),* you're far enough north to notice the difference in climate. It's warm and sultry, and rain forests and banana plantations cling to the flanks of mountains that plunge right down to the coast. The motels are gaudier, too. Coffs is the home of the **Big Banana** *(1.5 miles, 2.5 km, north of town on Route 1),* a monumental piece of roadside kitsch designed to draw tourists and celebrate the banana industry. Australians have a peculiar penchant for building giant objects. More than 60 of them have been constructed around the country, and they are so breathtakingly awful and shamelessly touristy that they make you laugh and pull over, camera in hand. Which, of course, is precisely what they are meant to do. The Big Crayfish (Kingston, South Australia), the Big Merino (Goulburn, New South Wales), the Big Pineapple (Nambour, Queensland), and the Big Ned Kelly (Glenrowan, Victoria) are among the best known, along with the Big Banana. Here at the Big Banana, you can tour a plantation, buy a banana smoothie, or browse in a souvenir shop whose entire theme is exuberantly tacky bananas.

The highway drifts inland north of Coffs Harbour. Much of the coast through here is national park land, and side roads lead to quiet lengths of beach. **Grafton** ❽, a genteel country town on the banks of the Clarence River, is kaleidoscopic in November (spring in Australia), when its jacaranda and flame trees are in full flower. You are starting to get into lush, tropical, sugar-growing country now, and as you go farther north you'll see more houses built Queensland-style—elevated on stilts to let cooling air circulate, and having wide wraparound verandas.

Not far south of the Queensland border, **Byron Bay** ❾ *(Visitor information, 80 Jonson St., tel (02) 6685 8050)* is one of the prettiest places along the north coast. This used to be a blue-collar town whose main industry was the abattoir, but now it is the most popular resort town on the coast, filled with crafts, galleries, vegetarian cafés, folk music, and organic markets. You can watch humpback whales off the coast of nearby Cape Byron in June and July. The lighthouse has one of the most powerful lights in the Southern Hemisphere. ■

Outlying territories

Australia has a number of far-flung territories, a legacy of the old days of the British Empire when it managed, on London's behalf, a swag of colonial islands and dependencies in this part of the world. In the Indian Ocean it has the lonely archipelago of the 27 Cocos Islands. Christmas Island, which is actually closer to Java than it is to Australia, is a sub-tropical paradise. In the Pacific lies Norfolk Island, first occupied by an overspill of convicts from Sydney. Lord Howe Island is on the World Heritage List and has become an exclusive vacation destination for walkers, bird-watchers, and lovers of water sports. In the sub-Antarctic waters of the southern Indian Ocean it has Macquarie Island (regarded as part of Tasmania) and Heard Island. Canberra claims nearly half of Antarctica as Australian territory, and it ruled Papua New Guinea until 1975. The easiest to visit of these territories are Norfolk and Lord Howe Islands. Accommodations are expensive, so many visitors come on a package deal. ■

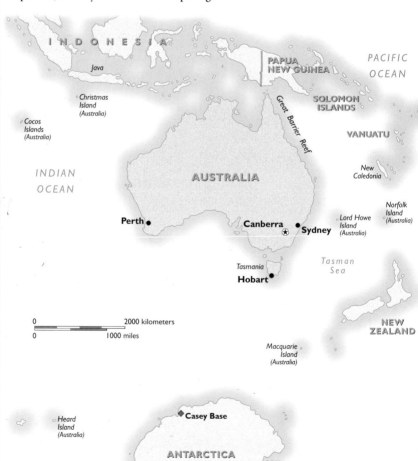

Lord Howe Island

ABOUT 500 MILES (800 KM) NORTHEAST OF SYDNEY, THE tiny volcanic speck of Lord Howe Island is a beautiful rain-forest-clad, mountainous tropical idyll. It is part of New South Wales (and a very expensive part at that), and so you do not need a passport to visit from mainland Australia. There are daily flights, but most visitors come on package tours.

Lord Howe Island
🗺 Map p. 122
Visitor information
✉ 91 York St., Level 1, Sydney
☎ (02) 9244 1777

The crescent-shaped island, with a wide lagoon tucked within its arms, was sighted by Lt. Henry Lidgbird Ball in 1788, on the way from Sydney to Norfolk Island. The first settlers arrived in 1833, and for the next 50 years it was a watering point for U.S. and British whaling ships. Millions of years of isolation have given rise to a unique ecology on the island, and it was listed as a World Heritage site in 1982.

The forested slopes of Mount Lidgbird offer fabulous hiking trails.

Eastern Australia
Airlines (part of
Qantas): flights daily
from Sydney
☎ 13 13 13

Tasman Australia:
flights from Port
Macquarie and Coffs
Harbour
☎ 1-300 361 153

Lord Howe Island is now a popular destination for ecotourists. More than 120 bird species can be seen here, including the flightless Lord Howe woodhen, one of the rarest birds in the world.

The waters around the island teem with fish and contain the world's southernmost coral reef, thanks to the tropical currents from Queensland's Great Barrier Reef. Diving and snorkeling are especially good. Hikers can scale the dramatic **Mount Gower** (2,850 feet, 866 m) for a stunning panorama of the island and the South Pacific. The slightly lower **Mount Lidgbird** is an extremely challenging, highly technical climb that is rarely attempted. ∎

Antarctica

If you want just to peek, Qantas (see p. 358) offers popular scenic flights over Antarctica during the Christmas holiday period; it is summer then, with 24 hours of daylight.

Actually getting to Australia's Antarctic Territories is more prob-lematic and a lot more expensive. Tours from New Zealand (which may also touch base in Hobart) go into McMurdo Sound and visit Australia's Casey Base or Macquarie Island. For information, check out www.antarcticaflights.com.au. ■

The volcanic hills of Lord Howe Island rise steeply from the sea, but shelter a quiet lagoon on the western side where snorkeling is good.

Norfolk Island

NORFOLK ISLAND IS A SELF-GOVERNING EXTERNAL TERRI-
tory of Australia, a tax haven about 1,100 miles (1,770 km) northeast
of Sydney. It was sighted by Captain Cook in 1774. Its Norfolk pines
(which could be made into masts) and wild flax (for linen sails) made
it strategically important to the British Navy.

Norfolk Island

▲ Map p. 122

Visitor information

✉ 91 York St., Level
1, Sydney 2000

☎ (02) 9244 1777

Getting there

✈ Norfolk Jet Express

☎ 1-800 816 947
(toll free). Flights
daily from Sydney
& 3 times a week
from Brisbane.

✈ Flight West

☎ 1-800 777 879 (toll
free). Flights four
times a week from
Brisbane.

The island was settled as a penal colony shortly after the First Fleet arrived in Australia in 1788, but it was abandoned in 1814 for several years. Then a new penal colony was established to be "a place of the extremest punishment short of death." In this it was wildly successful. In the hands of the sadistic governor John Giles Price, Norfolk Island became synonymous with cruelty and terror.

The penal colony was shut down in 1855, and the following year the descendants of Fletcher Christian and other mutineers of H.M.S. *Bounty* were resettled here after outgrowing Pitcairn Island. Today about 40 percent of the island's 2,000 inhabitants are descendants of the mutineers.

The chief settlement on this tiny volcanic island is **Burnt Pine. Kingston** is the island's main attraction, a historic settlement built largely by convicts. The convict cemetery in town is especially poignant. **Norfolk Island National Park** has bushwalks, and good fishing and diving, but the highlight for many visitors is the duty-free shopping. Getting here is an international flight—bring your passport and make sure you have a re-entry visa to return to Australia. ■

Christmas Island & the Cocos Islands

Christmas Island and the Cocos lie in the Indian Ocean off the northwest coast of Western Australia. Regular flights leave from Perth, which is about 1,600 miles (2,560 km) from Christmas Island and 1,700 miles (2,720 km) from the Cocos. Christmas Island *(Visitor information, tel (02) 9164 8392)* is covered with tropical rain forest and surrounded by coral reefs. Almost two-thirds of the island is national park. Deep-sea fishing, diving, and hiking are the main activities here—and gambling at the casino. Accommodations range from basic motels to the luxurious Christmas Island Resort Casino.

The Cocos Islands are an archipelago of 27 coral islands. Only two are inhabited—Home Island and Direction Island. A Scottish seaman, John Clunies-Ross, settled here in 1827 and began a coconut industry. For more than a century this was the fiefdom of the Clunies-Ross family, who were granted the islands "in perpetuity" by Queen Victoria. During World War II the Cocos Islands were an important flying-boat base. In 1955 the islands became an Australian external territory and in 1978 the Clunies-Ross family sold them for 6.25 million Australian dollars (U.S. $4 million dollars). In the 1980s the 600 islanders voted for Australian citizenship rather than independence. These islands are gaining reputations as tranquil tropical destinations for fishing and golfing *(for information on visits, tel (08) 9381 3644)*. ■

Smaller than some Outback stations, the Australian Capital Territory is little more than the city of Canberra. The seat of government, this modern city is home to Australia's National Gallery and the iconic War Memorial.

Australian Capital Territory

Inside the High Court of Australia, Canberra

Australian Capital Territory

AFTER THE SIX AUSTRALIAN COLONIES DECIDED TO FORM A NATION IN 1901, the next step was settling on a capital city—no easy task in a land notable for municipal jealousies, jump-and-bawl parochialism, and bickering politicians. Seven years of wrangling, two royal commissions, and numerous parliamentary debates followed, as the various civic authorities put forth their arguments. The new constitution decreed that the capital was to be somewhere in New South Wales, but at least 100 miles (160 km) from Sydney. This distance was a sop to the intense rivalry between Sydney and Melbourne, which was the stand-in capital until a permanent site was chosen and the capital built.

There was no shortage of candidates for the new capital. Even tiny Wentworth, in far western New South Wales, put in its oar, using a timeless argument that its position on the confluence of the Murray and Darling Rivers—two important steamboat routes—made it a natural capital.

In 1908 a parliamentary committee settled on a site diplomatically set between Sydney and Melbourne; as wits like to put it, the place was equally inconvenient to both cities. Although Limestone Plains, as the place was

Created by damming the Molonglo River in 1963, Lake Burley Griffin is Canberra's sparkling centerpiece.

called, would never otherwise have had a city on it, the setting was certainly pretty enough. Surrounded by mountains about 200 miles (320 km) southwest of Sydney, it sits on a plateau about 2,000 feet (608 m) up, high enough to get cold crisp winters and, occasionally, snow.

Two years later New South Wales ceded the 975-square-mile (2,526 sq km) parcel of land to the Commonwealth, and the Australian Capital Territory (A.C.T.) was formed. An annex at Jervis Bay on the New South Wales coast gave the A.C.T. a seaport. The same year an international competition was launched to find a designer for the new capital city.

The winner was Walter Burley Griffin, a Chicago landscape architect who had been Frank Lloyd Wright's chief assistant. His vision was for a city radiating out from the Parliament building and having a man-made lake at its heart. The design was controversial, and although construction began in 1913, bureaucratic resistance and World War I prevented much progress being made.

Griffin finally resigned in 1920 and went on to design other towns: Griffith and Leeton in New South Wales, the Melbourne suburbs of Heidelberg and Eaglemont, and the Sydney suburb of Castlecrag.

The seat of government was shifted to the new city in 1927, but Canberra's growth continued to be slow. Twenty years later it was still a country town of only 15,000. After the National Capital Development Commission was established in 1958, the city began to grow. Griffin's original vision of an artificial lake as the city's centerpiece was finally realized in 1963 when the Molonglo River was dammed to form Lake Burley Griffin. Handsome public buildings sprouted up. Suburbs grew and spread, and by 1967 Canberra was a fully fledged city of 100,000.

Today about 300,000 people live here, mainly politicians, civil servants, lobbyists, and diplomats. Now more than 70 years old, Australia's capital city is still struggling to achieve a lived-in look. ■

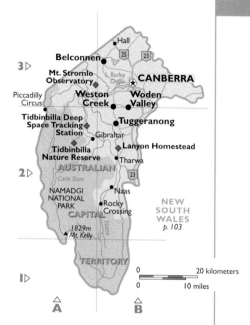

Area of map detail

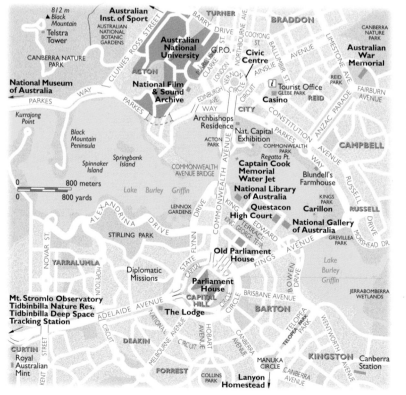

Canberra

CANBERRA IS A MUCH MORE ENGAGING CITY THAN YOU might expect. It is young, smart, sporty, and generally prosperous, with plenty of restaurants, nightclubs, and a casino. It also has the National Gallery and the Parliament House, where you can watch Australia's politicians fling earthy abuse at each other—possibly the liveliest show in town. Some of Australia's best hiking and skiing are only a short drive away, and the bush wildlife is even closer. This is the only city in Australia where you might encounter a kangaroo.

A good physical overview can be had from the top of **Black Mountain,** which dominates the city center. Its futuristic communications tower has observation galleries and a revolving restaurant giving good views of Canberra's formal design. At the foot of the mountain are the **Australian National Botanic Gardens** *(Black Mountain Dr., tel (02) 6250 9540),* which closely follow Walter Burley Griffin's original vision for a native flora garden. Its 125 acres (51 ha) hold more than 6,000 species of native trees, ferns, shrubs, and flowers, including a rain forest and 600 varieties of eucalyptus. Bus No. 904 takes you to the gardens, the summit of Black Mountain, and the **National Aquarium** *(Lady Denman Dr., tel (02) 6287 1211, $$).* A walking trail winds up Black Mountain from Frith Street.

Just north of Black Mountain is the **Australian Institute of Sport.** This multimillion-dollar modernistic facility was built in 1981, at a low ebb in Australia's athletic history, to turn out world-class athletes. An interactive sports exhibition lets you measure your sporting fitness and aptitude. Some of Australia's top athletes lead the daily tours of the facility.

Lake Burley Griffin sparkles at the center of Canberra. You can go boating on it, or cycle or jog around it. This is a particularly bicycle-friendly city, with more than 180 miles (290 km) of bike paths. Mr. Spokes Bicycle Hire *(near Acton Park ferry terminal, tel (02) 6257 1188),* on the north shore, rents bikes and in-line skates. Dobel Boat Hire *(Acton Park ferry terminal, tel (02) 6249 6861)* rents canoes. Beside the north end of Commonwealth Avenue Bridge, the **Captain Cook Memorial Water Jet** spurts a column of water 460 feet (140 m) into the air. Southeast around the lakefront on Aspen Island is the **Carillon,** with 53 bells in three towers.

Parkes Place, on the south bank of the lake, has the neoclassic **National Library of Australia.** Among its six million books are the journals of the explorers Burke and Wills (see p. 43) and Captain Cook's log. The library displays Australian photography, art, and a model of Captain Cook's *Endeavour.* It also has an Internet café with free access. The **Questacon**—the National Science and Technology Centre—is just across the road *(Parkes Place, tel (02) 6270 2800, $$).* Educational and fun, it has more than 200 hands-on exhibits. The **High Court building** sits beside the lake, a little farther east along Parkes Place, and beside it is the **National Gallery of Australia** (see p. 133).

The **Civic Centre,** around Vernon Circle on the north side of the lake, has most of the downtown

Canberra
- 129 B3

Visitor information
- Northbourne Ave.
- (02) 6205 0044

Australian Institute of Sport
- Leverrier Crescent
- (02) 6252 1111
- Tours 11 a.m. & 2 p.m.
- $
- Bus No. 431

National Library of Australia
- Parkes Place
- (02) 6262 1111
- Tours Tues.–Thurs. at 2 p.m.

shops, cinemas, and restaurants, and the main post office. The casino is nearby, on Constitution Avenue. The campus of the **Australian National University** *(Balmain Ave., tel (02) 6125 5111, closed weekends)* is just west of the city center, in the inner suburb of Acton. Nearby is **Screensound Australia,** with interactive displays of Australian film and sound recordings dating back to footage shot at the 1896 Melbourne Cup. The new **National Museum of Australia** offers a warts-and-all view of the nation's history, with eclectic exhibits including a large collection of Aborigine bark paintings, and clothes worn by baby Azaria Chamberlain, notoriously killed by a dingo at Uluru in 1980.

CANBERRA OUTSKIRTS
About 20 miles (32 km) southwest of Canberra on Paddy's River Road, **Tidbinbilla Nature Reserve** *(Tel (02) 6205 1233)*

has more than 10,000 acres (4,050 ha) of bushland with koalas, kangaroos, and birds, fine bush-walking trails, and facilities for picnics and barbecues. The **Tidbinbilla Deep Space Tracking Station** *(Tel (02) 6201 7880)*, a couple of miles farther north, is one of the most sensitive listening posts in the world. It operates in conjunction with NASA. The giant silver-domed **Mount Stromlo Observatory,** about 12 miles (19 km) west of the city off Cotter Road, houses the ANU astronomy department's 74-inch (1,880 mm) telescope, and it has a visitor center.

The National Trust-listed **Lanyon Homestead** *(Tel (02) 6237 5136, closed Mon., $)*, about 12 miles (19 km) south of the city and just off the Monaro Highway near Tharwa, has a museum on the history of the region before Canberra was built. You can visit its gallery of Sidney Nolan paintings. ■

Balloons drift over the fountain in Lake Burley Griffin, Canberra.

Screensound Australia
✉ McCoy Circuit
☎ (02) 6248 2000

National Museum of Australia
www.nma.gov.au
$ $$$

Parliament House

Parliament House
- ✉ Capital Hill
- ☎ (02) 6277 5399
- 🚌 Buses Nos. 901, 234, 352

AUSTRALIA'S BILLION-DOLLAR PARLIAMENT HOUSE ON Capital Hill, just south of Lake Burley Griffin, was opened in May 1988. Walter Burley Griffin's original vision for the city called for the parliament building to be sited on this hill, and he bitterly resented the decision of the authorities to situate the "temporary" seat of government lower down on King George Terrace. The Old Parliament House, completed in 1927, was actually used for more than 60 years.

The distinctive stainless steel flagpole atop Parliament House thrusts into the clear, cool evening skies over Canberra.

entrance is a mosaic called "Meeting Place," by Aboriginal artist Michael Tjakamarra Nelson. The foyer has marble staircases and green-gray marble columns that symbolize a eucalyptus forest. The floors are made of Australian native timbers, and the marquetry panels depict Australian flora. The **Great Hall** contains a 70-foot-long (21 m) tapestry based on a painting by Arthur Boyd. The 50-foot (15 m) tapestry in the public gallery above the Great Hall was created by 500 Australians. In the heart of the building you can see one of only four known original copies of the Magna Carta, the document signed by King John of England in 1215 that restricted royal power. You can take a free tour of this magnificent building. The grassy lawn (which sweeps back to cover the roof of the building) makes a lovely stroll.

Most of the city's 60 diplomatic missions are in **Yarralumla,** about half a mile (0.8 km) west. The U.S. embassy is housed in a Williamsburg-style colonial building. The Thai embassy resembles a temple. Greece's evokes the Parthenon, and New Guinea's is similar to an ornate spirit house. In the neighboring suburb of **Deakin,** the Australian prime minister lives in his official residence, **The Lodge.** Some of the embassies have open days, when you can visit. Ask at the Canberra visitor center (see p. 130) for details. ∎

The monumental new Parliament House, with its distinctive four-legged, 250-foot (76 m) flagpole, fits in beautifully with the city. Its design was the product of an international competition won in 1980 by Romaldo Giurgola from a New York firm. Parliament House took eight years to build, and naturally it was controversial.

Much of this beautiful building is open to the public. Outside the

National Gallery of Australia

THE NATIONAL GALLERY IN CANBERRA HAS AUSTRALIA'S most comprehensive collection of Australian and Aboriginal art. The gallery stands on the south bank of Lake Burley Griffin below Capital Hill. It has works by European masters (Monet, Rodin, Picasso), American pop artists such as Andy Warhol, and African and Asian art, but the main reason to go there is to see the art from down under.

National Gallery of Australia
✉ Parkes Place
☎ (02) 6240 6502
$ $

Twelve galleries spread over three floors. The **Art of Aboriginal Australia and the Torres Strait Islands gallery,** near the entrance, is the most popular. The displays change every few months. Typical exhibits are bark paintings from Arnhemland, burial poles of the Tiwi Islanders, and canvas paintings from central Australia and the Kimberley. One permanent feature is the **Aboriginal Memorial** (1988), which pays tribute to the Aborigines who suffered in the first 200 years of European settlement.

The upper level of the building contains the Australian art collection, including early colonial watercolors, the later 19th-century Romantics, and the nationalistic art of Tom Roberts, Arthur Streeton, Russell Drysdale, and Charles Conder. These artists were active from the late 1880s and were among the first to capture Australia's harsh landscapes and glaring light. Their paintings soon became some of Australia's best loved icons.

Another display with iconic status is Sidney Nolan's series of 25 paintings of bushranger Ned Kelly, which he turned out in the 1940s. There are also sculptures, prints, photographs, ceramics, and textiles. A sculpture garden overlooks the lake. ∎

Landscaped with native plants, the sculpture garden contains 24 art works such as these Tiwi Islands burial poles.

Anzac Day

If you visit Australia around Anzac Day—April 25— you'll quickly notice that it is not just another holiday on a calendar crowded with long weekends. On this day Australians commemorate those who served and died in their country's wars. While many countries set aside a day to pay tribute to their fallen, few do it with such style and depth of emotion as Australia. The dawn service and parade are especially moving. You'll learn much about the national character, although there's also a sense of sitting in on a family's grief that will make you want to be quiet and unobtrusive.

On April 25, 1915, 16,000 Australian soldiers of the Australia and New Zealand Army Corps (Anzac) waded ashore on the Turkish coast near the town of Gallipoli. The landing was an ill-conceived part of Britain's campaign to capture the strategically important Dardanelles Strait, and by nightfall more than 2,000 Australians had died trying to capture a small bay flanked by cliffs and well-prepared Turkish soldiers. For the next eight months, the troops clung precariously to the beach without ever being able to get a firm foothold. Thousands died before London issued the orders to withdraw under cover of darkness. The Anzac lost 8,587 men in the fighting. What is not often mentioned in the Anzac Day commemorations is that the French lost just as many soldiers at Gallipoli, England lost three times as many, and the Turks had 86,000 dead. Those ancient nations had long ago been blooded in battle; Australia and New Zealand hadn't, and so this battle took on deep mythological significance for them.

The first Anzac Day march took place a couple of years after World War I ended, and the occasion grew in stature with the passing

of the years. The motto for the day is "Lest We Forget." Ceremonies all over the country begin before dawn with a solemn religious service—always well attended despite the cold early hour—that progresses into a parade. If the word "parade" makes you think of floats and firetrucks on the Fourth of July, think again. There are a few martial bands, but mostly you see row after row of war veterans in Sunday suits and regimental ties, wearing their war medals and marching in step (as best they can) with their battalions. Crowds gather on the sidewalks, waving flags and calling out their thanks. It can be a haunting spectacle. Sometimes the only sound is the rasp of shoe leather and the clinking of hundreds of campaign medals. Later the gray-haired vets will gather at the local pubs, drink, and remember among themselves. Perhaps they will play a bit of Two-Up—an outback gambling game closely associated with Aussie soldiers.

In 1999 only five living veterans of Gallipoli were known, and even the ranks of World War II, Malayan, and Korean veterans are thinning. But the parades are growing larger as the children, grandchildren, and great-grandchildren put on the old campaign ribbons and step up to fill their ancestors' shoes, lest anyone forget. ■

The somber Byzantine lines of the Australian War Memorial in Canberra

Right: An old digger flies the flag at an Anzac Day parade to the cheers of thousands of his grateful neighbors, who line the streets to celebrate courage, heroism, and sacrifice.

Australian War Memorial

Australian War Memorial

✉ Anzac Parade
☎ (02) 6243 4211
🚌 Bus Nos. 901, 302

THE AUSTRALIAN WAR MEMORIAL, WITH ITS HEAVY Byzantine lines and vaulted mosaic dome, is the most poignant monument in Canberra, attracting more visitors than any other building in the city. It sits at the foot of Mount Ainsley. The monument was conceived in 1925, as a tribute to those who died in World War I, but it was not completed until 1941. By then the nation was in the midst of an even greater conflict and was threatened with invasion. The cloisters, reflection pools, and galleries are tributes to the soldiers who died.

The War Memorial also houses one of the world's great military museums. It charts Australia's involvement in conflicts from the Sudan campaign and the Boer War in the late 19th century, through both World Wars, Korea, the Malaya and Borneo campaigns of the 1950s and '60s, and Vietnam. Displays include

with all honors, in 1993. The ceremony was attended by the few surviving veterans of that war and left few eyes dry when the bent old soldiers—100 years old or close to it—saluted their fallen mate.

Canberra's Anzac Day ceremonies (see pp. 134–35) take place around the War Memorial. Tours of the War Memorial are free and quite frequent; call for details. The "Last Post" is played at closing. ■

The eternal flame illuminates the Pool of Reflection, the heart of the Australian War Memorial.

a Lancaster bomber, a Spitfire, and one of the two Japanese midget submarines that infiltrated Sydney Harbour in World War II.

More than a million visitors shuffle through the Hall of Memory every year. It houses Australia's Tomb of the Unknown Soldier— the remains of an unidentified Aussie killed in France in World War I and returned to Australia,

War memorials

Virtually every town and village in Australia has a cenotaph or spiked cannon as a war memorial. At first glance this seems a little out of place in such an isolated country. With the exception of a few bombing raids on Darwin and Broome in 1942, the continent itself has been largely untouched by the 20th century's wars. But Australia has never been slow to answer the call of duty, sending soldiers to every major conflict in which Britain was involved since the late 19th century—and paying heavily. More than 102,000 Australians were killed in these conflicts— catastrophic losses if you consider the proportion of young men this represents in a country with such a small population. ■

Home to the Great Barrier Reef and to the throbbing excitement of the Gold Coast, Queensland offers a tropical paradise for every taste. But its heartland is classic Outback, from northern savanna to the grazing lands of "Waltzing Matilda."

Queensland

Five-lined sweetlips swim together above reef corals.

Queensland

6 ▷

QUEENSLAND IS WHERE AUSTRALIA GOES ON HOLIDAY. THOUSANDS OF miles of beaches, forest-clad mountains, and hundreds of tropical islands scattered along the Great Barrier Reef provide a version of tropical paradise for every taste. In the south, the Gold Coast is like Miami with its amusement theme parks, nightclubs, Indy Car race, casino, and high-rise beachfront developments. The Sunshine Coast, just north of Brisbane, is a string of seaside towns and surfing beaches, basking in a climate that routinely appears on lists of the world's "most perfect." The Great Barrier Reef begins near the Tropic of Capricorn and stretches 1,300 miles (2,092 km) north to the tip of Cape York. Most of the 700 islands and cays here are uninhabited, but some have places to stay, from 5 ▷ camping and family-style accommodations to some of the world's most exclusive resorts.

Queensland's roots were nowhere near so glamorous. It started off in 1824 as a special hell for the worst sort (according to the authorities) of convicts in the New South Wales penal system. But by the 1840s free settlers were streaming in, taking part in one of Australia's biggest land grabs. In 1859 Queensland became a colony in its own right, severing its ties with New South Wales. Gold, cattle, sheep, and sugar soon made it wealthy. From 1863, in one of the colony's grimmer chapters, Pacific islanders—the Kanakas— were conscripted to toil on the sugar plantations in conditions of virtual slavery. The practice was known as "blackbirding," and it was abolished in 1905.

For much of the 20th century, Queensland had a reputation as an antipodean Dixie. Blackbirding had stopped, but the harsh treatment of Aborigines continued, as did redneck parochialism, heavy-handed policing, machine politics, and a deeply conservative outlook. This was particularly so during the 20-year reign of arch-conservative premier Sir Johannes Bjelke-Peterson. A former peanut farmer from Kingaroy, he kept Queensland in what the rest of Australia regarded as a time warp until he was voted out in 1989. (His party left a couple of years later.) A cathartic royal commission followed, as did a number of indictments, and these days Queensland is one of the most open and outward-looking parts of the nation, with an easy, down-home friendliness.

Although the beaches of southern Queensland and the Great Barrier Reef are the first things on most visitors' minds when they head north, Queensland offers much more. It is a huge state, almost four times the size of California, with only 3.2 million people—about half of whom live in Brisbane. In northern Queensland there are sweeping expanses of dusty Outback, the rugged wilderness of the Cape York Peninsula, the ancient rain forests of Cape Tribulation, the lush volcanic highlands of the Atherton Tablelands, mining towns, and frontier settlements along the Gulf of Carpentaria. ∎

▮ ▷

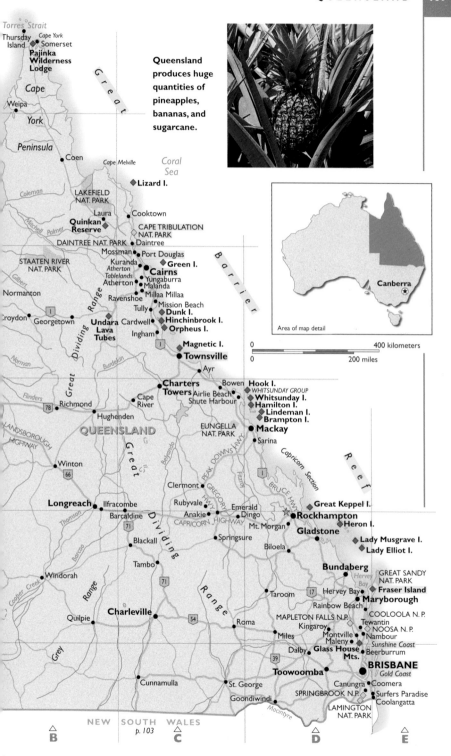

Queensland produces huge quantities of pineapples, bananas, and sugarcane.

Torres Strait
Thursday Island Cape York Somerset
Pajinka Wilderness Lodge

Cape

Weipa

York

Peninsula

Coen

Cape Melville

Coral Sea

◆ Lizard I.

Coleman
LAKEFIELD NAT. PARK
Laura Cooktown
Quinkan Reserve ◆
CAPE TRIBULATION NAT. PARK
DAINTREE NAT. PARK Daintree

Mitchell Palmer

STAATEN RIVER NAT. PARK
Mossman Port Douglas
Kuranda ◆ **Green I.**
Atherton **Cairns**
Tablelands Yungaburra
Atherton Malanda
Ravenshoe Millaa Millaa
Normanton Tully Mission Beach
Croydon Georgetown Cardwell ◆ **Dunk I.**
Undara Lava Tubes ◆ **Hinchinbrook I.**
Ingham ◆ **Orpheus I.**

Norman Burdekin

◆ **Magnetic I.**
● **Townsville**

Ayr

Flinders

Charters Towers Bowen ◆ **Hook I.**
Richmond Cape River Airlie Beach *WHITSUNDAY GROUP*
Hughenden Shute Harbour ◆ **Whitsunday I.**
◆ **Hamilton I.**
◆ **Lindeman I.**
QUEENSLAND EUNGELLA NAT. PARK ◆ **Brampton I.**
● **Mackay**

Sarina

Capricorn Section

Reef

Winton Clermont ◆ **Great Keppel I.**
Longreach Ilfracombe Rubyvale Emerald ☆ ● **Rockhampton**
Barcaldine Anakie Dingo ◆ **Heron I.**
CAPRICORN HIGHWAY Mt. Morgan ● **Gladstone**
Blackall Springsure ◆ **Lady Musgrave I.**
Biloela ◆ **Lady Elliot I.**
Tambo
Bundaberg
Windorah GREAT SANDY NAT. PARK
Taroom *Hervey Bay* ◆ **Fraser Island**
Hervey Bay **Maryborough**
Quilpie Rainbow Beach
Charleville Roma COOLOOLA N. P.
MAPLETON FALLS N.P. Tewantin
Kingaroy ◇ NOOSA N. P.
Miles Montville Nambour
Maleny *Sunshine Coast*
Dalby **Glass House Mts.** Beerburrum
Toowoomba ● **BRISBANE**
Gold Coast
Cunnamulla St. George Canungra Coomera
SPRINGBROOK N.P. Surfers Paradise
Goondiwindi Coolangatta
LAMINGTON NAT. PARK

Macintyre

NEW SOUTH WALES
p. 103

B **C** **D** **E**

Canberra ★

Area of map detail

0 _____ 400 kilometers
0 _____ 200 miles

Brisbane

Brisbane

⚠ 139 D1

Visitor information

www.visitbrisbane.com.au

✉ City Hall, George Sq.

☎ (07) 3221 8411

Fax (07) 3229 5126

Queensland Tourist & Travel Corporation

✉ Queen St. Mall Information Centre Corner of Adelaide & Albert Sts.

☎ (07) 3229 5918

BRISBANE IS A PLEASANT CITY OF 1.5 MILLION PEOPLE. IT sprawls around an elbow on the Brisbane River, about 20 miles (32 km) inland from the southern Queensland coast. Despite being Australia's third largest city, it has the relaxed feel of a big country town. Like Sydney and Hobart, it had to rise from hellish beginnings as a penal colony—in this case a dumping ground for hard cases and recidivists out of New South Wales.

By the early 1820s Sydney was becoming civilized enough to want to forget its brutal roots. So in 1821 Gov. Sir Thomas Brisbane sent north his surveyor-general, John Oxley, to scout out a new penal colony. He settled on Moreton Bay (20 miles/32 km from the modern city), and in 1824 a detachment of the 40th Regiment and a knot of Sydney's convicts arrived and set up camp near present-day Redcliffe.

Unreliable water supplies and hostile Aborigines forced them to shift the camp several times, and they finally went up the Brisbane River and established a settlement where Brisbane is today.

With the exception of the Old Windmill on Wickham Terrace, built in 1828, there are very few reminders of those bad old days in modern Brisbane. A fire leveled the city in 1864, and most of its elegant buildings date from the 1880s, when gold, wool, sugar, and beef were building the state's fortunes.

Brisbane dozed away much of the 20th century, with the exception of the 1940s, when it became Gen. Douglas MacArthur's headquarters after the fall of the Philippines. It resumed its slumbers after the war, and as late as 1960 the tallest building in town was the clock tower of City Hall. The Commonwealth Games in 1982 and the World Expo in 1988 were Brisbane's coming-out parties. More than 18 million people passed through the turnstiles at the World Expo and liked what they saw. Brisbane has hardly slept since.

By the early 1990s, when the rest of the nation was in recession, Brisbane's booming sunbelt economy was luring thousands of job-seekers north from Sydney and Melbourne. Its suburbs were the fastest growing in Australia, with jobs and new businesses sprouting like bougainvillea after tropical rain. Even if you couldn't find a job here—and most people could—this comfortable, nicely landscaped city with a low cost of living and 300-plus days of sunshine every year was at the very least a great place to spend your idle time.

Brisbane sprawls, but visitors find it easy to get around because it has a very good public transport system of trains, river ferries, and buses. The downtown hub sits on a neck of land formed by a loop in the river. This attractive, typically Australian city has the usual blend

South Bank Parkland across the river from Brisbane's business district has entertainment of all sorts, from the Queensland Cultural Centre to playgrounds.

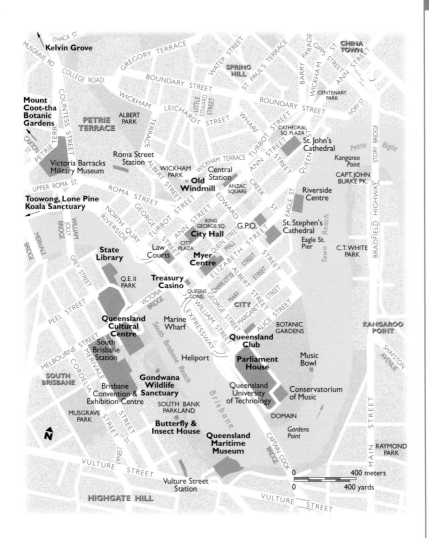

of Victorian architecture and modern office blocks. Its unique touches include the bougainvillea, palms, and (in the better suburbs) classic Queenslander houses—elevated wooden structures with verandas, designed to help air circulate.

It is a city of bridges. Seven span the river. The elegant Story Bridge, where the Bradfield Highway crosses the river, was designed by Dr. John Bradfield, architect of the Sydney Harbour Bridge. With its parks and gardens, jogging tracks and cycle paths, perfect winter climate and cosmopolitan style, Brisbane is a good base while you explore southern Queensland. The spectacular Glass House Mountains, Stradbroke Island, and the rain forest wilderness of the Lamington National Park are all easy day trips from here. The Gold Coast is only an hour away to the south, the Sunshine Coast a little farther to the north.

BRISBANE SIGHTS

Perhaps the best way to get a feel for Brisbane is to drive up **Mount Coot-tha,** about 5 miles (8 km) west of the city on the Western Freeway, and up the Mount Coot-tha Road. To get here via public transportation take bus 37-A from Ann Street, near King George Square. The hill is easily noticed from the city; it's the one bristling with TV towers. The view from its 800-foot (244 m) summit is spectacular—especially in the fine light just before dusk when the lights of the city are coming on against the gathering twilight over Moreton Bay. The Brisbane River shimmers its way through suburbs spread out like a jeweled blanket. On a clear day you can see the mountains behind the Gold Coast to the south, and the weird volcanic nubs of the Glass House Mountains to the north. A restaurant and a tearoom are up here, and both have superb views. There are also moderately strenuous bushwalking trails, the most popular being the hike to Slaughter Falls.

The **Mount Coot-tha Botanic Gardens** (*Mt. Coot-tha Rd., Toowong, information from Brisbane City Council, tel (07) 3403 8888),* at the foot of the mountain, have tropical plants in a postmodern dome, rain forests, a display of arid zone flora, and a Japanese garden. Also in the botanic gardens is the **Sir Thomas Brisbane Planetarium** (*Tel (07) 3403 2578, $$).* It is the largest in Australia, and an ideal way for Northern Hemisphere visitors to get acquainted with a sky full of new stars.

It is easy to explore downtown Brisbane on foot, and the City Council has free pamphlets of various heritage walking tours through the city. You can pick them up at City Hall. The commercial steel-and-glass heart of the city, and its historic districts, are in the blocks between Queen Street and the **Botanic Gardens** at the tip of the peninsula. These parklands (not the same as Mount Coot-tha Botanic Gardens) have 12,000 rose bushes, bamboo thickets, and poinciana trees. They are popular with in-line skaters, bicyclists, and office workers on their lunch hours. On summer evenings classical music recitals are given on an open-air stage.

Brisbane has dignified old architecture, much of it lining George, Queen, and Elizabeth Streets. The Treasury Building on Queen Street is a massive Renaissance-style edifice built in 1890. It now houses the **Conrad Treasury Casino.** At the southern end of George Street, adjacent to the Botanic Gardens, is Queensland's **Parliament House.** It was built in 1868 in French Renaissance style (with a few tropical touches, like shuttered windows), and a dome of Mount Isa copper. You can watch the political action from the visitors gallery when Parliament is in session. Just up the street is a row of Brisbane's most elegant Victorian mansions, trimmed with wrought-iron lace. They contain restaurants, bookshops, a National Trust gift shop, and a few professional offices.

For two blocks across the city center, Queen Street becomes an upscale pedestrian mall, with flower stalls and street musicians, all dominated by the huge five-story **Myer Centre** complex of department stores, boutiques, and cinemas. Two blocks north of the mall, on Albert Street, is Brisbane's opulent **City Hall** (*Tel (07) 3403 8888),* arguably the biggest and grandest city hall in a nation dotted with monumentally ornate shrines to municipal jealousy. Constructed in rich Italianate style in the Depression years, it has a beautiful circular concert hall, a cathedral-quality pipe organ, and a

Brisbane transportation
Trans-Info Service
☎ 13 12 30

Botanic Gardens
✉ Alice St.
☎ (07) 3221 4528

300-foot-high (91 m) clock tower that gives splendid views of the city.

One of the liveliest parts of Brisbane is across Victoria Bridge. Weekend crowds come to the 40 acres of **South Bank Parkland** to drink café latte, and to in-line skate, watch street musicians, and stroll along the artificial beach. At the **Gondwana Wildlife Sanctuary** here, you can see native birds, koalas, possums, and crocodiles. Other sights in the South Bank Parkland are the **Butterfly & Insect House,** and the **Queensland Maritime Museum,** which has a 1900 pearling lugger and a World War II frigate. An outdoor market stretches for more than half a mile on weekends. Nearby, along Grey Street, is the **Queensland Cultural Centre,** which includes the Queensland Art Gallery (mostly Australian artists), the Queensland Museum (dinosaurs, whales, and Melanesian exhibits), the Performing Arts Complex, and the State Library.

Brisbane started out as a river port, and the sluggish Brisbane River was once its lifeline to the outer world. These days most of the old wharves are idle and the river is more decorative than functional. A stylish Mississippi-style paddle steamer, the *Club Crocodile River Queen* (Tel (07) 3221 1300), does afternoon excursions and evening dinner cruises around the city from Eagle Pier. The large blue commuter catamarans known as the City Cat are an inexpensive way of getting to know the city and river. A $A3 (U.S. $1.50) ticket allows you to ride from Bretts Wharf up to the University of Queensland, a route that takes in the heart of the city.

A popular day trip is to the **Lone Pine Koala Sanctuary** *(Jesmond Rd., Fig Tree Pocket, tel (07) 3241 4419, $$),* with more than 150 koalas and other wildlife. For a feel of this river city, take the **M.V. Mirimar** *(Tel (07) 3221 0300)* upriver to the sanctuary. ■

Office towers back vibrant Brisbane's riverfront.

South Bank Parkland Visitor information
✉ Stanley St. Plaza
☎ (07) 3867 2051

Gold Coast

Gold Coast

139 E1

Visitor information

www.goldcoasttourism.com
.au

Cavill Ave. Mall,
Surfers Paradise

(07) 5538 4419

Surfers Paradise was just the name of a local hotel back in the 1920s. Today it is a glitzy international tourist destination where high-rise dwellings crowd the beach and cast afternoon shadows over sunbathers.

FOCUS OF SOUTHERN QUEENSLAND, THE GOLD COAST IS Australia's answer to Miami—without the art deco and happily without the vice. A relentless 25-mile (40 km) arc of surfing beaches, restaurants, motels, and developments, stretch from South Stradbroke Island, about 35 miles (56 km) south of Brisbane, to Coolangatta on the New South Wales border. The glittering, brassy heart of it all is Surfers Paradise, where high-rise developments crowd the foreshore so closely that much of the beach is in shade in the afternoon. It doesn't seem to matter. Although warm sands and surf are still touted as the Gold Coast's main attractions, these days they are really just backdrops for man-made amusements: nightclubs, theme parks, golf courses, boutiques, and Australia's largest casino.

The Gold Coast has been a vacation spot for Australians since 1884, when Cobb & Co. coaches made the trip down the coast from Brisbane to Coolangatta three times a week. But it was all pretty small scale until the 1950s, when the first high-rise beachfront apartments were built. These days more than 300,000 people live on this stretch of beach, and there are hotel beds, hostels, and campsites for another 100,000. More than a million overseas visitors come here every year, as well as several million Australians. Yet while the Gold Coast's population growth is three times the national average, a lot of locals are fleeing.

The Gold Coast is not for everybody. If you are searching for a lazy, unspoiled tropical paradise, keep going north, where you'll find miles

and miles of what you are looking for. But if your tastes run to high-octane entertainment, you've found the antipodean distributor.

Assuming you're driving south from Brisbane, here's a taster of what you'll find. **Dreamworld** *(35 miles, 56 km, south of Brisbane, tel (07) 5588 1122, $$$$)* is a theme park in Coomera where you can ride the Tower of Terror, reputedly one of the world's fastest and highest rides, play with a koala, and get jolted out of your seat at the IMAX theater. A mile down the road is **Warner Brothers Movie World** *(Tel (07) 5573 8485, $$$$).* Based on Hollywood movie sets, it has stunt and special effects displays, and a roller-coaster ride. Nearby is **Wet-'n'-Wild Water Park** *(Tel (07) 5573 2255, $$$),* Australia's largest aquatic park. **Sea World,** at Main Beach *(Tel (07) 5588 2205, $$$$),* is the biggest marine park in the Southern Hemisphere. It has whales, sea lions, helicopter tours, and amusement park rides. Surfers Paradise has the **Ripley's Believe It or Not Museum** *(Tel (07) 5592 0040, $$)* and the extravagant **Conrad Jupiter's Casino** *(Tel (07) 5592 1133).*

PEACE & QUIET

The hinterlands away from the coast are a subtropical paradise of smallish national parks, with rich rain forests, hidden waterfalls, and panoramic lookout views.

Burleigh Heads National Park is just off the Gold Coast Highway. **Lamington National Park,** one of Queensland's most popular, is about an hour's drive southwest of Surfers Paradise. This park has 3,500-foot-high (1,067 m) mountains in the rugged MacPherson Range, and densely forested valleys with lush subtropical vegetation. Two of the park's most popular sections, **Binna Burra** and **Green Mountains,** are both accessible from Canungra. More than 100 miles (160 km) of walking tracks lace these wilderness areas. One fine hike stretches 13 miles (21 km) between O'Reilly's Rainforest Guest House and the Binna Burra Mountain Lodge.

Another popular yet wild national park within an hour of the Gold Coast is **Springbrook National Park,** which has 3,000-year-old beech trees, gorges, and the 350-foot-high (106 m) Purling Brook Falls. ∎

Poised with their boards, Queensland's "iron men" prepare to compete in one of the many surf carnivals on the Gold Coast calendar.

Queensland National Parks & Wildlife Service
✉ Burleigh Heads National Park
☎ (07) 5535 3032

Lamington National Park
Ⓜ 139 D1

Binna Burra Visitor information
☎ (07) 5533 3584

Green Mountains Visitor information
☎ (07) 5544 0634

Sunshine Coast

SOUTHERN QUEENSLAND'S SUNSHINE COAST IS A STRING of vacation villages, white sand beaches, and coastal mountains about an hour's drive north of Brisbane. It starts at the Glass House Mountains and extends to the colored sands of Rainbow Beach 35 miles (56 km) farther north. Quieter than the Gold Coast, it has long been a vacation spot and is very popular with retirees from the cooler south. These days it is also a honey pot for families moving north from Sydney and Melbourne to enjoy Queensland's sunny promise.

Sunshine Coast
🗺 139 E2
Maroochy Shire Tourism
✉ Corner of 6th Ave. & Aerodrome Rd., Maroochydore
☎ (07) 5479 1566

Although it doesn't begin to be as glitzy and high-rise as the Gold Coast, the Sunshine Coast is still fairly heavily developed. The coast has its share of exuberantly tasteless Aussie kitsch too: the 50-foot-high (15 m) Big Pineapple at **Nambour** (and its neighboring Magic Macadamia), the tacky Ettamogah Pub, and the enormous Big Shell at **Tewantin.** The fashionable end of the coast is **Noosa Heads,** a rather exclusive seaside town flanked by Noosa National Park on one side and the Cooloola National Park on another. You're better off leaving the beaches alone until you get close to Noosa. In the lower part of the Sunshine Coast the hinterlands are far prettier, with their ginger, pineapple, and sugar-cane plantations, and rain forests.

Sixty miles (96 km) north from Brisbane on the Bruce Highway, the Glass House Mountains Tourist Road rises into tropical farmlands in the **Glass House Mountains.** This dramatic range is a series of 13 volcanic necks, as much as 1,000 feet high (303 m), rising from sugar-cane plantations. Captain Cook named them when he spotted the sunlight sparkling on their rock faces as he sailed up the coast in 1770. Four of the mountains— Connoorwin, Beerwah, Tibrogaran, and Ngungun—are national parks, and have good bush-walking trails. To get into the mountains, take the

14-mile (22 km) **Forest Drive** from Beerburrum. It is a spectacular route, winding through the peaks and giving gorgeous views.

The villages in the nearby **Blackall Range**—for example Mapleton, Flaxton, and Montville —are tranquil pockets that have a very 19th-century English feel. You will find arts and craft cottages, tearooms, antiques shops, and roadside fruit stalls sprinkled through here, in addition to several small but stunning national parks.

The 17-mile (27 km) scenic drive from **Maleny** to **Mapleton** is arguably the most beautiful in Queensland. It includes waterfalls, rain forests, and panoramic views of the mountains. Follow the Glass House Mountains Road to Landsborough and head east on the Landsborough–Maleny Road. Six winding miles (9 km) later, the Montville Road on your right is the start of the drive, but it is worth detouring 2 miles (3 km) farther east to the pretty village of Maleny *(Visitor information, 23 Maple St., tel (07) 5499 9033).* The lookout at **Mary Cairncross Park,** near the turnoff for the Montville Road, gives fine views of the Glass House Mountains. Once at Mapleton, the northern end of the drive, be sure also to stop at **Mapleton Falls National Park,** where a 400-foot (122 m) waterfall rushes into a deep, forest-cloaked valley. From

Mapleton follow the Nambour Road 8 miles (13 km) west to the Pacific Highway, and turn north for Noosa.

Noosa Heads has been a surfers' hangout since the 1960s. With admirable foresight the local town planners have ruled that no buildings can be higher than the trees, so though Noosa has smart restaurants and luxury hotels, it still has a small town feel.

Noosa is protected by the headlands of **Noosa National Park,** which has rain-forest trails, beaches, and views. Farther north are the beautiful colored sands of the **Cooloola National Park,** between Tewantin and Rainbow Beach. The park takes in a swath of hinterland, but it is the strikingly colored sandstone cliffs along 20 miles (32 km) of coast that catch the eye. You can see reds, ochers, yellows, and browns—more than 70 shades according to geologists, who estimate the age of the cliffs at 40,000 years. Scientists debate whether oxides in the rock or decaying vegetable matter give these cliffs their color. Local Aborigines have a more romantic explanation: The cliffs were colored by a Rainbow Serpent who was killed by a boomerang when he came to the rescue of a young woman. Spectacular walking trails run along the coast. The visitor center, at the northern end of the park, has details on the park and on neighboring Fraser Island. ∎

Noosa Heads

🅼 139 D2

Visitor information

✉ Hastings St.

☎ (07) 5447 4988

Queensland National Parks & Wildlife Service visitor information center

✉ Cooloola National Park

☎ (07) 5486 3160

The colored sands of Rainbow Beach at Cooloola National Park

Fraser Island

Fraser Island
🗺 139 E2
Visitor information
✉ Hervey Bay
☎ (07) 4124 8741

Ferries:
From Inskip Point:
Rainbow Venture
☎ (07) 5486 3154

From River Heads, Hervey Bay:
Fraser Venture
☎ (07) 4125 4444

From Urangan Boat Harbour:
Fraser Dawn
☎ (07) 4125 4444
foot passengers only

TO DESCRIBE FRASER ISLAND AS THE WORLD'S LARGEST sand island is accurate but misleading. Far from being just a big sandbar, this world heritage site is, in fact, a lush paradise of wildflowers, rain forests, colored sand cliffs, freshwater lakes, and a vast array of bird life. The waters of this 80-mile-long (128 km) island teem with fish, and in winter humpback whales shelter in Hervey Bay.

About 125 miles (200 km) north of Brisbane, this southern Queensland island is popular with bush walkers, four-wheel-drive enthusiasts, and surfers. Despite the fact that up to 20,000 vehicles tour the island each year, it manages to retain its pristine wilderness feel. Ferries to the island go from **Inskip Point** (*8 miles/13 km north of Rainbow Beach; see p. 147*), and from **Hervey Bay,** a pleasant city of 32,000 reached by turning off the Pacific Highway at Maryborough.

Fraser Island was formed over many millions of years by currents washing sands up the coast, where they backed up against the edge of the continental shelf. Its lushness is a tribute to nature's remarkable powers of adaptation. Some trees store nutrients in their trunks, rather than rely on the sands, while others have above-ground roots capable of feeding off windblown nutrients. Still other plants obtain nitrogen from insects instead of the soil. The result is a remarkable and ancient growth of palms, ferns, and rain-forest trees such as the satinay, which grows almost nowhere else and is highly sought after for its borer-resistant wood. The Suez Canal was lined with satinay.

Fraser Island was first recorded by Captain Cook in 1770. The

island was named for Eliza Fraser, the wife of a sea captain whose ship foundered farther north in 1836. Aborigines killed some of the survivors—including Eliza Fraser's husband. Eliza was captured, and two months later she was rescued by an unlikely alliance of escaped convicts and other Aborigines.

Getting your bearings on Fraser Island is fairly simple. **Great Sandy National Park** covers the northern third and has rocky outcrops and magnificent dunes. Most of the island's 40 or so lakes—including the jewel-like and often crowded **Lake MacKenzie**—are concentrated in the south. The razor-sharp line of **Seventy-Five-Mile Beach,** along the eastern flank, has become a playground for four-wheel-drive adventurers. The forested central part of the island is comparatively untouched and offers tranquil bush walking.

Plenty of organized tours of the island leave from Hervey Bay *(Visitor information, tel (07) 4124 8741).* You can also visit Fraser Island on your own. If you want to drive on the island, you will need a four-wheel-drive vehicle and a permit *(obtainable at the River Heads store, just south of Hervey Bay or from Hervey Bay City Council, tel (07) 4125 0222).*

A good place to start your exploration is **Central Station,** a former logging camp near the southern end of the island, where most of the tracks converge. You can get a taste of what's on the island by taking a short stroll along the astoundingly clear Wanggoolba Creek, through deep forests, prehistoric ferns, and enormous satinay trees. You are also likely to meet one of the island's other specialities—dingoes. Because of their island isolation, the dingoes of Fraser Island have never bred with dogs and are Australia's last genetically pure dingoes. Dogs are not permitted here in case they interbreed with the dingoes. In March 2001 dingoes killed a nine-year-old boy here. Take care, watch your children, and do not feed the dingoes. ■

Sunlight filters through the rainforest canopy above a creek on Fraser Island, a tropical paradise dotted with jewel-like lakes.

TROPIC OF CAPRICORN DRIVE

Tropic of Capricorn drive

Just the name Tropic of Capricorn conjures up the romance of faraway and exotic places. Otherwise known as the line of latitude at 23.5° south of the Equator, it slices through the northern third of Australia on maps. Here in Queensland you can drive along the Tropic of Capricorn for almost 500 miles (800 km).

The Capricorn Highway goes from the sparkling seas at the southern end of the Great Barrier Reef into the heart of the dusty, sun-burned Outback at Longreach. It starts at **Rockhampton ❶,** about a third of the way north along the Queensland coast. The Tropic of Capricorn actually runs a mile or so south of town, but enterprising locals have quietly nudged it to a more convenient location just outside the Capricorn information center on the Bruce Highway, 2 miles (3 km) south of the town center *(Tel (07) 4927 2055).* A large and ornate brass sundial is out front, and at a brightly colored plaque you can stand with one foot in the Earth's southern temperate zone and the other in the torrid.

Rockhampton is a very pleasant, small tropical city of about 55,000, set along the Fitzroy River about 25 miles (40 km) inland from the coast. The **Riverside Information Centre,** on elegant Quay Street, is a source of advice on local sights *(Tel (07) 4922 5339).* Quay Street has ornate 19th-century architecture, thanks to the wealth that passed through here in the Mount Morgan gold rush of the 1880s and later when Rockhampton blossomed into the center for Queensland's cattle industry. The **Cattleman's Club** is particularly handsome.

The local Aboriginal culture is explored at the **Dreamtime Culture Centre,** on the Bruce Highway about 4 miles (6.4 km) north of town *(Tel (07) 4936 1655, $$$).* On the south side of the city are the **Botanic**

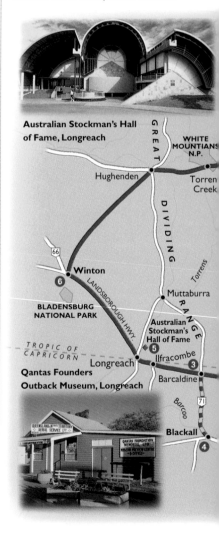

Australian Stockman's Hall of Fame, Longreach

Qantas Founders Outback Museum, Longreach

🅰 Also see area map 139 C2

▶ Rockhampton

↔ 966 miles (1,546 km)

⏱ 3 days

▶ Townsville

NOT TO BE MISSED
- Australian Workers Heritage Centre
- Australian Stockman's Hall of Fame
- Qantas Founders Outback Museum

Gardens (*Spencer St.*), where you can acquaint yourself with some of the tropical plants of Queensland's north.

You should keep a couple of things in mind before you drive into the Outback sunset on the Capricorn Highway. This is a genuine Outback highway—lonely, dusty, and narrow, with long stretches of nothing between small settlements and towns. Keep an eye on the gas gauge, always carry extra drinking water, and be sure to have some cash, because banks and ATMs are scarce out here. Be prepared for the road trains—huge triple-rigged trucks of up to 170 tons (173 tonnes)—hauling supplies to lonely settlements and stations. They are nothing to be afraid of—the drivers are very skilled—but the first time one sweeps by can be a little unnerving.

The highway starts at a roundabout just south of Rockhampton and heads due west, past the sprawling cattleyards of big-time cattle country and over the Great Dividing Range, into Outback Australia. The road rolls through the timber-milling town of Dingo, skirts Queensland's coalfields around Black-water, then climbs over more ranges as it goes farther into the Outback.

After 170 miles (274 km) you'll drive into **Emerald** (*Visitor information, tel (07) 4982 4182*), a pleasant town of fig-lined streets. The town's colonial railroad station has been listed by the National Trust. West of Emerald are what used to be the largest sapphire fields in the Southern Hemisphere. The Star of Queensland, regarded as the finest black sapphire in the

Tropic of Capricorn sundial

world, was found at Anakie and now resides in the Smithsonian Institution in the United States. You can visit a walk-in mine at **Rubyvale ②,** and you can get a fossicking (prospecting) license if you want to try to find some gems yourself.

The highway runs from Anakie through 180 miles (290 km) of mostly empty Outback before it reaches **Barcaldine ③** *(Visitor information, Oak St., tel (07) 4651 1724).* This town of 1,600 claims to be the birthplace of the Australian Labor Party. Striking shearers gathered here in the long hot months of 1891

A statue of an Outback pioneer, his saddle thrown over his shoulder, stands beside the the Australian Stockman's Hall of Fame.

to plan strategy in their bitter campaign against wealthy graziers. They met beneath a 150-year-old ghost gum (still standing) that became known as the Tree of Knowledge. The **Australian Workers Heritage Centre** on Ash Street tells the story of the struggle.

You can make an interesting detour from Barcaldine to the town of **Blackall ④,** an hour south on the Matilda Highway *(Visitor information, Short St., tel (07) 4657 4637).* Blackall was home to one of Australia's legends, Big Jackie Howe, the greatest shearer of them all. In 1892, at nearby Alice Downs Station, Howe set a record by shearing 321 ewes in the union-prescribed workday of seven hours and forty minutes, using crude iron hand shears. A statue of Howe stands at the corner of Shamrock and Short Streets. On Thistle Street

is another icon, a reproduction of the so-called Black Stump that surveyor Thomas Frazer used as his baseline for mapping the area in 1886. Anything beyond this marker was deemed to be "Outback," and Australians today still sometimes refer to the remote parts of their country as "beyond the Black Stump."

Return to the Capricorn Highway at Barcaldine and go west to **Longreach** *(Visitor information tel (07) 4658 3555),* home to the superb **Australian Stockman's Hall of Fame ⑤** *(Tel (07) 4658 2166, $$$).* You'll see it from the highway about a mile before you reach Longreach. It opened in 1988 with fanfares and some doubts that visitors would come this far to see it, but it has surpassed all expectations. It tells the story of Australia from the Dreamtime onward, and focuses on the settlement of the Outback. The excellent exhibits include photographs, videos, and slide shows of explorers and pioneers, Outback women, shearers, and cattlemen.

The Hall of Fame alone would be worth the drive out here, but Longreach has more. Qantas started here in 1920 as the Queensland and Northern Territory Air Service (it's the world's second oldest airline). The original hangar sits almost opposite the Stockman's Hall of Fame. Today it houses the **Qantas Founders Outback Museum** *(Tel (07) 4658 3737, $$)*, and its displays of early aviation history include the airline's first plane—an Avro 504K. The airline's original booking office, situated on the corner of Duck and Eagle Streets, is now Longreach's visitor information center *(Tel (07) 4658 3555).*

The **School of Distance Education** is nearby; you can see how children who live on remote Outback stations go to school by radio.

Longreach marks the end of the Capricorn Highway. From here the main highway veers north, away from the Tropic of Capricorn. Known as the Landsborough Highway, it runs 75 windswept miles (120 km) to the town of

The ancient Selwyn Ranges, near Cloncurry, are weathered nubs of an ironstone formation more than 600 million years old.

Winton ❻. This is where Banjo Patterson reputedly wrote "Waltzing Matilda." The truth about the origin of the song is lost in time and municipal rivalry, but according to legend it was performed publicly for the first time in Winton's North Gregory Hotel *(67 Elderslie St., tel (07) 4657 1375)* in 1895.

From Winton you can loop back to the coast via Hughenden, and then east on the Flinders Highway 240 miles (386 km) to the colorful gold-mining town of **Charters Towers ❼,** and then on to **Townsville ❽** (see p. 166) on the Coral Sea. If you don't go to Winton, you can vary the return journey by returning east from Longreach on the Capricorn Highway and turning north at Emerald, to follow the Gregory and Peak Downs Highways to the coast at Mackay. ■

Great Barrier Reef

Great Barrier Reef Marine Parks Authority

✉ P.O. Box 1379, Townsville, Queensland 4810

☎ 1-300 360 898

Queensland Government Travel Centre

✉ Corner of Adelaide & Edward Sts., Brisbane

☎ 13 18 01

THE GREAT BARRIER REEF IS AUSTRALIA'S CROWNING glory—the chain of coral reefs and lush tropical islands that flanks the Queensland coast, forming a very special vacation land. No adjectives or glossy underwater photographs can adequately prepare you for that magical moment when you don a mask and poke your face into the warm tropical waters of this seductive dreamscape.

The reef starts near **Lady Elliott Island,** offshore from Bundaberg, and stretches 1,300 miles (2,092 km) north to **Bramble Cay,** off the coast of Papua New Guinea. Although it is generally referred to as one reef, it is in fact a mosaic of more than 2,900 distinct reefs covering almost 90,000 square miles (233,100 sq km). The reefs change character along the way. In the south they form chains of sandy cays—coral outcrops that emerge above the water and have acquired a covering of vegetation. In the north, where the coral comes

PAPUA NEW GUINEA

Gulf of Papua

Torres Strait
MOA I.
PRINCE OF WALES I. Cape York

Shelburne Bay

Coral Sea

GREAT BARRIER REEF

CAPE

YORK

PENINSULA

Cape Direction

Princess Charlotte Bay
200m
Cape Melville

COOKS PASSAGE

HOWICK I.
LIZARD I.
Cape Flattery

●Cooktown

Cape Tribulation

DAINTREE N.P.

Mossman ●●Port Douglas

GREEN I.

Cairns
CAPTAIN COOK HIGHWAY

Mission Beach

Tully ●
DUNK I. 200m
Cardwell ● HINCHINBROOK I.
ORPHEUS I.
GT. PALM I.
MAGNETIC I.

Flinders Reefs

FLINDERS PASSAGE

QUEENSLAND

Townsville ●

Airlie Beach ●
Shute Harbour ●

HOOK I.
WHITSUNDAY I.
HAMILTON I.

GREAT BARRIER REEF

BRAMPTON I.
Mackay ● NORTHUMBERLAND ISLES

Cape Palmerston

200m

TOWNSHEND I.

NORTH KEPPEL ISLAND N.P.
GT. KEPPEL I.
HERON I.

Rockhampton ●

CURTIS I.

TROPIC OF CAPRICORN

Fitzroy

Gladstone ●

LADY MUSGRAVE I.
LADY ELLIOT I.

Bundaberg ●

FRASER I.

Hervey Bay

Brilliant sea fans and crinoids flourish in a gap in the reef where the currents can bring them nutrients.

Above: A brain coral. Left: See the reef from a glass-sided boat.

0 ————— 250 kilometers
0 ————— 150 miles

REEF FORMATION

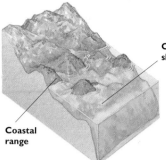

Coastal range

Coral growing in shallow water

As the last ice age ended and the Earth's climate warmed, Queensland's coast had a range of forested hills. Corals grew in the shallow waters of the continental shelf.

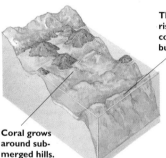

Coral grows around sub-merged hills.

The water level rises and the coral begins to build upward.

Glaciers and ice caps melted, raising the sea level slowly. As it rose, the coastal valleys filled leaving islands. Coral grew upward on the old, dead coral below.

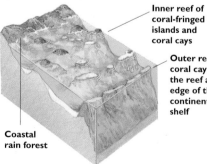

Coastal rain forest

Inner reef of coral-fringed islands and coral cays

Outer reef of coral cays on the reef at the edge of the continental shelf

Rising waters flooded farther inland. Fringing reefs grew around the inner reef islands; low coral cays developed on the spectacular reefs of the outer reef.

REEF INHABITANTS

Great white shark

Green turtle

Coral polyp tentacles catch prey during the day, retract at night.

Coral cod

Featherstar

Blue sea star

Giant clam

closest to the coast, it runs in long ribbons. Throughout its length the reef is a maze of sharp corals and shallow water, and it was a navigational nightmare for Australia's early explorers. French explorer Louis Antoine de Bougainville might have put in a claim to mainland Australia in 1768, had not the sound of waves washing against the corals put him off. Describing it in his log as the "voice of God," he kept going. Thirty years later Matthew Flinders compared navigating the reef to threading a needle. Some couldn't do it. The reef contains more than 30 wrecks and continues to be occasionally

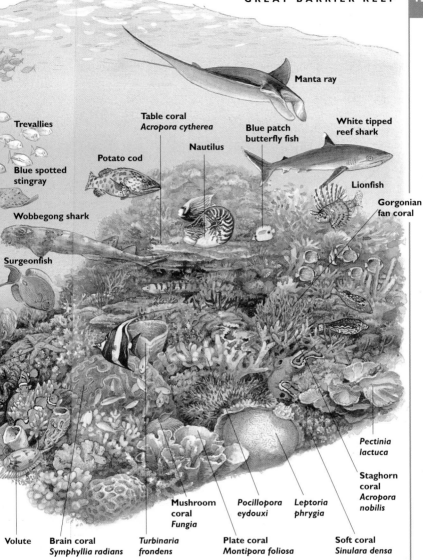

Manta ray

Trevallies

Table coral
Acropora cytherea

Blue patch
butterfly fish

White tipped
reef shark

Potato cod

Nautilus

Blue spotted
stingray

Lionfish

Wobbegong shark

Gorgonian
fan coral

Surgeonfish

Pectinia
lactuca

Staghorn
coral
*Acropora
nobilis*

Mushroom
coral
Fungia

*Pocillopora
eydouxi*

*Leptoria
phrygia*

Volute

Brain coral
Symphyllia radians

*Turbinaria
frondens*

Plate coral
Montipora foliosa

Soft coral
Sinulara densa

bruised by keels and hulls today.

A World Heritage site, the reef was built by a simple primitive organism, a marine polyp of the family Coelenterata. Billions of polyps huddle together in warm, salty, shallow water and grow toward the sunlight like brilliant flowers. When one dies, a new polyp grows on its skeleton. They are known as hard corals for the skele-tons they form. Over millions of years, a vast reef complex develops. Some parts of the Great Barrier Reef have been building for more than 18 million years. Much of the reef, however, dates from the end of the last ice age, about 15,000 years ago, when sea levels started to rise.

The reef is a world in itself, the coral colonies providing food, shelter, and hunting grounds for

billions of other creatures. In addition to 400-odd species of corals, the Great Barrier Reef has more than 4,000 species of mollusks, 350 species of echinoderms—sea urchins, sea stars, and sea cucumbers—and 4,000 varieties of sponges.

About 1,500 varieties of tropical fish swim around the reef, in almost every color imaginable. There are humpback whales, stingrays, giant tortoises, and dugongs—the sea cows that gave rise to myths of mermaids. No place on land, not even the wildest rain forest, supports this kind of diversity. One of nature's most spectacular sights occurs here beneath a full moon on a few nights each spring: The corals spawn, releasing billions of eggs in a rainbow of colors.

EXPLORING THE REEF

Diving and snorkeling are the best ways to explore the reef. If you don't dive, or don't want to, it's no problem. Anyone can learn to snorkel in five minutes, and the only thing you'll miss out on is a longer period under the water. Most of the best displays are shallow anyway, and if you simply paddle face down along the surface you'll be treated to vivid displays of tropical color and an eerie, dreamlike sensation of flying. You don't even have to get wet: many operators have glass-bottomed boats through which you view the reef.

If you do want to learn to dive, plenty of dive courses are available along the coast, particularly in tourist hubs like **Airlie Beach** and **Cairns** (see p.167). They vary greatly in professionalism and price, so shop around. You can also do a single escorted dive with an instructor for about $A50 (U.S. $25).

The Great Barrier Reef has been a protected marine park since 1975. It is managed by the **Great**

Barrier Reef Marine Parks **Authority** (GBRMPA), which tries to juggle the growing demands of tourism with the need to protect this ecosystem. One threat is the crown-of-thorns sea star, which eats coral and causes severe damage in its periodic outbreaks—but the damage that people do is far worse. Any dead or broken coral that you see has probably suffered from direct human attention or from tour-boat anchors. Consider this the world's greatest and most fragile china shop. Look, but don't touch. ■

Above: Spawn spews from a giant clam. Opposite: A hawksbill turtle swims with an unusual companion.

Great Barrier Reef islands

MORE THAN 700 ISLANDS DOT THE LEE SIDE OF THE GREAT Barrier Reef. Many of them are uninhabited, tropical paradises. Those that do have resorts offer varieties of paradise to suit every taste or budget. You can choose from family retreats, ecotourist lodges, some of the world's most exclusive resorts, or hard-partying college getaways. The Queensland Government Travel Centre (see p. 154) is a good source of information on the reef and its resort islands.

Queensland National Parks & Wildlife Service

✉ Shoreline Close, Rosslyn Bay

☎ (07) 4933 6595

✉ Centrepoint, Goondoon St., Gladstone

☎ (07) 4972 6055

Only a very few of the so-called Great Barrier Reef islands are on the reef itself. The majority are continental islands, which means they are ancient coastal hilltops that became islands at the end of the last ice age about 15,000 years ago, when the sea level rose. Magnificent fringing coral reefs have grown around these islands, which are often wooded, with high mountains and spec-

tacular views of the tropical seas and other islands nearby. Some are accessible by short ferry rides, others require a longer and more expensive journey. Three island resorts are actually coral cays themselves, and at low tide visitors can walk on the body of the reef. The islands are divided into three main groups: the southern islands, the Whitsunday Islands in the center

(see below), and the tropical north-ern islands (see pp. 164–65).

SOUTHERN ISLANDS

Most of the southern islands are clustered around the Capricorn Coast, between Bundaberg and Rockhampton. **Lady Elliott Island,** which marks the southern tip of the Great Barrier Reef, is a coral cay where divers stand a good chance of encountering loggerhead turtles and manta rays. In 1816 the seamen on the ship *Lady Elliott* made the first recorded sighting of the island, but it seems to have gone unsighted a little too often over the next 50 years. After an extraordi-nary number of shipwrecks, an ele-gant lighthouse was built here in 1866. It was a lonely place to be sta-tioned, and several early lighthouse-keepers reputedly committed suicide. The lighthouse still stands but is much less lonely these days, with the Lady Elliott Resort *(Tel 1-800 072 200, toll free)* catering to 140 people, and daily flights including from Bundaberg and Hervey Bay.

Neighboring **Lady Musgrave Island,** about 25 miles (40 km) farther north, is a tiny uninhabited mote popular with yachtsmen for its pretty turquoise lagoon formed by sheltering coral. It is a low island covered with grasses, pandanus palms, pisonia, and casuarina trees. In the early 1900s, goats released on Lady Musgrave and Lady Elliott Islands devastated the landscape. A revegetation program that was started in the 1970s has been fairly successful. These days Lady Musgrave is one of the best islands on which to camp in the southern reef, although light sleepers may be disturbed by the colonies of terns and other raucous seabirds. *(Arrange permits through the National Parks and Wildlife Service office in Gladstone. Only 50 campers are allowed on the island at a time.)*

You can get there by boat or sea-plane from Bundaberg. The **M.V. Lady Musgrave** *(Tel (07) 5152 9011)* makes day trips to the island.

Heron Island is another of the coral islands. Located about 70 miles (112 km) from Gladstone, it is also one of the best known islands on the reef—and with good reason. Its waters teem with coral and fish, making it a paradise for divers and snorkelers, and the island is a breeding ground for thousands of birds and turtles. Heron Island was first settled in the 1920s when a turtle cannery was set up. In 1932 the cannery closed and a tourism industry began to evolve. The island was declared a national park in 1943. Accommodations are at the Heron Island Resort *(Tel (07) 4972 9055)*. The island is small enough to stroll around in an hour, but you have to stay as part of a package deal.

The party is at **Great Keppel Island,** with its white-sand beaches and nightlife. Great Keppel is the biggest of a chain of 19 islands that make up **Keppel Group National Park.** These hilly, rain-forested islands are remnants of the ancient Queensland coast. You can enjoy great diving, bush-walking, and camping here. Access is by boat from the Rosslyn Bay ferry termi-nal, just south of Rockhampton. *(Tel (07) 4933 6744)*. Or you can take one of Qantas' twice-daily flights from Rockhampton. Other Keppel Bay islands can be visited by water taxi from the Keppel Bay Marina *(Tel (07) 4933 6244)*. Many of these islands are uninhabited, such as **Middle Island** and **Miall Island,** so campers have to take all supplies, including drinking water.

WHITSUNDAY ISLANDS

The Whitsunday Islands were named by Captain Cook, who sailed between the islands and the

Coral reefs lie beneath the sea. Debris builds up on the reef and catches sand, gradually forming islands that show above the water.

**Whitsunday
Islands National
Park**
✉ Shute Harbour Rd.,
    Airlie Beach
☎ (07) 4946 7022

Mackay
🗺 139 D3
Visitor information
✉ Nebo Rd.
☎ (07) 4952 2677

coast on Whitsunday in July 1770—
or at least thought he did. Although
the devout captain kept meticulous
logs, he had not allowed for the
international dateline and was
actually a day off.

The hundred or so Whitsunday
Islands are perhaps the most gorgeous of Queensland's tropical
paradises. These continental islands
formed when the sea level rose after
the last ice age, and they still resemble the mountaintops they once
were. They are steep and lush,
covered with dense pine forests.
Although the islands are more than
30 miles (48 km) from the reef, they
are fringed with coral. Many of
them became national parks in the
1930s and now collectively form
Whitsunday Islands National Park.
Although some of the islands have
resorts on them, most are uninhabited, and on several you can camp
on pristine beaches. Day cruises
through the Whitsunday Passage
(between islands and coast) and the
islands can be arranged in Airlie
Beach, Shute Harbour, and Mackay.

Brampton Island is the
southernmost of the Whitsundays,
only 20 miles (32 km) northeast of
Mackay, which is the departure
point for ferries *(Tel (07) 4955
3066)*. Most of the island is national
park, with seven coral beaches and
rain forests bright with rainbow
lorikeets and butterflies, although
tourist resorts have been here since
1933. You can hike to the summit of
Brampton Peak *(a one-hour hike,
very steep; take water)* for views of
the surrounding island-dotted seas.

Whitsunday Island is the
largest of the islands—almost
30,000 acres (12,150 ha)—and
probably looks much as it did when
Captain Cook sailed past in 1770.
The island has no resorts, just tropical forests, fjords, and unspoiled
Whitehaven Beach—arguably the
finest in the islands. If you want to

go back to nature, this is one of the
best places along the coast to do it.
Cid Harbour, on the island's west
coast, was an anchorage for part of
the U.S. fleet just before the Battle
of the Coral Sea (1943). Campsites
run by the national parks service
are there today. The Whitsunday
Islands National Park office at
Airlie Beach advises visitors on
campsites and on what to bring.

Hook Island, directly north of
Whitsunday Island, is the second
largest in the group. It has an
underwater observatory and a very
low key national park service
resort, the Hook Island Wilderness
Resort *(Tel (07) 4946 9380)*. Glass-
bottomed boats tour the island's
spellbinding coral reefs.

Lindeman Island is another
large member of the group—about
5,000 acres (2,025 ha)—and half is
national park. The snorkeling is
superb, as is the bird-watching in
the island's forests. Butterfly Valley
has rainbow lorikeets and spectacular blue tiger butterflies. You can see
much of the Whitsunday chain
from 700-foot-high (213 m) Mount
Oldfield. Most visitors to the island
stay at the Club Med Resort *(Tel 1-
800 801 823, toll free)*, but you can
also camp at the national parks service campsite at Boat Port.

Hamilton, Daydream, and
Hayman Islands are the most
developed of the Whitsundays.
Hamilton, about 10 miles (16 km)
south of Shute Harbour, is the most
built-over of all, with a high-rise
apartment tower, restaurants, marina, jetport, shopping boutiques,
and sports complex *(Tel 1-800
075 110, toll free)*. The ferries to
Hamilton Island leave from Shute
Harbour, or you can fly direct from
Sydney, Melbourne, or Brisbane.

Daydream Island is the smallest
of the developed islands, lying only
3 miles (4.8 km) from Shute
Harbour on the mainland. The

**Opposite:
Whitehaven
Beach on
Whitsunday
Island, one of the
loveliest of the
Great Barrier
Reef beaches**

Airlie Beach

🅰 139 C3

Visitor information

✉ Shute Harbour Rd.

☎ (07) 4946 6665

North Barrier Reef National Parks information

(for information on national parks on all the northern islands except Lizard Island)

✉ Department of the Environment, Cardwell

☎ (07) 4066 8601

family-style Daydream Island Travelodge Resort *(Tel 1-800 075 040, toll free)* occupies the northern end of the island.

Hayman Island is the Whitsundays' most luxurious resort. People who know regard it as one of the finest resorts in the world. The stunning design incorporates reflection pools and tropical gardens, a seawater lagoon, and an opulent octagonal freshwater pool. Everything here projects luxury and style. This place is for guests only; don't even think about day trips *(Tel 1-800 075 175, toll free).*

NORTHERN ISLANDS

In Far North Queensland—or FNQ for short—the reef veers closest to the coast, and the coral and fish life are most colorful and diverse.

Magnetic Island was named by Captain Cook, who had some problems with his compass when he sailed past in 1770 and decided the island must be magnetic.

Nobody else's compass has ever been troubled by it, but the name remains. You can get to it from Townsville in as little as 20 minutes —it is only about 7 miles (11 km) away. As a result, Magnetic Island is increasingly becoming a suburb to Townsville. It has more than 2,500 residents, some of whom commute to jobs across the bay. The island is ringed with white-sand beaches, and more than half of it is national park, with excellent bush-walking tracks, fine lookouts, and koalas in the wild. If you miss the wild ones you can visit a koala park or see aquatic creatures in the aquarium.

Orpheus Island, a small volcanic nub fringed by kaleidoscopic coral reefs, is 50 miles (80 km) farther northeast of Townsville. It is a national park, and its beaches have marvelous seashells.

Farther up the coast looms the formidable tree-clad mass of **Hinchinbrook Island,** just across a narrow channel from

Cardwell on the mainland. It is the largest island along this stretch of coast—about 250 square miles (648 sq km)—but was never settled, and today it is a nearly pristine wilderness of mangroves and white-sand beaches dominated by a line of steep, dark mountains rising to more than 3,000 feet (914 m). With the exception of the modest Cape Richards Resort *(Tel (07) 4066 8585)*, Hinchinbrook Island is still pretty much as it was two centuries ago. It can be visited on a day trip from Cardwell, but a better option if you have the time and energy is to walk the East Coast Trail or Thosborne Track (see sidebar this page).

Dunk Island is just 3 miles (4.8 km) off the Queensland coast near Tully, about 125 miles north of Townsville. It is one of the most popular resort islands in northern Queensland, rich in bird life, densely forested, and bright with tropical butterflies. You can fly there from Townsville or make a short crossing by ferry or water taxi from Mission Beach. Also in this group is little **Bedarra Island,** with a very exclusive resort *(Tel (07) 4068 8233)*.

Green Island, about 15 miles (24 km) from Cairns, is actually part of the reef. This coral island is less than half a mile (1 km) long, and Green Island Resort *(Tel 1-800 673 366, toll free)* takes up most of it.

Lizard Island, among the northernmost islands of the Great Barrier Reef, has some of the finest coral reefs. It lies about 60 miles (96 km) north of Cooktown. Captain Cook landed here in 1770 and climbed Cook's Lookout (as it is now called) to plot a way through the reef ahead. He named the island for the large but harmless monitor lizards that still bask here. Lizard Island Resort *(Tel (07) 4060 3999)* is luxurious and expensive. Or there is the national park campground *(book at Department of the Environment office in Cairns, see p. 167)*. ■

A national park since 1939, Lizard Island is an unspoiled pocket of grasslands, heath, and rugged granite promontories.

THOSBORNE TRACK

From Ramsay Bay to Zoe Bay on Hinchinbrook Island, the 20-mile (32 km) trek can be hurried through in two days or dawdled over in five, but book with the Department of the Environment Office in Cardwell—the number of hikers on the island is limited to 40. ■

Townsville

TOWNSVILLE IS AUSTRALIA'S LARGEST TROPICAL CITY, having more than 140,000 residents. Huddled under the 1,000-foot-high (304 m) Castle Rock, it is functional rather than scenic. The city is northern Queensland's industrial center, home to James Cook University, and one of Australia's biggest military towns.

Townsville

139 C4

Visitor information

Flinders Mall

(07) 4721 3660

Sunset over Townsville

Two entrepreneurs—a Scot named Melton Black and a wealthy sea captain named Robert Towns—sowed the seeds of Townsville. In 1863 they built a wharf and a rendering plant here for cattlemen who couldn't reach the port at Bowen when the Burdekin River was in flood. Gold rushes at Cape River (1867), Ravenswood (1869), and Charters Towers (1871) helped the city to prosper. During World War II Townsville was a strategic base for U.S. and Australian forces, and it was bombed three times by the Japanese in 1942.

Although Townsville is the administrative and commercial capital of northern Queensland, it struggles to hold the interest of tourists who prefer more fashionable Cairns and Port Douglas farther north. For one thing, it doesn't quite fit the image of a tropical city.

Visitors who expect lush rain forest are surprised to see typical olive-gray Australian scrub. The tropical heat and humidity are here, but the rain forests don't start for 100 miles (160 km) north along the Bruce Highway.

Townsville does have elegant tropical architecture and stately figs along the **Strand,** and the city has spent millions trying to entice tourists. A casino is now on the waterfront, along with a superb **aquarium,** part of the **Great Barrier Reef Wonderland** *(Flinders St. East, tel (07) 4750 0800)* that has reef coral, anemones, and schools of colorful tropical fish.

Townsville is also a base for visits to the Great Barrier Reef, and it is the only access point to **Magnetic Island** (see p. 164). Even so, most tourists continue to content themselves with a trip to the aquarium, a picnic on Magnetic Island, and a sunset view of the city lights from Castle Rock. Then they go on to Cairns and the north. ■

Cairns

CAIRNS IS THE MOST USEFUL BASE FOR VISITORS TO THE northern part of the Great Barrier Reef and to northern Queensland. Beneath a range of rain-forested mountains that rise steeply from the coast, this tropical city lives for the sea.

Cairns

139 C4

Visitor information

Calypso Plaza,
Esplanade

(07) 4031 1751

**Department of
the Environment
National Parks
Office**

10 Mcleod St.

(07) 4052 3096

**The Kuranda
Scenic Railway
winds up the
forested hillsides
behind Cairns.**

Cairns started out as a camp for trepang fishermen in the 1860s, but a succession of gold and tin strikes in the Atherton Tablelands (see p. 178), just over the mountain range, lured settlers from farther south, and the town was established in 1876. In 1924 the railway from Brisbane made its northern terminus at Cairns.

Until the tourism boom in the 1980s, Cairns was a sleepy sugar town and laid-back seaside resort popular with marlin fishermen. Seemingly overnight it became a throbbing, fast-paced tourist spot. Yet while the development has made Cairns one of Australia's most popular destinations, it has virtually destroyed the tropical laziness that gave Cairns its charm. These days quieter Port Douglas, where the trains and the jumbo jets that descend on Cairns never came,

has become the more fashionable vacation spot.

Nevertheless, Cairns is a convenient base from which to explore the region and a magnet for people who want adventurous activities—hang gliding, bungee jumping, white-water rafting, skydiving, and hot-air balloon rides. Visitors take day trips to the Great Barrier Reef, make excursions to the nearby islands, or charter deep-sea fishing boats. The National Parks office supplies information about hiking in the mountains around Cairns, and issues permits for camping on nearby islands. You can take a tour to the **Atherton Tablelands** rain forest or travel there by car, scenic railway, or 5-mile (8 km) cable-car ride (see p. 178). The Wet Tropics Information Centre *(Esplanade, tel (07) 4051 3588)* has information on the area's tropical rain forests. ∎

Port Douglas to Cape Tribulation

THE CHIC RESORT TOWN OF PORT DOUGLAS IS 40 MILES (64 km) north of Cairns on the Captain Cook Highway. This is an idyllic road, one of the most beautiful and seductive in Australia, rolling past isolated beaches and lush tropical hills. If you have the time and energy, do the journey on a bicycle.

Port Douglas, 3 miles (4.8 km) off the highway, was a sleepy seaside fishing village until the 1980s, when it was discovered by tourists and resort developers looking for something new. Set in the rain forest beside the Coral Sea, the little village (population 250) seemed to be almost everyone's idea of a tropical hideaway. Happily enough it still is, although its population is creeping toward 4,000.

Port Douglas is noted for five-star luxury resorts, such as the Sheraton Mirage *(Four Mile Beach, tel 1-800 818 831, toll free),* and for its golf course, marina, and upscale shopping complex. But while these developments may have brushed away the sleepiness, they haven't too badly bruised the town's easy tropical charm. It still projects that end-of-the-line feeling. Although it seems geared to the top end of the market (President Clinton has vacationed here), it has budget accommodations and eateries as well. Port Douglas is far more relaxed and cosmopolitan than Cairns and has plenty for visitors to do: walking the Mossman Gorge, taking trips into the Daintree rain forest, or exploring the northern end of the Great Barrier Reef.

Mossman is on the Captain Cook Highway around 9 miles (14 km) north of Port Douglas. It is still very much a small sugar town. Its major attraction is the lush, waterfall-laced **Mossman Gorge** about 3 miles (4.8 km) west. The

Kuku Yulanji people, a local Aboriginal tribe, guide tours through the gorge, or you can follow a 2-mile (3 km) walking track on your own.

The quiet village of **Daintree,** 22 miles (35 km) farther up the highway, is set on the edge of the rain forests of the vast **Daintree National Park** stretching to the north. The village was established as a timber camp to cut the prized red cedars that grew here. These days it is a base for cruises along the mighty **Daintree River—**a chance to putter through the tropical rain forest and spot saltwater crocodiles basking in the sun along the banks. One of the larger cruise operators is Daintree River Trains *(Tel 1-800 808 309, toll free).*

Cape Tribulation is 22 miles (35 km) north of Daintree. To get there take the ferry that crosses the Daintree River about 6 miles (9.6 km) south of Daintree. The ferries run every few minutes, from 6 a.m. to midnight *(Tel (07) 4098 7788, $A7/U.S. $3.50).* The road beyond the ferry is not bad, and, as long as there hasn't been particularly heavy rainfall, a conventional car can make it easily to Cape Tribulation. The **Daintree Rainforest Environmental Centre,** about 5 miles (8 km) past the ferry, is a worthwhile stop along the way *(Tel (07) 4098 9171).*

Cape Tribulation and nearby Mount Sorrow were named by Captain Cook, who was evidently depressed when his ship grounded

Port Douglas
🗺 139 C4
Visitor information
✉ 23 Macrossan St.
☎ (07) 4099 5599

Daintree
🗺 139 C5
Visitor information
✉ 5 Stewart St.
☎ (07) 4098 6133

Quicksilver catamarans: Cairns to Port Douglas
✉ Marina Mirage
☎ (07) 4087 2100
Offers a fast catamaran service to Cairns, also day trips to the Reef

The wettest corner of Australia, Cape Tribulation National Park is the last stronghold of the primeval rain forests that cloaked Australia 100 million years ago.

on a coral reef, forcing him to beach it near present-day Cooktown for repairs. For much of the next two centuries this lonely stretch of coastline was seldom visited. In the 1970s a few hippies arrived, and the area began to be better known. It still has a remote feel, although in holiday periods you'll see plenty of tourists and accommodations at Cape Tribulation often are full.

Cape Tribulation National Park is a spectacular paradise of mist-shrouded mountains tumbling down to the Coral Sea. One of the wettest corners on earth, the park has virgin tropical rain forest and coral reefs virtually side by side. It is the jewel of Queensland's 3,500 square miles (9,065 sq km) of wet tropics. Hidden in Cape Tribulation's dripping forests are primitive varieties of plants and flowers that are found nowhere else. Among them are species of angiosperms that are forerunners of all flowering plants. New species of ferns are

frequently discovered. Crocodiles lurk in the mangroves and estuaries, and the forests have 120 bird species, from rainbow honey-eaters to the flightless cassowary, which stands over 6 feet tall (2 m). Butterflies include the cobalt blue Ulysses and the huge Hercules moth, one of the largest in the world.

In the 1980s Queensland's tropics were the scene of confrontation between conservationists and the timber industry. A bitter campaign was fought over the building of the **Bloomfield Track,** a four-wheel-drive road that connects Cape Tribulation with Cooktown, 100 miles (160 km) north. The conservationists lost that battle, but the attention focused on the rain forests led the federal government to nominate the forests for the World Heritage List. Today logging is banned in the area, and because ecotourism is now the dominant industry in far northern Queensland, rain forests are a vital part of the economy. ■

Cape York Peninsula

Cape York

🗺 139 B6

Tourism Tropical North Queensland

✉ 51 The Esplanade, Cairns

☎ (07) 4051 3588

Pajinka Wilderness Lodge

✉ Cape York

☎ (07) 4069 2100

An Aborigine from Cape York Peninsula swims in a water hole or billabong.

Opposite: On Cape York rainless lightning storms may set the bush ablaze.

THE CAPE YORK PENINSULA IS ONE OF THE WILDEST corners of Australia. Driving up to the Tip, as Aussies call it, is one of the great four-wheel-drive adventures on the continent, a challenging 500-mile (800 km) trek to mainland Australia's most northerly point.

This is most definitely not a trip for beginners or the ill prepared. The roads and tracks are all dirt, and there are many river crossings. While it is possible under favorable conditions for a conventional vehicle to make it as far as the mining town of **Weipa,** about two-thirds of the way north, the final leg to the top is a very rough track, strictly for four-wheel-drive. You'll need a winch, chains, and plenty of experience in fording wild rivers. The banks on the rivers are steep and muddy, and crocodiles lurk in the water. And that's in the dry season. During the summer monsoons, forget it. Happily enough, if you lack the experience or gear, you can take one of a number of four-wheel-drive tours to the Tip, or get there by air or barge from Cairns. You can stay at the exclusive **Pajinka Wilderness Lodge,** owned by Aborigines, only a quarter mile from the top of Australia.

If air-conditioned travel to Cape York seems like roughing it, think how it was in 1848, when Edmund Kennedy led an ill-fated expedition to explore the peninsula. Of the fourteen people who started only three survived. Kennedy was speared by hostile Aborigines and died of his wounds. The only member of the party to reach the cape, where a ship was waiting, was the Aboriginal guide, Jacky Jacky.

In 1863 an adventurer named John Jardine established a pearling, coconut, and trading port called Somerset near the tip of the cape. His ambition was to make his little kingdom rival Singapore. In the fol-

lowing year, Jardine's sons Frank and Alexander drove a thousand head of cattle from Rockhampton all the way to the tip of the peninsula to help feed the struggling outpost. The remarkable venture opened up miles of new country, but in the end the termites and the attacks by hostile Aborigines proved too much. In 1877 the Jardines gave up on Somerset and relocated the little community of 200 to nearby Thursday Island.

By then, all the action on the Cape York Peninsula was taking place much farther south, along the Palmer River, where a gold rush drew thousands of prospectors. The diggings were marked by racial strife between the Australian and Chinese prospectors, and the Aborigines who did not care for either set of invaders in their territory.

Laura, about 200 miles (320 km) north of Cairns, was at the heart of the diggings, and 20,000 people a year passed through at the height of the boom. Laura is on the Peninsula Developmental Road, which you can join at **Mareeba,** west of Cairns on the Kennedy Highway. It is an easy drive, unless there has been heavy rain. There is not much to Laura itself, but it is the nearest township to the **Quinkan Reserve Aboriginal rock art galleries** near Split Rock, about 7 miles (11 km) south. The galleries are among the world's largest collections of rock art, with tens of thousands of paintings dating back more than 13,000 years. Most haunting are the Quinkans—gaunt, angular, sinister figures with staring eyes, whom the Aborigines believe lurk in cracks in the rocks. Tours to the galleries can be arranged at the Quinkan Reserves Trust *(Tel (07) 4060 3214)*. The **Aboriginal Dance Festival,** held in Laura in June of odd-numbered years, is a riveting spectacle, and worth arranging your itinerary around if you can be in Queensland then. The Ang-Gnarra Aboriginal Corporation in Laura *(Tel (07) 4060 3214)* has information on local rock art and on the dance festival.

Many people are attracted to **Thursday Island,** off the tip of the cape, simply because this tiny spot in Torres Strait is the end of the line. It is the most visited of the 60-odd Torres Straits Islands. Its residents are a multicultural swirl of Aborigines, Melanesians, Malay, Papuans, Chinese, and the descendants of Japanese pearl divers who worked here when the island was a pearling center. Today the clock with no hands in the local hotel says much about the present pace of life. Peddell's Ferry Service *(Tel (07) 4069 1551)* makes the crossing from Seisia, at the tip of Cape York, to Thursday Island. ∎

4WD tours:
Australian Outback Travel
☎ (07) 4031 6900
Oz Tours Safaris
☎ 1-800 079 006
The Adventure Company
☎ (07) 4051 4777

Rock-art tours:
Tresize Bush Guide Service
☎ (07) 4060 3236

National parks

Australia has 540 national parks, and they cover every kind of significant natural terrain in the country, including rain forests, deserts, islands, mountain ranges, and long stretches of haunting coastal dunes. Some are extremely remote, and visitors must travel across barren desert just to reach them, a journey that may be extremely dangerous for the inexperienced or the unprepared.

Not all of Australia's wild places require expedition planning. Some of the prettiest national parks are perched on the edge of cities. Royal National Park is on the coast just south of Sydney. In 1994 a bush fire in the Sydney suburbs destroyed about 90 percent of the park. Within a year, however, green shoots had appeared in the blackened soil, and the bush now is well on the way to recovery. Lush Dandenong Ranges National Park is only a suburban train ride from Melbourne.

Twelve of Australia's national parks have been included on the United Nations' World Heritage List. The Great Barrier Reef is among them. So is the Northern Territory's magnificent Kakadu National Park. This tropical wetland about three hours southeast of Darwin is the biggest tourist drawcard in the north. The main physical feature is the dramatic Arnhemland escarpment, a 400-mile-long (640 km) line of massive sandstone cliffs. During the summer wet season, runoff from the monsoon rains spills over the cliffs in a series of spectacular waterfalls. In the dry season, the shrinking waterholes are raucous with thousands of migratory birds. Kakadu is on the World Heritage List for cultural reasons as well. Aboriginal culture here dates back over 50,000 years, and thousands of rock-art murals decorate its hidden gorges, rock shelters, and caves.

The haunting monoliths of Uluru–Kata Tjuta National Park (Ayers Rock and the Olgas) are also on the World Heritage List for both cultural and natural reasons. Australia's other World Heritage sites include Shark Bay in Western Australia, popular with tourists for its friendly dolphins but famous among paleobotanists for the primitive blue-green algae

matting the rocks on the edge of Hamelin Pool. These algae, called stromatolites, are living fossils dating back 3.5 billion years.

Some of Australia's other World Heritage sites are wilderness islands. Fraser Island, midway up the coast of Queensland, is the world's largest sand island. It is forested with unique rain-forest plants and trees, such as the satinay. Lord Howe Island is a tropical paradise about 430 miles (692 km) off the coast of New South Wales. The southwest corner of Tasmania, also on the World Heritage List, is cloaked by some of the world's last great stands of virgin temperate forest.

The Central Eastern Rainforest Reserves is a group of 15 parks covering about 250,000 acres (101,250 ha) in the coastal highlands of New South Wales. The Fossil Mammal sites are widely scattered: One is at Riversleigh in Western Australia, and the other is more than 1,800 miles (2,896 km) away in the Narracoorte Caves of southeastern South Australia. As the name implies, these are treasure troves of fossil remains, revealing the history of Australia's unique fauna. The most obscure World Heritage site is Willandra National Park, a sequence of dry Pleistocene lake beds, 100 miles (160 km) northwest of Griffith in central New South Wales.

Visiting national parks

National parks are administered by the various states, and facilities vary. Some have resort accommodations inside or nearby, for example the Flinders Ranges in South Australia and Watarrka (Kings Canyon) in Northern Territory. Other parks have pit toilets and picnic tables, and some have no facilities at all. Contact the park in advance if you want to stay, as some parks allow only a few visitors at a time, and you may have to reserve a camping spot or accommodations. You also need to find out what equipment to take. *(The national parks agency in each state has details. For addresses and telephone numbers, see p. 366.)* ■

After the wet season, waterfalls pour over the escarpment in Kakadu National Park, Northern Territory.

Gulf of Carpentaria

Gulf of Carpentaria

🗺 138 A5

Visitor information

✉ Haig St., Normanton

☎ (07) 4645 1166

THE GULF OF CARPENTARIA AND QUEENSLAND'S RUGGED northwest are not for everyone. This is unvarnished Outback, with mining towns, isolated ports, and rough pubs. The landscape is blindingly hot savanna, studded with termite mounds capable of breaking the axle of a four-wheel-drive vehicle. Crocodiles inhabit the rivers and mangroves along the edge of the gulf, and the lonely towns can be cut off for weeks when the monsoons hit in summer. Despite all that, the area has an odd frontier appeal that pulls you on.

A road sign on the empty highway into Karumba. Flash floods happen in the monsoon season.

Undara Lava Tubes

🗺 139 B4

Lava Lodge Undara

☎ (07) 4097 1411 or 1-800 990 992 (toll free) Accommodations & tours of the lava tubes.

It's about 450 miles (720 km) from Cairns to Normanton on the lonely and evocative **Gulf Developmental Highway,** which runs down the western flank of the Atherton Tablelands and into the savanna country. The tourist make-believe falls away; you're on a lonely highway into an Outback barely changed from the days when explorers such as Burke and Wills passed this way. About 150 miles (240 km) southwest of Cairns the highway passes the **Undara Lava Tubes,** a vast series of hollow basalt chambers through which massive amounts of lava flowed in a volcanic eruption about 200,000 years ago. They are the largest such formation in the world and are well worth a visit.

Normanton is a rough old river port that over the decades has served the local cattle stations, the 1880s goldfields around Croydon,

and the silver mines in Cloncurry. The Norman River is rich with barramundi, tropical Australia's magnificent sweet-eating game fish. **Dorunda Station** *(Tel (07) 4745 3477),* deep in the wilderness about 100 miles (160 km) northeast of Normanton off the Burke Developmental Road, has barramundi fishing in lakes and rivers. If you decide to do a little fishing or boating, remember that these waters are home to some of the world's largest and most dangerous saltwater crocodiles. Check out the 28-foot (8.5 m) plaster cast of what was reputedly the biggest of them all— shot in the Norman River in 1957—near the town's garishly painted Purple Pub.

A 45-mile (72 km) side trip north from Normanton brings you to **Karumba,** a prawn-trawling port on the gulf. In the 1930s it was a refueling stop for the Qantas Empire Flying Boats that flew between Britain and Australia. These days fishing enthusiasts flock here to try their luck at what is said to be the best light tackle fishing in Australia. The gulf is filled with grunter, king salmon, blue salmon, and the famous barramundi. And, of course, saltwater crocodiles.

Except for the superb angling, you will find little else to do in Karumba. Sunsets over Karumba Point are gorgeous, as the blood red sun appears to melt into the gulf.

The beach is gorgeous, too, but don't even think about a dip unless you are into crocodile wrestling.

A 150-mile (240 km) dirt track leads west from Normanton to **Burketown,** population 230 and one of the loneliest towns in Australia, particularly during the wet season *(Oct.–April),* when it can be cut off for weeks. Although the road is bumpy, you normally do not need a four-wheel-drive vehicle in the dry season. The track runs through harsh spectacular country, past beautiful Leichhardt Falls.

If you are adventurous, you can drive to **Darwin** from Burketown along the **Gulf Track.** It is about 300 miles (480 km) of dirt track from Burketown to the next paved road, at Borroloola, and from there it is 600 miles (960 km) farther to Darwin. Attempt the Gulf Track only in the dry season. The less demanding **Wills Develop-**

mental Road, another dirt track, goes 75 miles (120 km) south from Burketown to **Gregory Downs** cattle station. There you can turn off for **Lawn Hill National Park** (see pp. 176-77) or take the Wills Highway 90 miles (145 km) southeast and turn south to Cloncurry.

The **Flinders Highway** runs east from Cloncurry to Townsville and the coast. West of Cloncurry, the highway runs 75 miles (120 km) to the sprawling mining town of **Mount Isa.** One of Australia's largest Outback cities, with a population of 21,750 (marginally fewer than Alice Springs), Mount Isa is the biggest city or municipal area in the world, covering almost 700 square miles (1,813 sq km). The main industry here is the giant silver-lead-zinc mine, also one of the biggest in the world. In August Mount Isa is host to Australia's

The McArthur River winds a serpentine course to the Gulf of Carpentaria.

MORNING GLORY

The atmospheric phenomenon called Morning Glory—a bizarre tubular cloud formation in the dawn skies in spring —is sometimes visible in the Gulf of Carpentaria. ∎

Mount Isa
⚠ 139 A3
Visitor information
✉ Marian St.
☎ (07) 4749 1555

Lawn Hill National Park

**Lawn Hill
National Park**
🅜 138 A4
☎ (07) 4748 5572

**Sheltered by
sandstone cliffs
and fed by
springs, Lawn Hill
Gorge is a hidden
tropical oasis of
fan palms,
parrots, and
freshwater
crocodiles amid
the harsh scrub of
northwest
Queensland.**

LAWN HILL NATIONAL PARK IS ONE OF AUSTRALIA'S JEWELS, an unexpected tropical oasis in the vast black soil plains of the gulf country. Locals and many visitors claim it is at least as spectacular as Kakadu (see pp. 186–89) and arguably more so, because its lushness is so surprising in the hot bleakness that surrounds it. It is a legacy of a time when all of northern Australia was covered with dense rain forests. When the climate grew warmer and drier the forests retreated.

These gorges, which are watered by a series of springs in the limestone hills along the nearby Northern Territory border, are the last secluded pockets of those ancient rain forests. They are lined with fan palms, fig trees, and ferns. The water attracts large numbers of mammals, birds, and reptiles such as water monitors, tortoises, and shy, freshwater crocodiles. The Waanyi people have been here for 30,000 years and the park is rich in rock art. Trails and boardwalks lead hikers to the **Wild Dog Dreaming** and **Rainbow Dreaming** rock-art sites. The park has about 15 miles (24 km) of walking tracks in all, but most visitors prefer to explore it by canoe or

pythons up to 25 feet (7.6 m) long. The fossil beds were actually a series of lakes where creatures came to drink. Fossilized remains have been extracted by blasting chunks out of the stubborn limestone beds. A roadside display contains some of the finds at the park. The fossil areas are a protected site.

In all, Lawn Hill is a hidden gem. Now comes the heartbreak part. There is a reason for the use of the adjective "hidden." This park is a long way from anywhere, and the final leg of the journey involves a long ride over a rough dirt track that is virtually impassable after heavy rains. A four-wheel-drive vehicle is recommended, although a conventional vehicle can make it through in dry weather, if the driver has experience on bush tracks. The park is about 250 miles (400 km) northwest of Mount Isa. The easiest drive there is to take the Burke Developmental Road north from Cloncurry to the Burke and Wills Roadhouse, and then go northwest on the Wills Highway. A 90-mile (145 km) drive will bring you to the Gregory Downs Hotel *(Tel (07) 4748 5566)*, an old Outback pub. You can buy food and fuel here, and the pub also has accommodations.

Access to the park is on a track by the pub, and this final leg is a tough 70-mile (113 km) ride. It would be nice to say that the scenery along the track into the park is stunning—but it isn't. In fact, it is positively apocalyptic in its bleakness, which is what makes Lawn Hill itself such a delightful surprise. Six miles (9.6 km) east of the park entrance is Adel's Grove Kiosk *(Tel (07) 4748 5502)*, where you can buy supplies and rent canoes. A national park service campsite is here, with another in the park itself. Despite its remoteness, Lawn Hill is popular and the campsites are often booked. Check with the park office. ■

Queensland's rain forests harbor the rare green python.

inner tube, floating in its clear, lime green waters looking up at the colored sandstone walls of the gorge rising 200 feet (60 m) above the pools. Although plenty of crocodiles live here, particularly in the lower parts of the gorge, these waters are safe for swimming. Freshwater crocodiles are smaller and much more timid than their saltwater cousins. In the southern end of the park, the staggeringly rich limestone fossil beds of the **Riversleigh Fossil Site** tell the story of the past 20 million years. The fossils reveal that this was once a scary little jungle filled with carnivorous kangaroos, marsupial lions, rhinoceros-size wombats, and relatives of the now extinct Tasmanian tiger. Also living here were birds, bats, and prehistoric

Atherton Tablelands

Atherton Tablelands
🗺 139 C4
Visitor information
✉ Corner of Mabel & Vernon Sts., Atherton
☎ (07) 4091 4222

Kuranda
🗺 139 C4
Visitor information
✉ Therwine St.
☎ (07) 4093 9311

Kuranda Scenic Railway
☎ (07) 4032 3964

SIMPLY GETTING TO THIS LUSH VOLCANIC HIGHLAND looming above Cairns can be as much fun as exploring it. The Kuranda Scenic Railway climbs the jungle-clad range that broods over Cairns to the cool moist heights of the Atherton Tablelands. The railway was built in 1891 to link the Herberton tin mines with the coast, and it is now one of the world's great short train journeys.

Pulled by a 125-year-old steam engine, the train skirts the coastline and then ascends the mountains in a series of switchbacks. It runs along a 600-foot (183 m) sheer precipice above the **Barron River Gorge** and through 15 tunnels cut into the stone. The 20-mile (32 km) ride ends at **Kuranda,** a rain-forest town with a famous crafts market and an arty atmosphere. Crowds and trashy souvenirs in the market

Having arrived by train, you need to rent a car to see the glories of the tablelands. Rain-forest towns such as Atherton and Ravenshoe (pronounced Ravens-hoe) attract artists, back-to-nature types, gypsies, and the just plain odd, and have a friendly offbeat style. The little village of **Yungaburra,** about 8 miles (13 km) east of Atherton on the Gillies Highway, is a central spot from which to explore. Two of the loveliest crater lakes you'll ever see—**Lake Eacham** and **Lake Barrine**— are east off the Gillies Highway. Both are national parks, with swimming holes and bush walks around their rims. A mile south of Yungaburra, on the road to Malanda, is the **Curtain Fig Tree,** a massive, much photographed tangle of roots and vines.

A few miles south of Atherton, off the Kennedy Highway, is **Mount Hypipamee National Park.** More than 300 species of birds have been found in this forest. A path leads a quarter mile (400 m) along Dinner Creek to a rather sinister volcanic cavity that plunges a sheer 200 feet (61 m) into a dark, algae-covered pool. The 10-mile (16 km) "waterfall circuit" drive around nearby **Millaa Millaa** (south of Malanda) takes in the best of the area's waterfalls. Take the Theresa Creek Road off Palmerston Highway toward Millaa Millaa Falls, the first and most magnificent. Then drive through dense rain forests and farmland to Zillie, Mungali, and Elinja. ■

The high, cool rain forests of the Atherton Tablelands shelter rare orchids, ferns, and brilliant tropical butterflies such as this coppery hued cruiser.

are lessening its charm, but it has gorgeous rain-forest walks close by. A track from the picturesque colonial station takes you into the wilds of **Barron Gorge National Park.** Another way to reach Kuranda is on the **Skyrail Rainforest Cableway** *(Tel (07) 4038 1555),* a 5-mile (8 km) cable-car ride that leaves from Cairns's northern suburbs.

Colloquially known as the "Never Never," Australia's remote Northern Territory is picture-book Outback and home to two of Australia's most cherished icons: Uluru in the Red Centre and the wild, monsoonal wetlands of Kakadu.

Northern Territory

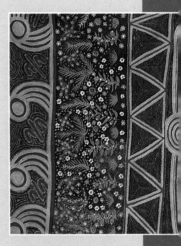

"Bush Medicine" by Sarah Morton

Northern Territory

THE NORTHERN TERRITORY IS THE AUSTRALIA OF MYTH. THIS IS WHAT most Australians think of as the real Australia, though few of them live there. Monsoon rains drench the tropical north, or Top End. The south is Australia's Red Centre, a desert of rock and dust in red and ochre. At 525,000 square miles (1,359,750 sq km), the territory is about the size of Alaska or six times the size of Great Britain, but with only 173,000 inhabitants it is one of the least populated places in the world. About half of its residents live in Darwin, in the tropical north, where Asia and Outback Australia meld in a bright, modern city. Alice Springs, in the Red Centre, is the other main population center. The rest of the population lives in Aboriginal communities, mining camps, or cattle stations.

The first settlements in the territory were on Melville Island and the Coburg Peninsula in the 1820s, when the British hastened to claim the northern coastline ahead of the French and Dutch. Malaria and cyclones put paid to these first settlements, and it wasn't until 1869, when Palmerston (later Darwin) was established, that Europeans took root.

The Northern Territory has the highest percentage of Aborigines in its population— about 22 percent—of any state in Australia. About 50 percent of the state is Aboriginal land. Much of it is remote and visitors require a permit. But some Aboriginal communities are opening up, inviting responsible tourism operators onto their lands, or starting their own operations, both to create jobs and to share their ancient knowledge and arts.

Many people visit the territory just to see Uluru (Ayers Rock) and the wetlands in Kakadu, but the Northern Territory has other sights, too. It has Kata Tjuta (the Olgas, near Uluru), the lost world of Watarrka, the MacDonnell Ranges near Alice Springs, and Nitmiluk Gorge near Katherine.

The tropical north has two seasons—the wet and the dry. The Wet runs through the summer, when heat, humidity, and monsoonal rain make life tolerable only to a special breed of frontier lovers. Bush tracks can be washed out for months, dry creek beds turn into cataracts, and wild tropical grasses grow as much as 30 feet (9 m) in a month. The Dry begins around April. The storms clear away, and for the next six months the country bakes beneath faultless skies. Daily high temperatures are in the high 80s°F (30°C). This is the best time to visit the Top End. The buildup to the Wet starts again in

Area of map detail

October, with heat and humidity rising unbearably, and dry thunderstorms that give no relief. In the central deserts, the weather is scorching during the summer and dry as parchment. Winters are cold and frosts are possible.

Visiting the Northern Territory requires planning because of the distances involved, but actually moving within it is fairly easy. The major highways are sealed and even the gravel back roads are generally graded. Flights go to Alice Springs, Darwin, and Yulara (the resort near Uluru) from all parts of Australia. Alice Springs is accessible from Adelaide by the Ghan train (see pp. 282–83). Some day the tracks may extend to Darwin. The government has been promising it a rail link since 1911.

The Northern Territory entered the new millennium as Australia's newest state, and the first new state since Federation. Statehood— the right to elect senators to Parliament and decide its internal affairs—eluded this vast area until August 1998, when the federal government agreed to make the Northern Territory Australia's seventh state by 2000. ∎

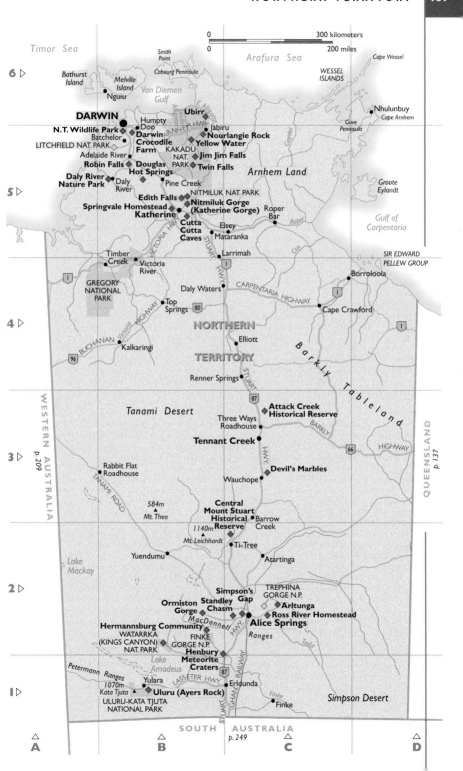

Timor Sea

Arafura Sea

6 ▷

Bathurst Island

Melville Island

Nguiu

Van Diemen Gulf

Smith Point

Cobourg Peninsula

Cape Wessel

WESSEL ISLANDS

Nhulunbuy

Cape Arnhem

DARWIN

Humpty Doo

Ubirr

Gove Peninsula

N.T. Wildlife Park

Batchelor

Darwin Crocodile Farm

Jabiru

Nourlangie Rock

LITCHFIELD NAT. PARK

KAKADU NAT. PARK

Yellow Water

Adelaide River

Jim Jim Falls

Groote Eylandt

Robin Falls

Douglas Hot Springs

Twin Falls

Arnhem Land

Daly River Nature Park

Daly River

Pine Creek

Gulf of Carpentaria

5 ▷

Edith Falls

NITMILUK NAT. PARK

Springvale Homestead

Nitmiluk Gorge (Katherine Gorge)

Roper Bar

Katherine

Elsey

Cutta Cutta Caves

Mataranka

Timber Creek

Victoria River

Larrimah

SIR EDWARD PELLEW GROUP

GREGORY NATIONAL PARK

Daly Waters

CARPENTARIA HIGHWAY

Borroloola

Top Springs

80

Cape Crawford

4 ▷

NORTHERN

Kalkaringi

BUCHANAN

96

Elliott

TERRITORY

Barkly Tableland

Renner Springs

87

Tanami Desert

Attack Creek Historical Reserve

Three Ways Roadhouse

BARKLY

Tennant Creek

66

HIGHWAY

3 ▷

Rabbit Flat Roadhouse

Devil's Marbles

TANAMI ROAD

Wauchope

584m Mt. Theo

Central Mount Stuart Historical Reserve

Barrow Creek

1140m Mt. Leichhardt

Ti-Tree

Yuendumu

Atartinga

Lake Mackay

2 ▷

Simpson's Gap

TREPHINA GORGE N.P.

Ormiston Gorge

Standley Chasm

Arltunga

MacDonnell

Ross River Homestead

Hermannsburg Community

Alice Springs

WATARRKA (KINGS CANYON) NAT. PARK

FINKE GORGE N.P.

Ranges

Henbury Meteorite Craters

87

Petermann Ranges

Lake Amadeus

1070m Kata Tjuta

Yulara

Uluru (Ayers Rock)

Erldunda

Simpson Desert

ULURU-KATA TJUTA NATIONAL PARK

Finke

1 ▷

SOUTH AUSTRALIA p. 249

△ A   △ B   △ C   △ D

WESTERN AUSTRALIA p. 209

QUEENSLAND p. 137

0   300 kilometers
0   200 miles

Darwin

Darwin
 181 B6
Visitor information
✉ Corner of Mitchell & Knuckey Sts.
☎ (08) 8936 2499

THIS PROSPEROUS MODERN CITY OF 80,000 CAN COME AS quite a shock to first-time visitors who have come to the rugged tropical north expecting a brawling frontier settlement out of the movie *Crocodile Dundee*. Darwin is Australia's most suburban city, a white-collar enclave with a low-rise skyline and sprawl of neat suburban homes, shopping malls, cinemas, a casino, and fast-food chains. All this newness is courtesy of Cyclone Tracy, which almost obliterated the city when it roared into town on Christmas Day in 1974, packing winds of more than 180 mph (290 kph). The city that was rebuilt from the wreckage is brighter, more cosmopolitan—and, one hopes, sturdier—than the ramshackle trading port that had grown up here.

Fish feeding at Aquascene in Darwin

In its better neighborhoods only the heat and the bright tropical flowers distinguish Darwin from, say, one of Melbourne's satellite residential suburbs. The elegant old-fashioned tropical-style houses, built of timber with sweeping verandas and elevated several feet off the ground to allow air to circulate, are mostly gone. In their place are brick ranch-style houses, less evocative than the old houses, but a lot more resilient in a cyclone. Darwin is the world's lightning capital, and the electric displays over the Arafura Sea beggar description.

This is a public service town at heart. Many of its citizens draw generous government paychecks, live in nice subsidized homes, and work in the huge air-conditioned office blocks downtown. You won't be popular, however, if you point this out. Territorians cherish their rough-and-tumble, maverick image. For all its white-collar homes and jobs, Darwin is genuinely a magnet for Australia's footloose—the adventurous, the restless, and the outcast (and the occasional wanted-by-police). It is a town of transients—whether public servants or teachers on a two-year contract, or drifters looking for a few weeks' or months' work in the mines. Most residents are from somewhere else and, as

often as not, somewhere far away. Darwin is exceptionally ethnically diverse, with more than 50 nationalities represented here.

It's a hard-drinking town that sometimes seems to be a parody of itself, self-consciously straining to maintain its frontier image. Tempers flare during the build-up to the wet season, when heat and humidity grab your temples like a vice, and the police logs fill up with petty assaults. Darwin's wet season is like the long Scandinavian winter in terms of dreariness and depression.

Darwin grew up with the gold rushes of the 1880s, when fortune-seekers from all over Asia flocked to the port. The settlement was founded as Palmerston, but it was renamed Port Darwin after the naturalist Charles Darwin, who passed through this harbor on the *Beagle* in 1839. In 1911 the name was simplified to Darwin. In the early days Darwin hoped it would become a rival to Singapore, but the harsh climate, sporadic tropical cyclones, and poor communications with the rest of the world were difficult obstacles to overcome.

World War II changed all of that when this isolated port suddenly took on significance as a key base for Allied forces. Hastily built highways to Alice Springs and Mount Isa linked Darwin with the rest of Australia, and airstrips were bulldozed in the bush nearby. Darwin suffered 64 air raids during the war, with the loss of 243 lives. It was the only part of Australia to be subjected to sustained attack. After the war, the bombed city was rebuilt, but reverted to its former torpor until Cyclone Tracy leveled it again in 1974.

Since then, huge amounts of government money have been poured into Darwin. Today it is an administration center, with government, mining, tourism, and the military the big local employers. Increasingly it is casting itself as Australia's gateway to Asia.

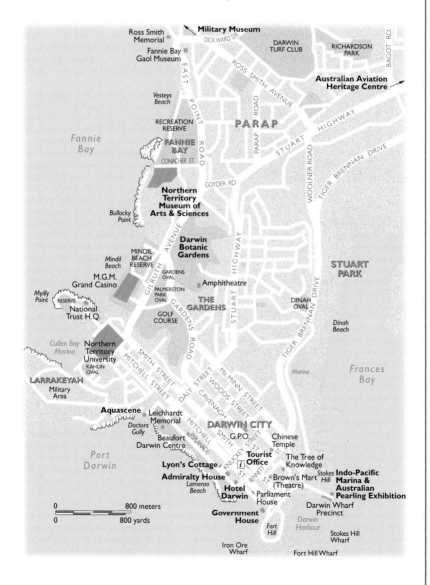

Northern Territory
Museum of Arts &
Sciences

✉ Conacher St.

☎ (08) 8999 8201

DARWIN SIGHTS

For most visitors Darwin is a base for sight-seeing expeditions to places such as Kakadu, Katherine Gorge, or Litchfield National Park, rather than an end in itself. The emphasis of the tourism industry in Darwin is on getting you into the

Lightning dances across the skies over Darwin. Storms from the summer monsoon can drop more than 6 feet (2 m) of rain on the city in a few spectacular weeks.

bush as quickly and often as possible. Nevertheless there are some very worthwhile things to see while you are in town.

Downtown Darwin is easy to get around—a simple grid of wide streets at the end of a peninsula jutting into the harbor. Although most of the early buildings were leveled, either by Japanese bombing or by Cyclone Tracy, some classic colonial tropical buildings are still standing on the Esplanade—**Admiralty House** and **Lyon's Cottage** (both 1920s), and the restored **Government House** (built in 1870). The National Trust *(4 Burnett Pl., tel (08) 8981 2848)* publishes a pamphlet, "A Walk through Historical Darwin," a useful guide to the old city. The Esplanade runs along the edge of the ocean and makes a lovely evening stroll. A huge embroidered **quilt,** hanging in the nearby library and crafted by people who lived here in the 1940s, tells the story of

Darwin during the dark days of World War II.

The **Northern Territory Museum of Arts & Sciences** overlooking Fannie Bay about 2 miles (3 km) north of the city center, is one of the best cultural attractions in Darwin. It was part of the massive rebuilding program after Cyclone Tracy, and it houses a major collection of Aboriginal and Pacific Islander art. The national Aboriginal Art Award is held here every September. The museum also highlights the contribution of Southeast Asia to the development of Australia's tropical north. Another display chronicles the terrible morning when Cyclone Tracy arrived in town, killing 66 people and effectively wiping out the old Darwin for all time. One of the most popular exhibits is the stuffed, late, and unlamented "Sweetheart," a 17-foot (5 m), 1,700-pound (770 kg) saltwater crocodile that terrorized local fishermen by attacking the outboard motors on their boats until he was captured in 1979.

Darwin has a number of very pretty beaches, but strong tides, crocodiles, and the presence of deadly box jellyfish six months of the year *(Oct.–April, during which swimming is banned)* have kept it from becoming much of a beach town. Nothing prevents you from rolling out your towel and catching some sun, but remember that you are in the tropics and put on plenty of sunscreen.

Mindil Beach has a lively open-air market on winter evenings *(May–Oct.).* The air is fragrant with the aroma of Asian food from scores of food stands. Families set up folding tables and elaborate picnics, kids play beach cricket, and crowds browse through racks of T-shirts, leather goods, velvet paintings, secondhand books, pinwheels, crafts, bush hats, and all manner of

other things. The nearby **Darwin Botanic Gardens** *(Geranium St., tel (08) 8981 1958)* have one of the finest collections of tropical plants—including more than 400 species of palms—in Australia.

Across town, the old wharf area has become a fashionable precinct, with upscale eateries, outdoor cafés, and live entertainment on weekends in the old shed at the end of Stokes Hill Wharf. Living coral can be seen at the **Indo-Pacific Marina,** and the **Australian Pearling Exhibition** *(Stokes Hill Wharf Rd.)* tells Darwin's story in the rough days of Australia's pearling industry. At **Aquascene** *(28 Doctors Gully Rd., tel (08) 8981 7837, open for an hour around high tide, call for times)* you can feed the fish—mullet, milkfish, rays, and many others—that come in on the tide.

WARTIME SITES
Darwin holds special memories for veterans who spent time here during World War II. You can do a self-guided tour of the old storage tunnels near the wharf, which were dug into the rock beneath the city to protect vital fuel during air raids. The **Military Museum,** on East Point Reserve *(Tel (08) 8981 9702),* tells the story of Darwin's World War II. The **Australian Aviation Heritage Centre** is on the Stuart Highway 5 miles (8 km) south of town *(Tel (08) 8947 2145).* It has a Japanese Zero that was shot down over Darwin on the first raid, but more spectacular is the huge B-52 bomber on loan from the U.S. Air Force.

The most poignant memories for those who served here may be triggered by driving south out of town to the abandoned airstrips. Signs by the side of the road point out which track to take. The strips themselves are just clearings now, with rusting fuel drums scattered in the bush, eerily still except for the birds chirping in the treetops. ■

Darwin's colorful Beer Can Regatta, usually held in July or August, brings out the city's rowdy style.

Kakadu National Park

Kakadu National Park

📍 181 B5

Visitor information

✉ P.O. Box 71, Jabiru NT 0886

☎ (08) 8938 1100

The walls of the Arnhemland Escarpment present a formidable barrier to the outside and lock away the lost world of Kakadu.

KAKADU NATIONAL PARK IS A WETLANDS MARVEL. IT stretches across 8,000 square miles (20,700 sq km) of remote tropical wilderness, about 95 miles (153 km) southwest of Darwin. Australia's largest national park encloses the entire drainage basin of the South Alligator River—so named by Capt. Philip King, an early explorer who confused the area's many crocodiles with alligators when he surveyed Van Diemen Gulf (just to the north) in 1818. In the river's short, 100-mile (160 km) run to the sea, it passes through rain forests, eucalyptus woodlands, swamps, and mangroves. The defining landmark is the huge sandstone escarpment over which the river and its tributaries spill in a series of cataracts and waterfalls during the monsoons, when the waters are swollen by heavy rains. During the long dry season the waters recede, leaving only a few billabongs—or water holes—that are usually carpeted with water lilies and teeming with birds. One of the most spectacular sights during the wet season is Jim Jim Falls, with its sheer drop of more than 500 feet (152 m).

Kakadu contains more than 280 species of birds (about one-third of all known Australian bird species), 25 kinds of frogs, 74 species of reptiles, 60 species of mammals, and about 5,000 varieties of insects. The list of Kakadu's flora and fauna is being lengthened all the time, and some species, such as the Oenpelli python (discovered only in 1977) are probably unique to the park. The wildlife provides some of the most enduring images of Kakadu: elegant Jabiru storks, thousands of galahs or magpie geese taking wing from a pool, and awesome giant saltwater crocodiles sunning themselves in the mud. About 3,500 salties live in the park, and every tour guide seems to have an inexhaustible stock of macabre

anecdotes about them. The park is not a great place for a dip.

Kakadu's human history dates back more than 20,000 years, and thousands of Aboriginal rock-art galleries can be found in the area's cliffs and rock shelters. More than 5,000 sites have been catalogued so far. Most are off-limits to visitors, either because they are too difficult to reach or because they have spiritual significance to the Gagadju people, who own the land and lease it to the government. Two accessible rock-art sites, however, are at **Ubirr** and **Nourlangie Rock.**

Controversy has raged over Kakadu's rich mineral resources for most of the park's history. Some of the world's richest uranium deposits are here, as well as gold, platinum, and palladium ore bodies in nearby Coronation Hill. The **Ranger Uranium Mine** has been in operation since 1979. The company, Energy Resources of Australia (ERA), is required to operate under strict environmental guidelines and set aside a trust fund for the eventual rehabilitation of the land when mining has stopped. Tours of the mine site include details of the environmental rehab program in addition to the company's (and some Aborigines') positive viewpoints on mining. So-called green groups are critical of the company's performance so far and are opposing plans for a new underground uranium mine at Jabiluka, which would include a 12-mile (19 km) road through the park.

Four miles west of the Ranger Mine is the township of **Jabiru** (population about 1,800). It was built in 1981 to service the mining operation, but the fast-growing popularity of Kakadu has made it something of a tourist center itself, complete with a luxury motel in the shape of a crocodile (see p. 376).

A hiker takes a break beside one of the termite mounds in Kakadu.

VISITING KAKADU

Getting to the park is easy. Drive along the Stuart Highway south of Darwin and take a left turn onto the Arnhem Highway. This highway takes you past the colorful old pub at Humpty Do and through the heart of the park to Jabiru. Getting around this vast wilderness is something else. Four-wheel-drive vehicles or light aircraft are the best bets for reaching the most interesting and remote places. Excellent tours leave from Darwin, and the visitor center at the park headquarters (see panel p. 186) has helpful pamphlets, information on ranger-led walks, videos, and a visitor's guide to help you get the most out of your stay.

When to go is another matter. The Aborigines distinguish six different seasons in the Kakadu calendar, but choosing between the wet and dry seasons is complicated enough for most people. The dry season (May–Oct.) is by far the most popular, with heat and humidity at tolerable levels and the wildlife concentrated around a few shrinking water holes. To see Kakadu during the Wet, however, is to see it in all its glory, with booming monsoonal thunderstorms sweeping over the plains, cataracts spilling over the escarpment, and lush tropical grasses running riot. Against this you have to weigh the crushing heat and humidity, the fact that the wildlife will be dispersed throughout the park, and the flash floods that make much of Kakadu inaccessible. Go when the dry season has just begun, and you may get the best of both. There's no perfect time. It's a judgment call.

The most popular attractions in the park are Aboriginal rock-art sites at Nourlangie Rock and Ubirr, the magnificent Jim Jim and Twin Falls, and Yellow Water, near the Gagadju Lodge, Cooinda, which is also the most convenient place to stay in Kakadu (Tel (08) 8979 0145). There are no real long-distance trails in this park—something of a surprise and disappointment to bush-walking visitors. Most of the trails are just short nature strolls, with the 7-mile (11 km) hike around Nourlangie Rock being the most challenging.

Nourlangie Rock is one of the easiest major sites to reach in Kakadu, only 20 miles (32 km) south of the park headquarters. It is a haunting deep-red sandstone formation, cloaked in forest, that falls away in steep cliffs with rock shelters clustered at its foot. A mile-long (1.6 km) walk takes you from the parking lot to **Anbangbang Shelter,** which has 20,000-year-old rock art. Nearby are sweeping views over the Arnhemland Escarpment. If you want to hike, follow the 7-mile (11 km) Barrk Walk around Nourlangie Rock. The park headquarters (see p. 186) has a leaflet on this hike.

Ubirr, about 25 miles (40 km) north of the park headquarters on a paved road, depicts numerous animals, including tortoises, goannas, wallabies, and some that are long extinct, such as the thylacine, or Tasmanian tiger. You will also see depictions of the Rainbow Serpent—a powerful female character in the Aborigines' creation story and a frequent rock-art motif—and of mischievous Mimi spirits who dwell inside the rocks. Artistic styles vary, ranging from more than 20,000 years ago until the mid-20th century. A trail (about a mile/1.6 km round-trip) takes you from the parking lot to the rock-art galleries and includes a spectacular lookout over the East Alligator River and the rocky crags of Arnhemland. A longer and less frequented 4-mile (6.4 km) hike called **Rockholes Walk** runs

along the river. **Guluyambi Cruises** *(Tel 1-800 089 113, toll free)* has a river trip with Aboriginal guides, from the start of the Rockholes Walk and upstream through dramatic scenery to the escarpment.

Jim Jim and **Twin Falls** are out of the way, about 70 miles (113 km) south of the park headquarters on a challenging four-wheel-drive track, but they are well worth a visit. They are best seen right at the beginning of the dry season, after the rains have stopped long enough for the road to be open and graded, but with enough water swelling Jim Jim Creek to make the falls an awesome sight. Water tumbles more than 700 feet (213 m) down the cliffs, including one unbroken 500-foot (152 m) fall, into a large pool at the base. As

the Dry takes hold, these falls can stop completely. Twin Falls is 6 miles (9.6 km) from Jim Jim, along an even trickier four-wheel-drive track and then a slippery climb up a forested gorge. The river cascades into an idyllic pool with a sandy beach. During the wet season, both of these spectacles are inaccessible.

For many people, **Yellow Water** is the highlight of their visit to Kakadu. It is a richly vegetated lagoon formed by Jim Jim Creek as it flows onto the floodplain about 30 miles (48 km) south of Jabiru. In the dry season it teems with many species of waterfowl, and saltwater crocodiles bask in the mud. Sunrise and sunset are the best times to be on the lagoon. Regular boat cruises leave from nearby Cooinda Resort. ∎

Yellow snowflake lilies create a kaleidoscopic carpet on one of Kakadu's billabongs in the aftermath of the monsoons.

Litchfield National Park

Litchfield National Park

🗺 181 B5

Community Education Information

☎ (08) 8976 0282

National Parks & Wildlife Service

✉ Desk at Darwin Tourism Association, Corner of Mitchell & Knuckey Sts., Darwin

☎ (08) 8981 4300

ONLY A TWO-HOUR DRIVE FROM DARWIN, LITCHFIELD National Park is a beautiful collection of waterfalls, sandstone formations, termite mounds, and crocodile-free swimming holes. Many people actually prefer this quieter and smaller park to the better-known Kakadu, and it is a popular day trip for locals. Plenty of organized tours leave from Darwin, or you can drive there yourself, down the Stuart Highway and through the old mining town of Batchelor. As is usually the case in the Northern Territory, access is much easier during the dry season, from May to October.

On the way you might want to stop at the **Darwin Crocodile Farm,** on the Stuart Highway about 25 miles (40 km) south of the city *(Tel (08) 8988 1450)*. This is a commercial crocodile operation with more than 7,000 animals. Some are breeders, others become handbags or the crocodile steaks that are served in certain Darwin restaurants. Rogue crocodiles that have been frightening communities are relocated here. Displays explain the difference between the extremely dangerous saltwater crocodiles ("salties") and the shy freshwater version ("freshies")—an important distinction to make if you do much swimming in the water holes up here. The farm has a souvenir shop, a café selling crocodile burgers, and some great photo opportunities. One star attraction is Burt, the monster saltie that appeared in the movie *Crocodile Dundee*.

The **Northern Territory Wildlife Park,** about 5 miles (8 km) farther along the highway *(Tel (08) 8988 7200)*, is another worthwhile detour, with an outstanding aquarium, aviaries, reptile house, and nature trails. Day tours leave for the park from Darwin.

Litchfield National Park is a 250-square-mile (648 sq km) parcel of rugged wilderness that takes in the Tabletop Range, a vast sandstone plateau covered by eucalyptus woodlands. A series of spring-fed rivers spill over the rim of the plateau in spectacular waterfalls that plunge into rain-forest valleys below. The park has two entrances: a gravel road from the north via the Berry Springs-Cox Peninsula Road and a paved road from the east that starts in the old mining town of Batchelor. The two roads link up inside the park so you can do Litchfield on a loop. The park's most popular attractions are Florence Falls, Wangi Falls, Tolmer Falls, and Sandy Creek Falls. There is no entry fee or visitor center in this park, although the national parks office in Darwin has information on bush walks, flora and fauna, the termite mounds, and the waterfalls. Litchfield Community Education Information is also helpful.

The 700-foot-high (212 m) **Florence Falls** is the first waterfall you'll come to if you enter the park through Batchelor, and the pool at the base is an excellent swimming hole. You can camp here or at the nearby Buley Rock Holes. The turnoff to **Tolmer Falls** is about 11 miles (17.7 km) past the turnoff for Florence Falls. Swimming is forbidden in the plunge pool here,

Cute now, but these baby saltwater crocodiles can grow up to be as much as 20 feet (6.1 m) long and weigh more than half a ton.

to protect the nesting site of the rare orange horseshoe bat.

Another 4 miles (6.4 km) will bring you to **Wangi Falls.** The year-round waterfalls are the most popular attraction in the park, with an idyllic tropical swimming hole and a rain-forest boardwalk.

One of the other great attractions in the park is the **Lost City,** an eerie collection of weathered sandstone columns that resemble ancient ruins. The turnoff is about 4 miles (6.4 km) past the turnoff for Florence Falls. To get there, you bump another 5 miles (8 km) along a steep, muddy four-wheel-drive track. The track will take you to **Sandy Creek Falls,** although it gets even more treacherous past the Lost City. It is easier to reach Sandy Creek Falls on a four-wheel-drive track leading directly off the main track through the park. ■

At Litchfield National Park, swimmers take a dip in the crystal clear waters beneath Florence Falls.

Nitmiluk National Park & Katherine

NITMILUK, OR KATHERINE GORGE (ITS OLD EUROPEAN name), is one of the three sights you should not miss in the Top End of the Northern Territory (the other two are Kakadu and Litchfield National Parks). It is a chain of 13 gorges carved out of the surrounding sandstone plateau by the mighty Katherine River during the past 25 million years or so. The whole chain now forms Nitmiluk National Park. In addition to the towering orange cliffs, there are spectacular Aboriginal rock-art galleries in the shelters tucked in the gorges. You can see them while on a canoe trip or cruising on the river.

Explorer John McDouall Stuart came this way in his epic south-to-north transcontinental trek in 1861. The river must have been the first permanent water he had seen in hundreds of miles, and he named it after the daughter of one of his friends. In 1871 the telegraph line was put through, and a couple called Frank and Kate Knott set up a pub and general store. The town of Knotts Crossing (later Katherine) sprang up here. It was a rough-and-tumble Outback settlement when a woman named Jeannie Gunn visited on her way to Elsey Station in 1902. Gunn wrote about Katherine's old pub, the Sportsman's Arms, in her classic novel about station life and Aborigines, *We of the Never Never*. For years the presence of reliable water made the Katherine settlement a major stopover point for drovers and prospectors crossing the desert.

By Northern Territory standards, **Katherine** is a bustling city of 8,500. The Tindal Air Force Base here is the main tactical fighter base for northern Australia, and the Royal Australian Air Force (R.A.A.F.) is the single biggest employer in town. The **School of the Air** on Giles Street gives tours of its facility so you can see how children in the Outback are taught.

Nitmiluk National Park and its chain of gorges are about 20 miles (32 km) northeast of Katherine, at the end of a highway that runs there from the town center. Most visitors come on a day trip during the dry season and go no farther than the second gorge. The river is flat, low, and calm at this time of

Katherine
⬛ 181 B5
Visitor information
✉ Lindsay St.
☎ (08) 8972 2650

National Parks & Wildlife Service
✉ Giles St., Katherine
☎ (08) 8973 8888

Nitmiluk National Park
⬛ 181 B5
Visitor information
☎ (08) 8972 1886

Canoeing is the most popular way to see Nitmiluk's ancient gorges.

Aboriginal guides offer visitors a glimpse of the way their people, the Jawoyn, lived along the Katherine River for more than 40,000 years.

year, and canoeists are impeded by piles of boulders that require portaging. If you are keen to see the Katherine River's entire baker's dozen of gorges, plan on doing an overnight trek. The first legal campsite is **Smith's Rock,** in the fourth gorge. You can camp anywhere beyond here. The uppermost gorges are most easily seen by beaching the canoe after the fifth gorge and scrambling over the rocks for the last couple of miles. During the wet season, however, the river becomes a formidable torrent. In 1998 Katherine experienced a flood, something that is expected to happen only once in 500 years.

Numerous walking tracks lead through the park's scenic bushland and down into the gorge itself. The longest and most challenging of

these is the 50-mile (80 km) hike to **Edith Falls.** The park visitor center has full details on hikes and canoeing the river, as well as maps and guides. A bus shuttles between Katherine and the national park.

Five miles (8 km) southwest of Katherine, just off the Victoria Highway, **Springvale Homestead** is supposedly the oldest station in the Northern Territory. Built in 1879, the homestead has accommodations and crocodile spotting tours, and local Jawoyn people put on corroborees, with demonstrations of dancing and spearthrowing. Still farther south is the **Cutta Cutta Caves Nature Park,** which has weird 500-million-year-old limestone formations and caves that contain rare orange horseshoe bats. ■

Arnhemland & the Tiwi Islands

ABORIGINES HOLD BIG TRACTS OF LAND IN THE TOP END— the primeval wilderness of Arnhemland, the Cobourg Peninsula, and Melville and Bathurst Islands. Much of this land is off limits to individual tourists. Aborigines have lived in these remote places for more than 40,000 years, and for the most part they do not wish to be disturbed. They are responding to the growing interest in their culture, though, and there are a few unique opportunities for travel.

Northern Land Council Office
✉ Jabiru
☎ (08) 8920 5100

ARNHEMLAND

The vast wilderness of Arnhemland is slowly opening its doors to controlled tourism. The main settlement is the bauxite mining town of **Gove/Nhulunbuy** in the northeast corner. You don't need a permit to fly there, but this port has little appeal. Independent tourism outside it is virtually impossible. Travel permits take up to a year to be issued, and most go to game anglers heading up to Smith Point. If you want to try anyway, contact the Northern Land Council Office.

A few organized tours are available. **Umorrduk Safaris** (Tel (08) 8948 1306), owned and operated by Aborigines, offers two-day safaris to the northwest corner, with visits to rock-art galleries and sacred sites. Expensive, but unlike anything else.

The most luxurious way to experience Aboriginal land is to go to **Seven Spirit Wilderness Lodge** (Tel (08) 8979 0277)—a five-star ecotourism resort, owned by Aborigines, on the tip of the Cobourg Peninsula, about 130 miles (209 km) northeast of Darwin. You can reach it only by light aircraft or boat. It offers guided bush walks and fishing trips.

TIWI ISLANDS

Bathurst and **Melville Islands**, about 50 miles (80 km) north of Darwin, are home to the Tiwi people. The Tiwi Land Council, which governs the island, has opened the island to small, carefully monitored tour groups (not individuals). **Tiwi Tours** (Tel 1-800 183 630, toll free), which employs many Tiwis, is the only accredited operator. It does day trips from Darwin and camping in the bush, which is some of the most remote territory in Australia.

Splendid isolation on these islands has meant that Tiwi language and culture developed independently of the rest of Aboriginal Australia. Features unique to this people include their *pukumani,* or burial poles, which are carved or painted with totems and motifs and set out around graves.

Tiwis have fiercely guarded their independence. The British attempted to settle on Melville Island in 1824, but their settlement, Fort Dundas, lasted less than five years. The Tiwis were never forced off their islands, and political control was formally returned to them in 1978. Most Tiwis lead nontraditional lifestyles in the main settlement of Nguiu on Bathurst Island. Much of the islands remains a wilderness. Visitors have a chance to buy local carvings and artwork, meet with community leaders, and then head out to the bush. Overnight visits can include lessons in digging wild pumpkins, hunting goannas, and spearing fish. The packages are fairly expensive, but this is not an everyday trip. ■

Opposite: Battered by centuries of monsoon storms and tropical cyclones, Cape Helvetius on Bathurst Island juts into the Timor Sea.

Alice Springs

Alice Springs

181 C2

Visitor information
✉ Gregory Terrace
☎ (08) 8952 5800

ALICE SPRINGS IS AN OASIS TOWN IN THE DRAMATIC rocky walls of the MacDonnell Ranges. It is a good base from which to visit most of the attractions in Australia's Red Centre—notably Uluru (Ayers Rock) and Kata Tjuta (the Olgas).

The Alice, as it is known, was settled in 1871 as a relay station for the Overland Telegraph Line that stretched from Adelaide to Darwin. The old stone-built **Telegraph Station,** now a restored historical reserve a mile (1.6 km) north of town, was built near a permanent water hole in the normally dry bed of the Todd River. (The river was named for Charles Todd, the superintendent of telegraphs in Adelaide; the nearby springs were named for his wife, Alice.) The station was one of 12 built along the telegraph line, which hooked up in Darwin with the undersea cable from Java to connect Australia with the rest of the world. You can walk to the station on a path by the riverbed. To drive there take the Stuart Highway north and turn right at the sign about half a mile (1 km) out of town. The

springs are a nice place for a cooling swim or a picnic.

The town was originally gazetted as Stuart, but the name was officially changed to Alice Springs in 1933. Nevil Shute's 1950 novel *A Town Like Alice* made it known across the world, but it wasn't until 1987 that you could drive here from Adelaide on a paved road. The Alice today is a modern little city of 22,000, laid out on a five-street grid between the bed of the Todd River and the Stuart Highway.

The **John Flynn Memorial Church** on Todd Street and a small museum in the old hospital *(Adelaide House, Todd St. Mall, tel (08) 8952 1856, closed Sun.),* commemorate the founder of the Royal Flying Doctor Service (R.F.D.S.). The R.F.D.S. base itself, over on Stuart Terrace, offers short tours of its facilities. The **Museum of Central Australia,** also on Todd Street *(Alice Plaza, tel (08) 8951 1121),* has excellent displays on local natural history as well as exhibits about Aboriginal art and culture of the area.

There is a great lookout over the city and the MacDonnell Ranges from the top of **Anzac Hill,** a steep but convenient rocky crag near the top end of Todd Street. You can drive up it.

The **Frontier Camel Farm** *(Tel 1-800 806 499),* south of the city, has camel rides and a camel museum. Camels were imported to Australia in the mid-19th century to help open up the country, and they were set free after trains and roads had made them obsolete. Now an estimated 15,000 camels trot around the Red Centre, and thousands more inhabit western Australia. **Camel Outback Safaris** *(Stuart Well, tel (08) 8956 0925),* about 55 miles (88 km) south of Alice Springs, does camel treks.

National Parks & Wildlife Service

✉ Off Stuart Hwy. (3 miles/4.5 km S of Alice Springs)

☎ (08) 8951 8211

The boisterous Camel Cup, held in Alice Springs each July, commemorates the days when the desert town depended on camel trains for its survival.

MACDONNELL RANGES

The Alice is the base for some great day drives through the deep, shady gorges and along the spectacular cliffs of the Eastern and Western MacDonnell Ranges. You'll need your own transportation to see these ranges unless you are in Alice as part of a tour.

There are excellent walks in **Trephina Gorge National Park,** about 40 miles (64 km) northeast of Alice Springs on the Ross Highway, and around the nearby **Ross River Homestead** (*Tel 1-800 241 711, toll free*), southeast of the highway a little farther on. Out here you'll have a fairly good chance of seeing a perentie—at up to 7 feet long (2.1 m) the largest lizard in Australia and second in the world after its cousin, Indonesia's Komodo dragon. Be careful if you encounter one. They are astoundingly fast and have powerful razor-sharp claws. If frightened they will run up the highest thing they can see—even if it is you.

The ghost town of **Arltunga** is in the far Eastern MacDonnell Ranges, 65 miles (105 km) northeast of Alice Springs on the Ross Highway. It was settled in 1887, when gold was mined here, but abandoned in 1912 when the gold finally ran out. It has an excellent visitor center *(Tel (08) 8956 9770)*, and guided tours on Sunday afternoon.

In the Western MacDonnell Ranges you will find **Simpson's Gap,** a deep cleft cut in the reddish quartzite walls by tiny Roe Creek, about 12 miles (19 km) west of Alice Springs on Larapinta Drive. It was made famous by the paintings of Aborigine artist Albert Namatjira, one of Australia's best known Outback painters and the first Aboriginal to be granted Australian citizenship. He died tragically of alcoholism in 1959 at the age of 57.

Twenty miles (32 km) farther west, turn north off Larapinta Drive for about 6 miles (9 km) to reach **Standley Chasm,** an incredibly narrow gap whose near-vertical walls seem little more than shoulder-width apart, and where the sun shines only for an instant around noon, illuminating the blood red stone. Three miles (5 km) west of the turnoff along Larapinta Drive, the road forks. The right (north) fork is Namatjira Drive. Appropriately enough for a road named after a great Aboriginal artist, it goes out to the **Ochre Pits,** about 40 miles (64 km) farther on, where ancient Aboriginal artists obtained their pigments. From there the road continues 10 miles (16 km) or so to rugged **Ormiston** and **Glen Helen Gorges.** If you stay on Larapinta Drive for 50 miles (80 km), you reach **Hermannsburg community.** This Aboriginal community was set up by South Australian Lutheran missionaries in 1877 and still has some of the original date palms they planted. The traditional German farmhouses have now been restored.

Finke Gorge National Park is 7 miles (11 km) on from Hermannsburg, and you need a four-wheel-drive vehicle to get there. In the park is **Palm Valley,** an isolated tropical pocket filled with Australian cabbage palms. The trees are unique to this gorge and have grown here since prehistoric times, when the climate was wetter.

Drive 60 miles (96 km) south on the Stuart Highway to reach the **Henbury Meteor Craters,** a few miles west off the highway on the Ernest Giles Road. The craters were formed several thousand years ago when a meteor broke into several chunks before slamming to Earth. The biggest crater is almost 600 feet (183 m) across. ∎

Opposite: Standley Chasm in the Western MacDonnell Ranges is a natural split in the rocks that glows red when the sun shines in briefly at midday.

Aboriginal art

Art has always played an important role in Aboriginal culture as a way of recording human events, honoring the land, and passing on to future generations the stories of creation and the deeds of supernatural beings. There are examples of paintings and rock engravings dating back at least 50,000 years. Some archaeologists think they could be much older—possibly over 100,000 years, if new dating techniques are correct.

The richest area for rock art is in northern Australia: in Kakadu and Arnhemland in the Northern Territory, and in the Kimberley region of Western Australia. Motifs include simple hand prints, complex hunting scenes, and fabulous renditions of Rainbow Serpents —deities who played crucial roles in Dreamtime creation stories. Art historians recognize several successive styles of rock art, starting with drawings of animals in what is known as the naturalist style. This was succeeded by the dynamic phase, in which motion, such as the trajectory of a spear, appears to be represented by scribbles, dashes, and dots. These paintings, the earliest of which are found in Kakadu and date from about 12,000 years ago, are the world's earliest forms of narrative art. Later came the curious "yam" style paintings, in which humans and animals were represented with yam-shaped symbols. Next came the X-ray style, in which the skeletal frames of people and animals appear. It is a tribute to the remarkable longevity of Aboriginal culture that today's elders can often look at a piece of art created by an ancestor a hundred generations before, and understand the story being told.

Aboriginal art gives a unique illustrated history of the continent over thousands of years. The earliest art in Kakadu, dated to the last ice age, shows an arid landscape in which hunters kill kangaroos with boomerangs. Later, trees and flowers begin to appear in the record as the ice age ended, and sea levels began to rise. Hunters are shown using spears, which were more reliable than boomerangs in the newly dense scrub. One 6,000-year-old rock mural, in a remote corner of Kakadu, illustrates what some art historians believe to be the world's

earliest battle scene. It shows 111 stick figures, apparently charging each other and hurling spears. Eight have fallen, and blood is gushing from their spear wounds. Scientists speculate that conflicts may have been caused by the slow rise of the sea, which over centuries forced coastal people to migrate inland and onto the higher territory of their neighbors. Aboriginal art of the 15th century represents the Macassar fishermen who arrived at that time from Indonesia, and art of the 18th and 19th centuries includes references to Europeans.

Many rock-art sites remain inaccessible to tourists, in some cases because they are so remote but also because after two centuries of disruption to their culture Aborigines wish to keep the sacred sites private.

Some particularly magnificent galleries that are open to the public are Ubirr and Nourlangie Rock in Kakadu (see p. 188), rock murals near the base of Uluru (see p. 206), and two of the Quinkan rock-art galleries near the town of Laura in Queensland (see p. 170). Totally different from anything in Kakadu, Quinkan art contains paintings of the region's wildlife, and illustrates the spiritual life of the Ang-Gnarra people. The spookiest images are those of the Quinkans, large and apparently malicious humanoid spirits who dwelled in fissures in the rocks. Only two of the Quinkan galleries are open to the public, Split Rock and Guguyalangi.

Since the 1980s, Aboriginal art has enjoyed something of a boom. Indigenous artists have found creative new ways to express and preserve their culture, and non-Aborigines have acquired a taste for Aboriginal art's unique and powerful style. Arnhemland's bark paintings and the abstract, dot-painted murals of central Australia are tremendously popular. Expect to pay good money for good art and be wary of imitations. Non-Aborigines have been caught turning out "Aboriginal" art. Whether that crosses any artistic boundaries—does any group actually own an artistic style?—is irrelevant; most buyers want their Aboriginal art to be made by an Aborigine, and the money to go to Aboriginal communities. Go to reputable dealers who know about the artists, and they will give you and the artists a better deal. ∎

Top: Aboriginal artists Glen Namundja and
Thomson Yulidirri, with paintings, from the
Arnhemland community of Oenpelli.
Above: An image of Barriginj, wife of a
spiritual being known as Lightning Man
from Anbangbang Shelter, Kakadu.
Right: Ceremonial boomerangs

Uluru-Kata Tjuta National Park

Uluru-Kata Tjuta National Park

🏕️ 181 B1

Visitor information

✉️ Uluru National Park Entrance

☎️ (08) 8956 2299

ULURU AND SYDNEY OPERA HOUSE SHARE THE DISTINC-tion of being the best known landmarks in Australia. Uluru (also known as Ayers Rock) attracts more than half a million visitors each year. This haunting monolith in central Australia, one of the world's largest, rising almost 1,150 feet (350 m) from the flat scrub, is a remarkable spectacle. Understandably, Aborigines consider this a holy site.

ULURU (AYERS ROCK)

The Rock lies about 200 miles (320 km) southwest of Alice Springs. It is the summit of a massive underground chunk of sandstone about 600 million years old. Geologists believe that only the top 10 percent of the rock is visible. Erosion over many millions of years has slowly exposed its mass, and weathering has revealed its characteristic red hue. Explorer Ernest Giles was the first European to set eyes on this wonder, back in 1872. The following year another adventurer, William Gosse, scaled the monolith with an Afghan camel driver and named it Ayers Rock after the premier of South Australia, Henry Ayers. In 1985 Ayers Rock was handed back to the Pitjantjatjara and Yankunytjatjara Aborigines, who promptly restored its ancient name of Uluru and

The haunting sandstone mass of Uluru, in Australia's Red Centre, glows a deep bloody orange in the dying rays of sunset.

leased it back to the government as a national park. The local Aboriginal communities get 20 percent of the gate takings and a royalty of $A75,000 (U.S. $38,000) a year.

Tourism at the rock has boomed since the 250-million-Australian-dollar (U.S. $125 million) Yulara resort complex opened in 1984. A local airstrip handles Qantas and Ansett jets from most major cities. Philip Cox, creator of Sydney's Darling Harbour Exhibition Centre and a major force in the 2000 Olympic Games, designed the resort village, whose canopies resemble sails in the desert. Yulara has a wide range of accommodations, from five-star luxury at the

Sails in the Desert Hotel to camping, and all of it is fairly expensive. The village is just outside the park boundaries, about 12 miles (19 km) from Uluru and a little over 30 miles (48 km) from Kata Tjuta.

The excellent visitor center at the park entrance has displays about the geology, flora, and fauna in the park, and you can book tours with the operators licensed to run tours from Yulara. **Anangu Tours** *(Tel (08) 8956 2123)* is owned and operated by local Aborigines. You can enjoy a nightly stargazing show with talks on Aboriginal legends about the constellations.

Everything here is about seeing Uluru. When all is said and done

Yulara Resort
181 B1
Reservations 1-800 809 622 (toll free)

Anangu Tours Night Time Sky Show
1-800 803 174 (toll free)
$$, includes transportation

To climb or not to climb

For more than a century tourists have clambered up the steep flank of the rock without ever bothering to ask Aborigines if they minded people climbing on their sacred monolith. When somebody did finally get around to posing this fundamental question, the answer turned out to be "yes."

Local Aborigines, who took possession of the rock in 1985, are seriously considering a permanent ban on climbing the rock after a temporary closure in 2001 in respect for an Aborigine leader who died. The climb is not really all that wonderful—except perhaps as a way of burning off 1,500 calories in a sweaty, heart-thumping half-hour. The initial pitch is extremely steep and exposed—terrifying to anyone with a bad head for heights—and the strain has induced some heart attacks. Every year, on average, somebody dies on the rock, either from heart failure or straying off the track. People used to put crosses at the foot of the climb to commemorate those who died and to

serve as a warning. Ironically they served as a challenge for tourists who posed for pictures by them and then started up the side of the rock. The crosses have been removed.

The biggest trouble with climbing the rock from a sightseer's point of view is that you lose sight of it. Its haunting mass is under your feet, not before your eyes. There's no longer a sense of its power and mystique. Presumably that is what has brought you out here—not an opportunity to gaze into a heat-warped horizon that, frankly, could be anywhere in the Outback, or Nevada for that matter. Far better to take the gentle 6-mile (9.7 km) walk around the base of the rock. Here you get an intimate sense of Uluru's shape, texture, and character, its weirdness as it rises up almost vertically from the desert floor, and an appreciation of its size. Best of all you'll be respecting the wishes of people who have loved and understood this marvel for many thousands of years. ∎

Opposite: Aborigines believe the route up the flank of Uluru follows the spiritual track of Mala, a sacred rock wallaby, and would prefer that visitors admire the rock from its base.

The Base Walk around Uluru displays the monolith's beautifully sculpted flanks.

Opposite: The ancient sandstones of Kata Tjuta colored by a setting sun. The name comes from a term meaning "many heads."

you can do so in three ways. You can gaze up at it, climb it, or see it from the air with the flat red desert spreading out to the curve of the horizon. Helicopter flights over Uluru and Kata Tjuta are organized locally by Rockayer *(Tel (08) 8956 2345)*. The 7-mile (11 km) driving loop around the rock has a sunset viewing area on the west side and a good sunrise viewing spot on the northeast. About 70 percent of visitors attempt to climb Uluru. It is a very tough hike (see p. 205). Bring a hat, carry water, and have a good head for heights. The extremely fit can do it in as little as 15 minutes.

A far better alternative to climbing Uluru is to take the pleasant and flat **Base Walk** that circles the rock. Walkers see some of the flora and fauna and there is Aboriginal rock art in shelters near the base of the rock. A good place to begin the walk is at the Mala parking area, near the climbing trail up Uluru. The park visitor center supplies a brochure on this walk and on shorter hikes near the base. You can also join a walking tour *(Anangu Tours, $$$$)* led by Aboriginal guides, and

learn about the ancient Aboriginal way of life and their uses for the various desert plants.

KATA TJUTA (THE OLGAS)

Kata Tjuta, or the Olgas, is a collection of sandstone and arkose (sedimentary rocks formed from granite sands) monoliths about 20 miles (32 km) west of Uluru on the Docker River Road. They form an eerie, hole-in-the-wall maze, and though they are not as well known as their world-famous neighbor, many visitors find them much more intriguing.

In 1873 the explorer Ernest Giles (see p. 43) was the first European to see Kata Tjuta. He waxed lyrical about these "rounded minarets, giant cupolas and monstrous domes" and named them after Queen Olga of Württemburg. To the Aborigines the rocks had always been Kata Tjuta, or "many heads," and they restored the ancient name once they had regained possession of this site.

The largest of the many heads—36 in all—is **Mount Olga,** which rises about 1,800 feet (549 m). Geologists believe the whole collection was once part of an enormous monolith ten times the size of Uluru. As with Uluru, the Aborigines regarded Kata Tjuta as a holy place, and the eastern side of the formation remains off-limits to visitors (and to Aboriginal women, for it is a men's sacred site).

Because much of the park is sacred, there are only two hiking paths through Kata Tjuta. The main attraction is the **Valley of the Winds Walk,** a spectacular 4-mile (6.4 km) loop that winds through ocher-red chasms, gorges, and cliffs. The way to the trailhead of this walk is clearly marked. For a shorter hike, there is a straightforward, well-marked trail into the Olga Gorge. ■

Watarrka National Park

Watarrka National Park
🅰 181 B2
Visitor information
✉ Uluru-Kata Tjuta National Park entrance
☎ (08) 8956 7488

WATARRKA NATIONAL PARK (FORMERLY KINGS CANYON) contains the deepest and most spectacular gorge in central Australia, with rocky pools, palms, and beehive-shaped outcrops that call to mind the Bungle Bungles (see pp. 234–35). The park has some superb walking trails, both around the rim of the canyon and up the gorge.

This desert canyon has been virtually inaccessible until recent years, although it is only about 150 miles (240 km) southwest of Alice Springs. Even in the early 1990s getting here meant traveling a rough dirt track, and facilities were few. That changed with the building of the **Kings Canyon Resort** *(Tel (08) 8956 7442)*. A paved highway now links Kings Canyon with Yulara Resort (see p. 205).

Two major walking trails both begin at the parking lot by the park entrance. The **Canyon Walk** is a three-hour hike that winds around the rim of the canyon, through a maze of rocky outcrops and the palm-filled Garden of Eden. Very different, is the hour-long **Kings Creek Walk,** a scramble up the narrow gorge, with its boulders and ghost gums, to the idyllic pool and waterfall at its head. ∎

Visitors on the rim of the 310-foot-high (95 m) walls of Watarrka

Australia's wild west is a colorful blend of frontier styles, from the gold mining town of Kalgoorlie to the remote pearling port of Broome. It is famous for its deep karri forests and its shining capital city of Perth.

Western Australia

A shaggy dryandra (*Dryandra speciosa*), one of Western Australia's multitude of wildflowers

Western Australia

THE FORTUNE-SEEKING DUTCH NAVIGATORS WHO SAILED ALONG WESTERN Australia's coasts early in the 17th century had no reason to suspect that it was one of the world's greatest mineralized zones. They did not know that these ancient formations contained a mind-boggling treasure trove of gold, silver, nickel, iron, and diamonds, and they could not foresee that its mineral-rich sands would prove to be one of the world's richest sources of valuable trace elements used in high-technology industries. Unknowingly they sailed over seabeds littered with fabulous pearls and beneath those, deep in ancient sandstone beds, billions, possibly trillions, of cubic feet of natural gas. The fabulous wealth of this land was hidden behind a mask of low, flat, sunburned scrub. They merely mapped the coast and moved on. So, too, did English buccaneer William Dampier, when he visited the area in 1688 and 1699. It was almost another hundred years before any European expressed interest in the place.

In 1779 the French explorer Louis François Alesno de Saint Allouarn sailed into what became Shark Bay, about halfway up the Western Australian coast, and laid claim to this half of the continent. But interest in the dry, barren land wasn't high enough for France to establish a colony—a key legal point in claiming new territory—and by the time it was, in the mid-1820s, Britain had moved both to claim the land and set up a colony near present-day Albany.

Because of its remoteness, vast size, and inhospitable deserts, Western Australia was the slowest of the colonies to develop. Not until the gold rushes of the 1880s and '90s—in Halls Creek, Coolgardie, and Kalgoorlie—did the colony begin to prosper. Even so, it retained its provincial, frontier atmosphere. As late as the 1960s, word that a family car had made the drive across the Nullarbor Plain was newsworthy enough to make the Perth papers.

It is still a long, desolate hike across the continent to Perth, which is one of the world's most isolated cities. The enormous empty distances around the state mean that visitors to Western Australia have to give some thought and planning to where they want to go. This state covers almost a million square miles (2.6 million sq km)—one third of the entire continent—yet has only ten percent of Australia's population.

Perth, the state's capital, has the easygoing atmosphere of an overgrown country town. The majority of Western Australia's 1.7 million inhabitants live within 50 miles (80 km) of this city, and almost all the rest live in communities along the coast. With its parks and gardens and dry, sunny Mediterranean climate, and with yachtie Fremantle nearby, Perth is a bit like a nautical version of Adelaide.

The southwest corner of the state is a green jewel, with deep, cathedral-like forests of majestic karri and jarra trees, fabulous caves, and some of Australia's finest surfing beaches. The small but prestigious wine region around Margaret River, 150 miles (240 km) south of Perth, is rapidly gaining a following among connoisseurs. Albany, the oldest settlement in Western Australia, is a fine old whaling port lying close to the dramatic wildflower-covered peaks of the Stirling Range.

A wheat belt surrounds Perth. Beyond it, to the east, are the goldfields and the brawling, redneck mining town of Kalgoorlie. Still farther out lies the empty, waterless waste known as the Nullarbor Plain, stretching to the South Australian border more than 500 miles (800 km) away. It is crossed by the lonely Eyre Highway and the Indian–Pacific Railway.

The northern part of the state is rugged wilderness, leavened with a few scattered mining settlements, cattle stations, old pearling ports, and Aboriginal communities. Some of its most dramatic scenery—for example, the gorges in the Pilbara—is too remote for most visitors. Other places, such as the pearling port of Broome, the wilderness of the Kimberley, the otherworldly Purnululu (Bungle Bungles), and the beach at Monkey Mia have developed a must-see cachet despite their isolation. ∎

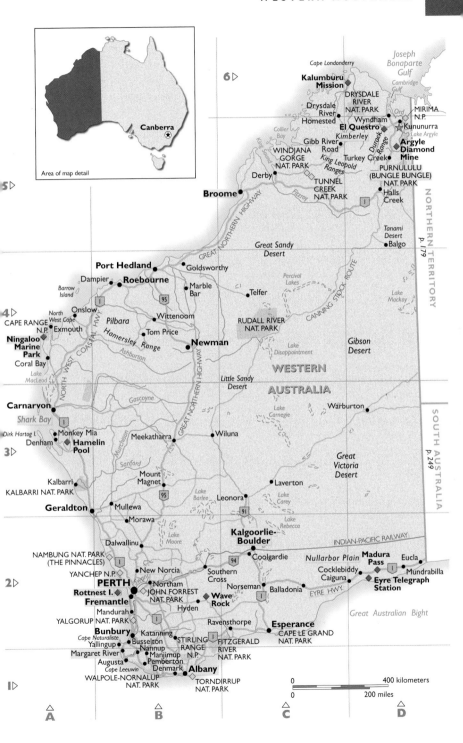

Area of map detail

6▷
Cape Londonderry
Joseph Bonaparte Gulf
Kalumburu Mission
Cambridge Gulf
DRYSDALE RIVER NAT. PARK
Drysdale River Homestead
Ord
Wyndham
MIRIMA N.P.
El Questro
Kununurra
Lake Argyle
Collier Bay
Gibb River Road
Kimberley
Durack Range
Argyle Diamond Mine
WINDJANA GORGE NAT. PARK
King Leopold Ranges
Turkey Creek
Derby
TUNNEL CREEK NAT. PARK
PURNULULU (BUNGLE BUNGLE) NAT. PARK
Halls Creek

5▷
Broome
Fitzroy
King Sound

Tanami Desert
Balgo

Great Sandy Desert

NORTHERN TERRITORY   p. 179

Port Hedland
Goldsworthy
Dampier   Roebourne
Marble Bar
Barrow Island
Percival Lakes
Telfer
CANNING STOCK ROUTE
Lake Mackay

4▷
North West Cape   Onslow
CAPE RANGE N.P.
Exmouth
Pilbara
Wittenoom
Tom Price
RUDALL RIVER NAT. PARK
Gibson Desert
Ningaloo Marine Park
Coral Bay
Homersley Range
Ashburton
Newman
Lake Disappointment

Lake MacLeod

WESTERN
Little Sandy Desert

Carnarvon
AUSTRALIA
Gascoyne
Lake Carnegie
Warburton
Shark Bay
Dirk Hartog I.
Monkey Mia
Denham   Hamelin Pool
Murchison
Meekatharra
Wiluna

SOUTH AUSTRALIA   p. 249

3▷

Sanford
Great Victoria Desert

Kalbarri
Mount Magnet
Lake Barlee
Laverton
KALBARRI NAT. PARK
Leonora
Lake Carey
Geraldton
Mullewa
91
Morawa
Lake Rebecca
INDIAN-PACIFIC RAILWAY

Lake Moore
Kalgoorlie-Boulder
Dalwallinu
Coolgardie
Nullarbor Plain
Madura Pass
Eucla
NAMBUNG NAT. PARK (THE PINNACLES)
New Norcia
94
Cocklebiddy
Mundrabilla
YANCHEP N.P.
Southern Cross
Caiguna
2▷
PERTH
Northam
Norseman
Balladonia
EYRE HWY.
Eyre Telegraph Station
Rottnest I.
JOHN FORREST NAT. PARK
Fremantle
Hyden
Wave Rock
Great Australian Bight
Mandurah
YALGORUP NAT. PARK
Ravensthorpe
Bunbury   Katanning
Cape Naturaliste   Busselton
STIRLING RANGE N.P.
Esperance
Yallingup   Nannup
FITZGERALD RIVER NAT. PARK
CAPE LE GRAND NAT. PARK
Margaret River   Manjimup   Pemberton
Augusta   Denmark
Cape Leeuwin
Albany
1▷
WALPOLE-NORNALUP NAT. PARK
TORNDIRRUP NAT. PARK

0   400 kilometers
0   200 miles

△   △   △   △
A   B   C   D

Perth

Perth

🗺 211 B2
Western Australia Tourist Centre
✉ Corner Wellington Place & Forrest Place
☎ 1-300 361 351

PERTH IS AUSTRALIA'S ANSWER TO DALLAS, WITH A HIGH-rise skyline of mining and oil company headquarters buildings. In the 1980s it was the base of high-rolling entrepreneurs whose dubious deals and shenanigans became known collectively as W. A. Inc. Even the most imaginative scriptwriter would have shied away from some of the storylines—outrageously rigged horse races, art fraud on the grand scale, and taxpayers' billions vanishing. The music stopped after the stock market crash in 1987, and the fallout led to royal commissions, indictments, ruined reputations, and prison terms for quite a few of the former high flyers, including Brian Burke, the state's dealmaking premier, and Alan Bond, the good-old-boy millionaire and yachtsman who won the America's Cup in 1983.

EXCURSIONS FROM PERTH

Popular excursions from Perth and Fremantle include Rottnest Island (see pp. 218–19). Farther afield but still an easy day-trip is New Norcia (see p. 217). The Pinnacles in the Nambung National Park are 156 miles (251 km) north along the coast. Here, hundreds of limestone pillars, from a few inches to 15 feet (5 m) high, stick up from a desert floor. Once thought to be fossil trees, they are now considered the result of wind erosion. Wave Rock (see p. 225) can be visited in a day (just), but allow longer for the southwest (see pp. 224–25) and Margaret River (see pp. 226–27). ∎

This is a city of 1.1 million inhabitants, with a futuristic skyline overlooking the Swan River and a Mediterranean lifestyle. It is frequently described as the loneliest city in the world. Adelaide, the nearest comparable Australian city, is almost 1,500 miles (2,400 km) away, and Canberra is more distant than the Indonesian capital of Jakarta. Perth's isolation has shaped the city's history and created a spirit of independence among West Australians, who occasionally talk of seceding from the rest of Australia.

Perth was founded by Capt. James Stirling, on August 12, 1829, as the Swan River Settlement. It had an inauspicious beginning. The idea was that the colony would be made up entirely of free settlers, but when word passed around that the isolated settlement was surrounded by swamps and mudflats humming with mosquitoes, migration slowed to a trickle. By 1850 a chronic labor shortage saw the colonists abandon their lofty ambitions and start importing convict laborers. Many of the city's grandest buildings—the **Town Hall, Supreme Court Buildings,** and **Government House**—were built by convict labor. In 1856 Perth

MUELLER PARK

MITCHELL FREEWAY

WELLINGTON STREET

HAY ST.

THOMAS STREET

HAY STREET

WEST PERTH   **Parliament House**

KINGS PARK ROAD

Legacy Lookout

MALCOLM ST.

HALE OVAL   Nursery

ARBORETUM

Mt Eliza Reservoir

KINGS PARK

MOUNTS BAY RD.

War Memorial

NARROWS BRIDGE

BOTANIC GARDENS

MOUNTS BAY ROAD

Mill Point

Flour Mill

KWINANA FREEWAY

Mosman Park

| 0 | | 800 meters |
| 0 | | 800 yards |

was proclaimed a city. Gold strikes in the 1890s caused the population to jump 700 percent and sparked a construction boom. Unfortunately, most of Perth's grand Victorian buildings were demolished during the 1960s, '70s, and '80s to make way for the skyscrapers that dominate the city today.

Finding your way around Perth is fairly easy. The compact city is set out along the banks of the Swan River, which is its southern boundary. The **Perth Tram** (it's actually a bus) takes visitors to Perth's major attractions. The 90-minute tours depart from 565 Hay Street.

Perth's main shopping and tourist thoroughfares are the Hay Street and Murray Street pedestrian malls, which are linked by modern arcades and department stores. St. Georges Terrace is where the mining and oil companies have their headquarters. **Parliament House** is at the western end of this street and you can tour the building when Parliament is not sitting.

Perth's railroad lines mark the northern boundary of the city. William Street arches over the downtown railway station via the Horseshoe Bridge and leads into raffish Northbridge, with its cafés,

Perth transportation (Transperth)

✉ Plaza Arcade, off Hay St. Mall

☎ 13 62 13

🕐 Closed Sun.

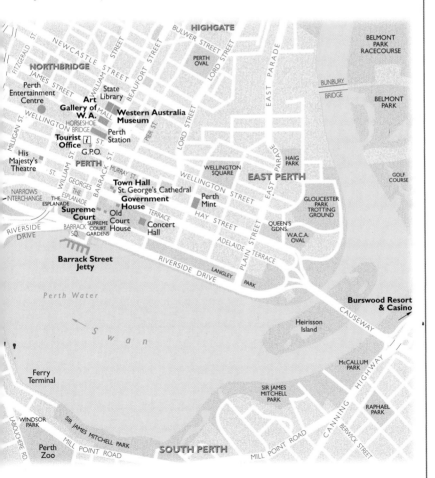

Western Australian Museum
✉ Francis St., Northbridge
☎ (08) 9427 2700

Art Gallery of Western Australia
✉ James St., Northbridge
☎ (08) 9492 6622

Botanic Garden
✉ Kings Park
☎ (08) 9480 3659
Free guided tours

The lovely Swan River reflects Perth's city towers.

pubs, nightclubs, and bistros. The state art gallery and museum are on this side of the tracks as well. The **Western Australia Museum** includes displays on Aboriginal culture, the marine life of the Western Australian coast, and meteorites (many have been found in Outback Australia). The **Art Gallery of Western Australia** has collections of Australian, Pacific, and European art.

In Perth's early days, steep Mount Eliza was regarded as a barrier to progress, and the city grew around it. As a result Perth now has a beautiful 2,500-acre (1,013 ha) park on its western edge. This is **Kings Park,** one of Perth's most scenic attractions. Within it is the 40-acre (16 ha) **Botanic Garden** that contains more than 2,500 different Western Australian plants. The park's noisy flocks of birds, and dazzling display of native wildflowers in spring are pleasing reminders

that Perth is perched on the edge of the Outback. Kings Park and much of the Swan River foreshore have excellent bicycle tracks, and given Perth's sunny climate, bicycles are a great way to get around. Bikes can be rented in Kings Park at Koala Bicycle Hire *(Tel (08) 9321 3061).*

The **Swan River** is the focus of the city, and it is set off by the green of Langley Park and the Esplanade. Although Perth is about 12 miles (19 km) inland, the river here is almost three-quarters of a mile (1.25 km) wide. Ferries from **Barrack Street jetty** (off the Esplanade) go to **Fremantle** (see p. 215) and **Rottnest Island** (see pp. 218–19). The Narrows Bridge (and ferries from Barrack Street) cross to South Perth, where **Perth Zoo** *(20 Labouchere Road, tel (08) 9474 3551, $$)* is set on well landscaped grounds. A mile or so upstream, **Burswood Resort & Casino** (see p. 376) is a rollicking 1980s memento. ∎

Fremantle

A TOUCH OF WESTERN AUSTRALIA'S COLONIAL MARITIME flavor has survived in Fremantle, despite the extensive renovations associated with Australia's unsuccessful defense of the America's Cup in 1987. An old working-class dockyard city, it lies about 12 miles (19 km) west of Perth, where the Swan River enters the Indian Ocean.

Fremantle
🗺 211 B2
Visitor information
✉ King Sq.
☎ (08) 9431 7878

Although Perth's sprawl has engulfed the port city over the years, Fremantle has retained enough of its identity to keep it from becoming just another suburb. It has more local color and sense of history, and a far more relaxed atmosphere than busier, nouveau-riche Perth. It was founded a few weeks before Perth, in 1829, by Capt. Charles Fremantle. His brief was simply to hoist the flag and create a British presence here ahead of the French.

Fremantle was an almost useless port until 1890 when a brilliant engineer named Charles O'Conner blasted out a rocky bar and built an artificial harbor to allow larger trading vessels in. Today a statue of O'Conner gazes out over his creation. Although known as a smart seaside and yachting town today, Fremantle is still a working port city with more than 2 miles (3 km) of docks (and a professional Aussie Rules football team called the Fremantle Dockers).

Visitors come to Fremantle for its cafés on **South Terrace,** interesting architecture, and artsy markets. This blue-collar port city of 25,000 exudes a sort of raffishness—but that's nothing new. This

With its old maritime flavor and elegant colonial streetscapes, such as this along Philmore Street, Fremantle is one of Australia's most fascinating port cities.

Western Australian Maritime Museum

✉ Cliff St.

☎ (08) 9431 8444

Fremantle Museum & Arts Centre

✉ 1 Finnerty St.

☎ (08) 9430 7966

The Western Australian Maritime Museum has a fine collection of marine artifacts, like this anchor.

is where Australia's only recorded formal duel took place, in 1832. On the weekends, **Fremantle Market,** on South Terrace at the corner of Henderson Street, is a colorful, noisy bazaar where you can buy craft goods, cheap clothing, fruits, vegetables, and other items. The town has a number of good restaurants and, as you might expect, the seafood is excellent. Sardines are a local specialty. Things to see in Fremantle include the 12-sided **Round House** *(High St.),* built in 1831 and used as a jail—but for the most part this is a leisurely, sun-splashed seaside town in which to stroll, take in the galleries and old buildings, sip cappuccino, and unwind. The Fremantle Tram makes a 45-minute loop through the city from the Town Hall, near the intersection of High and Adelaide Streets.

The **Western Australian Maritime Museum,** near the Round House, is one of Fremantle's highlights. Its excellent exhibits and displays tell the story of seamanship along the Western Australian coast, from the early days of the Dutch East India Company, through the era of clipper ships and whalers, to modern archaeologists' attempts to retrieve the old wrecks. Pride of place goes to the remains of the *Batavia,* wrecked off the coast near Geraldton in 1629 (see p. 228).

The sturdy-looking **Fremantle Museum & Arts Centre,** originally designed as the colony's lunatic asylum, was built by convicts in the 1860s. It has a fine collection of early Western Australian art and displays about the Dutch East India Company's role in exploring "New Holland" in the 17th century. ■

New Norcia

THIS IS ONE OF THE TWO EXTRA-SPECIAL DAY TRIPS TO make from Perth; the other is Rottnest Island (see pp. 218–19). They are very different, but both can feel like a little taste of heaven.

A visit to the Benedictine mission at New Norcia makes a fascinating—and unusual—day trip from Perth. It was established by Dom Rosendo Salvado, a Spanish monk, in 1846, and its unique blend of Byzantine, Gothic, and classical Spanish architecture is an exotic contrast to the miles of wheat fields and Australian scrub around it.

Dom Rosendo Salvado's mission was to convert Aborigines to Christianity, teach them European-style agriculture, and to rescue them from persecution. The monastery's gentle approach worked well with the Aborigines, producing a harmonious agricultural community in the 19th century. The flour mill opened here in 1879 is still going, the oldest operating mill in Western Australia. By the turn of the century the emphasis turned to education of European children. These days it is a meditative community, known for its museum and fine art gallery.

The monks have succeeded in balancing the needs of a contemplative religious community with those of a popular tourist attraction. Visitors can tour the **chapel,** take accommodations in old convent and college buildings, and browse in shops that sell olive oil pressed at the community. A more monastic-style retreat can be found at the **Benedictine Abbey Guesthouse.** The museum and art gallery have priceless collections of religious art and manuscripts, making them particularly worth a visit. Many of the pieces were given by Spain's Queen Isabella II (*R. 1833–1870*). A leaflet (*available at the museum*) gives details of a half-hour walk through the grounds of the monastery, starting just outside the museum.

The 80-mile (129 km) drive to New Norcia on the Great Northern Highway is particularly rewarding in spring when Western Australia's wildflowers are in bloom. The highway north of New Norcia rambles through the towns of Dalwallinu, Morawa, and Mullewa, all part of the **Wildflower Way,** which runs through a carpet of foxgloves, everlastings, and wattles—just some of the 7,000-plus species of wildflowers that carpet Western Australia. ∎

New Norcia
🄰 211 B2
Visitor information
☎ (08) 9654 8056
Ⓢ $$

Established by Spanish monks in 1846, the Benedictine mission at New Norcia is an exotic mix of Byzantine, Gothic, and classical Spanish styles.

Rottnest Island

Rottnest Island

211 B2

Visitor information

✉ Ferry Landing,
Thompson Bay

☎ (08) 9372 9752

ALTHOUGH HE DESCRIBED IT AS A TERRESTRIAL PARADISE, the Dutch mariner Willem de Vlamingh clearly did not have tourism marketing in mind when he visited this little island just off the southern coast of New Holland in 1696 and named it Rottnest ("rat's nest," in Dutch). The "giant rats" he saw are actually quokkas, which are smallish cousins to wallabies—not rats at all. He pegged the scenery correctly though.

A gregarious hare-size marsupial that lives in large colonies, the quokka has no natural enemies on the island. Opposite: Bathurst lighthouse guards the coastline on Rottnest Island's northern flank.

Rottnest is low and sandy, surrounded by turquoise waters with sparkling white beaches, and cooled by sea breezes. It has been a getaway for Perth's well-to-do since 1864, when the Rottnest Hotel was built as a summer retreat for the governor of Western Australia. These days the hotel is called the Quokka Arms.

The peaceful little island is about 10 miles (16 km) off the coast from Fremantle. Cars are not permitted, but wonderful bicycle and walking tracks (you can rent bicycles on the island) and a two-hour coach tour are available. The island is only 7 miles (11 km) long and 3 miles (4.8 km) across at its widest. The main settlement is at **Thompson Bay.** The visitor center is here, next to the ferry landing. It has brochures on the island's activities, and can arrange walking tours of the heritage buildings.

Visitors come here to unwind, mostly on day trips from Perth, though the island has camping, cabins, houses to rent, and other accommodations. Sprawling on the beach is the single most popular activity, although snorkeling on some of the world's southernmost coral is also big. There are dive shops on the island, a dive and snorkeling trail on **Pocillopora Reef,** just south of the island, and glass-bottomed tour boats. A historic train runs 5 miles (8 km) from Thompson Bay to the **Oliver Hill Battery,** in the center of the island, which was the site of gun emplacements in World War II. There are spectacular views from **Vlamingh's Lookout,** just south of the town.

Regular ferries run to Rottnest Island from both Fremantle and Perth, or you can fly here on the Rottnest Airbus (*Tel (08) 9414 7468*) from Perth's airport. This is a hugely popular place—more than 400,000 people visit every year—and it can be very crowded on sunny weekends. Be sure to make a reservation if you plan to stay on the island. ■

Wildflowers

Spring *(Oct.–Nov.)* is a magical time to visit Western Australia. More than 7,000 species of wildflowers burst into life, carpeting the deserts, plains, and mountains in a kaleidoscopic blaze of color. The rich golds of the feather flowers blend with the reds and pinks of boronias, and red-and-yellow clumps of blossom glow on the banksia trees. There are orchids, kangaroo paws, parrot bush, lilies, and foxgloves. The list and palette of colors just goes on, and most of the species are unique to Western Australia, a legacy of the area's long periods of isolation.

While you are still in Perth you can get a taste of what lies over the horizon by viewing the brilliant displays of wildflowers in Kings Park between August and October. Then head into the deserts, the wheat belt, or the Stirling Ranges in the mountainous southwest. Out in these places the flowering trees, bushes, and shrubs run riot. Jarrah forests, like those in John Forrest National Park only 15 miles (24 km) east of the city, are particularly rich. Red and green kangaroo paws, blue leschenaultia, and pink calytrix are the most prominent, but there are hundreds of other varieties. Yanchep

National Park, about 30 miles (48 km) north of Perth, is another good bet.

Or you can follow the Great Northern Highway 100 miles (160 km) northeast of Perth to the wheat-belt town of Dalwallinu, then drive along the Wildflower Way another 150 miles (240 km) to Mullewa. For much of this drive, the roadside will be carpeted by wildflowers, particularly a type known as everlastings, whose petals endure after the flower itself has died. Farther north, Kalbarri National Park is vibrant with flowering banksia, grevillea, and melaleuca, and the forest floor is littered with flowering twine rushes and sedges. This beautiful coastal park, at the mouth of the ancient Murchison River, is famed for its magnificent gorges and sweeping coastal views—the spring wildflower display only gilds the lily, so to speak.

Some of the finest displays can be found in the southwest corner of the state. The jagged peaks of Stirling Ranges National Park are rich with pink, red, and gold flowers beautifully offset by bald granite. More than 50 species of orchid are found in the karri forests, and some of the *Dryandras* and species of *Darwinia* grow no place else.

Above: Blushing mountain bells, *Darwinia lejostyla*
Right: The parrot bush, *Dryandra sessilis*, a member of the Proteaceae family
Opposite: Mulla mullas among the dunes of the Great Sandy Desert

Top left: The brushlike clusters of nectar-rich banksia flowers attract insects and birds. Almost all banksias are found only in Australia. Above: Grass trees in John Forrest National Park. Left: Yellow wattle, an acacia, is Australia's floral emblem.

The heaths at Torndirrup National Park and Walpole-Nornalup National Park, near the windswept coast of Albany, become a carpet of flowers each spring and seem to illuminate nearby dunes and granite outcrops. Fitzgerald River National Park, between

Albany and Esperance, harbors more than 2,000 species of flowering plants. Of these, about 80 or so species including oddities such as the flame orange royal hakea and the delicate pink quaalup bell, are found nowhere else in the world. In 1978 this spectacular park was declared a World Biosphere Reserve by UNESCO.

The Western Australia Tourist Centre in Perth (see p. 212) has a pamphlet on the state's wildflower trails. Most bookstores have illustrated guides to the myriad species and varieties you can see in the state. Remember that, tempting as it may be to pluck a few beauties, Western Australia's wildflowers are protected under the Native Flora Protection Act. Leave them for others to enjoy.

There are, however, increasing numbers of commercial wildflower farms around Australia—particularly Western Australia—as locals begin to capitalize on the growing international interest in Australian flowers. Australia now exports about 30 million Australian dollars (U.S. $15 million) worth of wildflowers, kangaroo paw, and Geraldton wax flowers each year. ■

The Southwest

ONE OF THE MOST BEAUTIFUL POCKETS OF FOREST IN Australia is in the southwest corner of Western Australia. This region has towering forests of karri and jarrah trees, gentle dairy country, rocky coasts, and the jagged expanse of the Stirling Range that riot with wildflowers every spring.

Denmark
🗺 211 B1
Visitor information
✉ Strickland St.
☎ (08) 9848 3888

Albany
🗺 211 B1
Visitor information
✉ Proudlove Parade
☎ (08) 9841 8599

A nice tour of the area can be had by driving the 150 miles (240 km) along the coast south of Perth to the lovely Margaret River wine and surf region. Then meandering another 200 miles (320 km) farther through the forests to the historic whaling port of Albany.

Nannup, Manjimup, and **Pemberton** are pleasant old timber towns, surrounded by forests of karri and jarrah trees. The pale-barked karri are among the world's tallest trees and can reach more than 300 feet (91 m) in height. What you don't see when you drive through these ostensibly virgin forests is the clear-cutting that goes on out of sight. This is why you can't take scenic flights over these ancient forests, but you can, say, in Tasmania's wilderness areas. It is a sensitive issue—jobs versus centuries-old giant gum trees—and the timber industry has skillfully put together material to make sure you have the benefit of their viewpoint. The Timber Park Complex in Manjimup *(Tel (08) 9771 1831)* has displays about the logging industry.

One of the most spectacular trees is the **Gloucester Tree,** north of Pemberton. If you have the nerve, you can make the

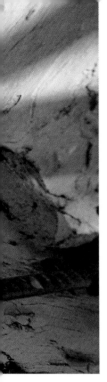

The Bicentennial Tree offers a scary climb and a spectacular view over the towering karri forests near Pemberton.

Top right: Looking like a surfer's dream, the Wave Rock is a granite wall sculpted by three billion years of rain and wind.

exposed climb almost 200 feet (61 m) up its trunk into what is said to be the world's highest tree-top fire lookout. The truly scary climb follows 153 spiraling rungs around the trunk. Not many people try to reach the top, but the view is remarkable. The tree was 50 feet (15 m) higher until 1947, when the top was lopped off to make way for the platform. Pemberton claims the tallest karri tree ever felled: a 343-foot (105 m) titan brought down in the last century.

Seventy miles (113 km) south-east of Pemberton is the **Valley of the Giants,** in Walpole National Forest part of **Walpole-Nornalup National Park** near the town of **Denmark.** The forest is filled with karri trees. Several species of eucalyptus grow here and nowhere else, including rare red, yellow, and Rates tingle trees, and the red flowering gum. Walking tracks here include the **Tree Top Walk,** a swaying wooden walkway (wheelchair accessible) through the canopy in the Valley of the Giants.

Albany is where the British laid claim to the western half of New Holland on Christmas Day in 1826. Soon this became a bustling whal-ing station, with French, U.S., and Australian whalers putting in here. Albany was Australia's last whaling station, ceasing operations only in 1978. The old Whaling Station, about 15 miles (24 km) to the southeast, is now the **Whale-world Museum** *(Frenchman's Bay Rd., tel (08) 9844 4021, $).* It gives a gory account of the days when around 850 whales were killed each season in these waters. Happily the whales have already begun returning, and southern right whales are often seen from the cliffs along the shore.

Albany itself, a pretty town of just under 20,000, having a vaguely New England, nautical feel, is one of Western Australia's most popular holiday destinations. It has a rugged coast, and the dramatic **Stirling Ranges** rise abruptly about 40 miles (64 km) northeast.

Another popular sight is **Wave Rock,** about 220 miles (350 km) east of Perth, near the wheat farm-ing town of Hyden. It is a block of granite, sculpted by three billion years of wind and rain to a perfect surfer's wave about 50 feet (15 m) high. It is an interesting geologic curio, but not really worth the long trip from Perth—although tour operators sell it as a day trip. ∎

Margaret River

THE MARGARET RIVER IS ONE OF WESTERN AUSTRALIA'S delights, an area of world-class wineries, karri forests, wildflowers, spectacular caves, and some of Australia's best surf beaches, only 150 miles (240 km) southwest of Perth. The region stretches about 60 miles (97 km) from Cape Naturaliste to Cape Leeuwin at the southwest tip of Australia, but skilled marketing has made the centrally located village of Margaret River the buzzword for the area.

This corner of Western Australia is as much a lifestyle as a holiday destination, although the Margaret River lifestyle means different things to different people. The past 30 years have seen this dairy farming area discovered by successive waves of hippies, surfers, upscale winemakers, artists, and urbanites seeking an alternative lifestyle. Most recently it has become a weekend getaway for Perth's well-to-do. It is still a major surfing hangout, because the beaches between Cape Leeuwin and Cape Naturaliste have some of the most powerful breaks in Australia.

Surfing tends to blur the social lines down here, and if you go to one of the beach parking lots you may see late-model Mercedes parked beside impossibly battered 1960s-vintage Kombi vans. Everybody looks the same in a wetsuit. Basically two kinds of people live here: surfers and windsurfers. Those with boards go out first thing in the morning, and those with sails head out in the afternoon. Life's that simple and sunny.

The spectacular coast is a lovely drive. Just follow the Bussell Highway south out of Perth, 140 miles (225 km) or so through the beach towns of Mandurah, Bunbury, and Busselton, and from there onto the scenic Caves Road. On the way south, you might stop at **Bunbury** for a swim with dolphins. A pod usually swims into the harbor once a day (they are lured

there with daily feedings). They seem happy to interact with swimmers. A leaflet from the Bunbury Information Centre explains the etiquette and ethics of contact with dolphins.

The turnoff to Caves Road is 5 miles (8 km) west of Busselton and takes you to the pleasant seaside town of **Dunsborough.** A worthwhile detour from here is the 8-mile (13 km) excursion down the Cape Naturaliste Road to the historic lighthouse *(closed Mon.)* on Cape Naturaliste and its sweeping views of the cape and Geographe Bay. In the winter this is a good spot for seeing humpback and southern right whales.

Five miles (8 km) farther along, the Caves Road from Dunsborough brings you to **Yallingup,** where huge Indian Ocean surf crashes almost constantly onto the beach. You don't need to surf to enjoy the pretty seaside resort village. **Yallingup Cave** has been a popular tourist attraction since 1899, and the Caves House Hotel *(Caves Rd., tel (08) 9755 2131)* opened in 1903. The **Gunyulgup Galleries** represent a number of local craftspeople and sells fine pottery, paintings, and furniture made from the prized jarrah wood.

WINERIES
Wineries can be found all along scenic Caves Road as it winds beside the coast. Although the wine region is generically called Margaret River,

Margaret River
△ 211 B1
Visitor information
✉ Corner of Bussell Hwy. & Tunbridge Rd.
☎ (08) 9757 2911

Bunbury
△ 211 B2
Visitor information
✉ Carmody Place
☎ (08) 9721 7922

most of the wineries are actually concentrated in a knot about 10 miles (16 km) south of Yallingup. The "Margaret River Regional Vineyard Guide," available at local visitor information offices, gives the rundown on what is where. You can choose from about 50. Names to look for include Cape Mentelle, Leeuwin Estate, and Cullens. Leeuwin Estate, which is just west of Margaret River, has particularly lovely grounds. Most of the wineries give free tastings. **Margaret River** itself is a funky little village of artists, surfers, and ageing hippies about 3 miles (4.8 km) off Caves Road.

CAVES

The scenic route through the region is called Caves Road because some of the most spectacular scenery south of Margaret River is underground. The limestone which helps make this a superb wine region is riddled with more than 150 caves. The best is **Jewel Cave,** about 25 miles (40 km) south of Margaret River, with its baroque formations and needle-like helictites. Fossilized remains of Tasmanian tigers have been found in nearby **Moondyne Cave** *($$),* which is unlit. **Lake Cave,** about 15 miles (24 km) south of Margaret River, has a Tolkienesque entrance. Despite its name, **Mammoth Cave,** close to Lake Cave, is the least interesting.

Guided tours are the only way to view these caves: information from the Cave Works Interpretive Centre *(Lake Cave, Caves Rd., tel (08) 9757 7411).*

Augusta is an old timber port. If you continue south along the road another 5 miles (8 km) you'll come to **Cape Leeuwin** lighthouse. Between May and September, the cape is good for whale-watching. It has a windswept, last-place-on-Earth feel to it, particularly when the sky is dark and threatening. ∎

Scenery along the old coast road between Augusta and Margaret River is a pleasing mix of cliffs and sheltered bays.

MARGARET RIVER WINES

The wines from the Margaret River wineries tend to be fairly expensive, compared with those of Australia's other premier wine districts, but there's no doubt about the quality. This small region accounts for about a fourth of Australia's premium-quality table wine. ∎

Shark Bay

Shark Bay

⚠ 211 A3

Visitor information

✉ 83 Knight Terrace, Denham

☎ (08) 9948 1253

Conservation Land Management Office

✉ Knight Terrace, Denham

☎ (08) 9948 1208

SHELTERED BY THE PERON PENINSULA AND A CHAIN OF desolate islands, Shark Bay is a World Heritage site 450 lonely miles (724 km) north of Perth. It has ancient life forms and some of Australia's oldest European history. The Dutch navigator Dirk Hartog landed here in 1616 on the island that now bears his name.

Shark Bay is best known today for the bottlenose dolphins that swim in the shallows to play with humans. The drive from Perth, on the Northwest Coastal Highway through the seaport of **Geraldton,** is bleak and windy, and in summer searingly hot. The coastline north of Geraldton was the scene of several Dutch shipwrecks in the 17th and 18th centuries, including that of the *Batavia* in 1629. The **Maritime Museum** has relics of later shipwrecks.

Kalbarri National Park is a worthwhile detour on the trek north. The turnoff is about 60 miles

(96 km) north of Geraldton on the Northwest Coastal Highway. The Murchison River runs through a spectacular series of deeply hewed gorges before it reaches the coast at Kalbarri, and the national park includes both gorges and coast. It is particularly beautiful in spring when the wildflowers are in bloom.

The turnoff to **Shark Bay** is about 110 miles (177 km) farther north on the Northwest Coastal Highway. The scenery along Shark Bay itself is lovely in an arid, under-stated way. The first turn off the road to Shark Bay goes 4 miles (6.4 km) to **Hamelin Pool.** The

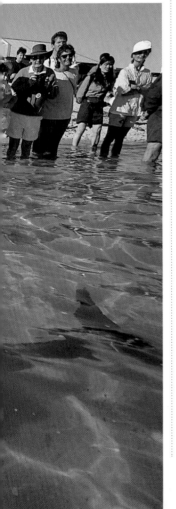

turquoise waters and the rocky coastline here are lovely, but what makes this place remarkable are the stromatolites, primitive blue-green algae that were one of the first life forms on Earth. These living fossils in Hamelin Pool are one of the most readily accessible populations of stromatolites in the world, and their presence was a big factor in giving Shark Bay its World Heritage listing. They thrive here because the sheltered waters are extremely clear and unusually saline. Fascinating as they undoubtedly are to paleontologists, the stromatolites look like blackened chunks of concrete matting. Information is available at the nearby historic **Telegraph Station** *(Tel (08) 9942 5905).*

Past the turnoff to Hamelin Pool, the road runs to Denham along the spectacular **Shell Beach,** a unique 70-mile (112 km) coast-line made up of countless shells packed in some places almost 50 feet (15 m) deep. **Denham,** the most westerly town in Australia, was once a pearling port and has become the main tourist town on the peninsula.

Fifteen miles (24 km) east of Denham is **Monkey Mia** and its famous beach where dolphins play. The interaction between humans and dolphins began in the early 1960s when a small pod of dolphins allowed themselves to be petted. As a result of this early interaction, and apparent willingness on the part of the dolphins, a great deal of valuable marine research took place. Then a major tourism indus-try grew up. Dolphins are coaxed into the bay with regular feedings, appearing most mornings in the winter months—less frequently in summer—while staff try to keep tourists from doing anything too silly. Sometimes you'll see just a solitary dolphin, and other times you can see a dozen. ■

Geraldton

◭ 211 A3

Visitor information

✉ Corner of Bayly St. & Chapman Rd.

☎ (08) 9921 3999

Maritime Museum

✉ Marine Terrace, Geraldton

☎ (08) 9921 5080

🕓 Closed Sun. a.m.

Kalbarri

◭ 211 A3

Visitor information

✉ Grey St.

☎ (08) 9937 1140

Winter mornings are generally the best time to encounter dolphins at Monkey Mia. As many as a dozen of these marine mammals have been recorded here at one time.

Ningaloo Marine Park

Ningaloo Marine Park
🅰 211 A4
Coral Bay
🅰 211 A4
Visitor information
✉ Coral Bay Arcade,
   Robinson St.
☎ (08) 9942 5988

Exmouth
🅰 211 A4
Visitor information
✉ Payne St.
☎ (08) 9949 1176

**Department of
Conservation &
Land Management**
✉ Maidstone Crescent,
   Exmouth
☎ (08) 9949 1676

NINGALOO REEF IS A SPECTACULAR, 160-MILE (257 KM) fringe to the rugged Northwest Cape, some 700 miles (1,126 km) north of Perth. Ningaloo is much shorter than the Great Barrier Reef but it is no less impressive. Unlike its better known cousin, Ningaloo Reef is easily accessible from the shore—never more than 2 miles (3 km) out and in some places only a couple of hundred yards out, within swimming range. The reef has been designated a national marine park, Ningaloo Marine Park, and the dry hills of the cape form the Cape Range National Park.

Getting to Ningaloo Reef from Perth is simple. Drive about 670 miles (1,078 km) north on the Northwest Coastal Highway to the isolated Minilya Roadhouse. From there a paved highway runs north, the length of the North West Cape, 50 miles (80 km) to pretty Coral Bay and another 90 miles (145 km) to Exmouth. Or you can take a Skywest plane (*Tel (08) 9478 9999*) from Perth to Learmouth (near Exmouth).

The quiet seaside resort of **Coral Bay** is at the southern end of the reef. It has pretty white beaches and is popular with divers and snorkelers. Glass-bottomed boat tours cater to nonswimmers.

Ningaloo Reef is Australia's longest continuous fringing coral reef. It is one of only two reefs anywhere in the world on a western coast. Among the rare marine life swimming in its warm waters are dugongs, humpback whales, manta

rays, and greenback turtles. But perhaps the most impressive creatures are the whale sharks. The largest fish in the sea, these gentle plankton-eating giants grow up to 50 feet (15 m) long and weigh up to 40 tons. Swimming with the whale sharks and "flying" with the manta rays are becoming popular things for tourists to do.

The waters of **Ningaloo Marine Park** are divided into recreational, general, and sanctuary zones. The sanctuary zones are completely protected, allowing visitors to see these delicate reefs and the cycle of rare marine life. Manta rays are around the peninsula from May to November, and humpback whales pass through in June and July. Turtles lumber onto the beaches at night, in the summer between November and January, to lay their eggs.

Whale sharks can be observed here from March to the end of May, when the coral spawns and plank-

ton bloom to give the behemoths a big feed. The best way to see them is with one of the specialist charter operators, who send up spotting planes to find them. The experience can be expensive, but you are paying for something unforgettable. The Diving Centre at Exmouth *(Tel (08) 9949 1201)* has a high success rate, but there are other reputable operators. Ask the tourist office at Coral Bay or the one at Exmouth for suggestions.

Exmouth, 90 miles (145 km) farther north up the peninsula, was built in 1967 to service the U.S. Navy's top-secret radio base, which communicated with American nuclear submarines patrolling the Indian Ocean. The base is closed now, but the 13 huge very-low-frequency transmitters that dominate the town are a charmless legacy of the Cold War. This town, too, has its share of dive and snorkeling operators and charter boats. ■

A diver floats among the corals and lemon damsel fish at Ningaloo Marine Park, one of Australia's hidden jewels.

The Kimberley

THE KIMBERLEY IN WESTERN AUSTRALIA'S WILD NORTH-west is generally regarded as Australia's last frontier. It is an ancient plateau, dissected by deep gorges, the craggy mountain strongholds of the Durack and King Leopold Ranges, and the bizarre sandstone formations of Purnululu (Bungle Bungle). The climate is savage, with violent storms during the summer monsoons. Lightning strikes in the dry season can spark awesome bushfires.

The Kimberley
🅰 211 C5
Visitor information
✉ Coolibah Dr.,
   Kununurra
☎ (08) 9168 1177

Opposite: The giant Argyle Diamond Mine, nestled in the southern edge of the remote Ragged Range, has produced more than five trillion stones since 1979.

Few people live here permanently —about 25,000 in an area larger than California. Most residents have come up for a few years of adventure or good paychecks at one of the mines. The region has a few scattered settlements, some far-flung Aboriginal communities, and a sprinkling of lonely cattle stations that can be bigger than some U.S. states. Saltwater crocodiles live in the rivers and estuaries along this ragged and barely explored coast, and bizarre boab trees dot the landscape. The Kimberley is hard to reach and challenging to explore, but is one of the world's truly wild places.

The frontier region's main road is the Great Northern Highway, which was paved only as recently as 1986. It links the Kimberley's three main towns—Kununurra, Derby (actually 20 miles off the highway), and Broome (see pp. 238–39)— with the cities of Perth and Darwin. The only other route through the Kimberley is the Gibb River Road, which crosses 400 miles (644 km) of wilderness (see pp. 236–37).

Kununurra—population 4,000—is the major town in the eastern part of the Kimberley and the best base for visiting the other-worldly Purnululu (see pp. 234–35) and the Argyle Diamond Mine. It is also a good jumping-off point for the Gibb River Road, which begins off the Great Northern Highway about 30 miles (48 km) west of town. Kununurra is the area's

newest town, built from scratch in 1961 to service the Ord River Irrigation Project that dammed the mighty Ord River. During the summer monsoon the Ord was pouring more than 15 million gallons (59 million litres) of water into the sea every second. By holding back some of that water in the giant man-made Lake Argyle and using it to irrigate crops, the project has turned 25,000 acres (10,125 ha) of arid scrub into sugarcane and banana plantations, mango orchards, peanut and melon fields, and vegetable gardens.

One of the most spectacular and easily accessible hikes in the Kimberley is within walking distance of Kununurra. Hidden Valley, in **Mirima National Park,** is a miniature version of Purnululu yet is only a mile from the center of town. Just follow Barringtonia Avenue to the edge of town and there it is, a maze of tiger-striped sandstone formations.

The **Argyle Diamond Mine,** about 100 miles (160 km) south of Kununurra, is the world's largest producer of diamonds. About 35 million carats a year, one-third of the world's production, come out of this giant open-cut mine. Most of its output is industrial quality, but it also produces spectacular jewels. They come in a suite of brilliant colors: champagne and topaz hues, blues, greens, and, rarest of all, pinks, lilacs, and reds. There is no public access, but the Kununurra tourist office can arrange tours. ∎

Purnululu (Bungle Bungle) National Park

IT SPEAKS VOLUMES FOR THE REMOTENESS AND INACCES-
sibility of the Kimberley that these spectacular sandstone ranges were
virtually unknown to non-Aboriginal Australians until the early
1980s, when a filmmaker who was doing a documentary for the
Western Australian government shot some aerial footage of them at
dusk. The haunting images seized the public's imagination, and
Purnululu's striped formations are now a symbol of the Kimberley.

**Purnululu
National Park**
🅰 211 D5
Visitor information
✉ Department of
Conservation &
Land Management,
P.O. Box 942,
Kununurra
☎ (08) 9168 7300

Aborigines have been coming into
these eerie ranges for more than
20,000 years. The park's name,
Purnululu, is the local Aborigine
term for "sandstone;" the name
Bungle Bungle may refer to a type
of grass. In Australia these rock formations are almost as well recog-
nized an Outback icon as Uluru.

The first European to see the
ranges was Alexander Forrest, who
explored the Kimberley in 1879. As
he was looking for prospective
cattle-grazing land, he dismissed
the spectacular ranges as useless
wasteland and moved on. Over the
next century, some of the big
Kimberley pastoral leases included
parts of the Bungle Bungle.

Many people who see images of
Purnululu resolve to go there, but
getting into this remote 750,000-
acre (303,750 ha) national park is
no mean feat. It is accessible only
during the dry season, and even
then you need a four-wheel-drive
vehicle or a helicopter and must
carry your supplies. Scenic flights
are easier. In 1997 about 40,000
tourists saw Purnululu, two-thirds
of them on sight-seeing flights out
of Kununurra, Turkey Creek, or
Halls Creek. The tourist office in
Kununurra (see p. 232) has details
of flights and tours into the park.

The vehicle turnoff to Purnululu
is about 150 miles (240 km) south
of Kununurra on the Great Northern Highway. From there you

follow a rough, bouncing 35-mile (56 km) track to a point called Three Ways. Here you can either head north to **Echidna Chasm** (about 12 miles/19 km) or go south to **Piccaninny Creek** (about 20 miles/32 km). The Echidna Chasm area has tall, narrow gorges and dramatic cliffs, while at the Piccaninny Creek area you will see the distinctive tiger-striped bee-hive-shaped sandstone formations for which Purnululu National Park is so famous. The tiger striping is the result of orange silica being interspersed with thin layers of black lichens. Climbing the sandstone formations is forbidden in the park because the ancient formations are so fragile.

Once in the park, visitors can stay in Kurrajong Camp or Wilardi Camp. Gungle Bungle is closed in the wet season *(Oct.–March).* ■

Alternating layers of lichen and weathered sandstone give the Bungle Bungle hills their unique tiger-striped appearance.

GIBB RIVER ROAD DRIVE

Gibb River Road drive

On a map of the Kimberley, the Gibb River Road looks like a handy shortcut between Kununurra and Derby, cutting 150 miles (240 km) off the Great Northern Highway route. But this rough track is emphatically not a shortcut; it is one of the great adventure drives on the continent. In the wet season *(Oct.–March)* it is impassable.

INDIAN OCEAN

Created in 1964 to bring cattle on the outlying stations to market, the Gibb River Road cuts 420 miles (676 km) through the heart of the Kimberley. It is still known as "the beef road" among locals, and travelers on it should keep an eye out for the massive road trains, loaded with cattle, booming along in a shower of gravel and dust. Also be wary of river crossings, for this is crocodile country. A conventional vehicle can make it along the Gibb River Road, with care, but a four-wheel-drive vehicle is preferable. Food, fuel, and accommodations are available en route but the distance between them can be great, so carry plenty of supplies, basic tools, and spares. If you don't want to drive yourself, you can join a four-wheel-drive safari from either end. Ask the tourist office at Kununurra (see p. 232) or Derby *(Tel (08) 9191 1426)*.

The road is described here from east to west, Kununurra to Derby. From **Kununurra ❶**, take the Great Northern Highway west for 25 miles (40 km) or so to the marked turnoff to the old seaport of **Wyndham ❷**. The Gibb River Road goes left off this road a couple of miles north of the turning, but before you take it, Wyndham is worth a visit. A quintessential Kimberley frontier town, Wyndham is surrounded by miles of shimmering tidal flats. It used to be known for bloodthirsty crocodiles that lurked in the marshes near the abattoir, waiting for offal. The meatworks closed in 1985, but Wyndham's tidal flats are still good for crocodile spotting.

One of the most spectacular views on Australia's wild north coast is from the **Five Rivers Lookout** on Mount Bastion, immediately behind Wyndham. You can drive up to the lookout 1,000 feet (305 m) above the tidal

Windjana Gorge is a haunting place.

King Sound

Mount Hart

Derby ❻ Meda Windjana Gorge ❹

WINDJANA GORGE N.P.

Tunnel Creek

GREAT NORTHERN HWY.

flats, and see five major rivers—the Ord, Pentecost, Durack, Forrest, and King—empty sluggishly into Cambridge Gulf. The Shell Service Station *(Tel (08) 9161 1281)* has local information. About 12 miles (19 km) west of town on the King River Road is the 2,000-year-old hollow boab tree that served as a prison in Wyndham's bad old frontier days.

The roughest stretch of the Gibb River Road is the first 150 miles (240 km). Some of the river crossings, such as the one through the Pentecost River, are potentially treacherous, but the countryside is magnificent. Fifteen miles (24 km) west along the Gibb River Road is a turnoff for **El Questro Station ❸** *(Tel (08) 9169 1777, April–Oct.)*, one of the most unusual resorts in Australia—a working cattle station 10 miles (16 km) south of the road. El Questro can organize fishing trips,

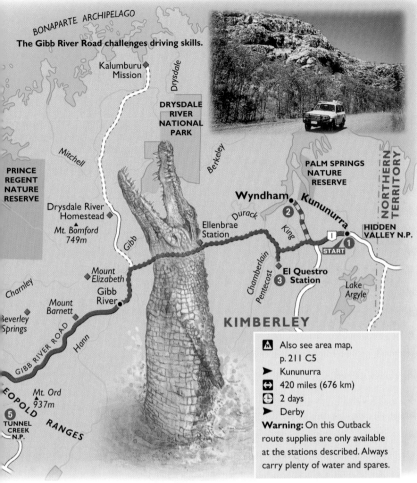

BONAPARTE ARCHIPELAGO

The Gibb River Road challenges driving skills.

Kalumburu Mission

DRYSDALE RIVER NATIONAL PARK

Drysdale

Mitchell

Berkeley

PALM SPRINGS NATURE RESERVE

Wyndham

Kununurra

NORTHERN TERRITORY

PRINCE REGENT NATURE RESERVE

Drysdale River Homestead

Mt. Bomford 749m

Gibb

Ellenbrae Station

Durack

King

HIDDEN VALLEY N.P.

START

Mount Elizabeth

Gibb River

Chamberlain

Pentecost

El Questro Station

Lake Argyle

Charnley

Mount Barnett

Beverley Springs

GIBB RIVER ROAD

Hann

KIMBERLEY

Mt. Ord 937m

LEOPOLD

RANGES

TUNNEL CREEK N.P.

Also see area map, p. 211 C5

▶ Kununurra

420 miles (676 km)

2 days

▶ Derby

Warning: On this Outback route supplies are only available at the stations described. Always carry plenty of water and spares.

camel and horseback rides, and four-wheel-drive treks for wildlife-watching or to see Aboriginal rock art. Accommodations vary from the luxurious to a campsite a half-hour hike from fern-filled **Emma Gorge.**

Sixty miles (97 km) farther on, you can buy food and fuel and get accommodations at **Jack's Waterhole,** 5 miles (8 km) on a marked sideroad *(Tel (08) 9161 4324).* The next refueling point is the **Mount Barnett Roadhouse** *(Tel (08) 9191 7007)* 140 miles (225 km) farther on. Two stations on tracks off the road have accommodations *(reserve in advance).* **Ellenbrae Station** *(Tel (08) 9161 4325)* is a few miles north of the road about 125 miles (200 km) from Kununurra; **Mount Elizabeth Station** *(Tel (08) 9191 4644)* is 20 miles (32 km) north of the road at Gibb River, 225 miles (362 km) from Kununurra.

West of Mount Barnett Roadhouse, the road enters the dramatic King Leopold Ranges. A turnoff goes 20 miles (32 km) to the spectacular **Windjana Gorge National Park** and 25 miles (40 km) farther to **Tunnel Creek National Park.** This range was once part of a vast coral reef and over the eons the Lennard River cut its way through the rock and formed gorges. At Tunnel Creek you wade through the tunnel to see flying foxes.

Supplies and accommodations are available at **Beverley Springs** *(Tel (08) 9191 4646, turn off 40 miles/64 km past Mount Barnett Roadhouse and go 40 miles/64 km north)* and at the **Mount Hart Homestead** *(Tel (08) 9191 4645, about 40 miles/64 km farther on and then 30 miles/48 km along a rough bush track).* The final 40 miles (64 km) of the Gibb River Road into **Derby** are paved. ∎

Broome

BROOME IS A FASCINATING OLD PEARLING PORT ON
Western Australia's remote northwest coast. One of the classiest
Outback towns you'll find anywhere, it has a lifestyle as lazy as tropical sin. Its chief attraction for visitors is Cable Beach, regarded by
aficionados as one of the world's most beautiful beaches. It would be
hard to argue against that. Imagine a 20-mile (32 km) stretch of gold-
en sand almost half a mile wide at low tide, offset against a shimmering turquoise sea so warm it is almost like a bath. All this only 2 miles
(3.2 km) from the center of town along Cable Beach Road.

Broome has a history that ought to
have come straight from a Joseph
Conrad novel. English buccaneer
William Dampier was the first
European known to have touched
base here, when he was dodging a
Spanish fleet in 1699. Almost 200
years passed before anyone realized
what treasures lay on the shallow
seabeds. The discovery of mounds
of pearl shell sparked a pearl rush
in the 1880s, and the coastal settlement that sprang up was named for
Frederick Broome, then governor of
Western Australia.

By 1910, Broome was the
world's pearling capital, accounting
for more than 80 percent of the
world's pearl shell (used to make
buttons). The town itself was a
brawling, bustling multicultural
mix of Malays, Chinese, Japanese,
Filipinos, Timorese, Arabs,
Aborigines, and Europeans, with a
fleet of more than 400 pearling lug-
gers. The best pearl divers came
from Japan, and the 600 graves in
the picturesque **Japanese cemetery** on Port Drive, at the edge of
town, bear testimony to the dangers
they faced. The pearling industry
fell into decline during the 1930s.

World War II saw Broome
bombed and strafed by the Japanese,
and the wrecks of a number of
Dutch flying boats sunk in the harbor during the raids can be seen
occasionally. One flying boat was
supposedly carrying a secret diamond shipment from Java when it
came to grief. Some of the diamonds
were recovered, but most were never
found. A beachcomber named Jack
Palmer was found with some of the
diamonds and arrested, but the
charges were dropped. After the war,
however, this easygoing soul developed a taste for expensive American-
made sedans. Palmer died in 1958
taking his secret with him.

Modern Broome still has much
of the flavor of the old days with its
airy bungalows, palm-lined streets,
and Chinese roofs. It went through
a redevelopment phase in the early
1980s, thanks to English Lord
Alistair McAlpine, who fell in love
with Broome and built, among
other things, the luxurious Cable
Beach Club. Economic recession
and McAlpine's financial misfor-
tunes then froze the development at
a perfect stage, in that the town of
9,000 retains its frontier character
but you can get a good cappuccino.

The heart of the downtown area
is the so-called **Chinatown** (really
only Carnarvon Street and
Dampier Terrace), which has old-
fashioned trading-post grocery
stores, modern boutiques, and
cafés. Here, in the hushed elegance
of Paspaley's Pearls, you can buy a
necklace of perfectly matched
Broome pearls—if you can meet the
$A200,000 (U.S. $100,000) price tag.

Broome
⚑ 211 C5
Visitor information
✉ Corner of Broome
   Rd. & Bagot St.
☎ (08) 9192 2222

The quaint **Sun Picture Gardens,** on Carnarvon Street, is reputedly the world's oldest outdoor movie theater. It was built by a pearling captain in 1916 and has barely changed since. You sit in old canvas sling chairs and take in the movie on a screen framed by palm fronds. You learn to ignore the occasional fruit bat fluttering across the picture, and if the monsoon rains are falling, you simply retreat into the covered part of the gallery.

Gantheaume Point, about 2 miles (3.5 km) west of town on Gantheaume Point Road, has a red sandstone headland, lighthouse, and 130-million-year-old dinosaur tracks that are visible at very low tides. The **Broome Crocodile Park,** on Cable Beach Road, has hundreds of saltwater crocodiles.

But Broome's best thing is still **Cable Beach,** so named because this is where the first overseas telegraph cable was brought ashore in 1889, linking Australia with Java and London. The beach is a crescent of sand facing the Indian Ocean rather than the bay. Sunsets here are incredible, and a crowd usually assembles on the grassy knoll overlooking the beach to watch. Or you can go for gentle camel rides along the sands *(book through the tourist office).* Don't be in a hurry to leave after the rim of the sun slides below the horizon—the most vibrant colors appear a few minutes later. If you are in Broome at full moon, you can see the Staircase to the Moon, an odd effect caused by reflected moonlight on the tidal flats. It resembles a golden staircase. ■

Strong winds have carved the rocks above the beach at Broome into fantastic shapes.

Broome Crocodile Park
- ✉ Cable Beach Rd.
- ☎ (08) 9192 1489
- 🕐 Closed Nov.–March, & a.m. Sat. & Sun.
- 💲 $$$

Kalgoorlie
🅰 211 C2
Visitor information
✉ Corner of Hannan &
Cassidy Sts.
☎ (08) 9021 1966

**West Australian
Museum
Kalgoorlie-Boulder**
✉ 17 Hannan St.
☎ (08) 9021 8533
💲 Donation

**Gold fever still
lures prospectors
to the region and
with good reason:
On December 31,
1990, a local
couple discovered
the Happy New
Year Nugget
containing 97
ounces (2.75 kg)
of gold.**

Kalgoorlie-Boulder

KALGOORLIE SITS ON THE GOLDEN MILE, AUSTRALIA'S richest vein of gold-bearing ore. This brawling frontier mining town is in the old Outback tradition, with tattooed, shirtless miners, and "skimpies" (scantily clad bar maids) in its pubs. It is also a much-anticipated stop on the Indian–Pacific train journey after the long westward trek across the Nullarbor Plain.

The town got its start in 1893 when an Irish prospector named Paddy Hannan stumbled across nuggets lying on the ground beneath a tree, where he'd pulled up with two mates to rest a lame horse. Having spent fruitless months at the gold diggings in nearby Coolgardie, the men could hardly believe their luck. They scooped up more than 100 ounces (2.8 kg) of gold in a few days and sparked the last of Australia's great gold rushes. The newly built railroad, which penetrated the desert as far as Southern Cross, made it easy to get to the diggings. Within a couple of months more than a thousand fortune-seekers came to the place known as Hannan's Find.

Later the fledgling town was given back its Aboriginal name, Kalgoorlie. By 1896 the town had a population of nearly 6,000 and a neatly arranged grid of tree-lined streets wide enough to allow camel trains to turn around. It was also providing the economic oomph to assure Western Australia's autonomy and eventual statehood. That year authorities began building a 350-mile (560 km) pipeline from Mundaring Weir to bring clean water to this desperately dry desert town. The pipeline was completed in 1903, by which time Kalgoorlie had grown to a small city of 30,000, with more than forty hotels and eight breweries (it wasn't just water they thirsted for). The extended rail line to neighboring Boulder was the busiest in the state.

Kalgoorlie's luck as well as its ore has lasted longer than that of any of the early eastern gold towns. While it is very much alive today, Kalgoorlie had a brush with oblivion in the years after World War I, when rising costs and the falling price of gold depressed the Outback community. A commodities boom in the 1970s, and new technology that enabled trace quantities of gold to be profitably extracted, gave Kalgoorlie a fresh lease on life. Today it is a bustling community of 30,000 (linked by a hyphen and municipal amalgamation to nearby **Boulder** in 1989). The town is Australia's largest gold-producer and one of the richest sources of gold in the world.

Hannan Street is lined with glorious gold-rush architecture, elegant old pubs, and the grandiose Town Hall. Kalgoorlie is very much a blue-collar town, although tourism is becoming important. The **West Australian Museum Kalgoorlie-Boulder** has excellent displays on the town's gold rush heyday, Aboriginal history, and the region's days as a sandalwood supplier.

The underground tour of **Hannan's North Tourist Mine** *(Broad Arrow Rd., tel (08) 9091 4074)* is one of the biggest drawcards in Kalgoorlie, and you can learn a bit about local culture at the **Two Up School,** in a corrugated iron amphitheater on Menzies Street on the outskirts of town. Two Up is a raucous Australian gambling game where bets are made on

the simultaneous toss of two coins.

A tourist train, the **Golden Mile Loopline** *(Tel (08) 9093 3055, $$)*, leaves from the former train station at Boulder for a tour of the workings in the **Super Pit,** the world's biggest open-cut gold mine, which is virtually a canyon. It is presently about 600 feet (183 m) deep and produces 800,000 ounces (22,676 kg) of gold each year. And there are plans for it to become much bigger over the years, as much as 1,500 feet (457 m) deep, a little over a mile (1.6 km) wide, and almost 3 miles (4.8 km) long. You can drive to the **Super Pit Lookout** on the Eastern Bypass Road just outside Boulder. For a sense of scale here, consider the fact that those "tiny" yellow dump trucks in that pit are actually the size of houses and carry more than 200 tons (203 tonnes) of ore at a time. The lookout is usually open from 6 a.m. to 6 p.m., but is closed when blasting is being done in the mine.

Coolgardie, 25 miles (40 km) away, where the first gold diggings in the area began in 1892, is now almost a ghost town—a sort of town-size mining museum, well worth a visit. The Warden's Court Building, the Town Hall, the Post Office, and the opulent Marble Bar Hotel attest to the prosperity this boomtown once enjoyed. The Old Courthouse in Bayley Street houses the **Goldfields Exhibition Museum,** an interesting collection of early goldfield artifacts. The old mining warden's residence—built in 1895—has been restored and listed by the National Trust. ∎

Kalgoorlie's main thoroughfare, Hannan Street, is lined with elaborate gold-rush architecture. The street was made wide to accommodate the turning radius of a loaded camel train.

Coolgardie
🗺 211 C2
Visitor information
✉ Bayley St.
☎ (08) 9026 6090

Eyre Highway
& the Nullarbor Plain

DRIVING THE EYRE HIGHWAY ALONG THE EDGE OF THE Nullarbor Plain is the classic Outback road trip—almost 1,500 miles (2,400 km) from Perth to Adelaide and most of it empty desert highway. Yet for all the barrenness of the landscape, you can enjoy remarkable views—the expanse of saltbush from Madura Pass, the cliffs along the Great Australian Bight. But it is the steady, relentless humming of tires on pavement that brings home the awesome size of this continent.

Norseman

🏔 211 C2

Visitor information

✉ 68 Roberts St.

☎ (08) 9039 1071

Strictly speaking, the Eyre Highway actually runs just south of the Nullarbor Plain (to cut directly across it you must take the train—see p. 248), touching the plain itself only briefly in South Australia. Australia's first transcontinental automobile journey was made in 1912 following camel tracks across the desert. World War II and the threat of invasion inspired the authorities to build a highway linking Perth with the rest of Australia. Even into the 1960s, however, the road was still little more than a rough track, and anyone who made it across in a car was likely to get a mention in the Perth newspapers. In 1969 the Western Australian government paved the highway to the South Australia border, and the last parts were paved in 1976.

The first stage, if you are heading east from Perth, is the 400 miles (640 km) or so to the goldfields around Kalgoorlie. It is probably the least interesting part of the journey, a typical Australian highway through wheat fields and arid scrub with lengthening stretches between towns. To anyone coming from Europe or North America it may even seem desolate. But this is the civilized part. The adventure doesn't really start until you drive through **Norseman,** past the red warning sign that little or no water will be available for the next 800

miles (1,287 km), toward a heat-warped horizon. You need to have done at least a bit of rudimentary preparation. Here the temperatures can soar to well over 120°F (48°C). Withering headwinds make your car work harder and chew up the gasoline, and the glare can be blinding. Be certain that your car is in good working order, that you have basic tools and spares, and above all, that you have brought extra water both for drinking and for the radiator. That said, the Eyre Highway is a reasonably well-used road that is paved and in good condition. It is the lifeline between Perth and the rest of the country, and if something went wrong you probably wouldn't have long to wait, but why take chances? Food and gasoline are expensive out here. Although the roadhouses can make electronic transactions, if the lines are down for any reason you will be stuck if you don't have some cash.

In a cloud of steam and coal smoke, the first Transcontinental Express steams into Kalgoorlie. It had left Port Augusta only two days earlier—a miracle in 1917.

Because no real towns are on the road between Norseman and the South Australian fishing port of **Ceduna,** 750 miles (1,200 km) away, you will find just a lonely archipelago of roadhouses generally between 80 and 120 miles (129 and 193 km) apart. The first of these, **Balladonia,** was a telegraph station in the early days, and the ruins of the old stone buildings can be seen a few miles past the modern roadhouse complex. The early part of the drive from Norseman is surprisingly well forested, but by the time you reach Balladonia you are well into the scrub. The nearby Balladonia sheep station is one of the oldest in this part of Western Australia, and it is still owned by the pioneering family that founded it. The sign behind the door at the roadhouse, giving Balladonia's population as "five" will give you a hint of just how lonely the drive ahead is going to be. It was near here in 1979 that the U.S. space station Skylab crashed back to Earth.

Just past the old station, the road makes a beeline for the **Caiguna** roadhouse *(Tel (08) 9039 3459),* about 100 miles (160 km) away. This rigid straightaway at 90 miles (144 km) is the longest in Australia, and while that fact may interest you for the first 10 or 20 miles, you'll have a big sense of relief when you finally reach Caiguna. You could adjust your watch 45 minutes forward at this point to accommodate the local time zone, or just ignore it because you are passing through and time is rather meaningless out here.

Cocklebiddy, 40 miles (64 km) east of Caiguna roadhouse, is famous for the labyrinth of limestone caves beneath its flat, almost featureless plain. The system has some of the world's longest underwater caves. In 1983 a French team set a world record for the world's deepest cave dive. Exploring these caves is difficult, dangerous, and best left to well-planned expeditions. What is easily accessible here is the **Eyre Bird Observatory** at the historic Eyre Telegraph Station *(Tel (08) 9039 3450)*, a few miles east of the Cocklebiddy roadhouse and down a track to the cliff-lined coast on the Great Australian Bight. It is a paradise for birdwatchers, and you can stay there.

Madura Pass is 340 miles (547 km) from Norseman. This is the most spectacular part of the drive, when the road suddenly starts down a steep, winding hill onto the **Mundrabilla Plains.** The views here are breathtaking and slam home the empty vastness of the country. A few miles past the Mundrabilla roadhouse the road starts to climb again, winding its way toward Eucla Pass. If it is night you'll be greeted by the sight of the illuminated Travellers Cross on top of the craggy pass.

Eucla, 103 miles (166 km) from Madura Pass, is worth a stop. The family-owned roadhouse and restaurant complex *(Tel (08) 9039 3468)* is easily the best on the route and one of the few roadhouses in Australia where you can actually get a fresh salad. The owners are friendly and can direct you to some of the

Abandoned in 1929, the old telegraph station at Eucla has been slowly engulfed by sand as the massive coastal dunes shift inland.

A quirky road sign at lonely Border Village gives directions and distances to far-flung points such as Capetown, Moscow, and the South Pole.

Ceduna
🅐 251 B4
Visitor information
✉ 58 Poynton St.
☎ (08) 8625 2780

Opposite: The Nullarbor Plain comes to an abrupt end at the 240-foot-high (73 m) Bunda Cliffs, over-looking the Great Australian Bight.

local sights and beaches, such as the picturesque ruins of the telegraph station, built in 1877 and now engulfed by dunes. Beyond the haunting dunes is the deep blue water of the **Great Australian Bight.** A weather observatory is also here—Western Australia's highest shade temperature (124°F, 51°C) was recorded at Eucla.

East of Eucla the highway dog-legs around a decent-sized meteor crater and 9 miles (14.5 km) later crosses the South Australian border at **Border Village.** If you are coming from South Australia, the agriculture checkpoint here requires you to surrender any fresh fruits, vegetables, or honey you might have with you. If you are going east, the South Australian authorities will get you just outside of Ceduna.

Border Village is a monument to roadside tackiness, the sort of place that would fit in well on Route 66 in New Mexico. You'll see a 20-foot (6 m) fiberglass kangaroo, bright murals on the diner walls, and a cheery sign warning you to be on the lookout for UFOs, a reference to an incident a few years ago when a family claimed their car had been towed by aliens.

The highway clings to the Great Australian Bight for much of the next 100 miles (160 km) and has plenty of turnoffs to spectacular cliff-top lookouts. The banded cliffs are up to 600 feet (180 m) high, and between June and October they make great viewing platforms for watching the annual migration of southern right whales.

The road veers inland to the Nullarbor Hotel/Motel *(Tel (08) 8625 6271)* and the only stretch of the Eyre Highway that is actually on the treeless Nullarbor Plain. It skirts it for 20 miles (32 km) or so, and then takes you back into saltbush scrub. A turnoff leads to the Head of the Bight, another good whale-watching vantage point, but because this is Aboriginal land you'll need a permit. Ask at the Nullarbor Hotel for details.

Ceduna is about 175 miles (280 km) ahead, through lightly forested country, and the line of white wheat silos along the port is a welcoming sight. This is the first town of consequence (population 2,750) after Norseman. From here the highway crosses the arid Eyre Peninsula, which is dotted with the ruins of stone cottages of settlers

**Indian–Pacific
Great Southern
Railway**

✉ 80 Williams St.,
Suite 206, 2nd
Floor, Sydney

☎ 13 21 47

who'd tried to scratch a living on this soil in the 19th century.

The Eyre Highway ends at **Port Augusta**—"Porta Gutta" in local speak. Adelaide is about 200 miles (320 km) south, through wheat and wine country. In Adelaide you can catch the Indian–Pacific train back to Perth—your car can ride as well—to save you from retracing your route and to cross the Nullarbor Plain. If you have developed a taste for Outback driving and roadhouse hamburgers you can always make a left turn at Port Augusta and head along the lonely Stuart Highway (see pp. 284–88) toward Alice Springs. ∎

Rails across the Nullarbor

The Indian–Pacific train crosses the continent from Sydney to Perth. It winds its way through the Great Dividing Range and rolls across the western plains to the frontier silver mining town of Broken Hill. Then it goes on to Port Pirie and down to Adelaide, before heading westward across the Nullarbor Plain.

At this point the great train really hits its stride—crossing the vast and waterless expanse whose name is a corruption of the Latin for "no tree" *(nulla arbor)*. For sheer size and scale no place else is like it—an 80,000-square-mile (207,200 sq km) limestone plateau, scoured by desert winds and scorched by temperatures that can easily exceed 120°F (48°C) beneath a pitiless summer sun. The plateau has no surface water at all, although an extensive system of flooded caves lies deep underground. Out here lies the world's longest stretch of straight railroad track—more than 300 miles (480 km) without so much as a kink.

The first European to cross the Nullarbor Plain was the explorer Edward Eyre, who barely survived his harrowing journey into ceaseless winds and deadly heat in 1841. Afghan camel drivers and telegraph linesmen helped forge a trail across it later in the century. A railroad was begun in 1911—partly as an inducement to Western Australia to join the federation. Six years later, on October 23, 1917, the nation's first transcontinental train rolled out of the South Australian town of Port Augusta.

Building the railroad was a logistical nightmare, akin to building a space station, because nothing there could sustain life. Everything had to be taken into the desert—food, housing, water, equipment, and building material. Provisions were sent out weekly from either Kalgoorlie or Port Augusta on what became known as the Tea and Sugar Train. Until recently that lifeline train still ran weekly out of Port Augusta, servicing the tiny isolated camps, where fettlers maintained the tracks, and the few inhabitants. The train took three days to make the crossing, bringing tankers of freshwater, freight, mail, a supermarket car, a post office, and news of the world.

The Indian–Pacific runs at a brisker pace, taking a little more than two days to cross the entire continent. Despite its epic stature —in part because of it—the train has been losing money for a good many years. A few years ago it was given an expensive facelift in a bid to make it a sort of Outback Orient Express. The result was tacky Aussie nouveau, although the club cars and sleepers are quite comfortable. But the scenery can't be replicated anywhere else. ∎

Vast tracts of desert, arid scrub, and salt pan cover 80 percent of Australia's driest state, but in the fertile southeast, where the Murray River flows, South Australia is a paradise of orchards, vineyards, and olive groves.

South Australia

Bottles in the Wine Museum, Yalumba Wines, Barossa Valley

South Australia

SOUTH AUSTRALIA IS A CORNUCOPIA OF MOST OF THE FINER THINGS IN life: Great food and world-class wines, a sunny cosmopolitan lifestyle, and a calendar crammed with events ranging from wine-tasting weekends to Australia's biggest arts festival. What makes this bounty all the more remarkable is that this is Australia's driest and most barren state. South Australia has a higher proportion of desert than any other state, with more than 80 percent of its surface receiving less than 10 inches (25 cm) of rain a year.

The vast majority of South Australians live in the southeast corner of the state, a fertile pocket of land watered by the Murray River. Adelaide, perhaps Australia's most gracious capital city, is here, forming an island of elegant homes and high Victorian architecture surrounded by leafy parklands.

The climate here is Mediterranean, and the rural scenery is elegant, with stately red gums, broad vineyards, and old stone cottages. The Murray River runs through deep sandstone gorges teeming with bird life, which you can see by steamboat. Victor Harbor, an hour or so south of Adelaide, is a popular seaside retreat, where southern right whales swim up to the coast during their winter migrations. Farther south the haunting sweep of coastline known as the Coorong is a bird-watcher's paradise. Naracoorte Caves, in the far southeast, is a World Heritage-listed fossil site and home to almost half a million bats. Kangaroo Island still has unspoiled bush, old-fashioned villages, and almost tame wildlife only two hours by ferry from Adelaide's suburb of Glenelg.

Glenelg was where the first European settlers landed from the *Buffalo* in 1836. The following year Col. William Light pegged out the city of Adelaide in lines as crisp and straight as an accountant's left margin. The colony itself was the vision of entrepreneur Edward Wakefield, who wanted it to be a model settlement. Migrants purchased their land from the South Australia Company at two pounds an acre and brought along capital to invest in the colony. They were guaranteed religious and civic freedoms. No convicts here, thank you. This is the only state never to have been a penal colony.

Many early settlers came from the English gentry. By 1839 large numbers of Prussian and Silesian Lutherans had arrived, fleeing persecution, and by 1842 were settling in the Barossa Valley. In 1841 the colony nearly went

Area of map detail

Canberra

bankrupt, and the experiment might have ended, had not rich copper deposits been discovered. From then on South Australia grew rich on copper and the steamboat traffic on the Murray River, taking wheat and wool downstream and fortune-seekers upstream to the goldfields. South Australia held to its tradition of libertarianism. In 1894 women here became the first in the world to stand for Parliament, and the second (after New Zealand) to be given the vote.

When you leave the state's southeast corner, the story changes, and South Australia quickly becomes one of the world's most inhospitable places—a scene of scrub, salt lakes, and arid mountain ranges. There are things to see here though. The desert bursts into flower in spring, and the folded rock formations of the Flinders Ranges have interesting wildlife. The Ghan train from Adelaide runs across the desert to Alice Springs in the Northern Territory. Or you can drive there on the Stuart Highway, through the opal-mining town of Coober Pedy, which has such savage desert heat that many residents live underground. Adventurous travelers can explore the Oodnadatta, Strzelecki, and Birdsville Tracks. To the west the Nullarbor Plain stretches into Western Australia (see pp. 242–48). ∎

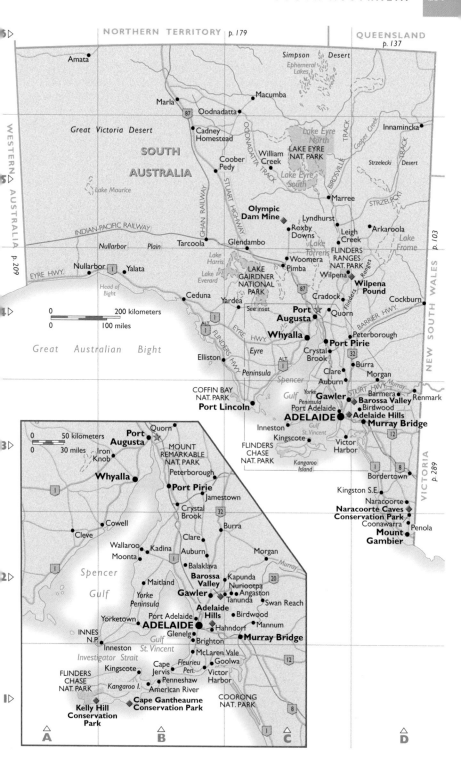

NORTHERN TERRITORY *p. 179*

QUEENSLAND *p. 137*

Simpson Desert

Ephemeral Lakes

Amata

Marla

Oodnadatta

87

Macumba

Cadney Homestead

Great Victoria Desert

Innamincka

William Creek

LAKE EYRE NAT. PARK

Lake Eyre North

Cooper Creek

Strzelecki Desert

SOUTH AUSTRALIA

Coober Pedy

Lake Eyre South

TRACK

BIRDSVILLE TRACK

STRZELECKI

OODNADATTA TRACK

Lake Maurice

GHAN RAILWAY

STUART HIGHWAY

Marree

Olympic Dam Mine

Lyndhurst

Arkaroola

INDIAN-PACIFIC RAILWAY

Roxby Downs

Leigh Creek

Lake Frome

p. 103

Nullarbor Plain

Tarcoola

Glendambo

FLINDERS RANGES NAT. PARK

WESTERN AUSTRALIA *p. 209*

Nullarbor

Yalata

Lake Harris

Lake Everard

Woomera

Pimba

Wilpena

Wilpena Pound

Ceduna

LAKE GAIRDNER NATIONAL PARK

Flinders Ranges

Head of Bight

EYRE HWY.

Yardea

See inset

Port Augusta

Cradock

Quorn

Cockburn

0   200 kilometers
0   100 miles

FLINDERS HWY.

Whyalla

EYRE HWY.

87

BARRIER HWY.

Great Australian Bight

Elliston

Eyre Peninsula

ALT 1

Crystal Brook

Clare

Auburn

Port Pirie

Peterborough

Burra

32

Morgan

NEW SOUTH WALES

COFFIN BAY NAT. PARK

Spencer Gulf

Yorke Peninsula

Port Adelaide

Gawler

STURT HWY.

Barmera

Renmark

Murray

Port Lincoln

ADELAIDE

Inneston

Barossa Valley

Birdwood

Adelaide Hills

Murray Bridge

Kingscote

Gulf St. Vincent

Victor Harbor

12

FLINDERS CHASE NAT. PARK

Kangaroo Island

Bordertown

8

VICTORIA *p. 289*

Kingston S.E.

Naracoorte

Naracoorte Caves Conservation Park

Coonawarra

Penola

Mount Gambier

Inset map:

0   50 kilometers
0   30 miles

Port Augusta

Quorn

MOUNT REMARKABLE NAT. PARK

Iron Knob

1

Peterborough

Whyalla

Port Pirie

Jamestown

1

Crystal Brook

32

Burra

Cowell

Clare

Cleve

Wallaroo

Kadina

Auburn

Morgan

Moonta

1

Balaklava

Murray

Spencer Gulf

Maitland

Barossa Valley

Kapunda

Nuriootpa

20

Yorke Peninsula

Gawler

Angaston

Swan Reach

Tanunda

1

Adelaide Hills

Birdwood

Port Adelaide

Yorketown

ADELAIDE

Hahndorf

Mannum

INNES N.P.

Glenelg

Brighton

Murray Bridge

Inneston

Gulf St. Vincent

McLaren Vale

12

Kingscote

Investigator Strait

Cape Jervis

Fleurieu Pen.

Goolwa

Victor Harbor

FLINDERS CHASE NAT. PARK

Kangaroo I.

Penneshaw

American River

COORONG NAT. PARK

8

Kelly Hill Conservation Park

Cape Gantheaume Conservation Park

1

A   B   C   D

Adelaide

ADELAIDE, ALSO KNOWN AS THE CITY OF CHURCHES, WAS planned as a utopia when Col. William Light surveyed it in 1836. He laid out a simple grid, surrounded by parklands, on a pretty site with a chain of "enchanted hills" on its western flank.

Adelaide

🅰 251 C3

Visitor information

✉ South Australian Visitor Information Centre, 18 King William St.

☎ (08) 8303 2249 or 1-300 655 276

The charming setting caused controversy at the time. The trouble was that Light had been given orders by Gov. John Hindmarsh to establish the city near the mouth of the recently explored Murray River, which authorities hoped would open the Australian continent as the Mississippi was opening North America. Light arrived only a few months before the first settlers were due and had to make his selection quickly. After examining the frequently silted mouth of the Murray and the treacherous coastline nearby, he decided to locate the new city about 60 miles (96 km) away, farther up the Gulf of St. Vincent and (even more controversially) on an inland plain. This action infuriated Hindmarsh and sparked bitter arguments between the two men and their supporters.

But Adelaide continued to grow and prosper, while settlements along the exposed coastline near the Murray mouth were troubled by numerous shipwrecks. In 1878 a railway spur linked Adelaide with the bustling inland river port of Morgan and resolved the issue. It was much too late for the tubercular Colonel Light, who had died a broken man in 1839. "The reasons that led me to fix Adelaide where it is I do not expect to be generally understood or calmly judged at present," he wrote shortly before his death. "I leave it to posterity to decide whether I am entitled to praise or blame."

Posterity has come down firmly in Light's favor. The grateful city has erected a bronze statue of him on

Montefiore Hill, where he gazed out on the gentle floodplain below and decided this would be the place. The hill itself is a grassy knoll in North Adelaide, just above the very pretty Adelaide Cricket Ground, and it is an ideal place to get a feel for the city. From here you

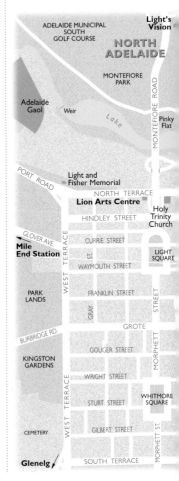

can see the breathing space of parklands that surround the inner city, the twin spires of the magnificent St. Peter's Cathedral, the graceful **Torrens River,** and the clean lines of the city skyline. The view is known as Light's Vision.

You can easily find your way around Adelaide, which is laid out in a grid exactly one imperial mile square. At the center of the grid is the grassy **Victoria Square,** where you can catch the tram to the beach at Glenelg. Tree-lined **North Terrace** is the cultural focus, with museums and fine colonial architecture. The main shopping precinct is along **Rundle Mall,** a sunny pedestrian way bright with flower stalls and lively with street musicians and jugglers (of markedly differing degrees of talent). **Hindley Street** is the town's red-light district, seedy in its way but very tame compared with Sydney's Kings Cross. On Gouger Street is one of Adelaide's gastronomic icons, **Central Market,** a paradise of local fruits and vegetables, cheeses, seafood, and meats. Gouger Street also boasts the highest concentration of restaurants in

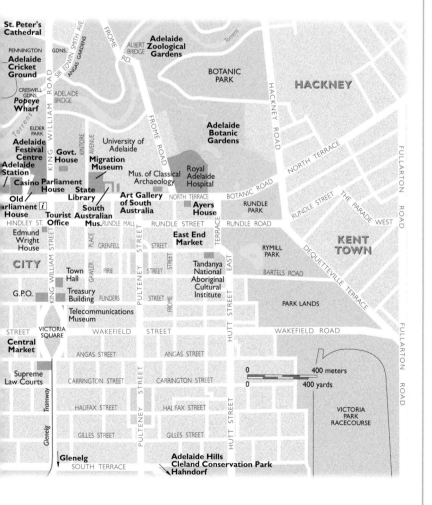

Lined with willows and gums, the Torrens River reflects the Adelaide skyline as it meanders through the parklands that surround the well-planned city.

Adelaide. **Rundle Street** is the artsy café district, lined with jazzy-cool winebars and bistros. This city is said to have more eateries per person than any other in Australia. O'Connell and Melbourne Streets in North Adelaide are also well known café strips, and Gouger Street has a veritable United Nations of ethnic restaurants.

Adelaide's character is hard to pin down. The city has a longstanding reputation for being conservative and even has a coterie of old, moneyed families known as "the Establishment." On the other hand, its Mediterranean climate, good food, and fine wine give it a hedonistic ambience at odds with its stuffy image. This is perhaps Australia's most vivacious city. The calendar is full of festivals, and the two professional Australian Rules football teams are cheered by crowds whose throaty parochialism would make a football-crazed Nebraskan blush.

ADELAIDE SIGHTS

On a map, downtown Adelaide resembles a lopsided hourglass set against a backdrop of green parklands. The larger portion is the commercial center, and the smaller section is North Adelaide, a leafy enclave set out by Colonel Light for the homes of the landed gentry. The two parts are connected by the elegant **Adelaide Bridge,** which spans the Torrens River. This river, once just a seasonal trickle, has been dammed to form a long lake through this part of the city.

The best place to start exploring the city is south of the bridge, at the corner of King William Street and North Terrace. Virtually every major attraction is only a few minutes stroll from here—the art gallery, festival center, South Australian Museum, Parliament House, Government House, casino, Botanic Gardens, and zoo. Most of them are on **North Terrace** itself, a grand tree-lined boulevard that showcases

**Adelaide Festival
Centre**
✉ King William Rd.
☎ 13 12 46

much of South Australia's solid colonial architecture.

Start on the west corner at the monumental **Parliament House,** with its massive marble Corinthian columns. This imposing building was started in 1883 but took more than 50 years to complete because of a dispute about a dome (which was never built). It is open to the public, and on days when Parliament is sitting you can watch South Australia's representatives sort out state affairs. Beside it is the beautifully restored **Old Parliament House,** completed in 1855, now a museum on the constitution. Next door, farther west, is the grand old railroad station, built of honey-colored sandstone in 1929. Although its imposing neoclassic lines suggest great rail journeys, only suburban lines depart from here. The Indian–Pacific (Sydney–Perth), the Ghan (to Alice Springs), and the Overlander (to Melbourne) all leave

from the soulless Keswick terminal at Mile End, just off Burbridge Road, west of the city.

The upper floors of the old railroad station were beautifully restored in the mid-1980s and turned into the elegant **Adelaide Casino** (open 24 hours). Abutting the casino are the convention center and octagonal towers of the Hyatt Regency Adelaide, arguably the city's most luxurious hotel. Still farther west is the **Lion Arts Centre** (*Morphett St. at North Terrace*), where the biennial Adelaide Fringe Festival is based. The center is a bright and airy building with exhibition galleries, theaters, bars, contemporary art galleries, and a cinema. The Jam Factory Craft and Design Centre in the Lion Arts Centre has high-quality glassware, pottery, and woodwork for sale.

The **Adelaide Festival Centre** is tucked in behind the Parliament House and the casino,

South Australian Museum

✉ North Terrace
☎ (08) 8207 7500

Art Gallery of South Australia

✉ North Terrace
☎ (08) 8207 7000

Central Market

✉ Gouger St.
☎ (08) 8203 7345
🕐 Closed Sat. p.m. & Sun.–Mon.

MARKETS

If you are planning a picnic, or just enjoy the sight of wonderful produce, check out Adelaide's **Central Market** on Gouger Street. More than 250 stalls sell exotic fruit, sheep cheeses, German pastries, smoked meats, fresh local produce, meats, fish, and more. Another good bet is the **East End** market on Rundle Street (*Fri.–Mon.*). ∎

Opposite: The conservatory in Adelaide Botanic Gardens re-creates a lush tropical rain forest in the Southern Hemisphere's largest greenhouse.

on the banks of the Torrens River. This boxy version of the Sydney Opera House has better acoustics. Built in 1977, the modernistic complex contains a 2,000-seat theater (the largest in Australia), smaller 600- and 380-seat theaters, and an 800-seat recital hall. Although the Adelaide Arts Festival runs only every second year, in February and March, the center itself is busy all year and is home to the South Australian Theatre Company, the experimental Space Theatre, and a small commercial art gallery. The sun-drenched plaza behind the complex, with its fountains and bright 1970-ish sculptures, is a popular place for office workers to bring a lunch. The manicured lawns that spill down to the riverbank are part of **Elder Park,** another popular picnic spot. There are brightly painted pedal-powered boats for hire along the bank, and a landing for the sight-seeing boat *Popeye,* an Adelaide institution since 1935. On Sunday mornings bands play in the lacy cast-iron Victorian-era rotunda.

If you head east on North Terrace from your original starting point *(corner of King William St. & North Terrace),* you'll come first to **Government House**—or rather an iron gate through which you get a glimpse of neoclassic stonework and ornamental gardens dating from 1836. The elegant mansion is the home of the governor of South Australia—the official representative of the British crown in the state—and is not open to the public. Nearby are the hallowed portals of the very exclusive **Adelaide Club**—the bastion of the city's old boy network.

The place next door, however, does welcome visitors. The **State Library** *(Tel (08) 8207 7250),* built in 1884, houses a vast collection of maps, the journals of early explorers,

and colonial records—as well as a large and very user-friendly public library. It adjoins the **South Australian Museum,** easily distinguished by the full-size whale skeleton in its front gallery window. The museum has the world's largest collection of Aboriginal artifacts and an extensive Melanesian collection as well.

Next door is the **Art Gallery of South Australia,** which recently underwent a 20-million-Australian-dollar (10-million-U.S.-dollar) upgrade and became the holder of the nation's largest collection of Australian art. Free audio guides to the museum's collection are available at the front desk; they are excellent. Or you can join one of the guided tours that meet at the entrance at 11 a.m. and 2 p.m. on weekdays, 11 a.m. and 3 p.m. on weekends.

Tucked away behind the library is the **Migration Museum** *(82 Kintore Ave, tel (08) 8207 7580),* a hidden gem with poignant displays about the lives of immigrants, who came to South Australia from a hundred nations. It is in the former Destitute Asylum, where homeless people of the last century were tucked out of sight and out of mind. The grounds behind the museum are part of the University of Adelaide campus.

Continue along North Terrace (and across the street), and you'll come to **Ayers House** *(Tel (08) 8223 1234, closed Mon., $),* which is said to be the finest example of Regency architecture in Australia. From 1855 to 1878 this 40-room bluestone mansion was the home of Henry Ayers, seven times premier of South Australia and the man for whom Ayers Rock (Uluru) was named. These days it is the headquarters for the South Australian chapter of the National Trust. Two elegant restaurants are here: the

Adelaide Botanic Gardens

✉ North Terrace

☎ (08) 8222 9311

💲 $ for Bicentennial Conservatory

Adelaide Zoological Gardens

✉ Frome Rd.

☎ (08) 8267 3255

💲 $$

café-style Conservatory and the sumptuous (and more expensive) Henry Ayers Restaurant (see p. 378).

The **Adelaide Botanic Gardens** are on the eastern end of North Terrace. Established in 1855, these formal gardens have been expanded to include a palm house and the Bicentennial Conservatory, holding a modest-size rain forest. From the Botanic Gardens you can continue to the **Adelaide Zoological Gardens**—a pleasant, if small, zoo—then return to your starting point on *Popeye,* along the Torrens River.

NORTH ADELAIDE

The enclave of North Adelaide was laid out by Colonel Light as the residential part of his utopian city, a small district surrounded by leafy parklands and within an easy stroll of downtown (just across the Torrens River). Some of the city's most gracious mansions are in North Adelaide, and there are rows of old bluestone cottages and some of the city's trendiest cafés and restaurants. The broad Adelaide Bridge is an open invitation to explore this part of the city.

The wide swath of manicured lawn to your left, after you cross the bridge, is **Pennington Gardens,** which also has walkways, ornamental trees, and flower beds. Looming above it are the twin spires of **St. Peter's Cathedral,** one of Australia's finest neo-Gothic buildings, which was built between 1869 and 1904. The cathedral has a powerful, but mellow, eight-bell carillon that is played on feast days. As the road goes up the hill, it becomes **O'Connell Street,** the heart of North Adelaide's café scene. Alternatively, if you follow Sir Edwin Smith Avenue, to your right as you cross the bridge, you'll come to **Melbourne Street,** another cavalcade of restaurants, cafés, and bistros. Veer to the left in front of the cathedral and you'll come to the **Adelaide Cricket Ground,** a pleasingly old-fashioned ground regarded as one of the prettiest in the world. Even if you know nothing about the game, it is worth sauntering this way if a match is playing.

At the top of the hill behind the cricket ground is **Light's Vision** and the bronze statue of the city's founder (see p. 252). This is a great place to get a photograph of the city, especially at dusk when the first lights are flickering on. You can understand Light's thinking. He hadn't yet created Utopia, but he could at least see where to put it. ■

Pie floaters

For all the elegant and innovative dining in Adelaide, one of the things Adelaideans love most is a "pie floater" from the humble pie cart that has been parked on North Terrace, just outside the railroad station, for as long as anybody can remember. Australians everywhere love their meat pies, consuming more than 260 million of them each year. Pies are generally served up in a paper bag with a squirt of tomato sauce (ketchup, to Americans) and a napkin to catch the gravy as it drips down your chin. South Australians have developed their own peculiar variation on the national dish. They float the meat pie in a bowl of pea soup, then add the tomato sauce (appetizingly called "dead horse"). You may not understand the appeal, but almost every South Australian swears a "pie floater" is food fit for gods. The station pie cart is the traditional place to buy one. Bon appetit. ■

Around Adelaide

TUCKED BETWEEN THE SEA AND A RANGE OF HILLS, Adelaide offers plenty of options for a day out when the summer city begins to stifle. Take the tram for a half-hour ride to Glenelg, or drive up to the Mount Lofty hills for marvelous views and a fresh tang to the air.

GLENELG & BEYOND

One of the quintessential Adelaide experiences is taking the restored 1929 tram from Victoria Square to the beach at Glenelg, 6 miles (9.7 km) away. Fifty years ago this quaint old beach town was where Adelaide went on holiday, and even today it has the feel of an English seaside resort, fading slightly but still immensely popular.

Glenelg was where South Australia's first settlers landed in 1836, and the gnarled gum tree where Gov. John Hindmarsh proclaimed the new colony into existence still stands on McFarlane Street. A full-size reproduction of the settlers' ship **H.M.S. *Buffalo*** sits in the harbor, and on board is a popular seafood restaurant (*Tel (08) 8294 7000*).

Glenelg has a bustling weekend atmosphere even during the week, but on the weekends it really hums. This beach is Adelaide's most popular and most accessible.

Umbrellas, deck chairs, boogie boards, in-line skates, and bicycles can be hired along the waterfront. Jetty Road is crammed with trendy cafés and bookshops.

Glenelg is one of a chain of beaches along the coast—running to the north are **West Beach, Henley Beach,** and **Grange Beach; Brighton** lies to the south. All have an old-fashioned, 1950s air to them.

You won't see much surf along here because these beaches are on the sheltered **Gulf of St. Vincent.** Older locals, though, can tell you about the wild storm of 1948 that virtually destroyed Glenelg's jetty. The water comes up from the southern Indian Ocean, and it can be surprisingly brisk at times. Occasionally sharks are spotted near the beach. Use caution, but don't let *Jaws* dissuade you from taking a refreshing dip. None of the locals do. Far more dangerous and ubiquitous are the deadly ultra-

The old tram, the beachside amusements, and the rambling hotels give **Glenelg the air of an English beach resort.**

Glenelg
⚑ 251 B2
Visitor information
✉ Behind the Town Hall
☎ (08) 8294 5833

violet rays of the sun, which here in South Australia regularly register as "extreme" or higher.

ADELAIDE HILLS

A 20-minute drive southeast of the city on Glen Osmond Road and the Southeastern Freeway brings you to the Adelaide Hills, the "enchanted hills" referred to by Colonel Light in his description of the city (see p. 252). It is easy to agree with him: They are leafy, green, and, on a hot day, as much as 15°F (8°C) cooler than Adelaide itself. As a consequence they have been a retreat for Adelaide's gentility for more than a century, especially since the Southeastern Freeway has provided quick access to the city, and today hill villages such as **Stirling** feel like genteel suburbs, or hobby farm

country. For the visitor the Adelaide Hills offer beautiful hiking trails and conservation parks, wineries, historic villages, and numerous festivals. A festival takes place almost every weekend in one village or another. Consult the helpful visitor center in **Hahndorf,** just off the freeway about 20 miles (32 km) southeast of the city.

The Adelaide Hills are a part of the **Mount Lofty Ranges,** and are dominated by the 2,362-foot (720 m) summit of Mount Lofty. (It's the tall one with the television antennas on it.) The Mount Lofty Ranges are believed to have originally been part of the Trans-Antarctic Mountains, which existed millions of years ago before the continents broke up and drifted apart. Mount Lofty's summit is

Adelaide Hills
🇦 251 B2
Visitor information
✉ 41 Main St., Hahndorf
☎ (08) 8388 1185, 1-800 353 323 (toll free)

German bands add to the fun at the festivals held around Adelaide.

The Cedars

✉ 50 Main St., Hahndorf

☎ (08) 8388 7277

🕐 Guided tours of house, studio, & grounds Sun.–Fri. 11 a.m., 1 p.m., & 3 p.m., closed Sat.

easily accessible by car and gives sweeping views over the city, the coast, and the country inland. Take the Summit Road exit off the freeway, just before the town of Crafers (about 10 miles/16 km out of Adelaide) and follow it north for about 3 miles (4.8 km). On the right shortly after you leave the freeway, you'll go past the beautiful **Mount Lofty Botanic Gardens** *(Summit Rd., tel (08) 8370 8370)*. The summit of Mount Lofty has a restaurant *(Tel (08) 8339 2600)*, and tourist office and interpretive center *(Tel (08) 8370 1054)*.

Two hundred yards farther along the road, on your left, is the **Cleland Wildlife Park** *(Tel (08) 8339 2444, $$)*, a conservation park where you can get close to a koala, hand-feed kangaroos and wallabies, or take a guided nighttime tour to see some of Australia's shy nocturnal wildlife.

Ten miles (16 km) farther east along the freeway is **Hahndorf,** the oldest German settlement in South Australia and one of the main attractions in the Adelaide Hills. Prussian and Silesian immigrants settled here in 1839, having come to Australia to escape religious persecution in their homeland. Today the village plays up to its colorful German heritage, perhaps a little too enthusiastically for some tastes; it borders on the kitsch. It is a lively place, with German bakeries, tearooms, galleries, and craft shops. One of the town's most famous residents was the noted early 20th-century landscape painter Hans Heysen, who lived and worked in an elegant home called **The Cedars,** still owned by his descendants. About 200 of Heysen's paintings are on display in the house

The Adelaide Hills have a long history of wine production (see p. 264) and are rich with vineyards.

Hiking

The area has excellent hiking, from afternoon strolls through the bush to extended treks of a week or more in the Mount Lofty Ranges. One of Australia's finest and longest trails, the 1,000-mile (1,600 km) **Heysen Trail,** named after Hans Heysen, winds through the Adelaide Hills on its way north from the tip of the Fleurieu Peninsula to the heart of the Flinders Ranges, across some of South Australia's finest countryside. Most hikers do just short sections as a day trip, but a few hardy souls have done the entire length. Maps of the trail are available in many of Adelaide's camping shops (which are concentrated on Rundle Street). The Youth Hostel Association operates several limited access hostels through the Mount Lofty Ranges, at convenient distances for hikers. Keys must be picked up at the YHA office in Adelaide *(38 Sturt St., tel (08) 8231 5583)*. The Heysen Trail is closed in summer because of potential bush fire hazards.

Going farther

The Adelaide Hills are a gum-tree-lined gateway north to the vineyards of the Barossa Valley or south to the Fleurieu Peninsula. To reach the **Barossa Valley,** take the Onkaparinga Road exit from the freeway near Bridgewater, about 12 miles (19 km) out of Adelaide, and go north for about 30 miles (48 km) through the villages of Oakbank, Woodside, Birdwood, and Springton.

To reach the **Fleurieu Peninsula,** take the Mount Barker–Strathalbyn Road south from Stirling through the stunning hills and farmland of the southern end of the Adelaide Hills to Macclesfield and Strathalbyn. From there it is an easy drive along the Goolwa Road to the pretty seaside towns of **Goolwa** and **Victor Harbor.** ∎

Australian wines

Since the 1980s Australia has emerged as one of the world's great winemaking nations, internationally lauded for its use of innovative techniques to produce bold, fruity, and affordable wines. Connoisseurs around the world recognize regional Australian names such as Barossa Valley, Coonawarra, Margaret River, Clare, and Hunter Valley. Australian labels have consistently pulled down some of the world's most prestigious awards. Penfold's 1990 Grange Hermitage—Australia's premier red—was judged by the influential *Wine Spectator* magazine to be the international Wine of the Year when it was released in 1995. In 1999 the magazine rated the '55 Grange among the 12 finest wines of the 20th century, ranking it with such luminaries as the '21 Château d'Yquem and the Château Mouton-Rothschild '45.

Although this success seemed to come suddenly, it was not a case of Aussie nouveau. Australian wines were winning international awards as long ago as the 1870s, and Victoria's Yerinberg winery took a gold medal at the Paris Exposition of 1889. Viticulture in Australia dates back to 1788, when the First Fleet brought vine clippings from South Africa. By the 1830s, the Hunter Valley in New South Wales was producing wine, thanks largely to the efforts of a Scot, James Busby, who had studied viticulture in France and imported hundreds of clippings from France and Spain. Prussian and Silesian immigrants began growing wine grapes in South Australia's Barossa Valley in the 1840s, almost as soon as they arrived. Victoria's wine industry was kick-started in the 1850s with 10,000 clippings from Bordeaux's Château Lafite-Rothschild.

These bold beginnings were put on hold, however, in part by the outbreak of phylloxera that ravaged much of the world's vineyards in the late 19th century, and in part by fashion. Tastes moved on to fortified wines and away from table wine. It wasn't until the 1960s that Australians began making table wine in quantity again. (Australia's total crush for Cabernet Sauvignon in 1959 was 69 tons/70 tonnes,

compared with 68,890 tons/70,000 tonnes, in 1996.)

Today Australia is the world's 11th-largest wine producer, with just over a thousand wineries producing more than 132 million gallons (500 million litres) of wine each year.

Grapes are grown in every state—there is even a vineyard near Alice Springs. Boutique areas such as Margaret River (Western Australia) and the Yarra Valley (Victoria) are on the cutting edge of fashion, but the lion's share of premium quality wine comes from South Australia. The Barossa and Clare Valleys, the McLaren Vale, and the Coonawarra region are the best known wine districts.

One of the main reasons for Australia's success is the willingness to use the latest technologies to blend whatever regional varieties of grapes they need to produce bold fruity flavors. The result of these so-called New World techniques is a clean-tasting wine that evokes Australia's bright sunshine and costs far less than a European vintage of comparable quality. Old World winemakers, on the other hand, have been bound by centuries-old traditions and prevented by law from taking such radical steps. But times are changing. These days Australian winemakers are in big demand in Europe, where they are helping some of the world's most famous houses develop their art into a science. In what would have seemed sacrilege only a few years ago, some European houses are now offering wines made "in the Australian style."

Penfold's Grange Hermitage may be Australia's greatest red wine, but at more than $A200 (U.S. $100) a bottle for the recent vintages (and into the thousands for some of the earlier ones), it is a little rich for most occasions. Even this outstanding red faces serious competition from other great Australian labels such as Henschke. The competition for best white wine is an open field, with runners from around the country.

VINTAGE YEARS

Australia's best recent vintages are 1971, '76, '80, '81, '86, and '90. The 1990 vintage was one of the truly epic years. ■

Above: Oak wine casks seasoning in the sun at Château Tanunda in 1923. A cooperage still operates in Tanunda today.
Left: A glistening vatful of grapes begins to ferment. Below: Brother John May tests the wine casks at the Seven Hills Winery in the Clare Valley.

Wine districts

THE BAROSSA VALLEY (SEE PP. 266–67) IS THE STATE'S MOST important wine district, but it doesn't have the field all to itself. Wine regions such as the Southern Vales, Coonawarra, and the Clare Valley are challenging its status, and new vineyards are being planted along the Murray River Valley, the Adelaide Hills, and near Port Lincoln on the Eyre Peninsula.

The **Southern Vales,** on the Fleurieu Peninsula about 20 miles (32 km) south of Adelaide, is the state's oldest wine district. The first winery here started in 1838, and now more than 50 wineries are in the area, which has gained a following for rich Shirazes and Cabernet Sauvignons. Chapel Hill, Hardy's Reynella, Hasle Grove, and Wirra Wirra are some of the better known labels. Most of the wineries are small, family concerns. The best time to visit is during the Wine Bushing Festival, late in October. There are tastings, feasts, and tours, and a special bus service goes around the wineries so visitors can drink and not worry about driving. The ideal base is the pretty little village of **McLaren Vale,** a rather trendy spot that has plenty of B&Bs, galleries, and craft shops. To get to the Southern Vales follow Main South Road out of Adelaide to Old Noarlunga and from there follow the Victor Harbor Road

another 3 miles (4.8 km) to the turnoff for McLaren Vale.

The **Adelaide Hills** (see pp. 260–61) also have a long history of winemaking. Australia's first known wine export went from here —an 1845 hock from Echunga was sent to England for Queen Victoria. These days 17 wineries are in the hills, which are becoming known for their Chardonnay. Petaluma and Karl Seppelts Grand Cru Estate are two prominent local labels.

Coonawarra, about 250 miles (400 km) southeast of Adelaide, produces excellent reds. More than 20 wineries are crammed into this narrow region (8 miles/12.8 km long and a little over a mile/2 km wide), and many more would like to be. Demand for Coonawarra's fabled *terra-rossa* soil has pushed prices for land to absurd levels—more than $A40,000 (U.S. $20,000) for a planted acre. Most of Australia's great Cabernet Sauvignons spring from this soil.

Wine district visitor information centers:

Southern Vales
- 🅰 251 B1
- ✉ Main St., McLaren Vale
- ☎ (08) 8323 9455

Adelaide Hills
- 🅰 251 B2
- ✉ 41 Main St., Hahndorf
- ☎ (08) 8388 1185 or 1-800 353 323 (toll free)

Coonawarra
- 🅰 251 D2
- ✉ 27 Arthur St.
- ☎ (08) 8737 2855

Around Coonawarra

The World Heritage-listed **Naracoorte Caves Conservation Park** is 25 miles (40 km) north of Coonawarra. The cave has a huge population of bats and appeared in David Attenborough's *Life on Earth* television series. But the main reason for its listing is the collection of Pleistocene fossils found here that contains the remains of extinct marsupials, from

a giant kangaroo to a wombat the size of a rhinoceros.

Six miles (9.7 km) south of Coonawarra is the village of Penola, where Mother Mary MacKillop did much of her early work with the poor and disadvantaged. Her works and subsequent miracles prompted the Roman Catholic church to beatify her in 1995—the last step before becoming Australia's first saint. ■

The **Clare Valley,** about 80 miles (128 km) north of Adelaide on Main North Road, has a lovely European feel to it and a lot less tourist hype than other districts. It was settled in the 1850s and named Clare by homesick Irish because its gentle landscape reminded them of County Clare. Winemaking in the valley began when Jesuit brothers grew grapes to make their own communion wine. They named their monastery Seven Hills after the line of seven hills around Rome. Today the Seven Hills winery, 6 miles (9.7 km) south of Clare, is still run by Jesuits, who continue their tradition of making sacramental wine but have diversi-fied into table wines, port, and sherry. Tours of the winery and old stone cellars are available by

appointment. Seven Hills is one of about 20 wineries in the region. They range from the small but highly regarded Grosset Wines, which is run out of an old butter factory in Auburn, to the giant, century-old Leasingham Wines near the town of Clare.

The **Murray River Valley** has long produced table grapes and cheap cask wine, but as the industry expands, an increasing number of big-name wineries are planting vines here. The Kingston Estate winery, 140 miles (225 km) north-east of Adelaide near Barmera, is the pick of the region, and its wines win gold medals. Boston Bay Wineries and Delacolline Estate are the two major winemakers in Port Lincoln. The sea view from the Boston Bay vineyard is stunning. ■

Vineyards in the McLaren Vale weave a gentle pattern in the foothills of the Mount Lofty Ranges.

Wine district visitor information centers:
Clare Valley
🔺 251 B2
✉ Town Hall, 229 Main North Rd., Clare
☎ (08) 8842 2131

Renmark
🔺 251 D3
✉ Murray Ave.
☎ (08) 8586 6704

Barossa Valley

Barossa Valley

▲ 251 B2

Visitor information

✉ Barossa Wine and Visitors Centre, 68 Murray St., Tanunda

☎ 1-800 812 662 (toll free)

THE BAROSSA VALLEY IS SOUTH AUSTRALIA'S PREMIER WINE area, producing almost one-fourth of the nation's wine output and accounting for about 70 percent of its wine exports. It is home to some of Australia's most respected labels, such as Penfolds, Henschke, Peter Lehman, Rockfords, and Seppelts—the only winery in the world with an unbroken line of vintage ports dating back to 1878. The district is also the closest thing Australia has to a distinct gastronomic province, producing smoked meats, pastries, and pickles that reflect its distinctive German heritage.

A butcher in the Barossa Valley town of Nuriootpa casts a critical eye over his next batch of smoked *mettwurst*.

The valley was settled in 1842 by Prussian and Silesian Lutherans who were seeking religious freedom. They were persuaded to come to Australia by George Fife Angas, a wealthy and philanthropic South Australian landowner, who underwrote the cost of their passage. It was the first time in Australia's

history that immigrants from somewhere other than England had been actively sought. In addition to their doughty work ethic, language, and culture, the newcomers brought their winemaking skills. Within a year grapevines had been planted along Jacob's Creek, and by 1850 the valley had begun its long tradition of winemaking. The Barossa Valley's isolation protected it from the outbreak of phylloxera in the 1870s that ravaged the rest of the world's grapevines. As a result some of the world's oldest Shiraz vines can be found here today.

There is still a strong German feel to the valley. Old stone Lutheran churches dot the countryside, and the villages have German bakeries and butcher shops where goods are made according to family recipes. On the subject of *mettwurst*, a friendly rivalry exists between two butcher shops, with some locals swearing by Linke's mettwurst in Nuriootpa and others insisting that Schultz's mettwurst, over in Angaston, can't be surpassed. (Both, by the way, are excellent.) The phone books here are crammed with old German names, and a few of the valley's older residents still speak an Australianized form of German known as Barossa-Deutsche.

The Barossa Valley is an easy 45-mile (72 km) drive north of Adelaide on Main North Road,

with ample signs to the valley's main towns of Tanunda, Nuriootpa, and Angaston.

Of the three towns, centrally located **Tanunda** is the one most geared to tourists, with a pleasant main street and a wide selection of craft galleries, cafés, and B&Bs. **Nuriootpa** is the valley's commercial hub. The small and quiet village of **Angaston,** off to the east, is perhaps the prettiest of the three. Angaston was founded by George Fife Angas in the 1830s. His magnificent estate, Lindsey Park, is now one of Australia's top racing stables. It is private and not open to visitors, but you can visit his son's mansion, **Collingrove** (6 miles/ 9.7 km via the road to Eden Valley southeast of Angaston), now owned by the National Trust.

Most of the 50-odd Barossa Valley wineries offer free tastings—although if you want to sample the priciest vintages and labels, you'll have to bring out your wallet.

Some, including **Seppelts** and **Château Yaldara,** are open for tours. Seppelts is one of the best, and the drive from Nuriootpa is exceptionally scenic. The route runs along a 2-mile (3 km) avenue of ornamental date palms, with a Doric temple on the hillside (the temple is the Seppelt family mausoleum). A variety of tours is available to the wineries (you can travel by minivan, luxury Daimler, or restored '55 Chevrolet limousine, among other vehicles), so everyone can partake in the tastings without fear of falling foul of Australia's strict drink-driving laws. You can also take a scenic day trip through the valley on the fully refurbished old *Bluebird* train from Adelaide (Tel (08) 8232 1255).

The Barossa Vintage Festival—held over Easter week on odd-numbered years—draws thousands of visitors to the valley for a week of parades and shows. It is just one of the many festivals held here. ∎

Judging the produce and jams at one of the annual shows in the Barossa Valley

VISITING WINERIES

The Barossa Wine and Visitor Centre (see p. 266) and the South Australian Visitor Information Centre in Adelaide (see p. 252) can advise on tours and visits. ∎

Festival State

South Australia's nickname is the Festival State. On its calendar are more than 400 festivals, carnivals, and sporting events. Depending on when you visit, you might take in events as varied as the Barossa Valley Vintage Festival (Easter in odd-numbered years), the Australian Camel Cup race in the Outback town of Maree (July), and the Schutzenfest (January, with oompah bands). Oakbank's Easter Racing Carnival is Australia's greatest picnic-day horse race, and the Bay to Birdwood Run is the biggest antique automobile rally in the Southern Hemisphere, attracting more than 2,000 entries from Australia and overseas.

The state's most famous event is the Adelaide Festival. For glamour, excitement, and size, it easily surpasses anything else of the sort in Australia. Held over three weeks in March, on even-numbered years, it attracts major artists from Australia and around the world. The festival began modestly in 1960 with 51 shows, but has burgeoned into a feast of more than 300 plays, concerts, films, dance performances, and cabaret acts. Ticket prices are quite reasonable—far more so than for shows in Sydney or Melbourne—and for those on a tight budget there are free weekend concerts and fireworks displays on the banks of the Torrens River. The weather in Adelaide in March is generally perfect, with hot days and warm starry nights that make outdoor performances a treat.

Coinciding with the official festival is the even more exuberant and sometimes very strange Fringe Festival. If the Arts Festival gives Adelaide a taste of Manhattan, the Fringe Festival is more like New Orleans, with offbeat artists, jugglers, comedy revues, musicians, experimental theater, and film festivals. Walk the café-lined streets on these summer evenings and you're likely to see anything. While all this is going on, Adelaide also hosts Writers' Week, during which well-known authors from Australia and overseas gather to discuss their works, launch books, and give readings. This one is free.

In odd-numbered years Adelaide hosts Womadelaide, an international music festival

held in the botanic gardens, with some performances taking place farther afield in the South Australian Outback. Another major music festival is the Barossa Music Festival, held in October each year in the Barossa Valley. The valley also hosts Barossa Under the Stars, in which international stars perform an open-air concert near one of the big wineries. This annual festival usually takes place late in January or early in February. The Country Music Festival is cele-

brated each June in the town of Barmera (140 miles/225 km) northeast of Adelaide.

Gourmet festivals are another South Australian tradition. Every August the Barossa Valley has a Classic Gourmet weekend, a sort of progressive luncheon in which visitors travel around the wineries sampling wines with dishes created by some of South Australia's best restaurateurs. McLaren Vale, 20 miles (32 km) south of Adelaide, has a similar fete,

The different faces of Adelaide: Elvises perform at the Fringe Festival, children watch the Feast for the Senses, and performers pose at the Womadelaide.

the Continuous Picnic, held each May. Clare, 75 miles (120 km) north, hosts a Gourmet Weekend in May. This is just a selection: Ask the South Australian Visitor Information Centre (see p. 252) for more. ■

Kangaroo Island

IF AUSTRALIA HAS BEEN AN ARK FOR UNIQUE FLORA AND
fauna, Kangaroo Island (or K.I.) has been its lifeboat. This surprisingly large island, barely 10 miles (16 km) off the coast of South
Australia, has remained an unspoiled haven for wildlife and a time
capsule of the way the rest of Australia was about 30 years ago. The
roads are mostly dirt, shops have oiled wooden floors, and drivers
have to be careful not to dent their fenders on the high stone curbs
in the villages. There are wallabies, kangaroos, koalas, platypuses,
and echidnas on land, and the sea has seals, dolphins, sea lions,
penguins, whales, and sharks; both have teeming bird life.

The island has 21 national parks or
conservation areas, covering about
a third of its total area. The largest
and best known is **Flinders
Chase National Park,** which
covers the western end of K.I. The
rest of the island has well-watered
forests and rolling farmland, with a
good reputation for such produce
as sheep milk cheeses, free-range
chickens, freshwater crayfish, rock
lobster, and King George whiting.
The island has the world's last pure
strain of gentle Ligurian honeybees—brought here from Italy in
the 1860s—and is increasingly
known for its honey.

Australia's third largest island
behind Tasmania and the Northern
Territory's Melville Island, K.I. is
about 90 miles (145 km) long and
up to 40 miles (64 km) wide. It is
sparsely populated, with only about
4,000 inhabitants. The dramatic
cliff-lined coasts and rocky shoals
have claimed more than 40 ships
since English navigator Matthew
Flinders set eyes on the island in
1802, a few weeks before French explorer Nicholas Baudin. Kangaroo
Island was uninhabited then.
Although Aboriginal artifacts dating back 30,000 years have been
found on the island, archaeological
evidence suggests the Aborigines
left around 7,000 years ago. No one
knows why.

The early European history
wasn't terribly genteel. Kangaroo
Island was settled in 1806 by an
assortment of escaped convicts and
deserters from Yankee whaling
ships. They camped near present-
day American River, built a 34-ton
(35 tonne) schooner out of local
materials, and set about the wholesale slaughter of the seal population. They also raided Aboriginal
camps on the mainland coast. By
1827 the island had acquired such
an evil reputation that the colonial
authorities sent in a military expedition and dragged almost the
entire population away in chains.

An official attempt was made in
1836 to set up South Australia's first
colony on the island (at Kingscote),
but attention switched to Adelaide
instead. Throughout much of the
next century Kangaroo Island
remained undeveloped. To remedy
that, authorities gave free land to
returned veterans from World
War I and World War II, and many
of the island's farmers are the sons
and grandsons of those soldiers.

Getting to the island is simple.
You can fly to Kingscote from
Adelaide Airport (see panel information, right) but most visitors go
by ferry. Kangaroo Island Sealink
(Tel 13 13 01) operates two vehicu-
lar ferries from Cape Jervis, about
an hour south of Adelaide at the tip

Kangaroo Island
⊠ 251 B1
Visitor information
✉ Gateway Visitor
Information Centre,
Howard Dr.,
Penneshaw
☎ (08) 8553 1185
email: t:ourki@ozemail
.com.au

**Flying to Kangaroo
Island from
Adelaide:**
Kendall Airways
☎ (08) 8234 4159
Albatross Airlines
☎ (08) 8553 2296
Emu Air
☎ (08) 8234 3711

Stokes Bay, on the northern coast of Kangaroo Island, is one of scores of secluded nooks and bays offering unspoiled swimming and fishing.

CAR RENTAL
Rental companies do not usually permit their cars to be taken to Kangaroo Island. The island's car rental companies are located in Kingscote. ■

of the Fleurieu Peninsula. The crossing takes about an hour and delivers you to Penneshaw. A bus service goes to Cape Jervis from Adelaide's central bus station on Franklin Street *(reservations necessary, contact Sealink, tel 13 13 01).* Once you are on the island, a Sealink shuttle can take you to Kingscote. For package tours to the island contact the South Australian Visitor Information Centre in Adelaide (see p. 252) or the Kangaroo Island Gateway Visitor Information Centre (see p. 270).

The island's three main settlements, Kingscote, American River and Penneshaw, are all on the eastern side. **Kingscote** is the island's commercial center, and by K.I. standards it's bustling and hectic, but with a population of about 1,500 it is hardly intimidating. All the towns have local attractions such as small museums, restored cottages, and the like, but the main reason people come to K.I. is to see

wildlife and the island's national and conservation parks, for which you need a pass (see sidebar, p. 272).

One of the most popular places on the island is the **Cape Gantheaume Conservation Park,** a haunting expanse of dunes and mallee scrub on the rugged south coast about a 30-mile (48 km) drive from Kingscote. Murray Lagoon has hundreds of bird species. Abutting the park is **Seal Bay Conservation Park,** with a resident population of several hundred sea lions. This colony somehow survived wholesale slaughter in the last century (and sporadic killings up until the 1950s). The sea lions are very tolerant of humans, and you can stroll quietly among them on tours with a park ranger.

Farther to the west along the south coast are the pretty beach at **Vivonne Bay,** the pure white dunes known as **Little Sahara,** and **Kelly Hill Conservation Park,** which has dunes and scrub

VISITING K.I.'S NATIONAL PARKS

An Island Parks Pass ($A20/U.S. $10) is required for entry to the national parks on the island. It covers camping fees and entitles you to "free" National Parks & Wildlife Service tours. The pass can be purchased only on the island, through any of the seven National Parks & Wildlife Service offices. The main office (37 Dauncy St., Kingscote, tel (08) 8553 2381) can also provide information on wildlife and hiking trails. ■

underlaid by limestone caves. The caves were discovered in the 1880s by a stockman named Kelsey and his horse Kelly, which tumbled into them through a sinkhole. The National Parks and Wildlife Service runs caving tours.

Flinders Chase National Park in the west has a dramatic rocky coastline, picturesque old lighthouses, and eucalyptus forests filled with wildlife. The park headquarters is at Rocky River Homestead. On the northwestern corner of the island, about 65 miles (105 km) west of Kingscote on the island's main highway, is the square **Cape Borda Lighthouse,** built in 1858. The wild southwestern corner has the elegant **Cape de Couedic Lighthouse,** built along a line of sheer cliffs in 1906. ■

Kangaroo Island's koalas

You are more likely to see a koala in the wild on Kangaroo Island than anywhere else. The island's resident koala population nudges 3,000 (nearly the same as the humans). The fact that the island has so many of these cuddly-looking marsupials is both a tribute to its qualities and a cautionary tale about well-meaning conservation.

Koalas are not native to the island. They were brought here in 1923, when it was obvious the species was in trouble. On the mainland, rapidly growing suburbs were gobbling up their habitat, and in Queensland they were being hunted as pests. More than three million koalas were shot in the decade following World War I, before they were finally protected in 1927. The seagirt wildlife stronghold of Kangaroo Island seemed a perfect place to relocate a few, and a group of 18 were released in Flinders Chase National Park.

The island was perfect for koalas because it had no disease, no predators such as dingoes, and a seemingly unlimited supply of manna gums—one of their favorite foods. The operative word is "seemingly." By 1996 the koala population had boomed out of control, stripping the stately century-old gum trees along the rivers and creating a potential environmental

nightmare. The suggestion that 2,000 or so koalas would have to be shot provoked an international uproar. On the other hand, letting them denude the forests until they starved seemed little better.

Relocation was not an easy option. Koalas are exceptionally finicky eaters. Their delicate stomachs can digest the leaves of only about a dozen of the 600-plus species of eucalyptuses. Those grow on well-watered soils along the coast—prime real estate for humans. Any small fragments of koala habitat that were left on the mainland were already fully populated by koalas. Instead, it was decided to use fertility controls to keep the population in check. The dominant males got vasectomies, and the females got hormone treatments. Some koalas were relocated to suitable homes. In three years the koala population has shrunk to a more manageable 3,000.

One of the best places to see koalas is the Flinders Chase National Park, or along the Cygnet River in the eastern half of the island. They can be a little difficult to spot, nestled in the forks of gum trees, because their gray coats meld perfectly with the gray of the bark. Look for an irregular bump when you run your eyes over a likely gum, and slowly a koala will appear. ■

Opposite: Comfortably perched in a fork of a gum tree, this koala seems oblivious of his admiring public.

Victor Harbor & Goolwa

Victor Harbor
📍 251 B1
Visitor information
✉ 10 Railway Terrace
☎ (08) 8552 5738

Goolwa
📍 251 B1
Visitor information & Signal Point River Murray Interpretive Centre
✉ Waterfront
☎ (08) 8555 1144

The paddle steamer *Mundoo* takes visitors up the Murray River from Goolwa.

THE 1870s WERE THE GLORY DAYS OF THE MURRAY RIVER, when steamboat traffic was at its height and civic boosters hoped that settlements such as Goolwa, Victor Harbor, and Port Elliott, near the river mouth, would one day rival New Orleans. Wool and grain from as far afield as Queensland would be floated down the river to these ports, where clipper ships could whisk them off to market in London.

Unfortunately, the exposed coastline was treacherous to shipping and the fickle Murray River had a habit of silting up at the mouth. Visions of an antipodean New Orleans faded completely in 1878 when a rail spur linked the river town of Morgan, about 150 miles (240 km) upstream, with the deepwater harbor at Port Adelaide. The beachside villages found their métier instead as vacation resorts. A century later these classic beach towns, about 60 miles (96 km) south of Adelaide, are still the weekend getaway of choice among South Australians.

VICTOR HARBOR

This is the biggest town on the Fleurieu Peninsula, and a weekend destination for thousands of Adelaideans. Although Victor Harbor is only 50 miles (80 km) south of the city, it is generally about 10°F (5.5°C) cooler. The drive from Adelaide, along Main South Road and Victor Harbor Road, takes you through the **McLaren Vale** wine country (see p. 264)—another great excuse to go.

Victor Harbor sits on pretty **Encounter Bay,** where, in 1802, English navigator Matthew Flinders

Scores of pelicans congregate on the Coorong's windswept dunes near the mouth of the Murray River.

met his French counterpart Nicholas Baudin while both were exploring the South Australian coast. The town was founded in 1837 as a whaling station, and today the **South Australian Whale Centre** (*Railway Terrace*) is the place to learn about southern right whales (an endangered species) and whaling. Better still, come to Victor Harbor between June and October and see these magnificent leviathans. No longer hunted, they come into Encounter Bay on their annual migration and can be observed from the bluffs overlooking the bay. A large colony of fairy penguins lives on nearby Granite Island. You can walk out there along the causeway—a pleasant stroll—or take one of the trams pulled by Clydesdale horses.

GOOLWA

With its beaches and rich beds of cockles, Goolwa became popular with homesick English migrants who could come down to gather cockles—just as they did on summer holidays back in the old country, in Brighton or Blackpool. The train bringing visitors came to be called the Cockle Train in the official railroad timetable. A restored

version of the old steam-powered train still runs between Goolwa and Victor Harbor on weekends and public holidays.

The town has a strong nautical feel. Beams from the wreck of the *Mozambique* hold up the bar in the **Goolwa Hotel** (*30 Cadell St.*), and restored 19th-century steamboats do tours of the lower lengths of the Murray River. The **Signal Point River Murray Interpretive Centre** (see p. 274), by the waterfront, has a museum covering Murray River ecology, the 19th-century river trade, and the history of the Ngarrinjeri Aborigines, who have gathered cockles on these beaches for more than 10,000 years. Steamboat cruises go from the wharf in front of the museum, as does the free ferry to **Hindmarsh Island,** a windswept island that almost plugs the Murray's mouth.

Goolwa is a good base for exploring the haunting sliver of sand dunes and coastal lagoons known as the **Coorong,** which extends 100 miles (160 km) along South Australia's southeast coast. Home to more than 240 species of birds, it was the setting of the 1976 film *Storm Boy,* about an Aborigine who befriends a pelican. ■

Lower Murray River

THE MURRAY RIVER IS THE LONGEST AND GRANDEST RIVER on the continent, and it is the only one that is navigable. It stretches 1,170 miles (1,883 km) from its beginnings in the Victorian high country to South Australia's windswept coastline. Like the child last in line for the bath, South Australia gets only the bottom 400 miles (640 km) of the river, but it gets the best scenery. The river here winds through sandstone gorges, past lagoons teeming with bird life, and along riverbanks lined with stately Murray River gums.

Mannum

🗺 251 C2

Visitor information

✉ Arnold Park, off Randell St.

☎ (08) 8569 1303

By Mississippi or Amazon standards, the Murray is a trickle—barely a couple of hundred yards wide. But on a continent as dry and dusty as Australia, it is life itself, accounting for more than half of the nation's fruit, vegetables, wine, meats, grains, cotton, and wool. In fact, you are likely to get your first experience of the Murray long before you see it. The quirky tasting drinking water for most of South Australia comes from the river.

South Australia was where the Mark Twain-style story of the Murray's steamboats began. In 1853, a flour miller named William Randell put a crude steamboat, the *Mary Ann,* on the water near the river town of Mannum. Randell had never even seen a steamboat before, but he could grasp the potential profit in being able to get his flour close to the Victorian goldfields, several hundred miles upstream. The *Mary Ann*'s boiler had been fashioned by the local blacksmith out of quarter-inch iron, and it swelled like a football once pressure built up, causing the ship's engineer to run in terror. But these were robust times, and Randell simply bound the dodgy boiler with chain and kept on steaming up the river. A few days later the *Mary Ann* was passed by a steamboat captained by a man named Cadell. The race was on. By the 1870s more than 250

steamboats were on the river, and Randell's hometown of **Mannum** was one of the nation's busiest inland ports, handling more than 20,000 bales of wool a year.

These days this quiet holiday town is a perfect place from which to get to know the river. It is an easy drive from Adelaide, following the Southeast Freeway 50 miles (80 km) to the old river port of **Murray Bridge** and then going 15 miles

(24 km) north on the Mannum Road. A restored 1897 steamboat, the **Marion,** has been converted to a floating museum next to the visitor center. The grand Mississippi-style stern-wheeler **Murray River Princess** ties up here between cruises *(Captain Cook Cruises, tel 1-800 221 080, toll free).* It does weekend and five-day sight-seeing cruises along the river, running upstream through the sandstone gorges near Swan Reach. Shorter excursions can be had on the **M.V. Lady Mannum** *(Tel 0427 813 576).* Another restored old steamer, the **Proud Mary,** offers three- and five-day cruises *(Tel (08) 8231 9472)* out of Murray Bridge. It is smaller and more intimate, and serves bush tucker, such as kangaroo. Both boats have air-conditioned cabins—an important consideration in summer when temperatures often top the century mark.

Murray Bridge is also home to the **Monarto Zoological Park** *(Princes Hwy., tel (08) 8534 4100),* a popular 2,500-acre (1,012 ha) big-game preserve.

The Murray is still a rural river, and the big steamboats simply tie up at a sandbar for the night. The stars are dazzling, and you wake up in the morning to a cacophony of galahs, cockatoos, and kookaburras. The crowds tend to be very Australian—the Murray River is a quintessentially Australian holiday spot.

If you want more independence, consider renting a houseboat. You'll get the same dramatic gorges, stars, and noisy bird life, but you'll have even more of a Huck Finn sense of freedom. The houseboats are comfortable but fairly spartan—a bit like a floating camper van—with a kitchen, bunks, and a living room. Naturally, because this is Australia, most include a barbecue. ∎

RENTING A HOUSEBOAT

Houseboats can be rented at Murray Bridge, Mannum, and a number of villages along the river. No license or special training is required, and river charts are provided. Information about rentals on the Murray can be obtained from visitor centers, or the Houseboat Hirer's Association *(Tel (08) 8395 0999).* ∎

A houseboat follows the Murray River around a bend near the village of Nildottie.

Flinders Ranges National Park

THE FLINDERS RANGES MAKE ONE OF THE MOST MAJESTIC national parks in Australia—an ancient folded landscape of craggy mountains and deep gorges, tinted purple and red in the clear desert light, and carpeted by wildflowers after the spring rains. With its vibrant hues, rich desert vegetation, and superb hiking trails, this spectacular Outback wilderness has long been a favorite haunt of hikers, photographers, and painters.

Aboriginal artists and artisans have been coming into this rocky fastness for thousands of years, to collect its rich ochers and workable stones. Matthew Flinders was the first European to see these mountains, when he sailed 200 miles (320 km) up Spencer Gulf in 1802. Within 40 years the first graziers were staking claims in the southern portion of the ranges and by the 1870s farm towns and wheat fields could be found deep in the heart of the mountains. The newcomers hadn't reckoned on the fickleness of South Australia's arid Outback, however, where a few seasons of gentle rains might be followed by a decade of implacable drought. Today the ranges are dotted with crumbling ruins of stone farmhouses and ghost towns.

The Flinders Ranges are one of those all-too-rare instances in Australia where dramatic Outback landscapes can be found a convenient distance from a capital city. A four-hour drive north of Adelaide on the Princes Highway will bring you to **Port Augusta.** Six miles (9.7 km) before the town a marked turn-off on your right leads 25 miles (40 km) to Quorn and the solitary highway that leads another 70 miles (113 km) through Hawker and into the heart of **Flinders Ranges National Park.** A far more scenic (and not much longer) option is to drive north out of

Adelaide on Main North Road, through the beautiful wine country around **Clare,** scenic wheat fields and historic towns such as **Mintaro, Melrose,** and **Laura.** A further 180 miles (290 km) will bring you to Wilmington, where a sign directs you to Quorn and the Flinders Ranges. **Quorn** itself is an interesting Outback town with a frontier history, and popular with vintage railroad buffs who come here to ride the Pichi Richi railroad *(Tel (08) 8276 6232).* This restored train makes the 20-mile (32 km) run from the town to Pichi Richi Pass. Because of fire danger in this tinder-dry part of the world, it operates only in the cooler, wetter months *(March–Nov.).*

The best known feature of the Flinders Ranges is **Wilpena Pound,** a vast amphitheater of red quartzite, purple shale, and cliffs that was formed by a dramatic upheaval of the Earth's crust about 450 million years ago. A quirk in the local climate gives the interior of Wilpena Pound considerably more rainfall than the surrounding desert. The floor of this lost world is covered with grasslands, native cypresses, casuarina trees, red gums, and, between September and November, a kaleidoscope of wildflowers in red, pink, mauve, yellow, and white. The pound is home to large numbers of wallabies, red kangaroos, and emus as well as

Flinders Ranges visitor information center

✉ 3 Seventh St., Quorn

☎ (08) 8648 6419

🕑 Closed weekends

huge flocks of rosellas, parrots, and galahs.

In the town of **Wilpena** is the Wilpena Pound Motel *(Tel (08) 8648 0004)* as well as a store and a campsite. The National Parks and Wildlife Service visitor center has information on the walking tracks inside Wilpena Pound itself.

Wilpena Pound is ringed by cliffs and is accessible only by foot, through a narrow gorge at Sliding Rock. Hikes in the pound can be challenging. The best known trail here (or in South Australia, for that matter) is the **Heysen Trail** (see p. 261).The most spectacular are the two steep trails that lead to the summit of **St. Mary's Peak** which, at 3,822 feet (1,165 m), is the highest point in Wilpena Pound. Other trails climb up **Mount**

Ohlssen Bagge and **Wangara Lookout.** Spring is by far the best time to do any hiking up here. In summer the temperatures are scorching, with the bare rocks only magnifying the desert heat. No matter what time of year, you should bring a hat, sunscreen, and carry plenty of water. Horseback-riding treks can be booked through the Wilpena Pound Motel, which also handles reservations for scenic flights over the ranges.

Not surprisingly the Flinders Ranges were significant to the Adnyamathanha ("hill people") who lived here before Europeans arrived, and the dramatic rock for-mations inspired some Dreamtime legends. There are rock-art galleries at **Arkaroo** and **Sacred Canyon,** both a short drive from Wilpena. ■

Eucalyptuses can often survive bush fires that would kill most other trees.

Flinders Ranges National Park
🅰 251 C4
Visitor information
✉ Wilpena
☎ (08) 8648 0048

Coober Pedy

THE APOCALYPTIC LANDSCAPE AROUND COOBER PEDY looks like the work of a disturbed mind, especially when you come upon it at dusk after a long drive across the desert. For miles in every direction the earth is covered by the sharp conical piles of clayish soil left by thousands of miners in their quest for opals. Australia produces 95 percent of the entire world's opals, and Coober Pedy is its richest field. The settlement's name comes from the corruption of a local Aboriginal phrase Kupa Piti, which means "white fellows in a hole."

Opal was discovered here in 1915 by travelers looking for water. Soon this remote wasteland became a magnet for fortune seekers, adventurers, and drifters from around the globe. It still is. Reputedly, about 40 languages are spoken in this double-tough mining town, but little is actually said. Locals tend to be gruff and tight-lipped. Exactly how much opal is mined here is a matter of great speculation, particularly by the Australian Tax Office, because lucrative finds are kept as secret as humanly possible. (One clue: seeing a stream of water leaking out of a garage where a lucky prospector is washing some rich earth.)

The town is located about 520 miles (850 km) north of Adelaide on the Stuart Highway. Although nobody would ever call this dusty, junk-strewn place charming, it has a certain weird fascination. The movie *Mad Max III* was filmed here. It is also a rare stopover on the long, empty drive along the Stuart Highway to the Northern Territory. There are shops where you can buy opals, craft galleries selling pottery made out of the local clay, motels, and organized tours of mines.

Buying opals

Australia's fiery opals are lovely and make wonderful souvenirs, but buying them in Coober Pedy or city jewelry shops requires care. You need to know what you are looking for.

Opal is made of delicate layers of silica that refract light like a prism and give the stone its fiery sparkle. Like other gems, opals are valued by their size, the strength and brilliance of their color, and their clarity. Flaws or cracks in a stone detract from its value. The brighter and clearer the stone, the higher the value.

Black and crystal opals are the rarest and most valuable, followed by semiblack opals. Milky opals, although still pretty, are the least valuable because they lack that special dark fire.

Shape is also very important. There are three categories of opal. Cabochon is a solid, domed piece of opal that is the most valuable shape. A less valuable "doublet" is a thin wafer of opal against a dark background, while a "triplet" has a quartz lens as well and is the least expensive. Unless you know opals very well, avoid deals with any kippered old characters you might meet down at the pub, however colorful such a transaction may seem. Stick to reputable dealers, shop around, and ask a lot of questions. ∎

Coober Pedy
🅰 251 B5
Visitor information
✉ Hutchinson St.
☎ (08) 8672 5298 or
1-800 637 076
(toll free)
🕐 Closed weekends

Summer temperatures here routinely hit 120°F (49°C). Many of Coober Pedy's residents escape the unrelenting heat by living underground in hand-dug caves. Far from being crude holes, these cave houses can be very stylish, with all the modern conveniences, and the temperature inside them stays at a constant 72°F (22°C). If you would like to visit some of these underground homes, the tourist office can arrange visits. For that matter, if you'd like a taste of cave living yourself, several motels in town are underground or offer underground rooms as options. Among them are **Radeka's Downunder Motel** *(Tel (08) 8672 5223)* and the ironically named **Desert View Underground Apartments** *(Tel (08) 8672 3330).*

If you are feeling lucky, have a go at fossicking (the Australian term for "prospecting"). There is no particular geological logic for where opal might be. Just sink a hole and hope for the best, or pick through the mullock heaps (spoil heaps) and look for flashes of color others have missed. If you want to dig, you must get a miner's permit *($A25, $13, from the Primary Industries & Resources Department, tel (08) 8672 5018)* and stake out a 60-square-yard (50 sq m) claim for yourself.

Be careful about walking in the opal fields because they are riddled with mine shafts. An area called the **Jeweler's Shop,** on the northeast side of town, has been set aside for visitors to poke around in, without danger of tumbling into an open mine shaft. ∎

Even the pub is underground at Coober Pedy.

Left: A handful of polished stones reveals some of the many opal colors.

The Ghan

THE GHAN RAILROAD RUNS 972 MILES (1,564 KM) FROM THE civilized skyline of Adelaide across the incredible harshness of the South Australian Outback, to the desert town of Alice Springs, in the heart of the continent's Red Centre.

Great Southern Railway

✉ 80 Williams St., 2nd Floor, Suite 206, Sydney

☎ (02) 9332 5133 Reservations: 13 22 32

The railroad was named after the Afghan camel drivers whose trains of camels (or single-humped dromedaries, to be precise) were Alice Springs' lifeline prior to the coming of the railway in 1929. The railway made the camels superfluous, and thousands of them were let loose in the desert, where their descendants still run wild today.

In the old days the Ghan was notorious for its unreliability. Its original course meandered through the outback to towns such as William Creek, Oodnadatta, and Finke. Unexpected downpours in the desert would wash away the tracks, stranding the train and its passengers. As a result, the route was altered and now sits firmly on high, dry ground. The typical journey time has been reduced from two days to a reliable 20 hours.

The train departs Adelaide's Keswick Train Station at 2 p.m. twice a week *(Mon. & Thurs.)* and

heads north through the wheat fields around Crystal Brook to the industrial city of **Port Augusta,** the gateway to the Outback. From here it rolls northwest, through the opal-mining town of **Coober Pedy** (see pp. 280–81), skirts the Simp-son and Great Victorian Deserts, and crosses the massive 15-span bridge over the **Finke River.** Although it is usually dry, this ancient river can become a raging torrent after heavy rains, which was one of the main reasons the train was delayed in the old days. The train pulls into **Alice Springs** (see pp. 196–99) at about 10 a.m. the next morning, and leaves Alice at 2 p.m. on Tuesdays and Fridays for the return trip to Adelaide.

The Ghan has first-class sleepers, holiday-class sleepers, and coach-class seats. First-class passengers have access to plush club cars, and dine in the Queen Adelaide Restaurant car. Holiday-class passengers dine in the Café Matilda, and coach-class passengers have a buffet car. The train also carries automobiles, so you can drive one way on the Stuart Highway (see pp. 284–88), and return by rail. There has been talk since 1911 that the line will one day extend to Darwin, and early in 2001, just 90 years after it was promised, the rail link to Darwin got the nod. The financing for the $A1.2 billion (U.S. $0.6 billion) project is sorted, and contracts have been awarded for the 1.2 million tons (1.4 million tonnes) of steel needed to build the line which developers hope to have in operation within three years. ∎

The sleek silver carriages of the Ghan rumble into Alice Springs after its 20-hour desert crossing.

Stuart Highway drive

The Stuart Highway runs through the outback from Port Augusta in South Australia to the Esplanade in Darwin—almost 1,700 miles (2,735 km) through the heart of the continent. It takes its name from the explorer John McDouall Stuart, who made an epic south-to-north crossing in 1861, and approximates his route and that of the Overland Telegraph Line, built in 1872. The highway rolls through the desolate saltbush country and glaring white salt pans of South Australia's deserts, into the opal-mining town of Coober Pedy, across the Red Centre to Alice Springs, and on through a lonely archipelago of Outback settlements in the Northern Territory.

The gas station, shop, café, and tourist office are all in one building in Outback settlements like Oodnadatta, which lies some 150 miles (240 km) off the Stuart Highway east of Marla.

PORT AUGUSTA TO ALICE SPRINGS

The paved, two-lane highway starts at **Port Augusta,** a truck-stop town (and also the start of the Eyre Highway, see pp. 242–48). It is a good road, and unless you are venturing off onto one of the lonely bush tracks, you need no special equipment beyond a few basic spares and extra water for yourself and the car.

When Port Augusta slips beneath your rearview mirror, you are alone with your thoughts and miles of saltbush until you reach the scruffy little settlement called **Pimba,** 110 lonely miles (177 km) later. A turnoff here leads to **Woomera,** once a top-secret rocket-testing base during the Cold War of the 1950s and '60s. The Heritage Centre *(Corner of Dewrang & Banool Aves., tel (08) 8673 7042)* has displays about Woomera's past and can arrange

tours of the still-active rocket range. If you stay on the road to Woomera, another 45 miles (72 km) will take you to the massive **Olympic Dam copper-uranium mine ❶.** For information about this giant mining facility, and to book a tour of it, contact the Olympic Dam Tours Office *(Tel (08) 8671 0788).*

- 🅰 Also see area map 251 C5
- ▶ Port Augusta
- 🔄 1,700 miles (2,735 km)
- ⏱ 7 days
- ▶ Darwin

NOT TO BE MISSED

- Coober Pedy
- Alice Springs
- Tennant Creek

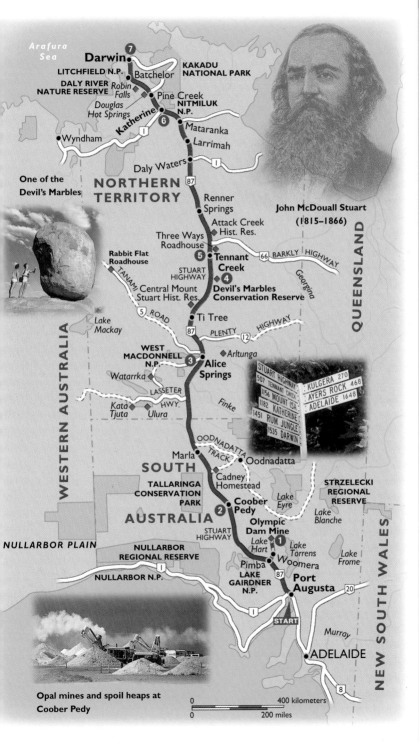

Arafura Sea

Darwin 7
LITCHFIELD N.P.
DALY RIVER
NATURE RESERVE
Robin Falls
Batchelor
KAKADU
NATIONAL PARK
Douglas Hot Springs
Pine Creek
NITMILUK
N.P.
Wyndham
Katherine 6
Mataranka
Larrimah
Daly Waters
87

One of the
Devil's Marbles

NORTHERN
TERRITORY

Renner
Springs
Attack Creek
Hist. Res.

Three Ways
Roadhouse 5
**Tennant
Creek**
66 BARKLY HIGHWAY
Georgina

Rabbit Flat
Roadhouse
TANAMI
Central Mount
Stuart Hist. Res.
STUART
HIGHWAY
4
Devil's Marbles
Conservation Reserve

5 ROAD
Lake Mackay
Ti Tree
87
PLENTY HIGHWAY 12

John McDouall Stuart
(1815–1866)

QUEENSLAND

WESTERN AUSTRALIA

WEST
MACDONNELL
N.P. 3
Arltunga
**Alice
Springs**
Watarrka
LASSETER HWY.
Kata Tjuta *Uluru*
Finke

STUART HIGHWAY
507 TENNANT CREEK
1156 MOUNT ISA
1182 KATHERINE
1451 RUM JUNGLE
1535 DARWIN

KULGERA 270
AYERS ROCK 468
ADELAIDE 1648

SOUTH

Marla
OODNADATTA
TRACK
Oodnadatta
Cadney
Homestead

TALLARINGA
CONSERVATION
PARK

**Coober
Pedy** 2

Lake Eyre

STRZELECKI
REGIONAL
RESERVE

Lake Blanche

AUSTRALIA

Olympic
Dam Mine 1

STUART
HIGHWAY
Lake Hart
Lake Torrens
Lake Frome

NULLARBOR PLAIN

NULLARBOR
REGIONAL RESERVE

Pimba
LAKE
GAIRDNER
N.P.
Woomera
87
**Port
Augusta**

NULLARBOR N.P.

NEW SOUTH WALES

20

START

Murray

ADELAIDE

8

Opal mines and spoil heaps at
Coober Pedy

0 ——— 400 kilometers
0 ——— 200 miles

Lake Gairdner National Park, a vast salt pan, sprawls off to the left as you drive north of Pimba. In recent years Lake Gairdner has become a venue for land-speed record attempts. More easily visited, however, is **Lake Hart,** a blinding white salt pan just off the highway to your right, about 30 miles (48 km) northwest of Woomera.

The rough and tough opal-mining town of **Coober Pedy ❷** (see pp. 280–81) appears on the horizon another 230 miles (370 km) up the highway, over a weirdly desolate landscape. Be particularly careful if you are driving this stretch of highway around dusk, because scores of kangaroos are about. Most people, whether they are going north or south on the highway, find Coober Pedy a convenient place to stop for the night. The town has plenty of good motels and some reasonably decent places to eat. (Outback Australia, as you'll quickly discover, is no gourmand's paradise. Anything more original than meat pies, sausage rolls, greasy chips, and spring rolls qualifies as haute cuisine.)

Coober Pedy is about 250 miles (400 km) from the Northern Territory border, with only the **Cadney Homestead** roadhouse and the tiny hamlet of **Marla** to break the scrubby monotony. The desert stretches of South Australia, it must be said, are the least interesting portions of the Stuart Highway. Marla has the dubious distinction of frequently being the hottest place in South Australia. At both Cadney Homestead and Marla you can take the rugged **Oodnadatta Track** into even more hostile—albeit scenic—Outback to the lonely bush town of **Oodnadatta.** Although a standard car in good condition can do this excursion during the winter months, it is a good idea to be well prepared, have some bush experience, and let responsible people know where you intend to go and when you plan to return. Many other tracks, leading to remote national parks such as **Lake Eyre** or the

St. Paul's underground church at Coober Pedy ministers to this remote Outback community.

Simpson Desert, are strictly for four-wheel-drive vehicles. Seek advice before venturing off the paved roads.

Fifty miles (80 km) after crossing the Northern Territory border, the Stuart Highway touches the Lasseter Highway, which heads 150 miles (240 km) west toward **Uluru** and **Kata Tjuta** (see pp. 202–207). This paved highway was named for the prospector Harold Lasseter, who supposedly found a fabulously rich gold reef out in the desert in 1897 but died trying to locate it again. The reef, if it indeed exists, has never been rediscovered, although not for want of trying. Also out this highway is the spectacular **Watarrka** (Kings Canyon, see p. 208).

Farther up the Stuart Highway, **Alice Springs** ❸ (see pp. 196–198) is an oasis

town in the heart of the dramatic MacDonnell Ranges. You are now in Australia's Red Centre, and are probably starting to feel as though you've come a long way. The Alice (as it is known) is an interesting town at the hub of a lot of Outback attractions and with scenic hiking trails nearby—and it is worth spending a few days here. If you want to return to Adelaide without driving back through South Australia's northern deserts, you can load your car onto the Ghan Train and ride back in style (see pp. 282–83).

The spherical boulders called the Devil's Marbles were thought by Aborigines to be the Rainbow Serpent's eggs.

ALICE SPRINGS TO DARWIN

The Stuart Highway continues another 950 mostly empty miles (1,529 km) north of Alice Springs to the end of the line in Darwin. From Alice Springs the highway rolls north across the reddish, stony immensity of the Northern Territory Outback, past the hamlet of **Ti Tree,** where Australia's first roadhouse was set up in the 1930s, and the **Central Mount Stuart Historical Reserve,** which marks the geographical center of Australia. Another 110 miles (177 km) brings you to the **Devil's Marbles Conservation Reserve** ❹. A campsite is here and you can walk among the eerily rounded boulders. Geologists say they are the weathered remnants of a 1.5 billion-year-old granite formation. Aborigines believe the boulders are the eggs of the Rainbow

Serpent. However you interpret them, they are a haunting spectacle, particularly in the dusk or early morning light.

Three hundred miles (482 km) north of Alice Springs is **Tennant Creek ❺**. It was the site of a lonely telegraph relay station in the 1870s, and in the 1930s it was the focus of Australia's last gold rush. One of the major workings was found by a dog named Peko. Another was discovered by a one-eyed prospector named Jack Noble and his blind partner William Weaber, and it went on to become Australia's biggest open-cut mine until it closed in 1985. The **Telegraph Station** is open for visits; so is the old **Tennant Creek Battery,** where gold-bearing ore was crushed and treated. Legend has it that Tennant Creek itself was settled when a wagon, loaded with beer, broke down here in 1933. The teamsters couldn't be bothered to fix it and built a pub on the spot. Look around. If a story like that about Tennant Creek isn't true, it ought to be.

Fifteen miles (24 km) farther north, at the **Three Ways Roadhouse,** the Barkly Highway runs east off the Stuart Highway across flat, spinifex-covered tablelands to the lonely Queensland border, about 280 miles (450 km) away. A further 25 miles (40 km) up the Stuart Highway, a sign marks the **Attack Creek Historical Reserve.** In 1860 the explorer John McDouall Stuart came here on his first attempt to cross the continent, but he was attacked by Aborigines ("tall, powerful fellows") who objected to his trespassing on their land.

The little settlement of **Renner Springs** is generally regarded as the point where the dry desert climate of the center yields to the seasonal wet–dry of the Top End (the north of the Northern Territory). Although scrubby, the bush becomes greener and taller as you continue north.

Daly Waters—another 150 miles (240 km) north—was a vital refueling stop for early aviators, such as Amy Johnson. During the 1930s Qantas flights refueled here, and passengers were given a meal at the **Daly Waters Pub** *(Tel (08) 8975 9927),* built in 1893 and said to be the oldest in the Northern Territory. It still serves good food and is filled with memorabilia from those early, seat-of-the-pants aviation days. The airfield (closed in

the 1970s) and a restored World War II hangar are a legacy of its days as a staging post for Allied fighters and bombers en route to Darwin and the Dutch East Indies.

Reminders of World War II become more frequent as you close in on Darwin. Signs point to abandoned bush airstrips or ammo dumps. The town of **Larrimah,** 60 miles (96 km) north of Daly Waters, was a major military post during World War II and the terminus of the North Australia Railway. This narrow-gauge line had been intended to link Darwin with Alice Springs, but it had not gotten beyond Larrimah when World War II broke out. The line was abandoned after Cyclone Tracy struck in 1974, and the tracks have been torn up. Little is here now but a friendly old pub and a plain but interesting museum. It covers the town's war years and the history of road trains in the Northern Territory.

Mataranka, 50 miles (80 km) to the north, has thermal springs in a pocket of rain forest about 5 miles (8 km) east of town. The film *We of the Never Never* (1982) was made near here. The hot springs are a relaxing soak but can be a little crowded. The **Mataranka Homestead Resort** *(Tel (08) 8975 4544)* has accommodations and a restaurant.

Katherine ❻ (see pp. 192–93) is the next town on the highway, and with a population of almost 10,000 it is easily the biggest metropolis you've seen since Alice Springs. The big attraction is **Nitmiluk National Park** (see pp. 192–93).

The last leg of the Stuart Highway—the 200 miles (320 km) to Darwin—crosses rolling bushland. At the old gold-mining town of Pine Creek, you can take a paved road into the heart of **Kakadu National Park** (see pp. 186–89). Ahead, turnoffs lead to scenic sites such as **Douglas Hot Springs,** the beautiful **Robin Falls,** and the **Daly River Nature Reserve.** Farther north, **Adelaide River** was a major military post during World War II, and a large cemetery commemorates those killed in air raids. The Batchelor turnoff brings you to **Litchfield National Park** (see pp. 190–91). Keep going and you'll notice the houses and buildings are crowding closer together. Suddenly you are at the end of the line: **Darwin's ❼** palm-fringed Esplanade and the Timor Sea (see pp. 182–85). ■

S mall, pretty, and prosperous, Victoria was built on the wealth of the 1850s gold rushes. If it is Australia's most industrialized state, it is also its most diverse, with old river ports, vineyards, rain forests, a beautiful coast, and alpine highlands.

Victoria

Door detail, Melbourne
Cricket Ground

Victoria

VICTORIA IS THE SMALLEST AND GREENEST OF AUSTRALIA'S STATES AND the only one without much "real" Outback. A history of gentlemanly farming and of vast wealth from the 19th century's fabulous gold rushes have given the state, and especially its elegant capital Melbourne, a patrician, old-money air. The richest gold diggings were in Ballarat, Castlemaine, and Bendigo—all discovered within a few weeks of each other in 1851—but dozens of rich strikes were made around the state.

The 19th century's heady combination of boomtime wealth and civic pride gave Victoria magnificent public architecture and elegant colonial mansions. It is not unusual in this state to drive into a farm town and see an Italianate city hall as grand as a European opera house, probably set among ornamental palms and landscaped gardens. When you see one of these grand rural palaces, just start looking for the historical marker that tells the story of the local gold rush.

No large-scale gold mining goes on here now. Victoria today is a combination of breadbasket and industrial heartland, producing about a third of Australia's gross domestic product. The Murray

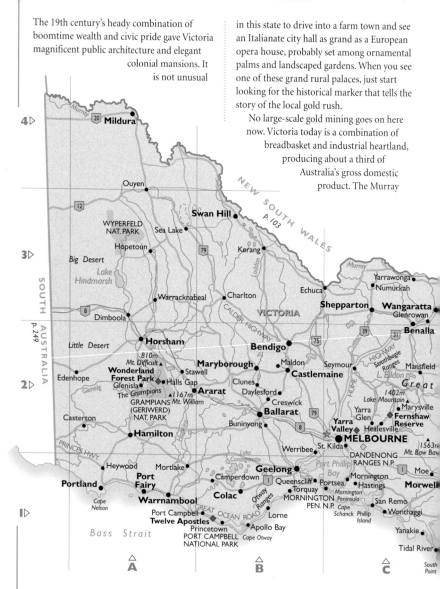

River forms its border with New South Wales and irrigates vineyards, market gardens, and vast orchards. Victoria is known as the Garden State. Shepparton, in the north, is a sort of Cannery Row. The dry country in the west is golden with wheat and has some of Australia's best wool-producing regions. The state is dotted with dairies and cheese factories. The dense forests in Gippsland feed a timber industry, coal is mined in the La Trobe Valley, and beneath the waters of Bass Strait lurk Australia's largest (by far) oil fields.

Victoria is Australia's smokestack industry hub, with car-manufacturing factories, chemical plants, and aluminum smelters. Port Melbourne is the world's fifth busiest waterfront. Headquarters to Australia's biggest mining houses, Melbourne was for decades the nation's financial and banking center, a role it has partly conceded to Sydney.

For such a small state, Victoria has an astonishing variety of scenery, from temperate rain forests along the eastern coast to dusty Outback scrub in the north to the sleek cafés of Melbourne's inner city suburbs. Australia's best skiing is on the powdery slopes of the Victorian Alps, and some of its finest surf can

Melbourne trams thread their way between skyscrapers and historic buildings, making getting around the city easy.

be found on the internationally famous Bells Beach. The Great Ocean Road, just west of Melbourne, is a fabulous coastal drive.

Melbourne itself—Australia's most European capital—has theaters, museums, and a sweeping range of cultures and cuisines. Unlike the rest of Australia, where interesting sights tend to be separated by hundreds of miles of dreary scrub, Victoria's attractions form a small neat package. Everything is an easy scenic drive from Melbourne, on excellent paved roads. ∎

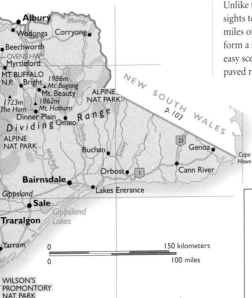

Area of map detail

Melbourne

Melbourne
290 C2

**Victorian Tourism
Commission
Visitor Inform-
ation Centre**
www.tourism.vic.gov.au
Town Hall,
Swanston St.
13 28 42

MELBOURNE LIKES TO AFFECT A BOSTONIAN AIR, WITH ITS Old World shadows, traditions, and sometimes chilly reserve. It matters here where you went to school and who your family is. This is a city of boulevards, parklands, and imposing churches and banks of the Victorian era. It calls itself the theater capital of Australia.

The elegant buildings along **Collins Street** form Melbourne's patrician soul. Here is where you'll find the headquarters of some of Australia's great mining houses and the stately **Melbourne Club.** The Southern Hemisphere's largest network of electric trams gives down-town a ringing-clanging feeling of old-fashioned efficiency.

Melbourne isn't stodgy, though it used to be. When Ava Gardner came here in 1959 to film *On the Beach*, she allegedly remarked that the movie was about the end of the world and Melbourne was the per-

fect place to film it, a crack that still rankles with Melburnians. That couldn't be said today. Melbourne is very much an international city, with café life and arts festivals. The trams are chic, and enhance the city. Sports are big. The city has nine major professional Australian Rules football clubs. It hosts the Australian Open tennis tournament, and the Melbourne Cup—Australia's greatest horse race.

Melbourne has a vibrant mix of ethnic communities—particularly Greek, Italian, and Asian—which give it bustling markets, restaurants, delicatessens, and bakeries. Just choosing a restaurant in Melbourne means sifting through a United Nations of culinary styles. There is even a restaurant tram giving evening sight-seeing tours around the city—a happy converging of several of Melbourne's strengths: excellent food, elegant architecture, and trams.

The city began in 1835 as a result of a dodgy land deal by two Tasmanian entrepreneurs, John Batman and John Pascoe Fawkner. They gave local Aborigines blankets, flour, axes, and trinkets in exchange for 500,000 acres (202,500 ha) of land around Port Phillip Bay. The unauthorized purchase annoyed the Colonial Office back in London, but they let it stand. Sixteen years later, fabulous goldfields were discovered around Ballarat, Bendigo, and Castlemaine, and the city's success was assured. Gold hunters flocked here—almost 2,000 a week at the boom's height—and by 1861 gold rush wealth had made Melbourne Australia's grandest city.

These days it comes a close second to arch rival Sydney as the nation's financial capital, and, with 3.3 million residents, Melbourne is a bit smaller. But Melburnians still claim their city is the nation's cultural capital and the better place to live. They have powerful voices to support them. The Washington, D.C.-based Population Crisis Committee ranked Melbourne as the world's most livable city in a 1991 survey.

Despite Sydneysiders' libel that Melbourne's climate is drizzly and bleak, the Victorian capital actually gets less rain than Sydney. In recent years, Melbourne has challenged its brash New South Wales rival on the glamour front as well, snaring such international events as the Australian Formula One Grand Prix and building Australia's largest and most glittering casino.

Colonial Tramcar Restaurant
☎ (03) 9696 4000

Formula One Grand Prix Information
www.grandprix.com.au
☎ (03) 9258 7100

A Vietnamese food stall brightens a sidewalk at one of Melbourne's multicultural festivals.

Left: Across the Yarra River from Melbourne's business district lie museums, concert halls, and historic houses, as well as gardens and sports grounds.

Visitor information booths

✉ Bourke Street Mall & City Sq.

Melbourne Observation Deck

✉ Rialto Towers, Collins St.
☎ (03) 9629 8222
$ $$

Queen Victoria Market

✉ Victoria St., West Melbourne
🕐 Closed Mon. & Wed.

Royal Melbourne Zoological Gardens

✉ Elliott Ave., Parkville
☎ (03) 9285 9300
$ $$$

MELBOURNE SIGHTS

It is easy to get around Melbourne on its network of buses, trains, and trams. The accommodating Victorian government runs a free tram that loops through the downtown core. The free tram is cream and burgundy. Regular trams are green and gold.

Melbourne's Central Business District—the CBD in local slang—is a pleasing mix of futuristic skyscrapers and Victorian-era sandstone facades. The city is set out on a grid and you need only remember a few key streets. Excellent information booths can help you plan your explorations.

The city's high point is the glittering **Rialto Towers,** a 1980s architectural marvel whose reflective glass sides subtly change hue as the sun marches across the sky. The observation deck on the 55th floor gives a breathtaking view of the city. Nearby, the former **Commercial Bank of Australia** building (333 Collins St.), with its high-domed banking chamber and massive vestibule, gives you an idea of the wealth that passed through this city in the glory days of the 19th-century gold rush and land boom. Bourke and Collins Streets are the main shopping thoroughfares, although La Trobe Street's glossy **Melbourne Central Mall—**anchored by the upscale Japanese department store, Daimaru—is shifting the focus somewhat.

Queen Victoria Market, which opened in the 1870s, is a Melbourne institution and an exciting place to buy ingredients for a gourmet picnic. You will find fresh produce just off the farm, interesting cheeses, sausages, breads, meats, fish, nuts, and cakes. Shopping here is never dull or quiet. A multicultural mix of shopkeepers and stand holders shout, cajole, and banter to move their goods. If you get there late on Saturday afternoon, when they must either sell their produce or throw it away, you have a lot of latitude for bargaining. This cornucopia is on the north side of the city, only a few minutes by tram along Elizabeth Street from the city center, although it's almost as easy to walk. The market is in a series of decorative old iron sheds, with the cheeses, meats, small goods, and fish spread out in the delicatessen hall. This is one of Melbourne's landmark buildings, distinctive for the livestock frieze above its portal. Tours of the market are available (Tel (03) 9320 5822).

Once you've bought your picnic ingredients—and you can even buy well-made baskets here—all you need is a convenient and elegantly landscaped park. A couple of good options are very close by. One is **Carlton Gardens** (Victoria St.), the grounds of the vast, high-domed Exhibition Building built for the Great Exhibition of 1880. Another is the zoo, the **Royal Melbourne Zoological Gardens,** established in 1862 and one of the oldest in the world, which is landscaped better than many cities' botanic gardens. It is about 2 miles (3 km) north of the market, in Royal Park, and you can reach it by tram No. 55 or 56 from William Street. The Australian fauna enclosure has a lake and bushland landscaping, where you walk among kangaroos and emus. The platypus house gives perhaps the best chance you'll have of seeing one of these elusive creatures, and the steamy tropical butterfly house is a delight. On certain summer weekend evenings there are free jazz concerts, and the picnicker-friendly zoo even has a hamper-check, where you can leave your picnic basket while you stroll among the exhibits before you take it in to the concert.

The **Crown Casino complex,** sprawled along the south bank of the Yarra River, has been a talking point among Melburnians since it opened with a star-studded extravaganza in 1997. It is Australia's largest casino, dripping with the sort of vulgar, overblown, glittering opulence you'd expect from Las Vegas or Australia's Gold Coast. This vast, multibillion-dollar development includes restaurants, bars, luxury boutiques, flashy nightclubs, and a thousand-room hotel—also Australia's largest. It is unlike anything Melbourne has ever seen, and even to a newcomer seems as out of place in this patrician city as a cocktail onion on a meringue. Nevertheless, if you are into Vegas-style gambling and entertainment, this is the place.

The Melbourne Cricket Ground is in **Yarra Park** and the National Tennis Centre is in **Melbourne Park,** both on the east side of the city. Melbourne's warren of inner suburbs is notably diverse. Brunswick Street, in **Fitzroy,** is one of the city's seedier spots, but with its bohemian cafés, alternative bookstores, and grunge chic, is also one of most interesting places to have a leisurely cappuccino and to people-watch on a Sunday afternoon. (The streets are dead quiet any earlier; they get out of bed at the crack of noon here.)

Victoria Street in **Richmond** could pass for a back street in Hanoi, with its bewildering jumble of Vietnamese apothecaries, family-run grocery shops, fruit stalls, and carcasses hanging in butcher-shop windows. Signs are in Vietnamese and the streets are lined with scores of cramped eateries. Yet just a few blocks away, on Swan Street, everything is Greek. Lygon Street, in **Carlton,** is Melbourne's Little Italy, full of Italian restaurants, pizzerias, and gelaterias.

On the south side, **Prahran** is an upscale version of Fitzroy, its boulevards lined with jazzy-cool bistros, antique shops, and funky boutiques. Even farther south, the bayside suburb of **St. Kilda** (see p. 302) has a profusion of bakeries along Acland Street, in addition to a breezy foreshore promenade.

In general, the Yarra River forms the social divide in Melbourne. Real estate southeast of the river tends to be richer, greener, and hillier. **South Yarra** and **Toorak** are Melbourne's wealthiest and most exclusive enclaves, with leafy streets and luxurious mansions tucked away behind high walls. Land northwest of the Yarra is flat and dry, and it is largely filled with industry, airports, and a mass of blue-collar suburbs. ∎

Picnickers beside the Yarra River in the Royal Botanic Gardens

Crown Casino
www.crownltd.com.au
✉ Southbank
☎ (03) 9292 8888 or 1-800 818 088 (toll free)
🕐 Open 24 hours

MELBOURNE WALKS

CENTRAL MELBOURNE

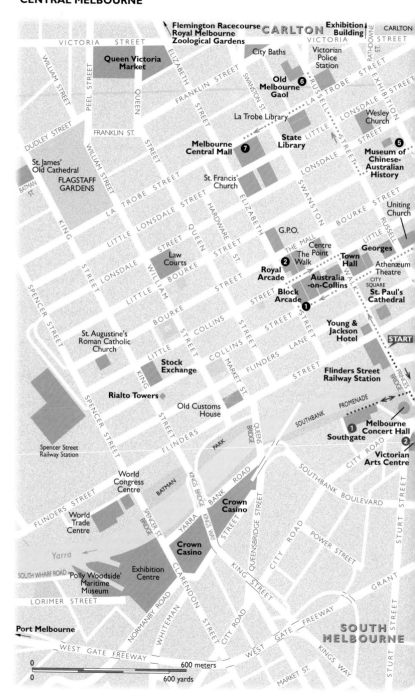

Flemington Racecourse
Royal Melbourne
Zoological Gardens

CARLTON

Exhibition
Building

CARLTON

VICTORIA STREET

VICTORIA

RATHDOWNE ST.

EXHIBITION STREET

Queen Victoria
Market

City Baths

Victorian
Police
Station

WILLIAM STREET

PEEL STREET

QUEEN STREET

ELIZABETH STREET

FRANKLIN STREET

SWANSTON ST.

Old
Melbourne
Gaol ❻

RUSSELL STREET

LA TROBE ST.

LONSDALE STREET

DUDLEY STREET

FRANKLIN ST.

La Trobe Library

LITTLE LONSDALE

Wesley
Church

St. James'
Old Cathedral

FLAGSTAFF
GARDENS

BATMAN ST.

LA TROBE STREET

Melbourne
Central Mall ❼

State
Library

Museum of
Chinese-
Australian
History ❺

KING STREET

LITTLE LONSDALE STREET

WILLIAM STREET

QUEEN STREET

St. Francis'
Church

ELIZABETH STREET

SWANSTON STREET

LONSDALE

BOURKE STREET

Uniting
Church

SPENCER STREET

LONSDALE STREET

Law
Courts

LITTLE BOURKE

G.P.O.

THE MALL

Centre
Point

The
Point
Walk

Town
Hall

LITTLE RUSSELL

Georges

Athenæum
Theatre

Royal ❷
Arcade

Australia
-on-Collins

CITY
SQUARE

St. Paul's
Cathedral

St. Augustine's
Roman Catholic
Church

LITTLE

BOURKE STREET

Block
Arcade ❶

QUEEN STREET

COLLINS STREET

Young &
Jackson
Hotel

START

Stock
Exchange

KING STREET

COLLINS STREET

MARKET ST.

FLINDERS LANE

FLINDERS STREET

Flinders Street
Railway Station

PRINCES BRIDGE

Rialto Towers

Old Customs
House

FLINDERS STREET

QUEENS BRIDGE

SOUTHBANK

PROMENADE

Melbourne
Concert Hall ❶

Southgate ❶

CITY ROAD

Victorian
Arts Centre ❷

STURT STREET

Spencer Street
Railway Station

World
Congress
Centre

BATMAN BRIDGE

KINGS BRIDGE

PARK STREET

BANK STREET

ROAD

SOUTHBANK BOULEVARD

World
Trade
Centre

FLINDERS STREET

SPENCER ST. BRIDGE

Crown
Casino

QUEENSBRIDGE STREET

KING STREET

CITY ROAD

POWER STREET

Yarra

Crown
Casino

YARRA

KINGS WAY

Exhibition
Centre

CLARENDON ROAD

SOUTH WHARF ROAD

'Polly Woodside'
Maritime
Museum

NORMANBY ROAD

WHITEMAN STREET

CITY ROAD

WEST GATE FREEWAY

GRANT STREET

LORIMER STREET

Port Melbourne

WEST GATE FREEWAY

KINGS WAY

SOUTH
MELBOURNE

STURT STREET

MARKET ST.

0 ——————————— 600 meters

0 ——————————— 600 yards

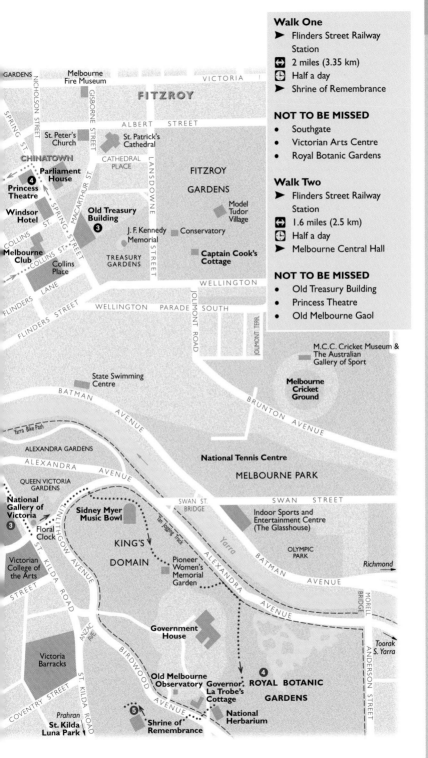

Walk One

► Flinders Street Railway
   Station

🚶 2 miles (3.35 km)

🕐 Half a day

► Shrine of Remembrance

NOT TO BE MISSED

- Southgate
- Victorian Arts Centre
- Royal Botanic Gardens

Walk Two

► Flinders Street Railway
   Station

🚶 1.6 miles (2.5 km)

🕐 Half a day

► Melbourne Central Hall

NOT TO BE MISSED

- Old Treasury Building
- Princess Theatre
- Old Melbourne Gaol

GARDENS

Melbourne
Fire Museum

VICTORIA

FITZROY

NICHOLSON STREET

SPRING ST.

GISBORNE STREET

ALBERT   STREET

St. Peter's
Church

St. Patrick's
Cathedral

CHINATOWN

CATHEDRAL
PLACE

FITZROY

LANSDOWNE   STREET

GARDENS

4 **Parliament
House**

MACARTHUR ST.

Model
Tudor
Village

4 **Princess
Theatre**

SPRING ST.

3 **Old Treasury
Building**

**Windsor
Hotel**

J. F. Kennedy
Memorial

Conservatory

COLLINS ST.

**Melbourne
Club**

COLLINS ST.

STREET

TREASURY
GARDENS

Collins
Place

■ **Captain Cook's
Cottage**

FLINDERS LANE

WELLINGTON

FLINDERS   STREET

WELLINGTON   PARADE   SOUTH

JOLIMONT ROAD

JOLIMONT TERR.

M.C.C. Cricket Museum &
The Australian
Gallery of Sport

State Swimming
Centre

**Melbourne
Cricket
Ground**

BATMAN   AVENUE

BRUNTON   AVENUE

Yarra Bike Path

ALEXANDRA GARDENS

ALEXANDRA   AVENUE

National Tennis Centre

QUEEN VICTORIA
GARDENS

MELBOURNE PARK

**National
Gallery of
Victoria**
3

LINLITHGOW AVENUE

SWAN ST.
BRIDGE

SWAN   STREET

**Sidney Myer
Music Bowl**

Tan Jogging Track

Indoor Sports and
Entertainment Centre
(The Glasshouse)

Floral
Clock

KING'S

Yarra

OLYMPIC
PARK

ALEXANDRA

Richmond

**Victorian
College of
the Arts**

ST. KILDA ROAD

DOMAIN

Pioneer
Women's
Memorial
Garden

BATMAN

AVENUE

MORELL BRIDGE

STREET

**Government
House**

ALEXANDRA   AVENUE

ANDERSON STREET

Toorak
S. Yarra

ANZAC AVE.

**Victoria
Barracks**

BIRDWOOD AVENUE

Old Melbourne
Observatory

Governor
La Trobe's
Cottage

4 **ROYAL BOTANIC
GARDENS**

ST. KILDA ROAD

COVENTRY STREET

Prahran

**St. Kilda
Luna Park**

5 **Shrine of
Remembrance**

**National
Herbarium**

Melbourne walks

Flinders Street Railway Station is a great place to start your walking tours of Melbourne. Set on the bank of the Yarra, this spectacular Edwardian railroad station, built of rich honey-colored sandstone in 1907, is the hub of Melbourne's commuter train system. Above its main portal is a row of clocks, and generally a knot of people is sitting expectantly on the steps below. "Under the clocks" has been a traditional meeting place for generations of Melburnians.

Those waiting steps look out on an interesting intersection. On the opposite corner is stately **St. Paul's Cathedral,** a neo-Gothic masterpiece completed in 1892 and the headquarters of Melbourne's Anglican church. Across the street is the **Young & Jackson Hotel,** one of the oldest pubs in Melbourne and the home of "Chloe," a full-length nude painted in Paris in 1875 by Jules Lefèbvre. In 1880 "Chloe" was sent to the Melbourne Exposition, where judges ruled the picture obscene. The drinkers in the Young & Jackson Hotel hadn't any

objections, and the painting has adorned the walls ever since. The pub is a bit rough, but it's worth going in to have a beer and see this Melbourne icon. She's on the second floor, in Chloe's Bar and Bistro.

There are two good walks from here (see map pp. 296–97). One takes you across the Yarra River to the Victorian Arts Centre, the cosmopolitan new Southgate shopping and café precinct, the botanic gardens, and some of Melbourne's oldest houses. The other walk explores "the Paris end" of town, as

Melbourne's Flinders Street Railway Station is still a focal point for the city, where bus, tram, and train interlink.

Melburnians are wont to call the elegant quarter at the eastern end of Collins Street.

WALK ONE: OVER THE YARRA

To take the first walk, simply follow St. Kilda Road across the Yarra on the ornate Princes Bridge. Ahead of you, the wide, tree-lined, and very European-looking St. Kilda Road runs to the massive Shrine of Remembrance, a brooding gray Romanesque war memorial that you can see more closely at the end of this walk.

Just across the bridge and on the right go down the steps to the sun-splashed promenade on the south bank of the Yarra. Just ahead is the classy riverbank development known as **Southgate** ❶. Perhaps the finest view of Melbourne's skyline in the city is from here. This spot was an industrial wasteland,

and its redevelopment in the early 1990s was the first real effort to make use of the Yarra River as a scenic feature in the city. It has been stunningly successful. Now it's the fashionable focus of town—for both visitors and locals—with five-star hotels, classy boutiques, bustling food courts, restaurants, and cafés catering to all tastes and budgets. An **aquarium** is also here. The enormous **Crown Casino complex** (see p. 295) is by the river on the far side of Southgate.

Return to Princes Bridge and on the right is the **Victorian Arts Centre** ❷, including the **Melbourne Concert Hall** and the **Theatre Building** (*St. Kilda Rd., tel (03) 9281 8000, tours Mon.–Fri. noon and 2:30 p.m., Sat. 10 a.m. and noon*), which is topped by a distinctive spire representing the pinnacle of the arts. Guided tours of the complex take about an hour. Also here is the **Performing Arts Museum,** a particularly entertaining shrine to pop culture, opera, television, and rock music *(Tel (03) 9281 8000).*

Next door is the **National Gallery of Victoria** ❸ (*closed for renovations; expected to reopen late 2003, tel (03) 9208 0222),* which has a superb collection of Australian art, rated higher by some than that of the National Gallery in Canberra. The collection ranges from early colonial watercolors to contemporary art, and includes paintings in the proudly nationalistic style that emerged in Melbourne in the late 1880s. Known as the Heidelberg school, after the little Yarra Valley village where they frequently took their easels, these plein-air painters were the first to paint the harsh Australian landscape as it really was, without trying to make traditionally "pretty" European scenes out of it.

A leading light of this school was Tom Roberts, whose 1890 painting "Shearing the Rams," capturing the camaraderie of the shearing shed, has become an Australian icon and is part of this gallery's collection. (The shed represented in the painting, by the way, was in Brocklesby, New South Wales, about 250 miles/400 km, northeast of Melbourne.) Alas, visitors who head out to Heidelberg, expecting the bush scenery seen in these early Australian paintings, will be in for a big disappointment: Heidelberg, which was the site of the Olympic village for the 1956 Olympic

Games, is now just another sprawling suburb.

Opposite the Victorian Arts Centre and the National Gallery is a wide swath of gardens: Alexandra Gardens, Queen Victoria Gardens, King's Domain, and the Royal Botanic Gardens. They meld together to form a delightful parkland flanked by the Yarra River. The **Royal Botanic Gardens** ❹ *(Birdwood Ave., South Yarra, tel (03) 9252 2429)*, near the southern end of this green space, may be the finest in Australia, and they are among the best in the world. Dotted with century-old oaks and ornamental lakes, they form a lush landscape that spreads over 100 acres (40 ha) by the river. These gardens were established in 1845, but it was the later 19th-century curators, Baron Sir Ferdinand von Mueller and then W.R. Guilfoyle, who created the present masterpiece.

You can explore the gardens on your own, run round them on a 3-mile (4.8 km) jogging track known as the Tan, or follow a self-guided walk. The elegant facade overlooking the gardens belongs to **Government House** *(for tours contact the National Trust, tel (03) 9654 4711)*, the residence of the British Queen's representative in Victoria. It is a copy of Queen Victoria's holiday palace on the Isle of Wight. The **Old Melbourne Observatory** *(Occasional openings, tel (03) 9669 9942)*, **Governor La Trobe's Cottage** *(for tours contact the National Trust, tel (03) 9654 4711)*, and the **National Herbarium** are clustered near the southern end of the Botanic Gardens. La Trobe's Cottage is a pre-fabricated dwelling sent out from England in 1840 to serve as the residence for the colony's first governor. The humble cottage is plainly furnished in period style, together with some of La Trobe's personal belongings.

A hundred yards west of La Trobe's Cottage, near St. Kilda Road, is the **Shrine of Remembrance** ❺. It was built in 1934 to honor the fallen of World War I. Its eternal flame is now also a tribute to the dead of World War II, Korea, Vietnam, Malaya and Borneo, and the Gulf War. It was positioned and designed so that a sunbeam passes over the inner sanctum at 11 a.m. on November 11 —the moment the armistice was signed in 1918 to end World War I. (Catch a tram on St. Kilda Road back to Flinders Street Station.)

WALK TWO: MELBOURNE'S PARIS END

This inner city stroll also begins beneath the clocks at Flinders Street Station. Cross Flinders Street and follow Swanston Walk into the heart of downtown. A few years ago Swanston Street was, in theory, closed to traffic to form a pedestrian mall, but taxis, buses, delivery vehicles, and 29.5-ton (30 tonne) trams are still allowed to use it, so you're safest on the sidewalks. A left turn and a short stroll down Collins Street takes you to the modernistic **Australia-on-Collins** shopping mall, and the elegant **Block Arcade** ❶, built with gold rush wealth in the 1880s and exquisitely restored in 1988. It has mosaic floors, an ornamental domed roof, and small shops. The **Hopetoun Tea Rooms** here also date from Victorian-era Melbourne. Nearby, the **Royal Arcade** ❷ on Little Collins Street was built in 1869. It is guarded by statues of the mythical giants Gog and Magog.

Take Little Collins Street back to Swanston Walk and go right for one block to continue along Collins Street, then go up a gentle hill to the grand **Old Treasury Building** ❸ on the far side of Spring Street. It was built in 1857 to hold the fabulous wealth coming out of the goldfields. Today it has exhibits on Victoria's history from precolonial times to the present. Tours of the old gold vault take place every day at 1 p.m. and 3 p.m. The area around this upper end of Collins Street is known as the Paris End, and has fashionable shops and galleries. The streetscape is particularly lovely at dusk, with fairy lights sparkling in the plane trees and shadows playing on the facades of the exclusive boutiques.

To the right of the Treasury Building as you face it are the beautiful **Treasury** and **Fitzroy Gardens,** a favorite spot for office workers to eat lunch. On weekends Fitzroy Gardens in particular are bright with picnickers and wedding parties having their photos taken among the flower beds or on the magnificent **Avenue of Elms.** This corridor of 130-year-old elms is one of the few in the world to have been spared Dutch elm disease. **Captain Cook's Cottage,** plucked from his native Yorkshire, was reassembled in the gardens in 1934 to help mark Melbourne's centenary—a rather odd tribute since Cook never set foot here.

The shot tower and atrium of the Central Mall shopping complex

If you turn left along Spring Street from Collins Street you'll pass the **Windsor Hotel,** opened in 1883. This old Melbourne icon has long been a favored haunt of royalty, prime ministers, visiting dignitaries, and old-money Australians. It is probably the last of Australia's grand hotels, and a lot of Australian history has taken place beneath these ornate ceilings, including the drafting of the nation's constitution in 1900. Afternoon tea at the Windsor is a Melbourne tradition that is well worth trying.

A little farther along Spring Street is the extravagantly ornate **Princess Theatre ❹,** built in 1886 and refurbished a century later for the *Phantom of the Opera.* It is now one of Melbourne's most stylish theaters. Turn left down Little Bourke Street and stroll through Melbourne's Chinatown, to the **Museum of Chinese-Australian History ❺** (*Cohen*

Place, tel (03) 9662 2888), which explores the role of the Chinese in Melbourne's growth.

Turn right along Russell Street. On the left between Little Lonsdale and La Trobe Streets is the **State Library.** Cross La Trobe Street and continue toward Victoria Street to reach **Old Melbourne Gaol ❻** (*Russell St., tel (03) 9663 7228),* one of the city's most popular—if ghoulish—museums. The notorious bushranger Ned Kelly (see pp. 322–23) was hanged here (and so were 134 other felons in the prison's 88-year history, which ran from 1841 to 1929). The gallows, three tiers of cells, Kelly's armor, death masks, and early penal records are among the exhibits.

From here, retrace your steps down Russell Street and turn right on La Trobe Street. At the **Melbourne Central Mall ❼** shopping center you can catch either a tram or the subway back to Flinders Street station. ■

St. Kilda

THE SUBURB OF ST. KILDA IS AN OLD-FASHIONED SEASIDE playground, with grand old hotels, a fading amusement park, and art deco apartments crowding a palm-lined esplanade and beach. It's shabby, but in a way that goes a long way toward being chic. It's also extremely popular and just a short tram ride from the city. Catch one of the trams (No. 16 or 96) clanging their way past Flinders Street Station, along St. Kilda Road, and 20 minutes later you're there.

Luna Park

✉ Lower Esplanade, St. Kilda

☎ 1902 240 112

🕐 Currently closed; call for latest information

St. Kilda's Acland Street is justly famous for its pastry shops with their tempting windowfront displays.

On sunny weekends it can feel like most of Melbourne is at St. Kilda eating ice cream, in-line skating along the foreshore, fishing off the pier, flying kites, or nibbling goat's cheese pizza at one of the restaurants along the bay. In a schizophrenic turn, by night these cheery streets become Melbourne's red-light district.

Acland Street is St. Kilda's main artery, famous for its glass-fronted continental cake shops and its ethnic eateries and take-outs. **Luna Park,** a small and tacky but much-loved old fairground, is just off the esplanade. It is modeled after New York's Coney Island, and the entrance is through a garish laughing clown's mouth. The rides are tame and old-fashioned—the Big Dipper roller coaster, bumper cars, and the Ferris wheel are the biggest attractions.

The beach is good, with a comfortable holiday atmosphere. On summer weekends, professional beach volleyball tournaments or Iron Man competitions are occasionally held here. Old men play chess on stone tables near the foreshore walkway. The pier, with the ornate kiosk at the end, attracts fishermen and Sunday strollers. It has a good view of the city skyline and the long curve of coastline of Melbourne's bayside suburbs. A bicycle path runs along this coast, from South Melbourne through St. Kilda and on to Brighton. ∎

Yarra Bike Path

MELBOURNE IS A BICYCLE-FRIENDLY CITY, WITH AN extensive network of flat bicycle paths to take an inquisitive cyclist through parklands, gritty inner-city streetscapes, and along the breezy foreshore of Port Phillip Bay. One of the most popular cycleways is the Yarra Bike Path, which runs beside the tortuous Yarra River from the heart of the city into suburban parkland. This 12-mile (19 km) path is an ideal way to get to know Melbourne.

On weekends the Yarra Bike Path is cheerfully busy with cyclists and picnickers, and the river and gum trees along the way make it astonishingly easy to forget you are in a city of three million. There are plenty of bike shops and bike rental businesses in Melbourne, including one right at the start of the path.

The Yarra Bike Path starts beneath the ornate Princes Bridge, across the river from the Edwardian Flinders Street Station in the heart of the city. A nice prelude to the ride is cake and cappuccino—which you'll ride off anyway—in one of the sunny cafés at the nearby Southgate complex (see p. 299). Then head upstream beside the river as it winds its way through leafy **Alexandra Gardens.** The riverside path goes south and east into some of Melbourne's most fashionable inner suburbs—park-like **South Yarra, Kew,** and **Hawthorne.** It elbows around a golf course in Hawthorne, then veers abruptly north into gritty working-class suburbs such as **Collingwood,** past some of the city's earliest industrial sites. Follow the path through more parkland, looking back occasionally for striking views of the Melbourne skyline, and on toward the **Fairfield Boat House.** Although the path continues for a few more miles, this quaint old tearoom, which overlooks the river, is a good place to stop. You can get a nice lunch here, or rent a punt and row a little on the river. There really is a country feel to this little enclave, and it is quite a shock to walk only a couple of hundred yards up a wooded path and step onto busy Heidelberg Road. Fairfield railroad station is a short ride away (across Heidelberg Road and up Station Street) and you can take the train to Flinders Street Station where you began. Another nice thing about cycling in Melbourne is that you can take your bike on the trains for free. ■

BICYCLE VICTORIA

Bicycle Victoria *(19 O'Connell St., North Melbourne, tel (03) 9328 3000)* publishes excellent cycling maps to take you around inner city Melbourne, with roads color-coded to indicate which are safest for cyclists. They also have information on rides out of the city. ■

The much loved Yarra Bike Path meanders along the river.

Melbourne Cup

The Melbourne Cup is the horse race that stops a nation. This prestigious handicap event is run on Melbourne's Flemington racetrack at 3:20 p.m. on the first Tuesday of every November, and for three minutes life across Australia is held in suspense. City traffic is reduced to a trickle as the post time nears. All around Australia—even in the most remote corners of the Outback—the pubs are full to bursting and latecomers stand on the sidewalk, craning their necks to see the TV screens over the crowd. Nothing beats being there at Flemington on race day, among hordes of partying racegoers, extravagant hats, and bookies surrounded by mobs of gamblers.

The first Melbourne Cup was run in 1861 and was won by a horse named Archer, who came back the next year and won it again. By 1888 the race was attracting crowds of over 100,000.

The Melbourne Cup is the highlight of Melbourne's Spring Racing Carnival, which spreads over a couple of weeks and includes other top races such as the Caulfield Cup. It is a race for stayers. It started out as a 2-mile (3,218 m) event but in deference to the metric system the distance was shortened to 3,200 meters when Australia went metric in 1972.

The most famous Cup winner was Phar Lap, a New Zealand-born gelding who won in 1930. This phenomenal chestnut horse won 37 of his 51 starts and was taken to North America in 1932 to prove his mettle there. He died mysteriously after winning a single race in Mexico, and his death has been fertile ground for Australian conspiracy theorists ever since, with American gangsters the popular villains. In 1985, however, Phar Lap's trainer, Tommy Woodcock, reputedly made a deathbed confession that he feared he might have accidentally poisoned the horse with arsenic-based tonic. Today Phar Lap's skeleton is in the National Museum of New Zealand; his hide is in the Museum of Victoria in Melbourne; and his huge heart rests in Canberra.

There may be some Australians who don't have a bet on the Melbourne Cup, but they are pretty rare. Even people who never normally follow horse racing, let alone place a bet, will have a flutter on The Cup. Most enter the office sweepstakes, where everyone in the office kicks in a few dollars, and the horses are chosen at random. That way nobody has to study a complicated form sheet—just kick back and wait for post time. ■

For a little over three minutes the eyes of a nation turn to the Flemington racecourse, where more than two million Australian dollars (one million U.S. dollars) in prize money and immortality await the winner. Melbourne Cup Day is the highlight of Victoria's social calendar, with its holiday atmosphere, champagne brunches, and tailgate picnics by the glamorous and not-so-glamorous alike.

Mornington Peninsula

TWO HOURS SOUTH OF MELBOURNE ARE THE FASHION-able beach towns of the Mornington Peninsula, where generations of well-heeled Melburnians have gone to escape the rush of the city—and often take a bit of the rush with them on busier weekends. A much loved crescent of beach runs nearly 60 miles (96 km) along the inner rim of the bay. The open ocean side has a dramatic rocky coastline and good surf on the "back beaches." About 30 small but superb vineyards and winemakers dot the boot-shaped peninsula.

**Mornington
Peninsula**
🅰 290 C1
Visitor information
✉ Nepean Hwy.,
Dromana
☎ (03) 5987 3078

**Greater Peninsula
Tourism
Association**
☎ 1-800 804 099
(toll free)

To get there, drive south on the Nepean Highway, along the bustling southeast flank of Port Phillip Bay, and past the bayside suburbs of Mordialloc, Carrum, and Seaford. **Mount Eliza** pretty well marks the outermost commuter suburb. It's a pleasant, prosperous, leafy town, noted by visitors for the **Omell Manyung Art Gallery,** which exhibits the work of new artists. The fishing port of **Mornington,** a few miles farther south, has a scenic esplanade and the **Mornington Peninsula Art Gallery**—one of the State of Victoria's 16 regional galleries. Every Wednesday there is a crafts fair on Main Street. **Dromana** is where the holiday feeling starts. The tourist office here has brochures and maps for the resorts all down the peninsula. The bayside beaches from Dromana to Rye are bright with colored wooden shacks—bathing boxes—where middle-class vacationers store their fishing gear, dinghies, and barbecues between getaways. **Arthur's Seat State Park,** a 1,000-foot-high (304 m) granite outcrop, is nearby, with sweeping views of the bay and peninsula. In 1802 the explorer Matthew Flinders climbed it to get his bearings (and learned from the view that he had sailed into the wrong bay). Today a chairlift climbs to the top.

Cape Schanck, a dramatic headland on the open ocean side of

the peninsula, is the site of a lighthouse built in 1859. Excellent beach walks can be taken here, including an 18-mile (29 km) trail through the **Mornington Peninsula National Park** toward Portsea. On the bay side, **Sorrento** and **Portsea** are both very fashionable little towns near the toe of the

peninsular boot. Even the ice-cream and fish-and-chip shops along the beach are upscale. The beaches are lovely, but take care, particularly on the open ocean beaches. In 1967 the Australian Prime Minister, Harold Holt, vanished while swimming in the surf here. Conspiracy theorists have had a ball with the incident, the most colorful theory being that he was taken aboard a Chinese submarine. The hard truth is that Holt, a powerful swimmer who disdained the rules and swam on unguarded beaches, was simply swept away by the ferocious riptides that sometimes scour these beaches. Swim between the lifesaving flags, and have a good, safe time.

Phillip Island, at the entrance to Westernport Bay, is another popular destination on weekends. It is famed for the sunset parade of the fairy penguins that live on the island. This has become a highly commercialized tourist must in Victoria. A bridge crosses from San Remo on the mainland to the island town of **Newhaven,** where the visitor center is close to the bridge.

The penguin parade takes place on Summerland Beach, at the western tip of the island. Every evening the penguins—sometimes a few, sometimes dozens—emerge from the sea and waddle up the beach to their nests, seemingly unconcerned about the throngs of camera bugs taking their pictures. This routine can attract thousands on busy weekends, so reserve a place *(Penguin Reserve, tel (03) 5956 8300).* ■

Newhaven
🗺 290 C1
Visitor information
☎ (03) 5956 7447

The surf of Bass Strait pounds on the outer shore of Mornington Peninsula National Park, but Port Phillip Bay on the inner side of the point has idyllic sheltered beaches.

Yarra Valley

MELBOURNE'S RURAL FRINGES—THE YARRA VALLEY AND the Dandenong Ranges—are well worth exploring. They have Victoria's best wineries, excellent bush walking, and some beautiful drives through tall forests.

Yarra Valley

🗺 290 C2

Visitor information

✉ Old Courthouse, Healesville

☎ (03) 5962 2600

A wedge-tailed eagle at Healesville. Australia's largest birds of prey, they are often seen in the Outback feasting on roadkills.

The Yarra Valley, only an hour's drive northeast from Melbourne on the Maroondah Highway, is best explored by car. This region is one of Victoria's oldest wine producers. Vines were first planted here in the 1860s by Swiss immigrants Paul and Hubert de Castella. In 1889 this wine region earned gold medals at the Paris Exposition. Then came the dreaded phylloxera outbreak that ravaged the world's vines in the late 19th century and struck Victoria particularly hard. Later, Australia's palate shifted to fortified wines, and under these twin blows winemaking in the valley seemed moribund. The last of the vines were pulled up in 1921.

These days the Yarra Valley is enjoying a renaissance, with more than 30 wineries spread through its length. One major presence is the French champagne-maker Moët et Chandon, whose **Domain Chandon winery,** near Coldstream, makes delectable sparkling wines. It has a delightfully airy tasting room with sweeping views of the vineyards. The **De Bortoli winery,** north of Yarra Glen on the Melba Highway, produces a dessert wine —called the Noble One—that is arguably Australia's best.

Healesville, about 12 miles (19 km) farther on the Maroondah Highway, has the **Healesville Wildlife Sanctuary** (*Badger Creek Rd., tel (03) 5957 2800*), established in the 1940s to care for injured or orphaned animals. Some are returned to the wild, and others are used for breeding programs to help endangered species. There are more than 200 species of birds, mammals, and reptiles here.

Beyond Healesville the Maroondah Highway twists its way up through the deep wet forests of the **Great Dividing Range.** The mountain ash here are incredibly tall, throwing the narrow road into cool green shade. The impression of driving through a cathedral would make you go at a stately pace even without the hairpin turns. It is luxuriant, with giant ferns, myrtle beech, manna gums, and small sparkling waterfalls that catch the corner of your eye as you pass. Although the road is narrow, there are pulling off points where you can stop and admire the scenery. ■

The Dandenongs

THE DANDENONG RANGES ARE MELBOURNE'S ANSWER TO
Sydney's Blue Mountains (see pp. 104–105) and, like them, are tinted blue by the mist of eucalyptus oil given off by the forests. In the
19th century, the cool and leafy Dandenongs were a favorite summer
retreat for Melbourne's moneyed set, and today they are popular for
days out. Drive 20 miles (32 km) southeast of town on the Burwood
Highway to Upper Ferntree Gully, and then turn north on the steep
and winding Mount Dandenong Tourist Road into the forests.

The mountains rise to more than
2,000 feet (610 m), and the area's
heavy rainfall means they are
cloaked with dense, lush growth.
Some of the gullies are shaded by
huge ferns, whose fronds form an
overhead canopy, blocking out the
sun and sheltering a rich growth of
mosses, smaller ferns, and flowers,
including more than 30 species of
orchids. The ranges have 100-odd
species of birds but are especially
known for lyrebirds. These skillful
mimics can re-create almost any
sound, including other birdcalls,
the motorwind on a camera, and
even a chainsaw. Three patches of
wilderness—Ferntree Gully

National Park, Sherwood Forest,
and Doongalla Reserve—have been
combined to form the **Dandenong Ranges National Park.** It
is popular with bush walkers and
has numerous short trails, many of
them giving views back to the city.

The restful villages up here are
well endowed with tearooms, craft
galleries, B&Bs, and gracious old
houses with beautiful gardens. At
Belgrave you can catch an old
steam train, *Puffing Billy (Reservations, tel (03) 9754 6800),* which was
built in 1900 to haul farm produce
to market and now winds along an
8-mile (12.9 km) track to Emerald
Lake Park. ∎

Puffing Billy now
hauls tourists
instead of its
original cargo of
farm produce.

**Dandenong Ranges
National Park**
🗺 290 C2
Visitor information
✉ 1211 Burwood
Hwy., Upper
Ferntree Gully
☎ (03) 9758 7522

**EXPLORING THE
DANDENONGS**
Hikers' guides to the
Dandenongs, detail-
ing paths and the
flora and fauna you
may see, are avail-
able in Melbourne.
Belgrave can be
reached by train out
of Flinders Street
Railway Station in
Melbourne. ∎

Great Ocean Road drive

Simply put, the Great Ocean Road is Australia's finest coastal drive. It starts at the seaside resort town of Torquay, about 60 miles (96 km) southwest of Melbourne, and hugs Victoria's spectacular, cliff-lined Shipwreck Coast for 150 miles (240 km) to the old whaling port of Warrnambool. From Melbourne, the direct route to Torquay is through Geelong, but the road down the Mornington Peninsula is more attractive.

Along the way this drive has perhaps the most magnificent mix of scenery anywhere in Australia: hauntingly long sandy beaches, miles of rugged cliffs, wildflowers, and pretty fishing ports, set against the backdrop of the steep, rain-forested Otway Ranges. The road's most famous landmarks are the Twelve Apostles, the much photographed series of dramatic rock pillars that rise from the sea near Port Campbell.

The road was built as a monument to the soldiers who had served in World War I. Construction began in 1918 and many of the 3,000 men who worked on it were themselves war veterans. It was completed in 1932, and since then it has been hugely popular with tourists and Victorians alike.

The Great Ocean Road officially starts in the old vacation town of Torquay, about 25 miles (40 km) south of Geelong. You can get

Beauchamp Fall in the Otway Range

The Twelve Apostles along the Great Ocean Road

there from Melbourne across the Westgate Bridge, following the Princes Highway 45 miles (72 km) to Geelong, and then taking the Surfcoast Highway to Torquay. It's a quick drive, but it isn't particularly scenic. Instead, you can detour on the Nepean Highway down Mornington Peninsula (see pp. 306–307) to Sorrento or Portsea, and then take the ferry across the mouth of Port Phillip Bay to the old maritime town of **Queenscliff** ❶. This pretty bayside town was founded in 1838 as a pilot boat station for ships entering the bay. Later it became a naval garrison town to protect Melbourne from the Russians. After the Crimean War (1854–56), Australia had a totally unfounded paranoia that Russia was going to invade. The railway arrived from Geelong in 1879, and the town became a fashionable

resort favored for its sea breezes, yachting, and grand hotels. Even today the **Queenscliff Hotel** (Gellibrand St., tel (03) 5258 1066), built in 1887, the **Vue Grand** (1884) on Hesse Street (Tel (03) 5258 1544), and the **Ozone** (1882) on Gellibrand Street (Tel (03) 5258 1011)

🅰 See also area map p. 290
▶ Melbourne
🔁 260 miles (418 km)
🕐 I day
▶ Warrnambool

NOT TO BE MISSED
- Lorne
- Cape Otway lighthouse
- Twelve Apostles

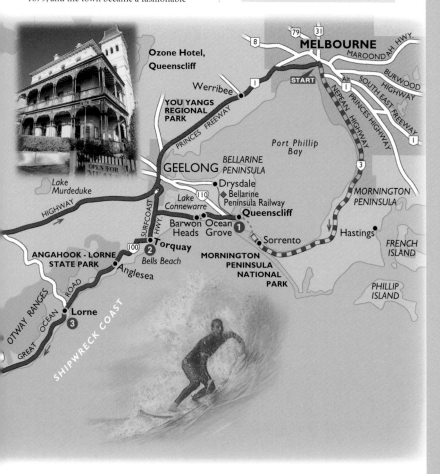

are very elegant retreats. From Queenscliff it is an 18-mile (29 km) drive via Ocean Grove and Barwon Heads to the Surfcoast Highway.

Torquay ② *(Visitor information, corner of Geelong and Beech Rds., tel (03) 5261 4219)* has been a vacation spot since the late 19th century, but the surfing culture of the 1960s made it famous outside Australia. Surf conditions along these beaches are close to perfect, and the Bells Easter Classic, held on nearby **Bells**

Shipwreck coast

If this coast is tough on drivers, it has been much more cruel to sailors. More than 80 vessels have come to grief along here, the most famous of which was the clipper *Loch Ard*. It went down on a cold, stormy night in June 1878, and of the 53 people on board, only two survived: an 18-year-old girl named Eva Carmichael and an apprentice seaman, Tom Pearce, also 18. They were washed into a long, narrow, high-walled gorge and sheltered in a cave until morning, when Pearce scaled the cliffs to summon help. The nation was stunned by the tragedy. Eva Carmichael lost both of her parents and five siblings in the disaster, and the

popular hope was that she would strike up a romance with the young seaman who had saved her life. It wasn't to be, however. She came from a prosperous family in Ireland and returned there, while Pearce went back to sea, where he survived two more shipwrecks.

Today scenic trails loop around Loch Ard Gorge, and wooden steps lead down to the tiny beach and cave—Carmichael's Cave— where the two castaways spent their miserable night. The *Loch Ard*'s anchor stands outside the visitor center in nearby Port Campbell, where the Loch Ard Shipwreck Museum tells the story of five other shipwrecks along the coast. ■

Beach, is one of the premier events on the world pro-surfing calendar. This is a surfer's town, its streets lined with surf shops and boardmaking companies.

The road veers inland for about 10 miles (16 km) before coming down to the sea again at **Anglesea,** but from there it diligently winds its way along the rugged coast past miles of beaches, through the picturesque seaside town of **Lorne** ❸ (about 25 miles/40 km from Torquay).

Lorne has been a popular holiday resort since the 1860s, when coaches brought visitors over the Otway Ranges on muddy bush tracks to stay in the town's growing number of guest houses and hotels. Today Lorne is one of the most fashionable retreats on the coast, popular with surfers and with bush walkers, who can scramble up the ranges behind the town to see the delightful **Erskine Falls** or just to get even more spectacular views of the coast. On a busy weekend, or around the Christmas holiday, its population can surge from 1,100 to more than 20,000. If you want to stay, avoid

Though called the Twelve Apostles, there are in fact only eight stacks—perhaps it seemed like twelve to the harried mariners on this stretch of the Shipwreck Coast.

busy times or reserve well ahead. The Lorne Visitor Information Centre *(144 Mountjoy Parade, tel (03) 5289 1152)* has details of accommodations.

The narrow and twisting 25-mile (40 km) stretch from Lorne to **Apollo Bay** is one of the most dramatic sections of the Great Ocean Road. It hugs steep cliffs, and winds around tight little inlets.The scenery is so beautiful that it can be hard to keep your eyes on the road—which is dangerous, because the road is incredibly curvy as it picks its way along the cliffs. Happily, there are plenty of lookouts where you can stop.

After Apollo Bay *(Visitor information, tel (03) 5237 6529)* the road veers inland, climbing into the Otway Ranges and giving spectacular views of the ocean and rolling green hillsides spreading out behind. These

steep mountains, clad in temperate rain forests, are the wettest parts of Victoria, averaging more than 80 inches (2,000 mm) of rainfall a year. Walking tracks go through the forests.

About 12 miles (19 km) after Apollo Bay, you can turn left (south) on a winding dirt track to **Cape Otway lighthouse 4**, built out of local sandstone by convicts in 1848, in response to a series of shipwrecks on the reefs near the coast. The lighthouse is a paragon of reliability, having never broken down in 150 years. There is no protection from bad luck or poor judgment, though. If you look at the rocks below the cape you can see the rusting anchor of a Cape Otway disaster—*Eric the Red,* which foundered here in 1880 with the loss of four lives.

The Great Ocean Road winds past the small but lovely **Melba Gully State Park,** with its luxuriant ferns, dense rain forests, and eerie evening displays of glowworms, and on through the old timber town of **Lavers Hill.** The highway rejoins the coast at **Princetown** and follows it for several miles through **Port Campbell National Park,** a strip of spectacular coastline *(Visitor information, tel (03) 5598 6089).* Storms over millions of years have eaten away at this coast, leaving the **Twelve Apostles 5**—enormous rock pillars, over 200 feet (60 m) high—in the sea. At numerous places you can pull off the highway to observe and photograph these striking formations from different angles. Early morning and late afternoon are the best times. The Great Ocean Road ends where it joins the Princes Highway, east of the old whaling town of **Warrnambool 6**. In winter months *(May–Oct.)* the southern right whales that use the shallows here as a nursery have become a popular attraction. Once hunted almost to extinction (they were the "right" whale to hunt, hence the name), their numbers are now slowly rebuilding, although there are still probably fewer than 2,000. Warrnambool's days as a whaling station are re-created at **Flagstaff Hill Maritime Museum** *(Tel (03) 5564 7841),* based around the lighthouse keeper's cottage, the lighthouse, and the fortifications

Between Lorne and Apollo Bay, the Great Ocean Road follows the seas with the Otway Ranges rising inland.

The cold seas of the Southern Ocean are a great place for fish.

built in 1887 to thwart Russian invaders.

One of Australia's most intriguing shipwrecks—and one of its great historical mysteries—is the "Mahogany Ship" that is reputedly buried in the sand between Warrnambool and **Port Fairy.** It was first sighted by a couple of whalers in 1836 and examined by the Port Fairy harbormaster, who thought its design antiquated and its timbers unlike any he'd ever seen, "like mahogany." There was no record of such a ship being lost in the area, and local Aborigines said the wreck had always been there. Then, in 1880, a series of great storms obliterated the mysterious remains and they have never been seen since. Some historians believe it may have been the skeleton of a shipwrecked 16th-century Portuguese caravel that had been sent by the Portuguese government to secretly reconnoiter the south seas, in violation of a treaty with Spain. The ancient Dauphin Map, reputedly based on information from Portuguese archives, appears to show the south coast of Australia. The archives were destroyed in the Lisbon earthquake of 1755, so the question of which Europeans first saw Australia remains open.

The **Mahogany Walking Trail 7,** a 12-mile (19 km) coastal walk to Port Fairy, takes you past the area where the Mahogany Ship was last seen 120 years ago. Warrnambool's Visitor Information Centre *(600 Raglan Parade, tel (03) 5564 7837)* has information on local walks and sights.

From Warrnambool you can head directly back to Melbourne on the Princes Highway. ■

Victoria's alpine country

THE HIGH COUNTRY OF VICTORIA HAS GREAT SCENERY for hiking in summer and some of Australia's best skiing in winter. It stretches from Mansfield—about 100 miles (160 km) northeast of Melbourne—to the New South Wales border. Most of the state's ski resorts are in this area. Picturesque villages, wineries, and small farms nestle in the valleys at the foot of the 6,000-foot-high (1,829 m) mountains and make it a delightful place to tour. Some of the towns, such as Bright, are lined with deciduous European trees and have a lovely Old-World melancholy when their leaves turn color in the fall.

Beechworth
🅰 291 D3
Visitor information
✉ 36 Camp St.
☎ (03) 5728 1374

The heart of the alpine country is around the **Bogong High Plains,** about a four-hour drive northeast of Melbourne on the Hume Highway. The drive itself is interesting. The highway runs through Kelly Country, where the bushranger Ned Kelly and his gang hid out and robbed banks (see pp. 322–23). In winter you can see the snowcapped mountains from the town of **Glenrowan,** where they fought their last battle.

At **Wangaratta,** leave the Hume Highway and follow the Ovens Highway up the picturesque Ovens River Valley. As with much of Victoria, it was gold that opened

up this neck of the woods. The town of **Beechworth**—a little north of the highway—was founded in 1852 on the heels of a big strike that produced more than 4 million ounces (113,400 kg) in the first 14 years alone. In its heyday it was a town of 42,000 with 61 pubs, and it was famous for its gaudy politics. Amid the brass bands, free drinks, mayhem, and vote buying of the 1855 election, one candidate, Daniel Cameron, reputedly paraded through town to the polls on a horse shod with solid gold.

These days Beechworth is a little more refined. It is one of the prettiest and best preserved of Victoria's

gold towns, its wide streets lined with honey-colored buildings, classy restaurants, galleries, and museums. The **Burke Museum** (*Loch St.*)—named for the explorer Robert Burke (see p. 43), who was Beechworth's police commissioner—tells the story of the gold rush. The 3-mile-long (4.8 km) **Gorge Scenic Drive** is good to drive but even better on a bicycle. It takes you through the old digging areas and past the Powder Magazine, now a National Trust museum.

The mountains start just past Myrtleford, with the spectacular **Mount Buffalo National Park.** It is known for wildflowers and waterfalls, and one of these, Crystal Brook, plummets almost 800 feet (243 m) in a single drop. There are nearly 90 miles (144 km) of hiking and cross-country ski trails on this mile-high (1.6 km) granite massif. You can drive to just below the summit of The Horn, and walk the last little bit to the top for a sweeping panorama of the Victorian Alps.

The 20-mile (32 km) drive up the valley from Myrtleford to **Bright** is lined with small farms growing tobacco, peppermint,

hops, and flowers. Bright has a lot of European trees and in autumn is famous for its New England-like foliage displays. (New Englanders may be a little underwhelmed.) Bright's tourist information center has a leaflet on some of the lovely bush walks in the area.

Beyond Bright the road forks, one branch leading to Mount Beauty and the ski resort of **Falls Creek,** the other winding its way to the 6,128-foot (1,862 m) summit of **Mount Hotham** and on to the alpine village of Dinner Plain. Falls Creek and Mount Hotham are both hugely popular ski areas. Mount Hotham has perhaps the best powder skiing in Australia, while Falls Creek has the best cross-country skiing. It is the only ski village in Australia where everyone can ski directly from their lodges to the ski slopes. In summer, there is magnificent hiking up here. **Mount Bogong** is a particularly nice—if somewhat steep—hike. Hikers with enough time and experience can tackle the 400-mile (640 km) **Alpine Walking Track,** which runs from Mount Baw Baw to the outskirts of Canberra. ■

Known as Australia's powder capital, Mount Hotham is one of Victoria's most popular ski resorts, with ten lifts and a vertical drop of more than 1,500 feet (457 m).

Bright
🅰 290 D2
Visitor information
✉ 119 Gavan St.
☎ (03) 5755 2275

Australian Rules football

For seven months each year suburban Melbourne becomes a patchwork of jealous footy fiefdoms—Collingwood, Essendon, North Melbourne, Carlton, and St. Kilda, to name a few. In all, this sports-mad city supports nine professional, big league Aussie Rules football clubs—ten if you count neighboring Geelong—and just as many professional minor league ones. Some clubs date back to the 1850s, which makes them the world's oldest football teams. Allegiances run in families, and after so many generations team colors can form far sharper social distinctions than race, class, or money. During the footy season about the only thing all these footy fanatics agree on is that it's sweet to see a Victorian team clobber one from interstate—especially one from South Australia.

Watching the big men fly. Footy creates a high-spirited tribalism with teams like Collingwood (in stripes) loved or loathed depending on where you live.

There is no more Melburnian activity than bundling up against the winter weather and heading down to the footy. If you're visiting Melbourne during the season—go! This is the real Victoria: a bleacher seat, a meat pie, and bone-crunching action. The plot is a little hard for novices to follow, because there don't appear to be any rules in Aussie Rules, other than that each side has 18 players on the field.

In a nutshell the object is to kick, bounce, and punch the ball up the field until you are close enough to boot it between the goal posts for six points. When that happens, the goal post referee—who looks like he's wearing a lab coat—struts between the posts and quick-draws two imaginary pistols. The crowd goes wild. If the player misses the two narrowest uprights, but gets it between the two wider ones, he gets a point for almost.

No doubt about it, this is one gutsy game. The players, who are built like basketball forwards with attitude, wear neither pads nor helmets, and they collide with reckless abandon—eyes only on the ball. They play at full tilt over four 20-minute quarters, leaping, kicking, chasing, wrestling, and tackling. Their athleticism is amazing. Imagine a bloke, maybe six feet eight (2 m) and 225 pounds (102 kg), leaping like a ballet dancer to snatch a football out of the air, then sprinting up the field, dodging tacklers, and booting the ball on a dead run 60 yards (55 m) for a goal. Injuries are common but the action never stops, not even when someone is being stretchered off.

The big game of the week is usually played at the Melbourne Cricket Ground (M.C.G.)—a sort of no-man's-land on the footy map, where both teams are visitors and 100,000-plus seats accommodate the crowd. Some of these clashes go down in footy history. But if you want to see a true suburban classic, get tickets for a match at Victoria Park. That seething cauldron is the home turf of the Collingwood Football Club, the most loved and hated team in the league. The atmosphere is throbbing, blindly parochial, yet still quite friendly. There's none of the hooliganism that plagues English and European soccer. The physical contact stays on the field. Aussies generally conduct their footy feuds with barbed wisecracks—often hilariously funny, even to the recipient.

The season stretches into the last week of September and culminates with the Grand Final. If you are lucky enough to be here then, and get a chance to go, or find yourself invited to a Grand Final party at a local's house—don't pass it up. ∎

Goldfields

A STRING OF FABULOUS GOLD DISCOVERIES IN THE MID-19th century transformed Victoria's economy and created huge wealth in gold-rush towns such as Ballarat, Castlemaine, and Bendigo. The nouveau-riche towns flaunted their incredible wealth with elaborate gardens, bandstands, statuary, and grandly frivolous architecture. A tour of the cities and the Victorian goldfields makes a delightful three-day (or longer) drive from Melbourne.

Ballarat

🅼 290 B2

Visitor information

✉ Corner of Albert & Sturt Sts.

☎ (03) 5332 2694

Daylesford

🅼 290 B2

Visitor information

✉ Vincent St.

☎ (03) 5348 1339

Castlemaine

🅼 290 B2

Visitor information

✉ Duke St.

☎ (03) 5470 6200

Maldon

🅼 290 B2

Visitor information

✉ High St.

☎ (03) 5475 2569

BALLARAT

Ballarat, the scene of the Eureka Stockade battle in 1854 (see pp. 45–46), is a good place to start. It is only an hour or so west of Melbourne. As you come into town from the east, the ornamental trees, ornate buildings, and brilliant flowerbeds give a taste of the elegance and wealth of this provincial city. The Western Highway on the other side of town is even more magnificent. It runs along a 14-mile (22.5 km) Avenue of Honor, flanked with trees, commemorating soldiers who died in World War I.

Gold was found at Ballarat in 1851, one of a series of strikes that sprang up like wildfires around central Victoria, and mining continued until 1918. Today mining companies are exploring the area again, armed with computer-age technology that could make this a gold town once again.

The center of town is rich with dignified old buildings, among them the classical revival **Town Hall**, the **Mining Exchange** building (1888), and the **Fine Arts**

Sovereign Hill at Ballarat is a living museum, re-creating life in gold-rush days.

Bendigo

🅰 290 B2

Visitor information

✉ Old Post Office building, Pall Mall

☎ (03) 5444 4433

EXPLORING THE GOLDFIELDS

The Victorian Tourism Commission Visitor Information Centre (see p. 292) has maps and suggestions for exploring the goldfields, nearby vineyards, and on into the Grampians Range (see p. 326), by bicycle or car. ▪

Gallery (1884, *40 Lydiard St. North*). The gallery has an excellent collection of Heidelberg school and colonial paintings (see p. 299), and the original Eureka Stockade Flag. Heritage tours of the town center (and of Bendigo), on old London buses, are available *(London Bus Company, tel 1-500 544 169).*

Beautiful though Ballarat's gardens, statuary, and architecture are, the main attraction is the living museum at **Sovereign Hill** *(Bradshaw St., tel (03) 5331 1944).* It re-creates the Ballarat of the gold-rush days, with coaches clattering down cobbled streets, old shops open for business, and gold diggings where you can try your luck. If you want to prospect further, the **Gold Shop** *(8A Lydiard St. N.)* can supply maps, metal detectors, and the required Miners Rights permit.

Follow the Midland Highway northeast to the gold-mining town of **Daylesford,** which these days is better known as a spa town. Eighty percent of Australia's known mineral springs bubble up in this old volcanic area, and for more than a century Victorians have come here to take the water. The town has a New Age feel, with organic eateries, alternative bookstores, and shops selling crystals and essential oils.

CASTLEMAINE

Castlemaine is farther north along the Midlands Highway. Reputed to have once had the richest shallow deposits of gold ever known, it is now one of Victoria's prettiest towns. Its streetscapes have not changed much since the 19th century because once the initial rush was over, the town settled into a quiet pastoral existence, with a few architectural marvels to remind people of the glory days.

The architectural show-stopper is the superb neoclassic-style

Castlemaine Market. Built in 1862, it is topped by a statue of Ceres, the Roman goddess of the harvest. The restored building is no longer used for selling fruits and vegetables, but has been turned into a gold-rush museum. Another jewel is **Buda** *(corner of Urquhart and Hunter Sts., tel (03) 5472 1032),* an example of colonial architecture now in the hands of the National Trust.

The nearby town of **Maldon** is considered to have the best preserved architecture of Victoria's goldfield towns. In 1966 the entire town was classified by the National Trust as a "notable town" for its unspoiled and intact streetscapes.

BENDIGO

Bendigo is where the gold rush began in 1851. Tremendous wealth came out of here in the 1850s, and its streets today are lined with imposing Victorian-era architecture. Its reputation for spectacular gold finds and overnight riches spread all the way to China, where Bendigo was known as the Big Gold Mountain. Thousands of Chinese prospectors came to the town in its boom days, and their arrival created a great deal of racial tension. After the initial alluvial strikes played out, gold continued to be mined in deep quartz reefs for over a century. The last large mine closed in 1956, but as in other goldfield towns, mining companies hope new technology will lead to hidden bonanzas.

Fabulous wealth and civic pride combined to make Bendigo an architectural jewel. One of the elegant buildings is the **Shamrock Hotel,** built in 1897 on the corner of Pall Mall and Williamson Street, with a marble staircase, polished wood, and stained glass in its lobby.

For a taste of life in an underground mine, try the 200-foot-deep (60 m) **Central Deborah Mine** *(76 Violet St., tel (03) 5443 8322).* ▪

Bushrangers

The gold rush days were also the glory days of the bushrangers, or highway robbers. They acquired the status of Robin Hood among the poorer people, especially Irish Catholics. Whether recent immigrants or descendants of convicts who had been transported for political reasons, Irish people had little reason to love English authority. They frequently sheltered and supplied the bushrangers, kept them apprised of police movements, and built them into folk heroes. Many bushrangers were of Irish stock themselves.

The first bushrangers were "bolters," or escaped convicts, who took to the bush and lived by robbing passersby. In 1814 the dripping rain forests of Tasmania sheltered so many armed bolters that the government declared martial law, fearing that the outlaws would help the captive convicts to rebel and take over the island.

In legend the bushrangers were dapper gentleman-robbers, but in reality they were frequently violent and thuggish. In the setting of Australia's brutal penal colonies, however, any flouting of authority must have seemed heroic. Some bushrangers really did have a certain gallant style. When Tasmania's Matthew Brady learned that there was a reward on his head, he jauntily tacked up notices offering 20 gallons of rum for the capture of the colony's lieutenant-governor. Brady went to the gallows a hero in 1824, his cell filled with flowers, cakes, and letters from admirers. "Bold Jack" Donohoe was lionized by the poorer Australians for his escapades. When he died in a shootout with New South Wales police in 1830, he became a martyr, remembered in ballads and in Bold Jack souvenir tobacco pipes sold by shopkeepers.

These heroes were eclipsed when Ned Kelly rode onto the scene. He was born in 1854 on a dirt-poor farm in northern Victoria, the son of an Irish convict. By the time he was 15, Ned had a conviction for assault. The next year he was sentenced to three years for horse theft, and in 1878 he gunned down three police officers who were coming to arrest him. With his brother Dan and two mates—Joe Byrne and

Steve Hart—he fled into the Strathbogie Ranges. Over the next 18 months the Kelly Gang conducted a series of dramatic raids. They once took over the town of Jerilderie, New South Wales, and held its citizens hostage. Here Ned dictated a rambling 10,000-word letter to the authorities justifying his actions, and described himself as an Irish Republican political activist. The authorities saw him as a murderous thief who had to be stopped.

In June 1880, the Victorian government dispatched a trainload of armed constables to track down the Kelly Gang. Tipped off that the law was coming, Ned and his cohorts took over the railroad town of Glenrowan and ordered workers to tear up the tracks. One of

the hostages managed to get away and signal a warning to the troopers. A gun battle erupted between the lawmen and the Kelly Gang, who were holed up in the Glenrowan Hotel. The fighting lasted all night, and toward dawn the police torched the place. Ned tried to escape in the suit of armor he had made for himself, but he was wounded and captured. The rest of the gang perished in the flames, although popular myth has one (or more) of them escaping and living in quiet anonymity. Old men were still claiming to be Dan Kelly as late as the 1930s.

Ned Kelly was taken to Melbourne for trial, found guilty, and hanged at the Melbourne Gaol on November 11, 1880. His last words were either "Such is life" or "So it has come to

Ned Kelly plays a key role in Australia's bush mythology. Artist Sydney Nolan did a series of Kelly paintings including "Death of Constable Scanlon" in the 1940s and '50s.

this." The authorities soon learned that Ned was bigger and more romantic in martyrdom than he had ever been in life. In 1906 the Kelly Gang was the subject of the world's first feature film. It was so sympathetic to Ned and his friends that the Victorian authorities banned it in Kelly's old stomping grounds for fear that it would cause a riot. As a writer in the *Bulletin* magazine noted: "These splendid bushrangers never came within a hundred yards of a woman without taking off their hats." ■

Murray River

THE MURRAY RIVER IS AUSTRALIA'S MISSISSIPPI, WITH A colorful history of paddle steamers and bellicose steamboat captains who took thousands of bales of wool downstream to railheads and ports, whence clipper ships whisked them to London. It is Australia's longest river, running 1,170 miles (1,883 km) from Victoria's alpine country to South Australia's coastline, the Coorong. For much of its length it forms the border between New South Wales and Victoria. In 1824 explorers Hamilton Hume and William Hovell were the first Europeans to see the river, near the site of modern Albury-Wodonga.

It was the key to unlocking much of inland Australia. By the 1860s hard-riding cattlemen had claimed a lot of the land along its upper reaches. Among them was Jack Riley, the model for Banjo Patterson's *The Man from Snowy River*. Dozens of steamboats were puttering up the river's lower reaches and along its major tributary, the Darling, bringing supplies to what had seemed useless land. In 1887 George and William Chaffee were invited by the Victorian government to set up an irrigation system in northern Victoria. After a very rocky start, and bankruptcy for the Chaffees, the Murray has become the life-blood for a good deal of Australia's agriculture. Its muddy waters sup-port thousands of acres of fruit orchards, vineyards, and cotton fields, and are controlled by a series of locks and dams. Although it is at most a couple of hundred yards wide, the majestic red gums along its bank, its serpentine curves, and the bright sunshine in the Sunraysia district have made the Murray River a classic Aussie vacation spot. Spring, autumn, or winter—anytime but the stagger-ingly hot summer—are the best seasons to visit here.

Mildura, about a six-hour drive north from Melbourne on the Calder Highway, is the river town where the irrigation scheme began. It is an oasis—and looks it, with ornamental palms along the

Mildura
🅰 290 A4
Visitor information
✉ 180–90 Deakin Ave.
☎ (03) 5021 4424 or 1-800 039 043 (toll free)

Echuca
🅰 290 B3
Visitor information
✉ Corner of Heygarth St. & Cobb Hwy.
☎ (03) 5480 7555 or 1-800 804 446 (toll free)

Walls of China

Mildura is a good base for visit-ing Mungo National Park *(Visitor information, tel (03) 5023 1278)*, about 70 miles (112 km) northeast and across the border into New South Wales. Part of Willandra National Park (a World Heritage site), it has spectacular wind-sculpted sand formations known as the Walls of China. They are on the bed of an ancient, dried-up lake that once teemed with fish and bird life. Animals gathered to drink at the lake, and Aborigines camped nearby and hunted them. In 1969 the world's earliest known formal burials were discovered here, the bones burned and covered with ocher before being interred about 30,000 years ago. (Archaeologists returned the remains to Aborigines for reburial in 1992.) Rich fossil beds have given paleontologists a glimpse of the bizarre fauna—including 10-foot-tall (3 m) kangaroos—that used to roam the lakeshore. A dirt track goes to the park although rains can make it impassable. ■

waterfront, landscaped gardens, golf courses, and lawn tennis courts that Australia's Davis Cup players have compared favorably with Wimbledon. Lush orange orchards and vineyards surround the town, and it is easy to forget that beyond the green fringe lie miles of harsh Outback mallee scrub and salt pan.

Several restored 19th-century paddle steamers offer cruises from Mildura, ranging from an hour to five days. A word to visitors expecting massive Mississippi-style steamboats: These are more like the *African Queen* in size (but considerably better appointed) because of the narrower confines of this shallow Outback river. Hot air balloon flights above the wine country and orchards are also available.

Echuca is a colorful old Murray River port about three hours north of Melbourne on the Northern Highway, and it is the most interesting town on the river. An ex-convict named Henry

Hopwood founded the town in 1853. He set a ferry crossing and in 1859 built the Bridge Hotel. By a shrewd contrivance, he fixed his ferry schedule so that travelers had to wait for their crossing, and they generally waited in the pub, buying drinks. Hopwood prospered, and so did Echuca.

The gold rushes and the booming wheat trade made it one of Australia's biggest inland ports, with a massive wharf more than half a mile long (800 m) built out of red gum beams. When the railroads came, the river trade declined and Echuca faded, but it has found new life in tourism. The wharf has been restored, and there are excellent restaurants and wood-carving galleries. A number of restored steamboats tie up at the old wharf for cruises along this pretty stretch of river, including one-hour excursions, lunch and dinner cruises, and overnight trips. Houseboats and canoe rentals are also available. ■

Echuca's massive wharf was built 42 feet (12.7 m) above the Murray River to allow for its frequent floods. The old wharf is still in business with antique paddle steamers offering cruises and sightseeing excursions.

Grampians National Park (Geriwerd)

Grampians National Park

📐 290 A2

Visitor information

✉ Dunkeld Rd., about 2 miles (3 km) south of Halls Gap

☎ (03) 5356 4247

THE GRAMPIANS—ALSO KNOWN BY THEIR ABORIGINAL name, Geriwerd—are a formidable series of folded and twisted sandstone ridges that rise to heights of more than 3,000 feet (914 m) in western Victoria. A national park of 500,000 acres (202,500 ha) incorporates these ranges, with cliffs, waterfalls, ancient rock shelters that have Aboriginal art, and a kaleidoscope of wildflowers. There are scenic drives through the park, bush-walking trails, great rock climbing, and the opportunity to see a lot of Australian fauna—koalas, kangaroos, and if you're very, very lucky perhaps even a shy platypus—in the wild. The park has around 200 species of birds.

It is an easy 170-mile (274 km) drive from Melbourne, through the goldfield town of Ballarat (see pp. 320–21), the Great Western sparkling wine district, and the wheat and grazing country in west-

The craggy outcrops on Mount Arapiles draw rock climbers from around the world. Here a climber scales Mitre Rock where a broad view of the Grampians awaits at the top.

ern Victoria. **Halls Gap** is the only town actually in the park. A picturesque spot, settled in 1840, it is a great place to base yourself while you explore the park. The national park visitor center has brochures, maps, and information about the Grampians' 400-million-year history.

The Grampians are actually a collection of mountain ranges bunched together, and a diversity of landscapes is found within the

park: hot, arid mallee scrub in the north, deep forests of stringy bark and red gums in the south, lush fern-filled gullies in the Wonderland Range, and even sub-alpine vegetation near the craggy exposed summit of Mount William. Hiking trails vary from half-hour strolls to strenuous overnight hikes on the aptly named **Mount Difficult.**

The best known drives and trails take in the **Wonderland Range,** close to Halls Gap. Many of the best viewpoints are accessible by car, with only a short hike to lookouts. The most popular viewpoint is the **Pinnacle,** hundreds of feet above the plains. To heighten the sensation, stroll out on the narrow ledge nearby, known as the Nerve Test. Another heart-stopping lookout is known as the Jaws of Death. The 3-mile (4.8 km) **Delley's Dell walk,** through lush cool ferns, is close to town. **Mackenzie Falls** nearby is awesome, particularly in the winter months, when rains swell the river.

The ranges have the best Aboriginal rock-art galleries in Victoria. More than 4,000 motifs, in red and white, are seen in rock shelters and caves throughout the park. Some are easily accessible. At **Gulgurn Manja,** in the northern

tip of the park near Mount Zero, a short signposted hike from the roadside goes to a shelter with depictions of Kartuk, the carpet snake. In the south, along the Henty Highway near **Glenisla,** the Billimina and Wab Manja shelters have handprints and figures of fish and lizards. The **Brambuk Living Cultural Centre** *(Tel (03) 5356 4452),* run by local Aboriginal communities, arranges tours of the rock-art sites. Brambuk is just behind the park's visitor center,

and has cultural displays, a shop selling books and music, and a little café specializing in westernized bush tucker, such as kangaroo burgers and cappuccinos with wattle seeds sprinkled on top.

The best time to visit is in the wet months of spring, when the waterfalls are flowing and the wildflowers are at their best. The park has more than a thousand species of ferns and wildflowers, and the Halls Gap Wildflower Exhibition is held here every September. ■

Wonderland Lookout offers a spectacular view. The Grampians are at their best from August to November when the wildflowers are in bloom.

Tug-of-war

Maj. Thomas Mitchell was the first European to explore these ranges, in 1836. He was one of the very few early surveyors who tried to maintain Aboriginal place names, but he named these ranges after the Grampian Mountains in his native Scotland, presumably not knowing that the Aborigines called them Geriwerd. Lately the ranges have been the center of a name-based cultural tug-of-war. In 1991 the Victorian government formally revived the Aboriginal name, but when a new administration took power they officially changed the name back to the Grampians. ■

Wilsons Promontory National Park

Wilsons Promontory National Park
🅰 290 C1
Visitor information
✉ Tidal River
☎ 13 19 63

ONE OF VICTORIA'S MOST POPULAR NATIONAL PARKS, Wilsons Promontory lies about 150 miles (240 km) southeast of Melbourne on the South Gippsland Highway and draws thousands of bush walkers and nature lovers on long weekends. This roughly heart-shaped promontory is the extreme southern tip of mainland Australia, jutting into Bass Strait and taking the full fury of its waters on the western flank while sheltering lovely beaches on the east. It has an astonishing variety of landscapes for its relatively small size: forests, heath and fern-lined gullies, salt marshes, sandy beaches, and granite tors. There are more than 100 miles (160 km) of hiking paths.

Wilsons Promontory is rich in wildlife, with kangaroos, wombats, wallabies, and koalas in plenty. It even has emus, which can often be seen feeding on the grasslands near

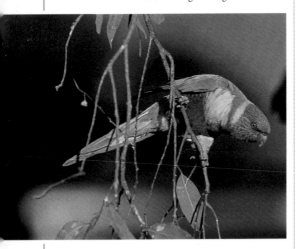

Hikers in Wilsons Promontory may see a rainbow lorikeet, Australia's most colorful bird. It has a brushlike tongue with which it extracts nectar from flowers.

the park entrance at Yanakie Isthmus, and many other birds— among them brilliantly colored lorikeets, rosellas, and kookaburras, which you can hear cackling away in the treetops.

Bush walking is the best way to see Wilsons Promontory. Those who do not have the time or energy for such pursuits can still get a taste of the place—one of the best views

over Bass Strait and some of the tiny coastal islands is from **Sparkes Lookout,** just off the road to the town of **Tidal River.** The national park office is at Tidal River. Hiking possibilities range from half-hour strolls to overnight hikes down to the old lighthouse, built in 1859 (see below).

Three very popular shorter hikes from Tidal River are the **Squeaky Beach Nature Walk,** where half an hour of walking brings you to a beach of quartz sand so pure it squeaks underfoot. The **Lilly Pilly Gully Nature Walk** is a bit longer—about three hours round-trip—with rain forest, ferns, and gum-studded bushland where you may spot a koala.

Another popular hike is to the top of **Mount Oberon.** The enjoyable 4-mile (6.4 km) round-trip takes about two hours. From the Mount Oberon car park it is possible to hike out to the light-house at Southeast Point. If you arrange it with the park office, you can visit the lighthouse. This hike takes pretty much a full day. You need a camping permit if you want to stay *(reserve it in advance because numbers are restricted and it is very popular),* and carry all your supplies, including water. ■

An island state set in stormy waters, Tasmania has two personalities: gentle English-style countryside on its east and brooding Gothic mountains, cloaked in forests, on its west. And everywhere reminders of its dark past.

Tasmania

The sturdy Tasmanian devil, a carnivore

Tasmania

TASMANIA IS ONE OF THOSE RARE islands that really feels like an island. The cities and towns along its storm-lashed coasts all have a strongly maritime flavor and a history of whalers, sealers, clipper ships, and, often, tragedy. It is aloof, far beyond the 200 or so miles (320 km) that separate it from mainland Australia.

After a few days here it becomes apparent that this is an island with two distinct personalities. There is the dark and tragic Tasmania of brooding mountains, rainy forests, and sandstone ruins left from a violent colonial past. The other Tasmania, existing cheerily, if schizophrenically, beside it, is the one of gentle English villages with sheep grazing on the common, quiet lanes, and apple orchards. Both are unlike anything you'll find elsewhere in Australia.

Dutch navigator Abel Tasman was the first European known to have sighted the island. He swept along its west coast in 1642, believing it to be a peninsula jutting out from main-

land Australia, and named it Van Diemen's Land, after the governor of the Dutch East Indies. His tales of rainy coasts, forbidding mountains, and savages on the beaches did nothing to kindle any enthusiasm for the place among his masters, both in Amsterdam and in Java, and when his subsequent voyage in 1644 turned up pretty much the same things, the Dutch gave up on Australia altogether.

In 1803 the British decided to establish a penal colony on Van Diemen's Land, partly to forestall French interest in the place. Hobart Town was established the following year as a place to send convicts who had re-offended. Van Diemen's Land quickly became a byword for sadism and terror, rum and the lash, a reputation augmented by the barbaric prison camps established at Macquarie Harbour in 1821 and Port Arthur in 1832. By the time convicts ceased to be transported here in 1852, the island's reputation was so ghastly that its residents decided to change its name to the friendlier sounding Tasmania.

Tasmania is a compact state, about the size of Scotland or Ireland. A third of its half-million residents live in Hobart. It is still very much an Anglo-Saxon community, with a deep social divide between the Greens and the predominantly blue-collar supporters of

With waters as smooth as glass, Bathurst Harbour mirrors Mount Rugby as the sun rises in Southwest National Park.

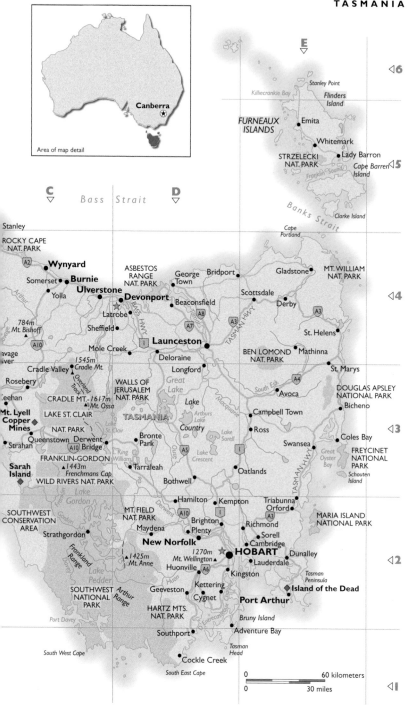

Area of map detail

Canberra ★

E

◁**6**

Killiecrankie Bay
Stanley Point
Flinders
Island

**FURNEAUX
ISLANDS**
Emita

Whitemark
STRZELECKI
NAT. PARK
Lady Barron
Cape Barren
Island
◁**5**

Franklin Sound

Banks Strait

Clarke Island

C
▽
Bass Strait
D
▽

Stanley
Cape
Portland

ROCKY CAPE
NAT. PARK

A2   **Wynyard**

Somerset   **Burnie**   Yolla

Ulverstone

ASBESTOS
RANGE
NAT. PARK

George
Town

Bridport

Gladstone

MT. WILLIAM
NAT. PARK

◁**4**

Devonport
Beaconsfield
Scottsdale
Derby

784m
Mt. Bishoff

Latrobe   A8
A7
A3

Sheffield   Mole Creek   **Launceston**

St. Helens

A10

Deloraine   Longford

BEN LOMOND
NAT. PARK
Mathinna

Roseberry

1545m
Cradle Valley   Cradle Mt.

WALLS OF
JERUSALEM
NAT. PARK

Great
Lake

St. Marys

Leehan   CRADLE MT.-1617m
Mt. Ossa

Lake

Arthurs
Lake

A4

Avoca

DOUGLAS APSLEY
NATIONAL PARK
Bicheno

◁**3**

**Mt. Lyell
Copper
Mines**

LAKE ST. CLAIR
NAT. PARK
Strahan

Queenstown   Derwent
A10 Bridge

TASMANIA
Country

Campbell Town

Ross

Coles Bay

Lake
St. Clair

Bronte
Park

Lake
Sorell
Swansea

FREYCINET
NATIONAL
PARK

**Sarah
Island**
FRANKLIN-GORDON
1443m
Frenchmans Cap

King
William

A5

Lake
Crescent

Great
Oyster
Bay

Schouten
Island

WILD RIVERS NAT. PARK
Tarraleah
Oatlands

Lake
Gordon

Bothwell

SOUTHWEST
CONSERVATION
AREA

MT. FIELD
NAT. PARK
A10

Hamilton   Kempton

Brighton

Triabunna
Orford
A3

MARIA ISLAND
NATIONAL PARK

◁**2**

Strathgordon

Maydena
Plenty

Richmond

Frankland
Range

New Norfolk

Sorell
Cambridge

Lake
Pedder

1425m
Mt. Anne

1270m
Mt. Wellington

HOBART
Dunalley

*Tasman
Peninsula*

SOUTHWEST
NATIONAL
PARK

Huonville   A6
Lauderdale

Arthur
Range
Geeveston   Kettering
Kingston

Island of the Dead

Port Davey
Cygnet

HARTZ MTS.
NAT. PARK
Port Arthur

South West Cape
Southport

Bruny Island

Adventure Bay

Tasman
Head

Cockle Creek

South East Cape

0   60 kilometers

0   30 miles

◁**1**

logging and mining. On the one hand, Tasmania has a higher percentage of its forests devoted to national parks and conservation than any other Australian state, and it is home to the Wilderness Society, one of Australia's most left-leaning Green groups. On the other hand, it is also a lumberjack state that consistently produces world-champion axmen—300 hundred pounds (136 kg) of hard red flesh and an awesome sight to see competing at the agricultural shows. Tensions continue to smolder.

Tasmania is small enough to drive across in a couple of hours, yet varied enough to hold your interest indefinitely. Hobart has gracious Georgian architecture and a scent of the sea, and it lies just a short drive from the scenic Huon Valley, which spills along the coast. The southwest coast bears the brunt of the Roaring Forties gales and storms driven north from Antarctica. This is a vast World Heritage-listed wilderness, still barely explored. There is challenging bush walking around Cradle Mountain and Lake St. Clair, and the central highlands have lakes filled with trophy-size trout. The pretty villages in the eastern half of

the state evoke old Britain with names like Swansea, Brighton, and Somerset, and have cream teas, antiques shops, and colonial B&Bs. The east coast has excellent surfing and the haunting ruins of Port Arthur.

TASMANIA'S ABORIGINES

Some of the ugliest chapters of Australian history were written in Tasmania in the 19th century, when the settlers made a concerted and largely successful attempt at genocide. When the first Europeans arrived in 1803, an estimated 4,000 to 5,000 Aborigines were living on the island. These were the descendants of the original inhabitants who came here more than 11,000 years ago during the last ice age, when it was possible to walk across the shallow plain that is now Bass Strait. The Aborigines' early grudging distrust of the newcomers turned to outright hostility when they realized that these interlopers had not come to share their land but to seize it. They fought, and the settlers fought back—brutally.

By the 1820s Aborigines were being shot on sight, poisoned with "gifts" of flour, or

The lightkeeper at Mersey Bluff lighthouse watches the *Spirit of Tasmania* set out from Devonport on its journey to Melbourne.

TASMANIAN FERRY

You can fly to Tasmania, but the most dramatic way to approach this storm-tossed island is by sea. On the sea you get a feel for its rocky fastness and insularity, not to mention a taste of the Roaring Forties—the region of heavy westerly winds between latitudes 40° and 50° south, which old mariners wrote about and feared. The English navigator Matthew Flinders discovered the strait between Tasmania and Australia in 1798, when he circumnavigated the island and established that it was not a peninsula. He named the waters for the ship's surgeon, George Bass. The new, stormy passage cut the sailing time between Sydney and India, or Capetown, by a week.

Every Monday, Wednesday, and Friday evening at six o'clock the *Spirit of Tasmania* slips away from its berth at Melbourne's Station Pier to make the 14-hour crossing over the Bass Strait to Devonport, Tasmania. The ship can accommodate 1,300 passengers and 600 vehicles, and has something of a family-style party atmosphere with its pubs, restaurant, poker machines, and promenade decks. A Tasmanian tourism office is on board, along with a surprisingly good museum of Tasmanian history. Reserve your ticket early, particularly during school vacations or if you want to take a vehicle (*Tel 13 20 10*).

The ferry gives fine views of Port Phillip Bay, and if you are heading to Tasmania in autumn or winter the lights of the receding Melbourne skyline are particularly pretty. The waters in the bay make smooth sailing, but this starts to change as the ship goes through the choppy seas out of the bay and into Bass Strait. If you are not a good sailor—or at least do not respond well to seasickness tablets—this voyage is not for you. The sea may be as smooth as a mill pond, but it is more likely to be rolling heavily, if not downright rough. Bass Strait has some of the world's stormiest seas, because it acts as a funnel, compressing the full strength of the Roaring Forties gales.

The *Spirit of Tasmania* has a range of accommodations, from luxury suites to hostel-style bunks. A buffet dinner and breakfast are included in the fare. Get up early the next morning to catch your first glimpse of Tasmania's rocky coastline and green hills. ■

trapped like animals. Their children were used for forced labor. Aboriginal women were raped and killed. In 1830 the authorities formed the infamous Black Line of more than 2,000 armed citizens, who for three weeks beat the bush, shoulder to shoulder, driving out the Aborigines. The 150 Aborigines who survived were transported in 1834 to stormy Flinders Island on Bass Strait, where they were forced to become Christians and faded away in disease, grief, and malnutrition. The pitiful handful who survived were later allowed to return to Oyster Cove on Tasmania. The last of the full-blooded Tasmanian Aborigines—a woman named Truganini—died in 1856. For the next 120 years her skeleton was in the Tasmanian Museum, until it was finally cremated and laid to rest on the waters of the D'Entrecasteaux Channel, off Oyster Cove, near where her people had lived.

Hobart

Hobart

🗺 331 D2

Tasmanian Travel & Tourism Centre

✉ Corner of Davey & Elizabeth Sts.

☎ (03) 6230 8233

🕐 Closed Sun. p.m.

AUSTRALIA'S SECOND OLDEST CITY (AFTER SYDNEY), Hobart looks far older because it has so many elegant, albeit convict-built, 19th-century buildings. The town evokes the age of sailing ships. Situated at the foot and lower flanks of Mount Wellington, it spreads out along both banks of the Derwent River, about 12 miles (19 km) from its mouth. Hobart's houses are mostly of timber, painted soft pastels, and call to mind places like Halifax, Nova Scotia, or St. John's, Newfoundland, rather than other Australian cities. Certainly the weather can be brisk enough to reinforce the image.

The Sydney–Hobart Yacht Race has been one of the world's most challenging races since its inception in 1945. In 1998 six sailors died, and many yachts were destroyed, when one of Bass Strait's signature storms raked the fleet.

The focus is the harbor and the century-old stone warehouses and wharves near Constitution Dock. Many of them have been restored and converted into restaurants and pubs. This quarter of town becomes one of the most boisterous spots in Australia over the Christmas–New Year's holiday, when the Sydney–Hobart Yacht Race enters the dock.

Hobart was founded in 1804 after an earlier attempt to settle at Risdon Cove, on the eastern side of the harbor, had failed. The new town, built on Sullivans Cove, was named Hobart Town after Lord Hobart, then Britain's colonial secretary. The name was streamlined in 1881. Although its founder, Lt.-Col. David Collins, had a poet's eye when it came to selecting a

lovely setting for the city, he had a laissez-faire attitude to town planning. When Lachlan Macquarie, the public-works minded governor of New South Wales, visited in 1811, he lamented the town's chaos and ordered that a simple grid of streets be laid out. Thanks to him, Hobart is today a very easy city to get about, with its downtown streets arranged in a grid around Elizabeth Street Mall. No place in the center is more than a few minutes walk from the waterfront.

Sullivans Cove and the bustling Franklin Wharf have been the town's commercial focus since the 1830s, when Hobart was one of the world's whaling capitals. Fortunes were made in whale oil, shipbuilding, and trading in wool, meat, and flour. Between 1835 and 1860, as the town grew wealthier, a new line of handsome sandstone warehouses was erected on Salamanca Place. These beautiful old buildings have been restored and converted into craft galleries, cafés, fruit and vegetable markets, and gourmet shops.

On Saturday mornings, on the plaza in front of **Salamanca Place,** a crowded market sells anything from healing crystals to velvet paintings of Elvis. If your taste for the bizarre isn't sated, you can always nurse a cappuccino at one of the sidewalk tables at the Retro Café and watch the Tasmanians.

A narrow stairway known as **Kelly's Steps** leads between two of the warehouses on Salamanca

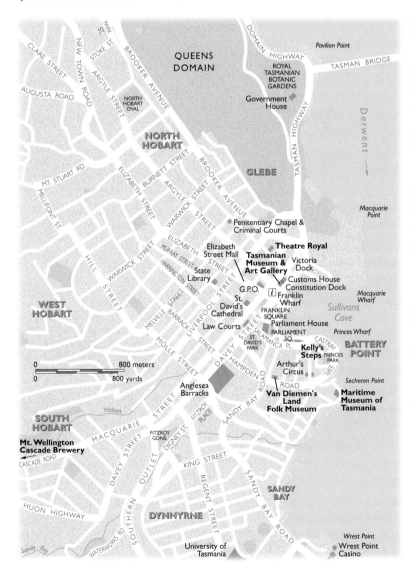

Hobart seen from Battery Point, with the snow-capped Mount Wellington in the background

Tasmanian Museum & Art Gallery
✉ 40 Macquarie St.
☎ (03) 6211 4177

Van Dieman's Land Folk Museum
✉ 103 Hampden Rd.
☎ (03) 6234 2791
🕐 Closed Sat.–Mon.
💲 $

Maritime Museum of Tasmania
✉ 16 Argyle St.
☎ (03) 6234 1427
💲 $

Place up to **Battery Point.** Named for the cannon that were set up in 1818 to protect the harbor, Battery Point became a blue-collar neighborhood for mariners, ship-wrights, sailmakers, coopers, and longshoremen. Later, as Hobart continued to prosper, wealthy mer-chants began building here as well. Hobart in general, and Battery Point in particular, has escaped the wrecking-ball-style of development. As you wander these 150-year-old tangled alleyways, with their stone churches, corner shops, and jumble of workers' cottages, it is easy to imagine the days of whaling.

More than 90 of Hobart's public buildings have been listed by the National Trust. About 60 of these buildings, including some of Australia's finest Georgian architec-ture, are along Macquarie and Davey Streets, which have almost unspoiled 19th-century street-scapes. Hobart's earliest surviving building is the Commissariat Store,

built by convict labor in 1808. Now it houses the **Tasmanian Museum & Art Gallery.** The gallery has fine displays on Tasmania's Aborigines and a good collection of colonial art.

The **Van Dieman's Land Folk Museum** is an elegant Georgian mansion built in 1836 on Battery Point, part of the Narryna Heritage Museum. The **Maritime Museum of Tasmania** occupies Secheron House, another National Trust building on Battery Point. The **Theatre Royal** on Campbell Street is Australia's oldest theater—built in 1837—and was praised by Sir Laurence Olivier as "the best little theatre in the world." The National Trust organizes Saturday morning walking tours of the colonial parts of the city and twi-light waterfront walks in the summer. It also sells *An Architectural Guide to the City of Hobart* and publishes guides to Battery Point to help you arrange your own walks.

MOUNT WELLINGTON

The best overview of Hobart is from the top of Mount Wellington, which looms more than 4,000 feet (actual height 1,270 m) above the city to the west and is sometimes covered with snow. This mountain dominates the city and draws visitors like a magnet, one of the most famous to climb it being Charles Darwin, who scaled it in 1836.

There are walking trails to the summit (it's about a two-hour climb), or you can drive up the winding auto road that turns off the Huon Highway. Just head inland, southwest of Hobart, along Cascade Road.

On the way you'll pass Cascade Gardens and the **Cascade Brewery,** which looks like a grand French château nestled in the foothills. This is Australia's oldest brewery—and its best, according to a sizable proportion of beer lovers. It began in 1832 and still makes beer in a traditional way, using the cold clear water that cascades down the mountainside. You might notice some childhood photos of actor Errol Flynn in the brewery museum. He grew up around here.

The stone **Pinnacle Observatory Shelter** on the craggy summit of Mount Wellington gives a stunning view of the city, out to the mouth of the Derwent River and over the wild countryside stretching out for miles in every direction.

The first European to climb this peak was the explorer George Bass, who stopped here in 1798 (and gave his name to the Bass Strait, see p. 354). The road to the summit was opened in 1937. The view is particularly dramatic when the valleys below are in broken mists or rain, as they often are. No matter what the weather, bring a jacket or sweater, even if it seems warm down in Hobart. ∎

Cascade Brewery
- ✉ Cascade Rd.
- ☎ (03) 6221 8300
- 🕐 Tours Mon.–Fri. at 9:30 a.m. & 1 p.m., reservations required

Mount Wellington has drawn sight-seers for 160 years, although English novelist Anthony Trollope dismissed it as "just enough of a mountain to give excitement to ladies and gentlemen in middle life."

Huon Valley drive

This is the heart of Tasmania's picturesque apple orchard district and is where the valuable trees called Huon pines were first discovered. You'll find fishing villages, dairies, tranquil island beaches, and the savage wilderness strongholds of the Hartz Mountains. You can see the valley on a day trip or over several days, depending on your pace and time. Either way, it's a particularly pleasant excursion from Hobart.

To begin, follow Davey Street south out of the city, where it becomes the Huon Highway. It is a hilly and scenic drive down into the Huon Valley, and in places you can look back and see Hobart spread out below along its harbor.

A settler named Silas Parsons planted the first apple orchard in the Huon Valley in 1841, and within ten years apples were being exported to New Zealand and India. By the 1920s nearly 30,000 acres (12,150 ha) of orchards in the valley were growing more than 500 varieties of apples. These days the valley has diversified into wine, salmon, and tourism, although apples and cider mills are still big. (Only eight varieties are grown these days, with Red Delicious the mainstay.) Although famed for its apples, the valley is also Tasmania's cherry-growing center. At Grove, 20 miles out of Hobart, you can visit **Huon Apple & Heritage Museum ❶** (*Grove, tel (03) 6266 4345*).

The town of **Huonville ❷,** 5 miles (8 km) farther south on the highway, is the commercial center of the valley. Timber became a big industry here when settlers discovered the Huon pines—or "green gold" in the eyes of the clear-cutting pioneers. This incredibly slow-growing softwood, unique to Tasmania, is nearly rot proof, and it quickly became popular with 19th-century shipbuilders. Thousand-year-old trees are hard to replace and few Huon pines are left standing in the valley today. You can arrange an exhilarating jet boat ride through the falls on the Huon River with Huon River Jet Boats *(Tel (03) 6264 1838),* which doubles as the town's tourist information center.

Another 15 miles (24 km) south on the Huon Highway will bring you to **Geeveston,** an old timber town and the gateway to the Hartz Mountain wilderness. The **Forest and Heritage Centre** *(Church St., tel (03) 6297 1836)* has displays on the timber industry and walking guides to **Tahune Forest Reserve,** where you can see magnificent stands of thousand-year-old Huon pines. Tahune Forest Reserve is about 15 miles (24 km) west of Geeveston on a marked road that is paved for about half the distance. By the road are picnic grounds, walking trails, and several good viewpoints. A scenic detour off the road leads to the **Arve Valley** and some of the world's largest hardwood trees. They are eucalyptuses of a stately variety that rises to nearly 300 feet (91 m) high.

The magnificent and wild Hartz Mountains loom just to the west. No less an authority than Sir Edmund Hillary described these mountains as some of the wildest country he'd ever seen. The **Hartz Mountains National Park ❸** has dense rain forests, snow-covered dolerite peaks, and rugged alpine moors. It is part of Tasmania's World Heritage area. The spectacular **Waratah Lookout,** about 15 miles (24 km) from Geeveston, is reached by a rough track off the road to the Tahune Forest Reserve. The walking tracks in the park are challenging but recommended, especially a six-hour (round-trip) hike to the 4,117-foot (1,255 m) summit of Hartz Peak. If you decide to do some of these hikes, be prepared for sudden and extreme changes of weather, and carry warm, waterproof clothing no matter how nice the day appears when you leave Hobart. For information on the trails contact the Forest and Heritage Centre in Geeveston.

Retrace your route as far as Huonville and then take the Channel Highway. It runs along the eastern bank of the Huon River, through the orchard town of **Cygnet,** which has black swans and old timber cottages, and along the D'Entrecasteaux Channel to **Kettering ❹,** about a 40-mile (64 km) drive from Huonville. Apple, cherry, and pear orchards, and fields of strawberries and raspberries surround this old fishing port. The waters of **Oyster Cove,** 3 miles (4.8 km) northeast of Kettering,

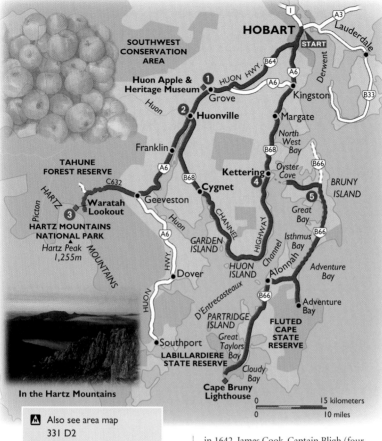

In the Hartz Mountains

NOT TO BE MISSED

- Huon Apple & Heritage Museum
- Waratah Lookout
- Adventure Bay

supported hundreds of generations of Aborigines, and it was to here that the last few Tasmanian Aborigines were allowed to return.

From Kettering, regular ferries make the short hop to **Bruny Island ⑤.** The Bruny D'Entrecasteaux Visitors' Centre *(Tel 1-800 676 740, toll free)* is next to the ferry terminal and sells ferry tickets. This elongated island was a veritable crossroads for 18th-century explorers, after being sighted by Abel Tasman in 1642. James Cook, Captain Bligh (four times), Matthew Flinders, John Cox, Bruni D'Entrecasteaux (for whom the island is named), and Nicholas Baudin all made visits here. A botanist on one of Bligh's expeditions is believed to have planted the first of Tasmania's apple trees. Later the island was a base for whalers. Today it is tranquil, with rain forests, guesthouses, and seafood restaurants. The island is about 30 miles (48 km) long, and most accommodations are at **Adventure Bay,** in the southern half, which also has the best scenery. The **Cape Bruny Lighthouse,** at the southwest tip reached via road B66 through Alonnah, is the second oldest in Australia. It was built in 1836—after several tragic shipwrecks, as is usually the case.

From Kettering drive back to Hobart through Margate and **Kingston,** which has the Australian Antarctic Division headquarters *(Channel Hwy.).* This has displays on early expeditions, as well as the latest information. ■

Port Arthur

"IT WAS ALL OUT OF KEEPING WITH THE PLACE, A SORT OF bringing together of heaven and hell," wrote American novelist Mark Twain when he visited Port Arthur on a world tour in the 1890s. Certainly it is hard to reconcile the gentle beauty of the countryside with the brutal past of the prison camp on this peninsula, about 70 miles (112 km) southwest of Hobart.

Baking bread in the Commandant's Cottage is one of the more palatable aspects of life in the brutal prison camp, which is re-created for visitors.

Port Arthur

🅰 331 E2

Visitor information

✉ Port Arthur Historic Site

☎ (03) 6251 2371

💲 $–$$

From 1832 until it was closed in 1877, Port Arthur was the final stop for many of the colony's most dangerous offenders. Its founder, George Arthur, decreed that "the most unceasing labour is to be extracted from the convicts, and the most harassing vigilance over them is to be observed." More than 12,000 passed through. Escape was almost impossible. The peninsula is linked to the mainland by a narrow isthmus barely 100 yards (92 m) wide, which was patrolled by guards and lined with savage dogs. The frigid waters that crash at the foot of these dolorite cliffs were believed to be filled with sharks.

Things got even worse in 1852, with the construction of the Model Prison based on a new concept of punishment devised in Britain: total sensory deprivation. Prisoners who had previously had the comfort of casting their eyes on soft green hills were now kept in tiny isolation cells for 23 hours a day. They were never permitted to speak, and during their solitary hour of exercise they were forced to wear hoods and shuffle around the yard in chains. Not surprisingly, many of the men went insane. No matter—the prison opened its own mental ward. The decision finally to close the prison is said to have been influenced by the dreadful publicity it received from Marcus Clarke's novel *For the Term of His Natural Life* (1874).

When fires swept through the place in the 1890s, there were few regrets, and locals hoped the flames would wipe the memories off the map completely. The major restoration effort begun in the 1970s has

preserved much of Port Arthur, and 200,000 visitors come here each year. It is Tasmania's biggest tourist attraction. More than 60 buildings are scattered around the site, including the **Lunatic Asylum,** which now holds a collection of chains, cat-o'-nine-tails, and crude convict uniforms. Some of the buildings have been fully restored, but others have been left as ruins amid the gardenlike setting. Visitors can wander around the penal colony at will; the entry fee gives access to all buildings in the complex.

Even in daylight Port Arthur can be a haunting place for a stroll, but things get eerie after dark, with ghostly apparitions and phenomena recorded since the 1870s. Guides carrying lanterns lead nightly ghost tours of the buildings and ruins. They are surprisingly spooky. Boat tours go from the main part of the prison to the **Island of the Dead,** where 1,769 convicts were buried. A solitary convict used to live on the island to dig the graves. "Australia has many parking lots but few ruins," wrote Robert Hughes in *The Fatal Shore.* "Port Arthur is our Paestum and our Dachau, rolled into one."

A terrible—and hopefully final—postscript to Port Arthur's brutal history was written one Sunday afternoon in April 1996, when a lone gunman named Martin Bryant killed 35 locals and tourists. The Broad Arrow Café, where he murdered 20 victims, was gutted and its ruins built in to a memorial garden to those who died. Bryant is now serving a life sentence in Hobart's Risdon Prison, without possibility of parole. ∎

The old Gothic-style church adds a touch of gentle melancholy to the ruins of Port Arthur.

Department of
Parks, Wildlife &
Heritage
📧 134 Macquarie St.,
    Hobart
☎ (03) 6233 6191

Southwest
Tasmanian Tourism
☎ (03) 6297 1836

Southwest wilderness

TASMANIA'S SOUTHWEST WILDERNESS IS ONE OF THE world's few remaining untouched places, with vast tracts of virgin temperate rain forests, swamp gums more than 300 feet (91 m) high, rare ferns and lichens, and wild rivers boiling through the gorges. Rain falls on more than 200 days a year. Viewed from the sea, the gloomy storm-lashed coastline of the southwest cape must be one of the world's most forbidding spectacles—virtually unchanged since Abel Tasman swept past these rocks in 1642.

Braving leeches and sudden savage squalls, a hiker scrambles up the flanks of 4,675-foot-high (1,425 m) Mount Anne in the wild Southwest National Park.

Opposite: Cushion plants on the north ridge of Mount Anne. The Southwest wilderness areas encompass a wide range of environments, from temperate rain forests to subantarctic tundra.

These days it is protected as **Southwest National Park** and the adjacent **Southwest Conservation Area**—together a 2.5-million-acre (1 million ha) wilderness stronghold with some of the most challenging and remote hikes on the planet. But these hikes should be attempted only by experienced bush walkers who are well equipped for sudden savage turns in the weather. This area is noted for violent storms, mists, and cold rain, even in summer.

The trails themselves scramble up steep muddy slopes, over rocky quartzite crags that may require ropes, and across miles of swampy buttongrass marshes infested by leeches. You'll have to carry everything, although you can arrange an airdrop of extra supplies if you are planning an extended hike.

The reward for all this hardship is immersing yourself in the solitude and isolation of a primeval world so fresh and new it seems to have the first dew still on it. If this sounds like you, consider tackling the **South Coast Track,** a 55-mile (88 km) trail that stretches from Cockle Creek to Port Davey. This moderate-to-difficult route is maintained and generally takes about a week to ten days to traverse. Most hikers fly into Malaleuca airstrip and hike east, back to Cockle Creek.

Other, even more imposing, challenges include the **Port Davey Track,** the **Western Arthurs Traverse,** and the **Mount Anne Circuit.** Some of these tracks can be linked up for an expedition-length trek. Unless you are flying in, or starting your walk at Cockle Creek, you'll reach the park via the Strathgordon Road and the rough sidetrack to Scotts Peak, where the trails begin. Always register your intentions with the park ranger at Mount Field, or with the police, and ask about conditions before heading out. Specialist hiking maps and guidebooks for this wilderness are on sale in outdoors shops in Hobart. Two airlines *(Par Avion, tel (03) 6248 5390, and Tas Air, tel (03) 6248 5088)* fly hikers in and out of the park.

Scenic flights are a less strenuous way of enjoying this magnificent wilderness. Par Avion also operates a wilderness camp and runs a tour boat, the *Southern Explorer,* on the Davey River into the heart of the national park. ■

Tasmanian Greens

When you look at a map of Tasmania, the first thing you notice is the huge swath of green covering the lower left quarter of the state. Tasmania has a higher percentage of its land set aside for conservation and national parks, much of it World Heritage listed, than any other state in Australia—and a legacy of bitter environmental protests.

The story of Tasmania's strident environmental movement begins at Lake Pedder, which sprawls along the edge of the vast southwest wilderness. Before 1972, this was a tiny jewel of a lake accessible only by light plane. But then the Tasmanian Hydro Electric Commission dammed the nearby Gordon River, flooding the lake and surrounding valleys to create Australia's largest inland freshwater catchment. Conservationists, who had lost their battle to stop the dam, formed the Wilderness Society in 1976 to be better organized for their next confrontation. They didn't have to wait long.

The Hydro Electric Commission's next plan was to dam the Franklin River, the last major wild river in Tasmania. This sparked a bitter and divisive campaign in Tasmania, which snowballed into international protest when the Tasmanian government continued with its proposal even after the river and surrounding wilderness received World Heritage listing in December 1982. Protesters came from around Australia and overseas to throw up a human blockade to the bulldozers. Hundreds were arrested. A new Labor government came to power in Canberra in March 1983, and it promptly used its federal powers to stop the building of the dam.

The environmental movement remains a major social force in Tasmania, which has elected a Green senator—Dr. Bob Brown, a veteran of the Franklin Blockade—to the federal parliament. Pulp mills and wood chipping are the biggest Green topics in Tasmania these days, but calls are growing for Lake Pedder to be drained and returned to its natural state. In 1995 the Wilderness Society began a campaign to drain the lake, optimistically calling it Pedder 2000. Although this did not happen by the proposed date, the group has kept the name and continues the fight. ∎

Protestors take to the water in a demonstration against the Franklin River dam.

Franklin-Gordon Wild Rivers National Park

FRANKLIN-GORDON WILD RIVERS NATIONAL PARK EXISTS pretty much for itself. Many of its million acres are covered by dense rain forest and rugged mountains, and they are virtually inaccessible on foot. Boats or scenic flights are really the only way to see the park.

The Franklin River draws the adventurous from around the globe to test their skills in its thunderous rapids.

GORDON RIVER

The most leisurely view can be had on a scenic cruise up the Gordon River. The cruises go out of **Strahan,** a remote town of 600 on the central west coast near Macquarie Harbour. Most visit **Sarah Island** and the ruins of its notorious prison camp, then putter up the tannin-rich waters of the Gordon another 20 miles (32 km) or so. The Gordon is Tasmania's largest river, and the reflections of ancient Huon pines on its mirror-smooth surface make evocative photographs. Seaplane tours of the park and of Southwest National Park leave from Strahan on Wilderness Air *(Tel (03) 6471 7280)*. The Strahan Wharf Centre *(Tel (03) 6471 7488),* combining tourist information center and museum, can help with information on the park.

FRANKLIN RIVER

The more adventurous way to experience the wilderness is to raft the wild Franklin River. The full trip takes 14 days, through some of the world's most challenging and most remote white water. It starts on the Collingwood River, about 30 miles (48 km) west of Derwent Bridge, and ends many rapids later at Heritage Landing, where you are retrieved by seaplane.

This is emphatically not a trip to attempt independently, unless everyone in your party is extremely experienced. A number of outfits run trips on the river (see right)

Participants do not need to be experienced rafters—just fit and adventurous. Those on a time budget can do an eight-day trip.

HIKING

Although rivers are the main thoroughfares in this park, the trail up the spectacular, 4,734-foot-high (1,443 m) Frenchmans Cap gives some breathtaking views. The southeast face is a sheer 1,500-foot (457 m) cliff of white quartzite, and the mountain is prone to mists and violent storms. The hike is for experienced bush walkers only. It starts at the Lyell Highway, about 25 miles (40 km) west of Derwent Bridge. The 33-mile (53 km) round-trip takes three to five days. ■

Rafting
Tour operators offering rafting packages on the Franklin include:

Peregrine Adventures
✉ 258 Lonsdale St., Melbourne
☎ (03) 9662 2800

Rafting Tasmania
✉ Summerleas Rd., Fern Tree
☎ (03) 6239 1080

Tasmanian Expeditions
✉ 110 George St., Launceston
☎ (03) 6334 3477

Cradle Mountain-Lake St. Clair National Park

CRADLE MOUNTAIN-LAKE ST. CLAIR NATIONAL PARK IS Tasmania's most popular wilderness park. Its deep gorges, mountain peaks, glacier lakes, and broad expanses of alpine moorland are challenging enough to excite any bush walker, yet it is still (at least by Tasmanian wilderness standards) fairly accessible. Its southern end is only a two-hour drive north from Hobart on the Lyell Highway, and its northern one is about 50 miles (80 km) from Devonport.

An Austrian naturalist named Gustav Weindorfer first saw the area's potential and began campaigning for its preservation. "This must be a national park for the people for all time," he wrote in 1910. "It is magnificent and people must know about it and enjoy it." Weindorfer built himself a little chalet in the Cradle Valley in 1912, and he lived long enough to see 130,000 acres (52,650 ha) of the valley set aside as a scenic reserve in 1927. The park has since grown to 315,000 acres (127,575 ha) and has been World Heritage listed. It contains Tasmania's highest country—including 5,305-foot (1,617 m) **Mount Ossa,** its highest peak—and the beautiful **Lake St. Clair,** Australia's deepest freshwater lake (more than 600 feet/183 m deep).

Many exciting trails cross through these mountains, but the **Overland Track,** easily the most famous bush-walking trail in Australia, is the biggest draw.

Hundreds of bush walkers flock here each summer to trek the 50 miles (80 km) from Cradle Mountain in the north down to the southern tip of Lake St. Clair. It is a stunning trail, through wildflower-dotted high country meadows, buttongrass marshes, and deep forests of beech, Tasmanian myrtle, and pandanus. It typically takes five or six days, and is a satisfying challenge for the experienced and well-equipped hiker. Side trips as well—up Mount Ossa, for example—can easily double your time in the wilderness. You're limited only by the amount of supplies you can carry. A dozen huts along the trail provide accommodations, but because these are likely to be full, you are strongly advised to bring your own tent. Reservations for the huts are made through the park visitor center at the northern entrance to the park.

Don't let the popularity of the trail lull you into thinking this must be a cakewalk. The weather here is notoriously fickle, and the sudden storms on these exposed ridges can easily trap the unwary or the foolish. Snow is possible even in summer. Rain, mud, and leeches are near certainties at all times. By the same token, the scenery and sheer exhilaration of being in this wilderness is well worth any hardships. Late summer is the best time to go, although some exceptionally experienced and hardy hikers have enjoyed the challenge of winter traverses.

Most hikers start from the northern end of the park and go down to Lake St. Clair in the south. If you want to save yourself the last day's hiking around the edge of Lake St. Clair, or get another perspective, you can arrange to have a boat, the M.V. *Idaclair (Tel (03) 6289 1137),* pick you up at

**Cradle Mountain
Northern entrance**
🗺 331 C3
Visitor information
✉ Cradle Valley
☎ (03) 6492 1110
ranger station:
(03) 6492 1133,
hut reservations:
(03) 6289 1137

Southern entrance
🗺 331 C3
Interpretive center
✉ Cynthia Bay,
Lake St. Clair
☎ (03) 6289 1172

Narcissus Hut and take you to the trailhead at Cynthia Bay.

The lake cruise itself is stunning and a great way to get a taste of the Tasmanian wilderness if you can't spare the six days for the hike. Or you can do a day trip on the Overland Track by taking the boat to the northern end of the lake and hiking back along the track—a very scenic six-hour walk. **Cynthia Bay** at the southern entrance has a ranger station and an interpretive center, a kiosk, a restaurant, and a fishing lodge with luxury and budget accommodations. If you do not have your own transportation, you can reach it by Redline bus from Hobart to Derwent Bridge and then a local taxi service (which meets the bus) to Cynthia Bay.

At the northern end of the Cradle Mountain-Lake St. Clair park, daily buses run between Launceston, Devonport, and Burnie to the park entrance in Cradle Valley. *(In winter the schedule is reduced to three days a week.)* Besides being in a stunningly beautiful rain forest, this end of the park has excellent—and less energetic—ways to savor the wilderness. The half-mile (800 m) **Rainforest-Pencil Pine Falls Walking Track** is not only spectacular, but also accessible for visitors in wheelchairs or those pushing prams. Scenic flights are flown by Seair, which can be contacted at Cradle View Restaurant *(Tel (03) 6492 1132).* There are also shorter day and half-day hikes. Information is available at the interpretive center. ■

Called the Acropolis, this rock formation rises to 4,839 feet (1,475 m) in the heart of Cradle Mountain-Lake St. Clair National Park.

Scenic loop drive

Tasmania's compactness, the fact that it is an island, and the scenic loop of highway that stands out on the map makes circling the island by car the most obvious and rewarding way of getting to know the place. The scenic loop is about 600 miles (960 km) in all, although with side trips to the Huon Valley, Port Arthur, and Macquarie Harbour on the rugged west coast, you'll likely add a bit more.

Tasmania's diversity is astonishing. The drive takes in primeval rain forests and brooding mountain ranges, wild rivers, towering trees, and lakes filled with trout. There are mining ghost towns, ruined penal colonies, and the maritime charm of Hobart. Along the north and in the midlands, gentle landscapes with old stone churches and cottages call to mind England rather than Australia.

NORTH & WEST COASTS

You could begin this tour almost anywhere in Tasmania—Hobart, Launceston, or straight off the ferry at Devonport, if you brought a car. Start in **Devonport ❶,** a bustling port and tourist town, and go counter-clockwise.

Follow the coastal highway northwest out of town, along the coast to the logging and paper milling port of **Burnie,** named after William Burnie, a director of the Van Diemen's Land Company. This enterprise was founded by well-connected gentlemen in London in 1825, with a million pounds (1.6 million U.S. dollars) in capital and a grant of about 300,000 acres (121,500 ha) in northwest Tasmania.

The company got off to a rocky start. Prized sheep, horses, and cattle died, European agricultural equipment—imported at great cost—proved unsuitable, and the Aborigines fought bitterly to keep their land. In its first 32 years the company paid only two small dividends. While shareholders lost money, the company's exploration of the rugged wilderness opened up the northwest. The discovery of tin at nearby Mount Bischoff sparked a rush to the northwest, and the deepwater seaport at Burnie flourished. Unfortunately, it makes better history than it does sight-seeing, because Burnie itself is a dreary smokestack city despite its beautiful pastoral surrounds. Better to skate through the old port and onto **Wynyard** *(Visitor information, corner of Hogg and Goldie Sts., tel (03) 6442 4143),* a

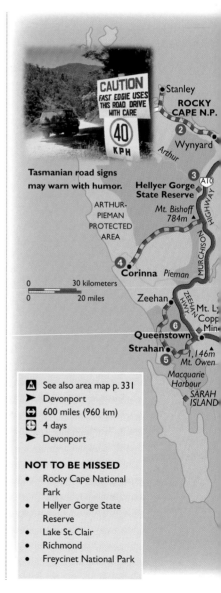

Tasmanian road signs may warn with humor.

See also area map p. 331
▶ Devonport
↔ 600 miles (960 km)
⏱ 4 days
▶ Devonport

NOT TO BE MISSED
- Rocky Cape National Park
- Hellyer Gorge State Reserve
- Lake St. Clair
- Richmond
- Freycinet National Park

pleasant seaside community just 12 miles (19 km) farther along the highway. This dairy town is a good place to catch a flight to King Island (see p. 354), or visit **Rocky Cape National Park ❷,** with its profusion of wildflowers, including rare native orchids, and white sandy beaches. The place has a long human history. For more than 8,000 years Aborigines sheltered in caves in these quartzite hills. Two major caves— **North** and **South Caves**—contain huge shell middens, bones,

and tools. There are plenty of trails in the park, but no toilets or water supplies.

A detour can be made by following the Bass Highway northwest for about 40 miles (64 km) to reach **Stanley,** a picturesque fishing village at the foot of a dramatic volcanic neck known as the **Nut.** This is where the Van Diemen's Land Company set up its headquarters in 1826, and built its slate-roofed store in 1844. The building has been restored and is now open to the public. The **Nut Chairlift**

A thylacine, called the Tasmanian tiger

BASS STRAIT

Burnie

Devonport

❶ **START**

Tamar

TASMAN HWY.

A3

St. Helens

BASS HWY.

Launceston

❶❷

North Esk

CRADLE MOUNTAIN - LAKE ST. CLAIR N.P.

OVERLAND TRACK

DOUGLAS- APSLEY N.P.

Bicheno

❼ **Lake St. Clair**

Friendly Beaches

Swansea

Coles Bay

Wineglass Bay

❶❶ **FREYCINET NATIONAL PARK**

Derwent Bridge

LYELL

A10

Ouse

In the mountains near Queenstown

SCHOUTEN ISLAND

Lake Gordon

Strathgordon

HWY.

Richmond

New Norfolk

❾

Orford

TASMAN HWY.

A3

MARIA ISLAND

Sorell

❶⓿ **MARIA ISLAND NATIONAL PARK**

B61

Gordon

❽ **Hobart**

A6

Battery Point

A9

Port Arthur

The ruins of Port Arthur prison

(Browns Rd., tel (03) 6458 1286), also the area's tourist information center, gives access to the top of the Nut. The view is spectacular.

The loop drive goes south on the Murchison Highway, which leaves the Bass Highway between Wynyard and Burnie. After about 30 miles (48 km) you will reach the **Hellyer Gorge State Reserve** ❸, with its deep rain forest of sassafras, giant myrtle, blackwood, and huge ferns. Forests such as these used to be the haunts of the now (presumably) extinct Tasmanian tiger. At one time many of these striped, carnivorous marsupials roamed the wilderness—the Van Diemen's Land Company lost much livestock to Tasmanian tigers. A bounty was placed on them and they were hunted to presumed extinction, with the last supposedly dying in a Hobart zoo in 1936. But there have been persistent reportings of Tasmanian tigers—scientific name, *Thylacine* —in recent years, and it is just possible that a few still live in the wilder corners of the northwest. If there are any, one likely spot is the almost untouched **Arthur-Pieman Protected Area,** a rain-forest wilderness on the west coast. It is accessible by a 45-mile (72 km) each way detour off the highway to the nearly deserted gold mining town of **Corinna** ❹, where you can take wilderness cruises *(Pieman River Cruises, tel (03) 6446 1170)* through the spectacular deep gorges on the Pieman River.

The Murchison Highway becomes the Zeehan Highway 50 miles (80 km) farther south of the turning to Corinna. A turnoff at this point leads to the colorful old mining town of **Zeehan** *(Visitor information, Main St., tel (03) 6471 6225).* This was a boom town mining silver, lead, and zinc around the turn of the century, with enough money for the local Gaiety Theatre to draw the likes of Dame Nellie Melba, Enrico Caruso, and Harry Houdini. Today it is a quiet village of 1,200. You can continue through Zeehan to **Macquarie Harbour** and **Strahan** ❺, the only town on the west coast and the base for visiting the remains of the penal colony on **Sarah Island** and the Gordon River (see p. 345).

The Zeehan Highway runs 20 miles (32 km) south to **Queenstown** ❻, a mining center built up around the **Mount Lyell Copper**

Mine. The apocalyptic moonscape left by its busy mining and smelting industry has become an attraction in its own right: bare hills tinted pink, gold, gray, and purple.

From Queenstown the highway winds a tortuous 50 miles (80 km) through mountains to Derwent Bridge. A very short—3-mile (4.8 km)—detour here will bring you to the jewel-like **Lake St. Clair** ❼. A lodge has accommodations and meals, and the launch trip across the lake gives some breathtaking glimpses of Tasmania's pristine wilderness.

The highway continues to **Hobart** ❽ (see pp. 334–36) through the hop-growing center around **New Norfolk,** settled in 1808 and now a very English-style town. Take the Tasman Highway out of Hobart. A very worthwhile short detour (8 miles, 12.8 km, north from Lindisfarne) goes to **Richmond** ❾ *(Visitor information, 48 Bridge St., tel (03) 6260 2132),* a well-preserved colonial village, with Georgian cottages and old stores. The four-span stone bridge, built by convicts between 1823 and 1825, is the oldest in Australia. A short drive back to the highway leads to **Sorell,** a historic village founded just after Hobart in 1805.

The drive along Tasmania's east coast is nothing like the drive through the west. The eastern countryside is gentle, with a mild climate and seaside villages arranged around secluded beaches. Forty miles north of Sorell on the Tasman Highway is **Orford,** a pleasant little seaside town and the jumping-off point for the ferry (*Eastcoaster Express, tel (03) 6257 1589*) to **Maria Island National Park** ⑩—a penal colony of the 1820s but a wildlife reserve popular with bird-watchers today (*Ranger's office, tel (03) 6257 1420*).

Highlight of the east coast is **Freycinet National Park** ⑪ (*Visitor information, tel (03) 6257 0107*), which includes Schouten Island and the Friendly Beaches. To get there you follow the highway 50 miles (80 km) past Orford, through Swansea, to a turnoff on your right to Coles Bay, the headquarters for the park. Cape Freycinet has hiking, bird life, and camping on **Schouten Island.** Sheltered **Wineglass Bay,** with shimmering beaches of white quartzite sand, is about an hour's hike from the parking lot on a well-marked trail.

Going north, the highway hugs the coast for 40 miles (64 km), then veers through an old whaling town, **St. Helens,** and rolls

With its crescent of shimmering quartzite beach and sparkling waters, secluded Wineglass Bay in Freycinet National Park is accessible by foot or by boat.

inland through a mix of farmland, dairies, and rain forests. After 100 miles (160 km) you reach **Launceston** ⑫, Tasmania's second city, with a population of about 70,000 (*Visitor information, corner of St. John and Patterson Sts., tel (03) 6336 3133*). It is set near the confluence of the North Esk, South Esk, and Tamar Rivers. **Cataract Gorge,** where the South Esk tumbles into the Tamar through a gorge, is a big attraction about ten minutes out of town.

Although it is almost as old as Hobart, Launceston (founded 1805) is a high Victorian town—a legacy of its glory days when prospectors came to Tasmania in the hopes that its forests hid gold. For information about Launceston's architecture, go to the **Old Umbrella Shop** (*60 George St., now a National Trust center*), built in the 1860s and lined with rare Tasmanian blackwood.

From Launceston the highway circles back toward Devonport, about 70 miles (112 km) east, and closes the scenic loop of Tasmania. ∎

Trout fishing

Thanks to the persistence of the 19th-century amateur naturalists who brought brown and rainbow trout eggs out from England, Tasmania is today an excellent trout-fishing destination. Its highland lakes host world fly-fishing championships.

Trout are not native to Australia. Amateur naturalists of the 19th century, with a Victorian-era notion that a bit of England could improve any landscape, began trying to import trout and trout eggs in the early 1860s, but they were defeated by the long sea journey. In 1864, however, a man named James Youl succeeded in getting a batch of eggs out from England in an ice chest. The eggs survived a remarkable 91-day relay of clipper ship, steamer, riverboat, and finally horseback, to be released in a few ponds near the Tasmanian town of Plenty.

Youl was later knighted—in part, for his efforts in bringing this gentleman's gamefish to Tasmania. (Later, the descendants of these fish stocked New Zealand as well.) The town of Plenty, about 30 miles (48 km) northwest of Hobart, has a fishing museum *(Salmon Ponds, tel (03) 6261 1614)* set on English-style grounds.

Trout occupy an unusual niche in Australia's ecology mindset. Introduced species have been almost invariably a disaster for local wildlife. The introduction of rabbits for sport shooting in 1859 and European carp into the rivers in 1872 are the most famous and catastrophic environmental blunders in the continent's history. These days a more environmentally aware Australia spends millions trying to eradicate nonnative species such as rabbits, foxes, carp, blackberry vines, and cane toads, which were introduced with harmless intention. But trout have a certain élan, and although they are believed responsi-

Cold clear waters and hard gravel river-beds made Tasmania the perfect place to introduce trout.

southeast wilderness area). They flourished in the nutrient-rich waters, and there are (possibly apocryphal) tales of anglers catching 45-pound (20 kg) brown trout out of Lake Pedder. Whatever the truth of those boasts, the average size for brown trout in this lake is a very respectable 10 pounds (4.5 kg).

The midlands of Tasmania have trophy fishing lakes and spectacular scenery. Great Lake, Arthurs Lake, Lake Sorell, and Lake

A fly fisherman casts in the cool dawn light over Lake King William in the central part of Tasmania.

ble for putting heavy competitive pressure on already threatened native species, they nevertheless enjoy a sort of honorary "native" status. They are seen as genteel, they don't muddy the rivers and lakes they swim in, and they contribute more than 30 million Australian dollars (15 million U.S. dollars) to the Tasmanian economy. Thousands of anglers flock to the state from all over the world, where their patience can be rewarded with trophy-size brown, rainbow, and lake trout.

There are a lot of good fishing holes and a number of professional guides around the state to help you find them. Back in the early 1970s, more than 350,000 brown trout fingerlings were released into Lake Pedder, and another 500,000 rainbow trout were put into Lake Gordon (both are on the edge of the

Crescent are some of the most productive, although the area has numerous smaller lakes and fishing holes. Trout were released here not long after they arrived from England, and by 1868 trout weighing nearly 10 pounds (4.5 kg) were being caught in Arthurs Lake. To get an idea of what is in those waters, stop in at the old Castle Hotel in Bothwell. While you'll no doubt hear a lot of fisherman's lies, the stuffed and mounted 25-pound (11 kg) trout over the bar offers its own mute testimony.

Tasmania's trout season opens early in August, although a few rainbow trout waters do not open until early October. The season lasts until April. The Inland Fisheries Commission (127 Davey St., Hobart, tel (03) 6233 4140) has information on bag limits, licenses, and minimum-size regulations. ■

Bass Strait islands

TASMANIA INCLUDES TWO OUTER ISLAND GROUPS IN THE
violent waters of Bass Strait—the Hunter Islands off the northwest
coast and the Furneaux Islands off the northeast. They are well off the
usual tourist routes.

HUNTER ISLANDS
Famous for its luscious cheeses,
King Island is the largest of the
Hunter Islands. This low, green, 40-
mile-long (64 km) island is blessed
with lush pasture grasses that are
found nowhere else in Australia. It
produces incredibly rich handmade
cheeses and thick double creams.
Legend has it the grasses came from
seeds in the straw-filled mattresses
washed ashore from shipwrecks, of
which the island has had more than
any other part of Australia. The

*Flinders Island
presents an aloof
face to the Bass
Strait and the
rest of the world.*

worst was when an immigrant ship,
the *Catarqui,* foundered in 1845
with the loss of 399 lives.
  Today the island has four lighthouses. **Cape Wickham** lighthouse in the north is the tallest in
the Southern Hemisphere and gives
a splendid view of the island.
  The island's biggest attraction,
the **King Island Dairy,** is on
North Road about 5 miles (8 km)

north of Currie. It gives tours
and free tastings. This island is
also noted for its smoked meats,
crayfish, and oysters. Howell's
Auto Rent *(Tel (03) 6462 1282)*
has rental cars. The island has no
public transportation.

FURNEAUX ISLANDS
The 52 islands of the Furneaux
group are at the eastern end of the
Bass Strait. The biggest is **Flinders
Island,** which was charted by
Matthew Flinders in 1798. It
became a base for sealers, who vir-
tually wiped out the local seal pop-
ulation and then turned to piracy.
Later, in 1834, the 135 Tasmanian
Aborigines who survived the Black
Line were sent here (see p. 333).
  Flinders Island has granite
mountains, secluded beaches, and
excellent fishing, scuba diving, and
rock climbing. There are numerous
bush-walking trails in **Strzelecki
National Park,** including a hike
to the wind-scoured summit of
Mount Strzelecki. You can look for
Killiecrankie "diamonds"—actually
a form of local topaz—on the
beach at Killiecrankie Bay.
  Like King Island, Flinders is
noted for its farm produce, and also
for handmade chocolates and fine
woolens. The main settlements are
Whitemark on the west coast
and **Lady Barron** on the south.
The **Emita Museum,** about 12
miles (19 km) north of Whitemark,
tells the story of the Aborigines'
time on the island. For car rental,
contact Bowman Transport *(Tel
(03) 6359 2014)* or Flinders Island
Car Rentals *(Tel (03) 6359 2168).* ∎

Travelwise

**A four-wheel-drive with a
'roo bar on front is favored
Outback transportation.**

TRAVELWISE INFORMATION

PLANNING YOUR TRIP

WHEN TO GO

Australia is good for vacations year-round. For a short trip without a fixed itinerary, spring and autumn give the most flexibility. There are no extreme weather conditions or temperatures to contend with, and no significant school holidays to push prices up and availability of travel and accommodations down. The wildflowers in the west are particularly beautiful in the spring.

CLIMATE

The Australian spring runs from September through November, summer from December until March, autumn from March through May, and winter from June until September. Seasonal weather varies widely in the different parts of Australia.

The best summer weather is in the southern states: Everyone seems to live outdoors and take to the balmy seas. The center is scorchingly hot in summer and the flies are at their worst. In the far north, temperatures may be slightly cooler, but the tropical humidity and monsoon downpours can be depressing, and poisonous box jellyfish make the sea too dangerous for swimming. On the other hand, some choose to head north in summer to escape the crowds and the cities, and see the Top End luxuriantly green and in full flood. The electrical storms are fantastic, and the barramundi fishing is superb.

In winter the southern states have snow, and some tourists come for the skiing. In the north the humidity and water levels drop. Travel is simpler, and wildlife is easier to spot, as it clusters around the remaining watering holes. This is the best time of year to see crocodiles.

CALENDAR OF EVENTS

See also National Holidays (p. 363)

January
Perth: Western Australia Cup (January 1)—*premier horse-racing event*
Tasmania: Huon Valley Folk Festival
Sydney: Festival and Carnivale—*three weeks of arts, music, food, and dance*
Tamworth, New South Wales: Australasian Country Music Festival (weekend nearest to Australia Day, January 26)
Montsalvat, Victoria: Jazz Festival
Thredbo, New South Wales: Alpine Wildflower Festival

February
Hobart, Tasmania: Royal Hobart Regatta
Sydney: Gay and Lesbian Mardi Gras
Perth: Festival of Perth—*three weeks of cultural events*
Melbourne: Music Festival
Hunter Valley, New South Wales: Vintage Festival (through February and March)

March
Adelaide Arts Festival (biennially, occurring in even-numbered years)—*three-week festival of the arts*
Melbourne: Moomba—*week-long festival ending with a street parade*
Port Fairy, Victoria: Folk Festival (Labor Day weekend)
Melbourne: Australian Formula One Grand Prix
Eastern Creek, New South Wales: Australian Motor Cycle Grand Prix

Easter
Sydney: Royal Easter Show—*livestock, sideshows, ring events, and rodeos*
Bells Beach, southwest of

Melbourne: Bells Beach Surf Classic

April
Melbourne Comedy Festival: *three-week event*

May
Longreach, Queensland: Outback Muster—*three-day festival with events related to droving*

June
Melbourne: International Film Festival

July
Northern Territory Royal Shows—*agricultural shows at Darwin, Katherine, Tennant Creek, and Alice Springs*

August
Darwin: Rodeo
Darwin: Beer Can Regatta Races—*for boats made entirely out of beer cans*
Sydney: City to Surf—*8.75-mile (14 km) fun run between Hyde Park and Bondi Beach*
Broome, Western Australia: Shinju Matsuri (Festival of the Pearl)—*week-long festival*

September
Melbourne: Australian Rules Football League (AFL) Grand Final
Melbourne: Royal Melbourne Show—*livestock, sideshows, and rides*
Perth: Royal Perth Show—*livestock, sideshows, and rides*
Adelaide: Royal Adelaide Show—*agricultural and horticultural show*
Birdsville, Queensland: Birdsville Races—*weekend of horseracing, in aid of the Royal Flying Doctor Service (see p. 18)*

October
Melbourne: International Music Festival—*opera, theater, dance*
Melbourne: Fringe Festival—*three-week alternative celebration of the arts*
Alice Springs, Northern Territory: Henley on Todd

Regatta Boat Race—*in dry riverbed, using leg-powered bottomless boats*
Bathurst, New South Wales: Toohey's 1000 Touring Car Race, Mount Panorama circuit
Hobart & Launceston, Tasmania: Royal Shows—*agricultural and horticultural shows*
Western Australia: Queen's Birthday First Monday in October: *state holiday in Western Australia*

November
Flemington, Melbourne: Melbourne Cup First Tuesday —*Australia's premier horse race*
Adelaide: Indigenous Arts Festival —*week-long Aboriginal festival*

December
Sydney to Hobart Yacht Race (leaves Sydney on December 26, Boxing Day)—*Australia's leading ocean race*

TRAVEL INSURANCE

Always take out adequate insurance when you travel, especially for medical needs. Costs for ambulance or helicopter rescue, emergency surgery, or travel home can be exorbitant. Ensure that the policy covers the activities that you are likely to undertake.

ENTRY FORMALITIES

Visas
Many travelers may now obtain authority to enter Australia through the Electronic Travel Authority (ETA) system, which replaces the need for an Australian visa. The tourist ETA is valid for multiple entries into Australia (each entry to a maximum of three months) over a period of one year and costs $A20 (U.S.$10). A business ETA can be purchased for $A80 (U.S.$40), allowing multiple entries into Australia for the life of your passport. Restrictions apply. ETAs can be obtained through your travel agent (who may charge a fee), from your

airline, or via the internet on www.immi.gov.au. Apply at least seven days before departure.

Travelers not eligible for an ETA, and those wishing to stay for longer than three months, or to work, must obtain a visa. Further advice and application forms may be obtained from your travel agent, or from the Australian embassy, high commission, or consular office. Further information at www.austemb.org.

Customs
Items brought in for personal use, for example cameras, laptops, radios, and film, are exempt from duty. If you take a laptop, it is a good idea to register it with your own customs officials before leaving for Australia. You should also be prepared to "boot up" the laptop on request. Travelers over the age of 18 may bring one liter of alcohol into Australia, 250 cigarettes, or 250 grams of tobacco, and gifts to the value of $A400 (U.S.$200) duty free. Travelers under 18 may bring gifts to the value of $A200 (U.S.$100) without attracting duty.

Currency restrictions
There are no restrictions on the amount of Australian or foreign currency you can import, although sums exceeding A$10,000 (U.S.$5,000), or its equivalent, should be declared on the appropriate inbound customs forms. If you wish to export hard currency exceeding the value of A$5,000 (U.S.$2,500), you must gain prior permission.

Quarantine
Australia has very strict quarantine laws designed to keep out pests and diseases. Planes are routinely fumigated by the cabin staff. Do not attempt to bring any fruit, seeds, vegetables, foodstuffs, or animal or plant products into the country. (Similar border controls are also in place between Australian states.) If you inadvertently carry

any such item into the control zone, place it in one of the many clearly labeled disposal bins. Do not attempt to take it through customs and if in doubt, declare it. Sniffer dogs check for foodstuffs as well as drugs. If you have hiking boots, expect to produce them for inspection. Any soil adhering to the soles must be cleaned off. Also expect items such as straw hats and wooden clogs to be scrutinized.

Drugs & narcotics
Sniffer dogs check for drugs and narcotics. Such checks are commonplace and penalties are severe. Medicines for personal use should be clearly labeled. Obtain a statement from your doctor if you are importing a large number of pharmaceuticals or if they are of a restricted type.

For detailed information on visas, customs controls, and restrictions, contact the relevant Australian high commission, embassy, or consular office listed below, or check out www.immi.gov.au.

United States
1601 Massachusetts Ave., N.W.
Washington, D.C., 20036
Tel 202/797-3000
Fax 202/797-3168
Offices also in Atlanta, Boston, Chicago, Denver, Honolulu, Houston, Los Angeles, New York, & San Francisco

Canada
50 O'Connor St., Suite 710, Ottawa, Ontario, K1P 6L2
Tel 613/236-0841
Fax 613/236-4376
Also in Toronto & Vancouver

United Kingdom
Australia House
The Strand, London, WC2B 4LA
Tel 020-7379 4334
Visa information 0906 550 8900
Also in Edinburgh & Manchester.

Australian Dept. of Foreign Affairs & Trade
www.dfat.gov.au

HOW TO GET TO AUSTRALIA

CHOOSING A TICKET

Australia is so far away from just about anywhere else in the world, that most people arrange in advance to go there, rather than making it an optional part of an itinerary. It is not a cheap destination, but you can save money by shopping around for your ticket, going out of season, and planning ahead. At the minimum you should investigate the savings available through advance purchase ticketing, such as Apex. Major carriers include:

Qantas
www.qantas.com

United States
Tom Bradley International Terminal,
380 World Way,
Room 4124
Los Angeles
CA 90045.
Tel 1-800/227-4500

United Kingdom
395 King St.,
London W6 9NJ
Tel 020-7497 2571 or
08457 747767

Air New Zealand
United States: 1-800/262-1234
Canada: 1-800/663-5494
United Kingdom: 020-8741 2299

British Airways
United Kingdom: 08457-222111

United Airlines
United States: 1-800/538-2929

The options for ticketing are endless. You may want to travel at a set time or for a limited period, or fly with a certain carrier, or go direct. There are free stopovers along certain routes, for example Hawaii or New Zealand out of Los Angeles, Singapore or Bangkok out of London. One of the cheaper options is a multi-carrier ticket that stops off for refueling, but not disembark-ation, at half a dozen stops along the way. You have to decide what comforts you will and won't compromise on, and what you can and can't afford in time and money. You may also wish to buy air and bus discount passes before you go (see Getting Around, below.) Check with your travel agent, and don't forget the consolidators, who often offer the best bargains. Always check for conditions and restrictions, and be prepared to negotiate.

PACKAGE TOURS

There are three main options for package tours (and endless variations within them). The first is to fly independently but spend your time with a tour company, for example:

AAT Kings
U.S.: 9430 Topanga Canyon Blvd.,
    #207, Chatsworth, CA
    91311, tel 1-800/353-4525
Australia: 29 Palmerston
    Crescent, South Melbourne
    3205, tel (03) 9274 7422 or
    1-800 334 009

Thomas Cook
Australia: Level 4f, 355 Bulwara
    Rd., Ultimo 2007, tel (02)
    8585 7300 or 13 17 71

Contiki
U.S.: 300 Plaza Alicante #900,
    Garden Grove, CA 92640,
    tel 714/740-0808 or 1-
    800/266-8454
Australia: Level 7, 35 Spring St.,
    Bondi Junction 2022, tel (02)
    9511 2200

Second, you can buy a vacation package that includes flights, hotels, and rental cars or sight-seeing, with **Qantas, British Airways,** or **United Vaca-tions** (in U.S., tel 1-800/328-6877) for example.

Third, there are customized package vacations with companies such as
Fishing International
U.S.: Box 2132, Santa Rosa, CA
    95405, tel 1-800/950-4242
ITC Golf Tours
U.S.: 4134 Atlantic Ave., #205
    Long Beach, CA 90807, tel
310/595-6905 or 1-800/257-4981.
Check the newspapers and ask your travel agent.

AIRPORTS

Most visitors arrive in Sydney, though international flights also arrive at Perth, Melbourne, Adelaide, Cairns, and Darwin airports.

Sydney International Airport, Kingford Smith, is 7 miles (11 km) south of the city and can be reached by bus, rail, and taxi. International and Domestic flights have separate terminals. Shuttle buses (Nos. 300 or 350) link the terminals to each other and to the Central Railroad Station, Town Hall, and Circular Quay. Many city hotels operate their own shuttle buses. A taxi to the city center costs around $A15 (U.S.$7.50) and takes about 30 minutes. Rail services go to Central station.
Note: a departure tax is assessed. This is usually pre-paid as part of your air ticket.

GETTING AROUND

BY AIR

Australia has an excellent network of domestic air services linking the main cities, Outback communities, and vacation islands off the Northern Territory and Queensland. The competitors for domestic services are Qantas and Ansett, both of which operate with a number of associate airlines. Short term, special fares are available throughout the year and are widely advertised in the media. International travelers may also be able to obtain a 20 percent (Ansett) or 30 percent (Qantas) discount on the purchase price of a full-economy domestic fare on presentation of their international ticket.

Discount air passes are also available, but you must buy them

before you enter Australia. The Qantas **Boomerang Pass** lets you buy a minimum of two coupons (one coupon per flight) for economy air travel. Two price levels ($A220/U.S.$110, or $A275/U.S.$140, one way) apply to Australian cities and other Qantas destinations depending on travel between fare zones within Australia. The Ansett **Visit Australia/New Zealand Pass** works in a similar way. Both have various restrictions, but these passes are good value if you are sure of where you want to go, cannot tag your preferences onto your inter-national ticket, and have only a limited amount of time available. Full details of passes and restrictions may be obtained from your travel agent, or contact Qantas or Ansett direct.
Qantas
For overseas offices, see p. 358.
Australia: Tel 13 13 13 (calls charged at local rate)
Ansett
U.S.: Tel 800/366-1300
Canada: Tel 800/366-1300
U.K.: Tel 020-8741 2299
Australia: Tel 13 13 00

BY CAR

Drive on the left and overtake on the right. Remember to give way to traffic coming from the right at traffic circles. (Pedes-trians should remember to look right for traffic when crossing a road.) Roads are generally well kept. You need to take special care if driving long distances, though, especially if you use Outback dirt tracks. (See Driving Safely, below.)

RENTING A CAR

Rental costs vary according to season, demand, availability, and the size and type of car required. Check whether the cost covers unlimited mileage. Certain companies add an additional charge for miles traveled over a stated limit. Prices start at around $A40 (U.S.$20) a day or $A250 (U.S.$125) a week for a manual

gear shift, economy car. There may also be local or airport surcharges. Always check the condition of the car before you drive away and report any concerns immediately. Normally you must return the car to the place it was rented from. Occasionally cars may be dropped elsewhere (for a fee).

You may get a cheaper rate if you book the car before you leave home. Most major agencies, for example Avis, Hertz, and Budget, have an international booking section. They give advice on rates, restrictions, and availability at your chosen destination and, if you choose, reserve a car for your arrival.
Avis, Level 2, 15 Bourke Rd., Mascot 2020, tel (02) 9353 9033 or 1-800 225 533
Hertz, 10–16 Dorcas St., South Melbourne 3205, tel (03) 9222 2523 or 13 30 39, 1-800 550 067
Budget, 128 Jolimonet Rd., East Melbourne 3202, tel (03) 9206 3222 or 1-300 362 848

Rental conditions
You must have a valid driver's license and be at least 21 years of age (a premium may be charged for any driver under 25). Third party insurance and collision damage waiver are compulsory and are included in the cost of the rental. Comprehensive coverage and personal accident insurance are available at extra cost, but do check the coverage provided by your home car and travel insurance policies. Nearly all companies will insist that you pay for the rental with a major international credit or charge card. You may well find additional insurance protection on the card you use for payment.

Four-wheel-drive
A four-wheel-drive (4WD) is essential for Outback travel. Rental companies usually rent them only to those with previous four-wheel-drive experience. The rental and

insurance costs are higher than for an ordinary car. Damage to the vehicle caused by the driver is not covered by insurance.

Motorhomes & camper vans
These may be rented locally in all states. The minimum rental period is usually a week, and good reductions may be obtained for longer periods. Rates are highest in the main holiday season of December and January. Motorcycles may be rented only in New South Wales and Western Australia.

DRIVING REGULATIONS
The use of seat belts is compulsory in Australia. Drivers must ensure that passengers wear them—failure to do so results in a fine. Fines may follow you home, because car rental com-panies will supply customer address details to the authorities.

ROAD SIGNS
Signs are easy to understand. Speeds and distances are given in kilometers. Speed limits are set at 60 kph (37 mph) in urban areas, 100 kph (62 mph) on highways and country roads, and 110 kph (68 mph) on freeways. The Northern Territory has no speed limits. Elsewhere they are strictly enforced.

FUEL
Fuel (leaded, unleaded, or diesel) is sold by the liter. Expect to pay around 85 Australian cents a liter (U.S.$3.50 a U.S. gallon) in the city and around $A1 a liter (U.S.$4.50 a U.S. gallon) in the outback.

ALCOHOL
Permitted blood alcohol limits are low, and it is wise to avoid all alcoholic drinks when in charge of a vehicle. Police checks are frequent and the penalties severe.

DRIVING SAFELY
Long-distance driving has its own hazards in Australia. Although the main highways are well

maintained, they can be very tiring. Always build sufficient rest periods into any journey time, and do not underestimate the draining power of the sun and its glare. Always carry a good supply of water and snacks.

If planning to use dirt tracks, ensure that the vehicle is suitable and that you are prepared for emergencies. Check the weather forecast and road conditions with the local police before setting out. Deep, fine "bulldust" can prove impassable for even an experienced four-wheel-driver. Flash floods and dust storms are common in season (which varies from area to area; check with local police offices for information). Be wary of animals on the road, particularly at dawn and dusk.

The need for care cannot be over emphasized. Know where you are on your maps. Break-down or other assistance may not be easy to attract. As well as water and snack foods to sustain you in case of emergency or delay, take warm blankets. A flashlight (with spare batteries) will help if you are stranded overnight. Use common sense and have a healthy respect for an unforgiving environment. Carry a good first aid kit, spare fuel, and adequate tools to make basic repairs to your vehicle.

If you are planning to visit a remote national park, find out from locals and police at your starting point about road conditions, what gear to take, and what to do if things go wrong. Listen to advice and always leave word with a responsible person or the local police about where you are going and when you expect to return.

AUTOMOBILE ASSOCIATIONS

The Australian associations provide services to members of most foreign motoring organizations as they would

to their own members. You need to have a valid membership card from your own organization if requesting a service. Breakdown assistance may also be available.

A.A.A. (Automobile Association of Australia)
21 Northbourne Ave.
Canberra
ACT 2601
Tel (06) 6247 7311

N.R.M.A. (National Roads and Motorists' Association)
92 Northbourne Ave.
Canberra
ACT 2601
Tel (06) 6243 8958

WHAT TO DO IN AN ACCIDENT

Take the names and addresses of any witnesses, the driver of the other vehicle, and the owner if different. Note the make, model, and registration number of the other vehicle. Exchange insurance information and contact details. Make a note of damage to the vehicle and any injuries to yourself and other persons. Record details of the scene—visibility, traffic flow, road details, and surface conditions. Record details of the collision, including speed of travel and point of impact.

All accidents unless they are minor scrapes must be reported to the police. Cooperate with the police officer. Make a note of the officer's name, number, and where he or she may be contacted. Draw a sketch of the accident showing the layout of the road and the position and movement of the vehicles involved. Keep all of these details for the insurance report.

BUYING A VEHICLE

Before you buy a motor vehicle in Australia, check that it has a current annual Roadworthiness Certificate (RWC), in addition to making the obvious safety checks. When you want to resell a car, it is advisable to return to the state in which you bought it.

LONG DISTANCE BUS ROUTES

If money is a constraint, or if you have the time and want to get a feel for the immense size and geography of the country, go by bus. Traveling the long distance bus routes is usually the cheapest way of getting around Australia. All the major cities and highways are serviced by large express companies that link up with regional operators serving smaller communities. All the major carriers have comfortable buses with onboard sanitary facilities. Air-conditioning is the norm, and drivers often run videos on overhead monitors.

Discount fares and passes are cheaper if you buy them before you leave home, but you can still buy them in Australia. The main operators are Greyhound Pioneer and McCafferty's.

Greyhound's Unlimited Travel Pass gives you a fixed number of days of travel in a given period. You can travel on any route. The minimum is 7 days travel within 30 days (cost around $A450/U.S.$225). The long-est is 90 days within 6 months (around $A2,225/U.S.$1,110). This facilitates extensive travel but is normally more than most people want. The more popular set route passes allow you either 6 or 12 months to cover a route. There are 33 routes to chose from, including Cairns to Perth via the Top End (one way, around $A490/U.S.$245) and a Sydney–Sydney loop through Melbourne, Alice Springs, Cairns, and down again along the east coast (around $A690/U.S.$345). The **All Australia Pass** takes you around the country and north or south through the center for $A1,200 (U.S.$600). Discounts of up to 20 percent are often available on these prices.

Greyhound Pioneer
From outside Australia,

tel 0061 7 3258 1736, fax 0061 7 3258 1910.

From within Australia, tel 13 20 30 (calls charged at local rates) or try www.greyhound.com.au

McCafferty's has 15 set routes to choose from, and they are designed and priced to compete with Greyhound. McCafferty's **Travel Australia Pass,** for example, is similar to Greyhound's All Australia Pass, and costs around $A1,160 (U.S.$580). The set-route pass for the **Nullarbor Plain** includes travel on the Indian–Pacific train service between Adelaide and Perth. The **Tassie Discovery** pass allows a circuit of Tasmania over 7, 14, or 30 days, and includes the ferry passage from Melbourne.

McCafferty's
From outside Australia, tel 0061 7 4690 9809, fax 0061 7 4638 3815.
From within Australia, tel 13 14 99, or try www.mccaffertys .com.au

BUS TOURS
Many Australian travel operators run bus, or coach, tours. These range from a few days in luxury, air-conditioned buses and hotels, to several weeks camping out of a beaten-up jalopy. The former provides interesting narration, a minimum of physical activity, and every creature comfort. On the latter, everyone is expected to lend a hand and enjoy a sleep under the stars. Some of the most popular tours run out of Darwin and Adelaide to Alice Springs and Uluru (Ayers Rock). Other popular routes are Cairns–Brisbane and Brisbane–Sydney. Check with your travel agent for further information, or with the Australian Tourist Commission.

BY TRAIN

LONG DISTANCE TRAIN ROUTES
The Indian–Pacific runs twice a week from Sydney to Perth (and vice versa) via the Nullarbor Plain, with a running time of 65 hours (see p. 248). The Ghan train runs twice a week from Adelaide to Alice Springs (and vice versa) through the Outback, with a running time of 20 hours (see pp. 282–83), and once a week to Melbourne in 36 hours. The Queenslander runs daily from Brisbane to Cairns (and vice versa) and takes 32 hours. All these services have luxury packages that include sleeper accommodations and meals.

Rail passes may be valid across Australia or in just one state. You can get reductions of up to 30 percent by booking at least 7 days in advance. There are several passes to choose from, but the following are the most popular:
The **Austrail Pass** lets you travel anywhere on the rail network over a set number of days within a fixed period, in either economy or first class. To travel 8 days over 60 you would pay $A320 (U.S.$160) economy or $530 (U.S.$265) first class; for 15 days over 90 $A475–750 (U.S.$238–375). You have to buy this pass before leaving for Australia. The **Austrail FlexiPass** allows you to travel the whole network, with 8 (excluding Adelaide–Perth and Adelaide–Alice Springs), 15, 22, or 29 days travel over a 6-month period. An 8-day pass for economy class travel costs around $A360 (U.S.$180) (first class $A620/U.S.$310); a 15-day pass costs around $A520 (U.S.$260) (first class $A870/U.S.$435).

You can book at any railroad office or direct with either:
ROA Rail Australia
1 Richmond House, Keswick, SA 5035, tel (in Australia) 13 22 32; or **Great Southern Railways** P.O. Box 445, Marleston S.A. 5033. Or visit their website at www.gsr.com.au.
Great Southern Railway also operate the Overlander, a weekly overnight service from Adelaide to Melbourne and return.

BY BOAT

The only regular maritime service in Australia is the *Spirit of Tasmania* car ferry that sails between Melbourne and Devonport, Tasmania (see p. 333). The sailing takes around 14 hours and is often cursed by rough seas.

Some international cruise liners, for example Holland America Lines, P&O, and Princess Cruises, sail around Australia. Typically they dock at Sydney and continue along the coastline stopping at Brisbane and Cairns to the east, Melbourne, Adelaide, and Hobart to the south, or Fremantle in the west.

Numerous pleasure boats, catamarans, and yachts operate out of the mainland towns along the east coast and islands on the Great Barrier Reef, and out of Exmouth on the west coast, for Ningaloo Reef. Some give a day's island hopping, with dolphin-watching and whale-watching, snorkeling, and scuba diving. Others go for up to a week of diving and sailing out at sea.

There are river cruises along the Murray River in South Australia (see pp. 276–77) and Victoria (see pp. 324–25), Mayall Lakes in New South Wales, and the Hawkesbury River north of Sydney.

PRACTICAL ADVICE

CHILDREN

Most hotels allow children under a certain age to stay in their parents' room for free or at a discounted rate. The cut-off age varies considerably (the average is 12). Australia's Hyatt hotels do not charge for children under 18 staying with their parents. A few hotels still charge for children as if they were adults. The Australian suburbs have a large number of family restaurants, with special menus for children, high chairs, and booster seats.

COMMUNICATIONS

MAIL

Stamps may be purchased from post offices, hotels, and many shops. The rate for domestic letters is 45 Australian cents (23 cents). Rates to North America are 95 Australian cents (48 cents) for an airmail postcard and $A1.05 (53 cents) per 20 grams for an airmail letter. Rates to the U.K. are $A1 and $A1.20. Heavier packages may be sent by sea mail, economy air, or airmail.

Poste restante

Larger offices have a free poste restante (general delivery) service (as do some Outback offices). Take proof of identity, such as a passport or driver's license, when collecting. American Express has a client mail service at its main city offices.

TELEPHONES

Australia has an excellent telephone system and modern exchange. There are numerous public telephones that take both coins and prepaid phone cards. Many city telephones also accept credit cards. Phone cards are readily available and are sold in 5, 10, 20, and 50 Australian dollar units. Local calls from public phones cost 40 Australian cents (20 cents) for an unlimited amount of time. The same call from a private phone costs 30 cents.

You can make a long-distance call from virtually any public telephone, with a minimum charge of $A1.20 (60 cents). Calls to the U.S., Canada, and U.K. cost around $A1 (50 cents) per minute in off-peak hours (the cheapest time is 10 p.m. to 8 a.m.).

Toll-free numbers in Australia have the prefix 1-800. Six-digit numbers starting with 13 are charged at local rates, regardless of where the answering office might be.

Mobile phones are charged at special rates and can prove expensive.

To call from Australia to the U.S. or Canada use 00 11 1.
To call from Australia to the U.K. use 00 11 44.

FAX

Overseas fax services cost around $A10 (U.S.$5) for the first page and $A4 (U.S.$2) for each page thereafter.

E-MAIL & ON-LINE SERVICES

All the big cities have on-line services at Internet cafés. These allow you to use the internet and send e-mail at a half-hour or hourly rate (around $A10/U.S.$5 an hour). You do not have to be a member and you may use the café address for responses to your mail, but there will be a charge for search and retrieval, or printouts. If you are traveling with a laptop, check with your local provider before leaving for Australia. Several larger service providers, such as AOL, have local Australian numbers that you can access from your hotel.

CONVERSIONS

Australia uses the metric system. Useful conversions are:

Weights & Measures
1 mile = 1.61 kilometers
1 kilometer = 0.62 mile
1 pint = 0.47 liters
1 liter = 2.12 pints
1 U.S. gallon = 3.78 liters
1 pound = 0.37 kilos
1 kilo = 2.20 pounds
1 ounce = 31 grams
1 foot = 0.30 meters
1 meter = 39.37 inches

Clothing
Women's clothing

American	8	10	12	14	16	18
Australian	10	12	14	16	18	20

Men's clothing

American	36	38	40	42	44	46
Australian	92	97	102	107	112	117

Men's shirts

American	15	15.5	16	16.5	17
Australian	38	39	41	42	43

Women's shoes

American	6	6.5	7	7.5	8	8.5
Australian	6.5	7	7.5	8	8.5	9

Men's shoes

American	8	8.5	9.5	10.5	11.5	12
Australian	7	7.5	8.5	9.5	10.5	11

ELECTRICITY

Australian electrical appliances have plugs with three flat pins. Electrical voltage is 240 AC, 50 cycles. Most visitors need to use an adapter.

GAY & LESBIAN TRAVELERS

The Australian Gay and Lesbian Tourism Association promotes gay and lesbian travel within Australia, and it is an excellent source of help and information. A.G.L.T.A., P.O. Box 208, Darlinghurst, NSW 2010 Tel (02) 9955 6755 Fax (02) 9922 6036

LIQUOR LAWS

It is against the law for anyone under the age of 18 to buy alcohol or consume alcohol in public. Serving hours for public bars are usually 10 a.m.–10 p.m., Monday through Saturday, Sunday hours vary. Restaurants, clubs, and hotel lounges have more flexible hours. Alcohol is sold at liquor stores, hotels, and other licensed premises (not at supermarkets).

Many restaurants are licensed to sell alcohol, but some may only be able to sell it to you if you are having it with a meal. Others are BYO (bring your own). Most restaurants will allow you to BYO; they may charge a small corkage fee for opening the bottle and serving it to you.

MEDIA

NEWSPAPERS

News International's *The Australian* and the *Daily Telegraph* are the only newpapers available country wide. Otherwise, each state has its own daily paper: the *Sydney Morning Herald* and from Melbourne *The Age* are the best known.

TV CHANNELS

There are three commercial networks (Seven, Nine, and Ten), plus the Government owned but substantially independent Australian Broadcasting Corporation channel (Channel Two) and the similarly established multicultural channel, SBS. There are two cable networks, Foxtel and Optus Vision, which feature sports channels, movie channels, and news channels such as CNN.

RADIO

There are numerous radio channels on the AM and FM bands. 2GB and 2BL have news and talkback programs, 2WS, 2-DAY-FM, and MMM play popular music, jjj is the youth station, and ABC-FM and 2MBS are devoted to classical music.

MONEY

The unit of currency is the Australian dollar, which consists of 100 cents. The 1 cent coin is no longer in circulation and prices are rounded up or down to the nearest 5 cents. Coins are available in 5, 10, 20, and 50 cents, and 1 and 2 dollars. Bills are in 5, 10, 20, 50, and 100 dollar denominations. Different colors and sizes make them easy to identify.

Traveler's checks are a straight-forward and secure way to carry money. You may change traveler's checks at almost any bank or licensed money changer, using your passport and/or driver's license as proof of identity. Fees vary from bank to bank, as do commission charges.

The major international credit cards are widely accepted throughout Australia, and even small towns seem to have an ATM allowing Mastercard or Visa cash withdrawals. Major charge cards, such as American Express, are also widely accepted. You should carry cash on long journeys in the outback. In all cases it is sensible to carry a mixture of traveler's checks, credit cards, and cash.

NATIONAL HOLIDAYS

January 1 (New Year's Day)
January 26 (Australia Day)
March/April (Good Friday, Easter Saturday, Easter Sunday, and Easter Monday)
April 25 (Anzac Day)
Second Monday in June (Queen's Birthday national holiday except Western Australia)
December 25 and 26 (Christmas Day and Boxing Day)

NATIONAL TRUST

The National Trust is dedicated to preserving historic buildings throughout Australia, many of which are open to the public.

Membership gives you free entry to any National Trust property. Helpful leaflets on historic buildings and walks around many towns and cities are available at National Trust offices.

Australian Capital Territory
2 Light St.
Griffith, ACT 2603
Tel (02) 6239 5222

New South Wales
Observatory Hill
Sydney, NSW
Tel (02) 9258 0123

Northern Territory
4 Burnett Place
Darwin, NT 0800
Tel (08) 8981 2848

Queensland
Old Government House

George St.
Brisbane, QLD 4000
Tel (07) 3229 1788

South Australia
2/27 Leigh St.
Adelaide, SA 5000
Tel (08) 8212 1133

Tasmania
Brisbane St.
Hobart, TAS 7000
Tel (03) 6223 5200

Victoria
Tasma Terrace
4 Parliament Place
Melbourne, Vic. 3002
Tel (03) 9654 4711

Western Australia
Old Observatory
4 Havelock St.
West Perth, WA 6005
Tel (08) 9321 6088

OPENING HOURS

Shop hours vary from state to state, but the core opening hours are Monday to Friday 9 a.m. to 5 p.m. and Saturday 9 a.m. to 1 p.m. Many towns have late night shopping Thursday and/or Friday to 9 p.m. Shops in many tourist areas also open for a short time on Sunday.
Banks are open Monday to Thursday 9:30 a.m. to 4 p.m., and Friday 9:30 a.m. to 5 p.m. In some states banks are also open on Saturday mornings.
Post offices are open Monday to Friday 9 a.m. to 5 p.m. Many post offices open on Saturday mornings as well.

PHOTOGRAPHY & VIDEO

Quality film and processing are available throughout Australia. Take extra care in the tropical heat, which may affect the life and quality of your film and batteries. The intense glare from the sun and its reflection on the water may bleach your photographs of color. The best light for photography is in the early morning and late afternoon.

SENIOR TRAVELERS

There are various discounts for senior citizens in Australia, but senior citizens from abroad cannot claim them. However, it is always worth asking about discounts or promotional rates, particularly at hotels, with tour operators, and at car rental agencies.

SWIMMING & BEACHES

Australia has some very fine beaches and swimming holes. As always when swimming off unfamiliar beaches, take notice of tides, currents, and forecast weather conditions. It is advisable to swim only on beaches that have lifeguard support or supervision. A red-and-yellow flag indicates that it is safe to swim. A red flag warns that you should stay out of the water because of strong currents, rough seas, or less obvious dangers, such as sharks, blue-ringed octopuses, or scorpion fish.

Between October and May, the seas of the tropical north may contain poisonous box jellyfish (stingers). All year round the saltwater crocodile poses a serious danger to swimmers. Always heed signs warning of crocodiles. If you are camping, keep at least 50 yards back from the water's edge, and don't follow the same route when going to fetch your water.

TIME DIFFERENCES

Australia has three time zones. **Eastern standard time** East coast states—Tasmania, Queensland, Victoria, & New South Wales: 10 hours ahead of Greenwich Mean Time (GMT) and 15 hours ahead of U.S. Eastern standard time. **Central standard time** South Australia & Northern Territory: 9.5 hours ahead of GMT. **Western standard time** Western Australia: 8 hours ahead of GMT.

During the summer most states observe Daylight Savings Time, moving the clock forward by one hour. If used, Daylight Savings Time begins in October or November, depending on the state, and ends in March.

TIPPING

Tipping is not an Australian tradition. It is a matter of choice. A waiter at a quality restaurant, however, would anticipate a gratuity of up to 10 percent of the total bill if you have been satisfied with the service.

TRAVELERS WITH DISABILITIES

The Australian Tourist Commission has Consumer Helplines around the world and provides a fact sheet, called "Travel in Australia for People With Disabilities," with the addresses of helpful organizations in each state or territory.

N.I.C.A.N., National Information Communications Network, P.O. Box 407, Curtin, ACT 2605, tel (02) 6285 3713, fax (02) 6285 3714, provides an Australia-wide directory of accessible accommodations, and sporting and recreational facilities.

A.C.R.O.D., Australian Council for the Rehabilitation of the Disabled, P.O. Box 60, Curtin, ACT 2605, tel (02) 6282 4333, fax (02) 6281 3488, offers advice on state-based help organizations, accommodations, and specialist tour operators.

Air travel All of Australia's airports have facilities for travelers with disabilities. Certain Qantas jets carry skychairs and have an accessible toilet on board.

Trains Facilities vary. On the Indian–Pacific (Sydney–Perth), for example, one cabin in each carriage provides wheelchair access. A skychair is used for boarding and movement

between carriages. Conditions may not suit everyone. For further information, contact the Passenger Services Manager in Sydney, tel (02) 9255 7833.

Car rental Avis and Hertz have cars with hand controls. They must be reserved in advance but can be collected from major airports at no extra charge.

Parking & public toilets Major city councils provide mobility maps.

Ferry The *Spirit of Tasmania* (see p. 333) has four wheelchair-accessible cabins and provides access to the public areas on the ship.

VOLUNTEER VACATIONS

The Australian Trust for Conservation Volunteers, P.O. Box 423, Ballarat, Vic. 3350, tel (03) 5333 1483 organizes practical conservation projects for volunteers. Projects run from two days to a week and provide all food, transportation, and accommodations in return for your work and a contribution toward costs (around $A120/U.S.$60 a week). The work varies—typically, volunteers might find themselves planting trees, conducting fauna surveys, or clearing tracks. You can sign up for a Banksia Package, which is a six-week series of projects.

EMERGENCIES

EMERGENCY TELEPHONE NUMBER

Throughout Australia, the toll free emergency services number for fire, ambulance, or police is **000.**

EMBASSIES & CONSULATES

Most countries have an embassy or high commission within

Canberra and a consular office in the major cities. Visa applications are generally handled in Canberra. For consulates, consult the local telephone directory.

United States
21 Moonah Place
Yarralumla
Canberra
ACT 2600
Tel (02) 6270 5000

Canada
Commonwealth Ave.
Yarralumla
Canberra
ACT 2600
Tel (02) 6273 3844

United Kingdom
Commonwealth Ave.
Yarralumla
Canberra
ACT 2600
Tel (02) 6270 6666

HEALTH

Medical care in Australia is excellent and not expensive. A doctor's appointment typically costs around $A35 (U.S.$18). The U.K., New Zealand, Sweden, and the Netherlands, have reciprocal health care arrangements with Australia, and residents from these countries are entitled to free or heavily subsidized medical treatment at public hospitals and certain clinics.

Inoculations
None are essential. Cholera, malaria, and yellow fever are unknown, though tropical diseases such as dengue fever are a problem (see Insects, below). It is sensible to be vaccinated against tetanus, and hepatitis (A and B)—but that is true whether you are traveling or not.

Spiders & snakes
Thirteen of the most poisonous snakes and spiders in the world live in Australia. Snakes live in the water as well as on the land,

but both prefer to stay out of your way and usually go before you've had a chance to spot them. If you are bitten by a snake, try to remember what it looked like (but never pursue it), and go straight to the hospital for anti-venom. Most snake venom needs a few hours to take hold, but the shock of the bite can be as dangerous as the bite itself.

The most dangerous spiders in Australia are the red back and funnel web. The latter is most common and most poisonous in the suburbs of Sydney. Again, if bitten, try to remember the features of the spider and go straight to the hospital.

Sunburn
Do not underestimate the power of the sun. Australia has the highest incidence of skin cancer in the world. The hole in the ozone layer is directly above Australia, and its clear blue skies offer very little protection from the sun's burning ultraviolet radiation. Try to stay out of the sun between 11 a.m. and 3 p.m. Always wear properly applied, high-factor suntan lotion and a hat. Keep neck and arms well covered. Protect your eyes with quality sunglasses that fit well.

Insects
Flies can be a horrific nuisance in the Outback, where they will settle on you by the hundred, seeking moisture from your ears, eyes, and nose.

Mosquitoes can also be a real problem in Australia, not just for the irritation of their bites, but because they may be carrying the Ross River virus or dengue fever. These can be as debilitating as malaria, or worse.

Ask advice locally and use an effective insect repellent or fly net when necessary.

INFORMATION OFFICES

The Australian Tourist Commission (A.T.C.) runs tourist information offices in most countries.

United States
2049 Century Park East
Ste. 1920
Los Angeles, CA 90067
Tel: 310/229-4870
Fax:(301/552-1215

United Kingdom
Gemini House
10-18 Putney Hill
London SW15 6AA
Tel 09068 633235 (cost 60p per minute)
Fax 020-8780 1496

INTERNET INFORMATION

The Australian Tourist Commission and the Office of National Tourism give travel and reservation advice at the following addresses:
www.australia.com
www.aussie.net.au
www.tourism.gov.au

For up-to-date news, weather, finance, and sports information, as well as shopping and fashion, try: www.ninemsn.com.

Telephone numbers for the whole of Australia can be checked out on:
www.telstra.com.

STATE TOURIST OFFICES

Each state in Australia runs a central visitor information office. These are generally open Monday to Friday 9 a.m. to 5 p.m., and on Saturday mornings. They give information, maps, and brochures.

Local tourist offices (addresses and telephone numbers on the relevant pages in text) may also reserve accommodations, tours, and transportation.

Australian Capital Territory (ACT)
ACT Tourism Commission
CBS Tower (8th Floor)
Akuna & Bunda Sts.
Canberra, ACT 2601
Tel (02) 6205 0666

New South Wales
NSW Tourism Commission
19 Castlereagh St.
Sydney, NSW 2000
Tel 13 20 77

Northern Territory
Northern Territory Tourism
Commission
43 Mitchell St.
Darwin, NT 0800
Tel (08) 8999 3900

Central Australian Tourism
Industry Association
Corner of Gregory Terrace &
Todd St.
Alice Springs, NT
Tel (08) 8952 5199

Queensland
Queensland Tourist & Travel
Corporation
Corner of Adelaide &
Albert Sts.
Brisbane, QLD 4000
Tel (07) 3229 5918

Gold Coast Tourism Bureau
Level 2, 64 Ferny Ave.
Surfers Paradise, QLD 4217
Tel (07) 5592 2699
Fax (07) 5570 3144

South Australia
South Australian Travel Centre
18 King William St.
Adelaide, SA 5000
Tel (08) 8303 2033 or
1-800 882 092 (toll free)
Fax (08) 8303 2231

Tasmania
Tasmanian Travel
& Information Office
20 Davey St.
Hobart, TAS 7000
Tel (03) 6230 8233

Victoria
Tourism Victoria
Level 12, 55 Swanston St.
Melbourne, VIC 3000
Tel (03) 9653 9777

Western Australia
Western Australia Tourism
Commission
Albert Facey House
Forrest Place
Perth, WA 6000
Tel (08) 9483 1111

NATIONAL PARKS OFFICES

Every state also has offices for
the departments in charge of
the national parks, the environment, natural resources, &
heritage. These are variously
named, but all offer information
and advice on visiting national
parks, heritage sites, and nature
reserves. The larger national
parks have their own information offices. Details of those are
given on the relevant pages.

New South Wales
National Parks & Wildlife
Service
43 Bridge St.
P.O. Box 1967
Hurstville, NSW 2220
Tel (02) 9585 6333
www.npws.nsw.gov.au

Northern Territory
Parks & Wildlife Commission of
the Northern Territory
Gaymark Building
Mansfield Lane
Palmerston, NT 0830
Tel (08) 8999 4401

Queensland
Department of Environment &
Heritage
160 Ann St.
Brisbane, QLD 4000
Tel (07) 3227 8186

South Australia
Department of Environment
& Natural Resources
77 Grenfell St.
Adelaide, SA 5001
Tel (08) 8204 1910

Tasmania
Department of Parks, Wildlife
& Heritage
134 Macquarie St.
Hobart, TAS 7000
Tel (03) 6233 6191

Victoria
Department of Conservation &
Natural Resources
240 Victoria Parade
P.O. Box 41 East Melbourne,
VIC 3002
Tel (03) 9412 4011

Western Australia
Department of Conservation
& Land Management (CALM)
50 Hayman Rd.
Como
Perth, WA 6152
Tel (08) 9334 0333

HOTELS & RESTAURANTS

Australian accommodations and restaurants are probably more sharply divided between city and small town than in most other countries. Cities have a wide choice of hotels from luxury to modest and a huge variety of restaurants. In the country, except in tourist areas, both accommodations and food are basic but adequate. An Australian specialty is the backpackers hostel, offering cheap but clean beds, sometimes in a dormitory. Aimed at traveling students, they also accommodate many a middle-age visitor on a budget.

ACCOMMODATIONS
Hotels
All the state capitals have luxury hotels belonging to international chains. Hotel groups providing high quality accommodations are easily accessible. Rooms may usually be booked through the hotels' international network. In both town and country areas throughout Australia more modest hotel accommodations are also available. In the Outback the only hotel is the local pub. The mainland coasts and the islands of the Great Barrier Reef have resort hotels, with a wide range of recreational activities.

Hotel rates
The ranges of prices given for hotels are based on the standard full price for a double room. Off season, many hotels are prepared to offer guests special rates. It is always worth asking if any such arrangements are available.

Motels
Travelers on a budget find these establishments good value. They offer comfortable bedrooms, sometimes with small kitchen-ettes and often with a single as well as a double bed. Most are located on main roads on the outskirts of towns and cities, but some are in city centers. Prices range from $A40–100 (U.S. $20–50) per night per room.

Guesthouses & homestays
These accommodations range from a simple bedroom in a family home to a fully converted barn or a romantic country house. Prices range between $A40–100 (U.S.$20–50) a night, per double room, with breakfast. Book directly or through an

agent. For information contact:
Bed and Breakfast Australia
P.O. Box 727, Newport Beach,
NSW 2106
tel (02) 9999 0366

Hostels
Australia has an extensive and competitive network of hostels. The Australian Youth Hostels Association, 10 Mallett St., Camperdown, NSW 2050, tel (02) 9565 1699 has hostels nationwide. Standards vary considerably, from the rustic cabin with water drawn from a creek, to the 500-bed modern building, with air-conditioning, swimming pool, sauna, launder-ette, and state of the art kitchen facilities. Top end prices hover at A$20 (U.S.$10) per night, for a bunk in a dorm. Hostels are aimed at young, independent travelers, although no age restrictions apply. Guests tend to be members of one or more hosteling organizations. Membership privileges include reservations, discounts on travel, activities, and basic supplies. Further details of membership and travel centers may be obtained from the address above.

Farm stays
Visitors can watch the everyday work on a farm, explore the surroundings, and enjoy hearty farm cooking. One agency that can arrange farm stays is Australian Farmhost & Farm Holidays, P.O. Box 41, Walla Walla, NSW 2659, tel (02) 6029 8621. Holders of a visitor's visa are not officially permitted to take paid work on a farm, but voluntary work is possible: see Volunteer Vacations (p. 364).

see Volunteer Vacations (p. 364).

PRICES

HOTELS
An indication of the cost of a double room without breakfast is given by **$** signs.

$$$$$	Over $280
$$$$	$200–$280
$$$	$120–$200
$$	$80–$120
$	Under $80

RESTAURANTS
An indication of the cost of a three-course dinner without drinks is given by **$** signs.

$$$$$	Over $80
$$$$	$50–$80
$$$	$35–$50
$$	$20–$35
$	Under $20

Cottages
York Mansions, York St., Launceston, Tas 7250, tel (03) 6334 2933, arranges rental of 19th-century houses and cottages, furnished in traditional style, throughout Tasmania.

Camping, RVs, motorhomes
The majority of parks are well equipped, with power hook-ups, hot and cold water, toilets, showers, waste disposal, and coin-operated laundry facilities. Many also have public telephones, television and recreation rooms, a swimming pool, and conven-ience stores. Occasionally it may be possible to rent bed linen. Site-owned RVs or cabins, often with private sanitary facilities, may also be rented.

The New South Wales N.R.M.A. (National Roads and Motorist Association, 388 George St., Sydney, NSW 2000, tel 1-800 251 574, toll free) publishes an annual list of Australian camping and RV parks.

RESTAURANTS
Major cities have a huge variety of eating places: hamburger joints, vegetarian cafés, ethnic restaurants from a bewildering

---

number of countries, right up to the newest of celebrity chef-owned elegant restaurants. Small towns, particularly Outback ones, will not be able to offer much more than basic eateries.

Closings for holidays may vary from year to year. It is advisable to check, and to reserve a table.
L = lunch
D = dinner

AE American Express, DC Diners Club, MC Mastercard, V Visa.

In the following selection, hotels are listed under each location by price, then in alphabetical order, followed by restaurants also by price and alphabetical order.

SYDNEY

🏨 THE OBSERVATORY
$$$$$
89–113 KENT ST., THE ROCKS
TEL (02) 9256 2222
FAX (02) 9256 2233
Only a few minutes from downtown, this hotel in the historic Rocks area has every conceivable luxury, including a beautiful star-ceilinged indoor pool and deep spa baths. Each of the sumptuous guest rooms has a marble bathroom and a balcony.
🛏 100 🚉 Wynyard 🅿
🔃 Ⓢ Ⓢ 🔲 🔲 🗠 All major cards

🏨 PARK HYATT SYDNEY
$$$$$
7 HICKSON RD., THE ROCKS
TEL (02) 9241 1234
FAX (02) 9256 1555
One of the most luxurious hotels in Sydney, with good views of the Opera House. The spacious, extremely comfortable rooms have marble bathrooms and walk-in closets. The service is faultless.
🛏 158 🚉 Circular Quay
🅿 🔃 Ⓢ Ⓢ 🗠 🔲
🗠 All major cards

🏨 RUSSELL
$$–$$$$
143A GEORGE ST., THE ROCKS
TEL (02) 9241 3543
FAX (02) 9252 1652
Room styles, sizes, facilities, and rates vary considerably at this small, friendly hotel. There is a pleasant roof garden with views of the harbor. No air-conditioning.
🛏 30 🚉 Circular Quay 🅿
🗠 All major cards

🏨 HUGHENDEN BOUTIQUE
$$–$$$
14 QUEEN ST., WOOLLAHRA
TEL (02) 9363 4863
FAX (02) 9362 0398
This prettily renovated hotel is close to Sydney's main concentration of antique shops and art dealers. A cooked breakfast is included in the basic rate.
🛏 36 🅿 16 Ⓢ Ⓢ
🗠 All major cards

🏨 VICTORIA COURT SYDNEY
$$–$$$
122 VICTORIA ST., POTTS POINT
TEL (02) 9357 3200
FAX (02) 9357 7606
Small, 19th-century terrace house, with comfortable rooms; the best ones have balconies. Breakfast in the courtyard conservatory.
🛏 25 🚉 Kings Cross 🅿 4
Ⓢ Ⓢ 🗠 All major cards

🍴 ROCKPOOL
$$$$$
107 GEORGE ST., THE ROCKS
TEL (02) 9252 1888
Possibly the best restaurant in Australia, and the most expensive. The outstanding cooking is Australian with Asian, Chinese, and European influences, such as Chinese roast pigeon with shiitake mushroom lasagne. Glamorous environment. Reservations essential.
🍽 100 🕐 Closed Sat. L & all Sun. 🚉 Circular Quay
Ⓢ Ⓢ 🗠 All major cards

🍴 BATHER'S PAVILION
$$$$–$$$$$
THE ESPLANADE, BALMORAL BEACH
TEL (02) 9968 1133
A restored turn-of-last-century beach house, converted to a restaurant, the Bather's Pavilion serves up tasty seafood in a delightful setting. Its weekend champagne breakfasts are legendary indulgences.
🍽 85 Ⓢ Ⓢ 🗠 All major cards

🍴 BENNELONG
For a special experience dine under the small sails of the Opera House. Dishes run the gamut from baked eggs for a weekend brunch to a memorable sautéed lobster with anchovies and rosemary.
$$$$
SYDNEY OPERA HOUSE BENNELONG POINT
TEL (02) 9250 7548
🍽 140 🚉 Circular Quay
🅿 🕐 Closed Sun. D Ⓢ
Ⓢ 🗠 All major cards

🍴 CLAUDES
$$$$
10 OXFORD ST., WOOLLAHRA
TEL (02) 9331 2325
Relaxed, elegant dining, and the best French cuisine in Sydney. Business attire. Reservations essential.
🍽 40 🚉 Bus 389 (Bondi Bus) 🕐 Closed L, Sun.–Mon. D, & 4 weeks Christmas Ⓢ Ⓢ 🗠 All major cards

🍴 UNKAI
$$$$
ANA HOTEL, LEVEL 36, 176 CUMBERLAND ST., THE ROCKS
TEL (02) 9250 6123
There is a beautiful view of the harbor from this excellent Japanese restaurant. The sushi is heavenly. Formal attire. Reservations essential.

🏨 90 🚇 Circular Quay West 🅿 🕐 Closed Sat. L 🚭 ❄ 🔑 All major cards

🍴 DARLEY STREET THAI
$$$
28–30 BAYSWATER RD.,
KINGS CROSS
TEL (02) 9358 6530
A lot of hype surrounds this modern Thai restaurant, but the excitement is fully deserved: The food is adventurous and richly rewarding. Reservations essential.
🏨 80 🚇 Kings Cross 🕐 Closed L 🚭 🔑 All major cards

🍴 ELENI'S
$$$
185A BOURKE ST.,
EAST SYDNEY
TEL (02) 9331 5306
Inspired modern Greek cuisine, and reinvigorated traditional favorites such as slow-braised lamb shoulder. Reservations essential.
🏨 34 🚇 Kings Cross 🕐 Closed L Sat. & Sun. 🚭 ❄ 🔑 AE, MC, V

🍴 LORD NELSON
🏨 BREWERY
$$
CORNER OF ARGYLL & KENT STS., THE ROCKS
TEL (02) 9251 4044
This is one of Sydney's oldest pubs—licensed since 1841—and beside the meals in its brasserie, serves up an interesting blend of beers brewed on the premises. (Some of these brews are surprisingly potent, with over 10 percent alcohol content!) If the brasserie's closed, you can still get snacks at the bar.
🏨 80 🕐 Closed L Sat. & all Sun. 🚭 ❄ 🔑 All major cards

🍴 GOLDEN CENTURY
$$
393–9 SUSSEX ST.
TEL (02) 9212 3901
Top-notch Cantonese-style cooking. Take your pick of seafood from the huge surrounding tanks.

🏨 600 🚇 Central Town Hall 🚭 ❄ 🔑 All major cards

NEW SOUTH WALES

BLUE MOUNTAINS

SOMETHING SPECIAL

🏨 LILIANFELS BLUE MOUNTAINS
Small, luxury resort in a turn-of-the-century guesthouse with sumptuous rooms and a tranquil atmosphere. In the heart of the Blue Mountains with wonderful valley views. Elegant dining at Darley's Restaurant. Afternoon tea here is an institution. Reservations essential.
$$$–$$$$$
LILIANFELS AVE., ECHO POINT, KATOOMBA
TEL (02) 4780 1200
FAX (02) 4780 1300
ℹ️ 86 🅿 60 🍴 🚭 🔥 🚇 🔑 All major cards

🏨 PEPPERS FAIRMONT RESORT
$$$–$$$$$
1 SUBLIME POINT RD., LEURA
TEL (02) 4782 5222
FAX (02) 4784 1074
Large hotel with very comfortable rooms. Access to the Leura golf course. Magnificent mountain views.
ℹ️ 210 🅿 200 🍴 🚭 ❄ 🔥 🏊 🚇 🔑 All major cards

🍴 CAFÉ BON TON
$$
192 THE MALL, LEURA
TEL (02) 4782 4377
The restaurant and its menu have Italian influences. Nice atmosphere and good food.
🏨 100 🅿 6 🕐 Closed Tues. D 🚭 🔑 All major cards

🍴 PARAGON CAFÉ
$
65 KATOOMBA ST.,
KATOOMBA
TEL (02) 4782 2928
Delightful café serving satisfying, home cooked, comfort foods and great coffee. It also sells delicious chocolates.
🏨 50 🕐 Closed D & Sun.–Mon. L 🚭 🔑 AE, MC, V

HUNTER VALLEY

🏨 PEPPERS GUEST
🍴 HOUSE HUNTER VALLEY & RESTAURANT
$$$$
EKERTS RD., POKOLBIN
TEL (02) 4998 7596
FAX (02) 4998 7739
Guesthouse set in extensive gardens, with comfortable, unfussy accommodations. The in-house restaurant ($$$) has a reputation for fine wines and serves good Asian/ Mediterranean-style cuisine.
ℹ️ 47 + homestead 🅿 17 🚭 🔥 🔑 All major cards

🏨 OLD GEORGE &
🍴 DRAGON INN
$$$–$$$$
48 MELBOURNE ST.,
EAST MAITLAND
TEL (02) 4933 7272
FAX (02) 4934 1481
The inn at this former convict settlement exudes old wealth and Victorian charm. Rates include all meals. The **Old George & Dragon Restaurant,** in a separate building, is regarded as one of the best restaurants outside Sydney. Classic Anglo-French dishes on the menus—perhaps sautéed kidneys with mustard sauce or gamey venison—are fittingly accompanied by some of Hunter Valley's best wines.
ℹ️ 5 🅿 14 🚭 ❄ 🔑 All major cards

HOTELS & RESTAURANTS

🏨 **CONVENT AT**
🍴 **PEPPER TREE**
$$$
HALLS RD., POKOLBIN
TEL (02) 4998 7764
FAX (02) 4998 7323
This converted Roman
Catholic convent is about
100 years old, and has a
pretty vineyard setting.
Charmingly old-fashioned
rooms, each with a porch. The
complex also contains
Robert's Restaurant
($$$$) recommended for its
excellent Mediterranean
menu. Breakfast is included in
the basic rate.
🛏 17 🅿 17 🔘 🔘 🏊
🚭 All major cards

**COAST: NORTH
OF SYDNEY**

🏨 **TAYLORS**
$$$-$$$$
MCGETTIGAN'S LANE,
EWINGSDALE
TEL (02) 6684 7436
FAX (02) 6684 7526
Elegant guest house with
spacious rooms in pleasant
garden surroundings. Breakfast
included in the basic rate. No
children.
🛏 6 🅿 15 🔘 🏊

🏨 **PELICAN BEACH
CENTRA RESORT**
$$-$$$$
PACIFIC HWY., COFFS
HARBOUR
TEL (02) 6653 7000
FAX (02) 6653 7066
Warm Mediterranean-style
resort with massive,
landscaped, saltwater
swimming pool.
🛏 12 🅿 111 🔁 🔘 🔘
🏊 📺 🚭 All major cards

🍴 **FIG TREE, BYRON BAY**
$$
4 SUNRISE LANE, EWINGSDALE
TEL (02) 6684 7273
Impressively set old farm-
house serving Mediterranean-
style cuisine. A few miles out
of Byron Bay, but worth the
drive.
🔲 80 🅿 30 🕐 Closed

Sun.–Wed. D & Sun.–Thurs. L
🔘 🚭 All major cards

**COAST: SOUTH
OF SYDNEY**

🍴 **WHITE HORSE INN**
$$-$$$
MARKET PL., BERRIMA
TEL (02) 4877 1204
A beautifully restored 19th-
century inn serving tasty, light
daytime fare and more
substantial (and expensive)
formal dinners.
🔲 120 🅿 🕐 Closed
Sun.–Thurs. D 🔘 🚭 All
major cards

SNOWY MOUNTAINS

🏨 **PERISHER VALLEY**
🍴 **$$$-$$$$**
MOUNT KOSCIUSZKO RD.,
PERISHER VALLEY
TEL (02) 6459 4455
FAX (02) 6457 5177
This luxury hotel has
sumptuous suites, fabulous
food, sauna, and spa. Rates
include breakfast, dinner, and
transfers to the hotel.
Snowgums Restaurant for
excellent dining.
🛏 31 🕐 Open ski season
only 🔘 🚭 All major cards

🏨 **BERNTI'S MOUNTAIN**
🍴 **INN & RESTAURANT**
$$$
MOWAMBA PL., THREDBO
TEL (02) 6457 6332
FAX (02) 6457 6348
There are delightful mountain
views from this friendly inn
with sauna and spa. As well
as winter, it is open for school
summer holidays when it is
cheaper.
🛏 30 🅿 15 🕐 Open ski
season & school holidays
🔘 🚭 All major cards

**AUSTRALIAN
CAPITAL TERRITORY**

CANBERRA

🏨 **HYATT CANBERRA**
$$$$
COMMONWEALTH AVE.,

YARRALUMLA
TEL (02) 6270 1234
FAX (02) 6281 3598
Within the Parliamentary
Triangle, this beautifully
restored hotel is an elegant
example of Australian art
deco. Extensive landscaped
gardens. See the Oak Room
restaurant (below).
🛏 249 🅿 🔁 🔘 🔘
🏊 📺 🚭 All major cards

🏨 **CAPITAL PARKROYAL**
$$-$$$
1 BINARA ST., CANBERRA
TEL (02) 6247 8999
FAX (02) 6257 4903
Modern hotel with
comfortable, spacious guest
rooms in pleasing muted
tones.
🛏 293 🅿 110 🔁 🔘 🔘
🏊 📺 🚭 All major cards

**SOMETHING
SPECIAL**

🏨 **OLIMS CANBERRA**
Heritage-listed split-level
executive apartments
around a landscaped central
courtyard. Cheaper rates on the
weekend.
$-$$
AINSLIE & LIMESTONE AVES.,
BRADDON
TEL (02) 6248 5511
FAX (02) 6247 0864
🛏 126 🅿 50 🔁 🔘 🔘
🚭 All major cards

🍴 **OAK ROOM**
$$$$
HYATT CANBERRA,
COMMONWEALTH AVE.,
YARRALUMLA
TEL (02) 6270 8977
The elegant dining room
of the Hyatt Canberra
complements the Hyatt's art
deco style. Refined menu,
wonderful French/Asian
influenced food. Business
attire. Reservations essential.
🔲 100 🅿 🕐 Closed
Sun.–Mon. D 🔘 🔘
🚭 All major cards

PRICES

HOTELS

An indication of the cost of a double room without breakfast is given by $ signs.

$$$$$	Over $280
$$$$	$200–$280
$$$	$120–$200
$$	$80–$120
$	Under $80

RESTAURANTS

An indication of the cost of a three-course dinner without drinks is given by $ signs.

$$$$$	Over $80
$$$$	$50–$80
$$$	$35–$50
$$	$20–$35
$	Under $20

VIVALDI
$$$
UNIVERSITY AVE., ACTON
TEL (02) 6257 2718
The cooking style is modern Australian at this restaurant in the National University's Arts Centre. Tasty food, big portions.
120 Closed Sat. L & all Sun. All major cards

TOSOLINI'S
$$
EAST ROW & LONDON CIRCUIT
TEL (02) 6247 4317
Popular Italian brasserie with tables both inside and out on the sidewalk. Try the agnoletti with spinach and sugo.
40–90 Some Closed Sun. & Mon. D All major cards

OUTSIDE CANBERRA

BRINDABELLA STATION
$$
BRINDABELLA VALLEY, BRINDABELLA, 2611
TEL (02) 6236 2121
FAX (02) 6236 2128
Lovingly restored historic homestead in a classic Australian bush setting. There are just four very comfortable private rooms. Rates are fully inclusive.
2 cottages Closed Dec. 25 MC, V

QUEENSLAND

BRISBANE

CONRAD TREASURY HOTEL & CASINO
$$$$–$$$$$
WILLIAM ST.
TEL (07) 3306 8888
FAX (07) 3306 8880
A fine, sandstone example of Edwardian baroque. Suites are individually decorated and rooms have antique furnishings.
96 All major cards

BEAUFORT HERITAGE
$$$$
BOTANIC GARDENS, EDWARD ST.
TEL (07) 3221 1999
FAX (07) 3221 6895
In the downtown district by the botanic gardens, this is probably Brisbane's top luxury hotel. All of the elegant guest rooms overlook the river. Siggi's Restaurant is one of Brisbane's most popular eating places.
252 250 All major cards

CARLTON CREST
$$$–$$$$$
KING GEORGE SQ.
TEL (07) 3229 9111
FAX (07) 3229 9618
Refurbished in 1995, this twin-towered hotel is opposite City Hall.
438 All major cards

SHERATON
$$$–$$$$$
249 TURBOT ST.
TEL (07) 3835 3535
FAX (07) 3835 4960
This quiet, high-rise hotel has airy, elegant rooms with marble bathrooms. Floors 27 to 29 form the more expensive and luxurious Sheraton Towers.
410 130 All major cards

ALBERT PARK
$$
551 WICKHAM TERRACE
TEL (07) 3831 3111
FAX (07) 3832 1290
Just a short walk from the city center with park views. Excellent service.
95 50 All major cards

BELLEVUE HOTEL
$$
103 GEORGE ST.
TEL (07) 3221 6044
FAX (07) 3238 2288
Good value accommodations right in the heart of town (opposite the casino).
99 30 All major cards

INN ON THE PARK
$$
507 CORONATION DR., TOOWONG
TEL (07) 3870 9222
FAX (07) 3870 2246
The inn is a traditional Queenslander-style building in a tropical garden, connected to the city by a 2-mile walk along the river.
32 20 All major cards

MICHAEL'S RIVERSIDE
$$$$
RIVERSIDE CENTRE, 123 EAGLE ST.
TEL (07) 3832 5522
Wonderful seafood restaurant. Reservations essential.
150 200 Closed L & Sun. D All major cards

ABOUT FACE
$$$
252 KELVIN GROVE RD., KELVIN GROVE
TEL (07) 3356 8605

One-time finalist for Restaurant of the Year, About Face draws on Asian, French, and Australian influences. Reservations essential.

🍴 150 🅿 8 🕐 Closed Sat.–Thurs. L 🚇 💳 🗝 All major cards

🍴 TABLES OF TOOWONG
$$$

85 MISKIN ST., TOOWONG
TEL (07) 3371 4558
This restaurant in a converted Queenslander-style house has an exciting menu combining Asian flavors and French influences with Australian ingredients. Reservations essential.

🍴 85 🕐 Closed Sat.–Thurs. L & Sun. D 🚇 💳 🗝 All major cards

🍴 ECCO BISTRO
$$

CORNER OF BOUNDARY & ADELAIDE STS.
TEL (07) 3831 8344
Once an old tea warehouse, now a stylish bistro with Mediterranean cuisine. Bug (a local crustacean) and fennel risotto is popular.

🍴 85 🕐 Closed Sun.–Mon. & Sat. L 🚇 💳 🗝 All major cards

🍴 PIER NINE OYSTER BAR & SEAFOOD GRILL
$$

EAGLE ST. PIER
TEL (07) 3229 2194
Freshly shucked oysters and other quality seafood such as grilled reef fish, served with wine on the waterfront.

🍴 130 🚇 💳 🗝 All major cards

🍴 GOVINDA'S
$

UPSTAIRS AT 99 ELIZABETH ST.
TEL (07) 3210 0255
Cheap, filling vegetarian meals.

🍴 100 🕐 Closed Mon.–Thurs. D & Sun. L 🚇 💳 🗝 Credit cards not accepted

🍴 KIM THANH
$

93 HARDGRAVE RD., WEST END
TEL (07) 3844 4954
A variety of delicious Chinese and Vietnamese dishes at very reasonable prices.

🚇 💳 🗝 All major cards

GOLD COAST

🏨 HYATT REGENCY SANCTUARY COVE
$$$$$

MANOR CIRCLE, CASEY RD., HOPE ISLAND
TEL (07) 5530 1234
FAX (07) 5577 6161
This huge, but exclusive, resort has a large number of facilities including two golf courses.

🛏 247 🅿 50 ⬍ 🚇 💳 🌊 📺 🗝 All major cards

🏨 SHERATON MIRAGE GOLD COAST
$$$$–$$$$$

SEA WORLD DR., BROADWATER SPIT, MAIN BEACH
TEL (07) 5591 1488
FAX (07) 5591 2299
Set among beautiful gardens, this luxury development has every comfort, its own secluded beach, and a number of fine restaurants. The Marina Mirage, a luxury shopping complex, is nearby.

🛏 293 🅿 ⬍ 🚇 💳 🌊 📺 🗝 All major cards

🏨 SURFERS PARADISE MARRIOTT RESORT
$$$–$$$$

158 FERRY AVE.
TEL (07) 5592 9800 OR
1-800 809 090 (TOLL FREE)
FAX (07) 5592 9888
A grand hotel, with spacious, pleasant guest rooms including 13 suites. Private beach.

🛏 330 🅿 280 🚃 ⬍ 🚇 💳 🌊 📺 🗝 All major cards

🏨 ISLE OF PALMS
$$

COOLGARDIE ST., ELANORA
TEL (07) 5598 1733 OR
1-800 074 283 (TOLL FREE)
FAX (07) 5598 1653
A resort offering suites in luxury town houses, with heated pools and private beaches.

🛏 175 🅿 🌊 🗝 MC, V

🍴 OSKAR'S ON BURLEIGH
$$$

43 GOODWIN TERRACE, BURLEIGH HEADS
TEL (07) 5576 3722
A well-known restaurant that overlooks the beach. Good wine and delicious seafood.

🍴 150 🅿 🚇 💳 🗝 All major cards

🍴 SHOGUN, SURFERS PARADISE
$$$

90 BUNDELL RD.
TEL (07) 5538 2872
Classic Japanese dishes served with flair.

🍴 100 🕐 Closed L 🚇 💳 🗝 All major cards

SUNSHINE COAST & FRASER ISLAND

🏨 HYATT REGENCY COOLUM
$$$$–$$$$$

WARREN RD., COOLUM
TEL (07) 5446 1234 OR
1-800 637 876 (TOLL FREE)
FAX (07) 5446 2957
Private Mediterranean-style villas and rooms near the beautiful Coolum beach.

🛏 324 🅿 200 🚇 💳 🚃 🌊 📺 🗝 All major cards

🏨 NOOSA SHERATON RESORT
$$$$

HASTINGS ST., NOOSA HEADS
TEL (07) 5449 4888
FAX (07) 5449 2230
Everything you would expect from a luxury hotel, plus a number of themed suites.

🛏 169 ⬍ 🚇 💳 🗝 📺 🗝 All major cards

🏨 KINGFISHER BAY RESORT
$$$
FRASER ISLAND
TEL 1 800 072 555
The only luxury accom-
modations on this world-
heritage island, the Kingfisher
Bay Resort's modern
buildings, built of timber and
finished in natural colors, are
strung along a pretty bay on
the island's west coast.
🛏 153 🅿 50 🚭 ❄ 🌊
🔲 All major cards

🍴 CHILLI JAM CAFE, NOOSAVILLE
$$
195 WEYBA RD., NOOSAVILLE
TEL (07) 5449 9755
Thai restaurant above a
corner store.
🕐 Closed L & Sun.–Mon.

GREAT BARRIER REEF: SOUTHERN

🏨 GREAT KEPPEL ISLAND RESORT
$$$$$
TEL 1-800 245 658 (TOLL FREE)
This beach resort is popular
with young families and can
be reached by small aircraft
or ferry. Meals in the Admiral
Keppel restaurant. Inclusive
packages are available. The
island is some 25 miles from
the outer reef.
🛏 193 ❄ 🌊 🔲 All
major cards

🏨 HERON ISLAND RESORT
$$$$$
P&O RESORTS, LEVEL 10, 160
SUSSEX ST., SYDNEY, NSW 2000
TEL (07) 4972 9055
Right on the reef, this island
is a diver's paradise and ideal
for snorkeling, with the
clearest waters in June and
July. Accommodations
range from basic cabins to
comfortable suites. One
beach house is also available.
Meals are included in the
basic price.

🛏 116 🌊 🔲 All major cards

🏨 LADY ELLIOT ISLAND RESORT
$$$
BOX 206, TORQUAY, QLD.
TEL (07) 4156 4444
Accommodations are in
simple, waterfront cabins on
this 100-acre coral cay with
good diving and white coral
beaches. Sea turtles visit from
October through March.
Breakfast and dinner are
included in the basic price.
🛏 49 🌊 🔲 All major
cards

GREAT BARRIER REEF: WHITSUNDAY ISLANDS

🏨 HAMILTON ISLAND RESORT
$$$$
PMB, POST OFFICE,
HAMILTON ISLAND
TEL (07) 4946 9999
FAX (07) 4946 8888
Accommodations range from
privately owned homes to
rooms in high-rise towers at
this popular resort which
offers plenty of activities
including outstanding sports
facilities. The basic price is for
room only. Food and activities
are extra.
🛏 680 🍴 🚭 ❄ 🌊
🏋 🔲 All major cards

🏨 HAYMAN ISLAND RESORT
$$$$
GREAT BARRIER REEF
TEL (07) 4940 1234
FAX (07) 4940 1567
An unbelievably luxurious
resort. The very stylish, three-
level complex includes
tropical gardens, huge salt
and freshwater pools, and
lagoons. Children welcome.
The basic price includes
breakfast; full-board packages
are available.
🛏 214 🍴 🚭 ❄ 🌊
🏋 🔲 All major cards

🏨 DUNK ISLAND RESORT
$$$–$$$$$
DUNK ISLAND, PMB 28, VIA
TOWNSVILLE
TEL (07) 4068 8199
FAX (07) 4068 8528
Dunk is one of only three rain
forest islands on the reef.
The popular resort has four
levels of accommodations:
Bayview Villas, Beachfront
Units, Garden Cabanas and
(least expensive) Banfield
Units. Full-board packages
and childcare facilities are
available.
🛏 148 ❄ 🌊 🏋 🔲 All
major cards

🏨 HORIZON AT MISSION BEACH
$$–$$$
THE POINT, MITCHELL ST.,
SOUTH MISSION BEACH
TEL (07) 4068 8154 OR
1-800 079 090 (TOLL FREE)
FAX (07) 4068 8596
A resort in a rain forest
setting with private beach.
Overlooks Dunk and Bedarra
islands.
🛏 54 🅿 50 🚭 ❄ 🌊
🔲 All major cards

GREAT BARRIER REEF: NORTHERN

🏨 GREEN ISLAND RESORT
$$$$$
PO BOX 898, CAIRNS
TEL (07) 4031 3300
FAX (07) 4052 1511
This coral cay and its
surrounding reef are a
national park. The luxury
Green Island Resort houses
92 guests and is reached by
catamaran out of Cairns.
🛏 46 ❄ 🌊 🔲 All major
cards

🏨 LIZARD ISLAND LODGE
$$$$$
PMB 40, CAIRNS
TEL (07) 4060 3999
This lodge has everything that
you might expect at an
exclusive resort. The rate
includes all meals (but not

HOTELS & RESTAURANTS

drinks) and the use of all facilities which include tennis courts, windsurfers, dinghies, and fishing equipment.
[i] 40 [S] [≈] All major cards

TOWNSVILLE & MAGNETIC ISLAND

JUPITERS TOWNSVILLE HOTEL & CASINO
$$$–$$$$
BOX 1223, SIR LESLIE THIESS DR., TOWNSVILLE
TEL (07) 4722 2333 OR
1-800 079 210 (TOLL FREE)
FAX (07) 4772 4741
This busy waterfront hotel has spacious and surprisingly quiet rooms and a good restaurant. Views to Magnetic Island.
[i] 192 [P] 300 ⬌ [S] [S] [≈] [W] All major cards

ISLAND LEISURE RESORT
$$
4 KELLY ST., NELLY BAY, MAGNETIC ISLAND
TEL (07) 4778 5000
FAX (07) 4778 5042
A resort with self-contained cabins set in tropical gardens.
[i] 17 cabins [P] 9 [S] [S] [≈] [W] All major cards

MAGNETIC INTERNATIONAL RESORT
$$
MANDALAY AVE., NELLY BAY, MAGNETIC ISLAND
TEL (07) 4778 5200 OR
1-800 079 902 (TOLL FREE)
This 11-acre garden resort is just over a mile back from the beach.
[i] 96 [P] 20 [S] [S] [≈] [W] All major cards

TOWNSVILLE REEF INTERNATIONAL
$$
63 THE STRAND
TEL (07) 4721 1777 OR
1-800 804 812 (TOLL FREE)
A pleasant Best Western hotel, with good service. On the sea front.

[i] 45 [P] 50 ⬌ [S] [S] [≈] [W] All major cards

CAIRNS

REEF HOTEL CASINO
$$$$–$$$$$
CORNER OF SPENCE & WHARF STS.
TEL (07) 4030 8888
FAX (07) 4030 8788
Part of a 200-million-Australian-dollar (100 million U.S. dollar) complex opened in 1996. Each suite has a jacuzzi and the services of a butler. There are six restaurants to choose from, and the casino is on the spot.
[i] 127 suites [P] ⬌ [S] [S] [≈] [W] All major cards

PACIFIC INTERNATIONAL
$$$–$$$$
ESPLANADE & SPENCE STS.
TEL (07) 4051 7888 OR
1-800 079 001 (TOLL FREE)
FAX (07) 4051 0210
The guest rooms in this hotel on the sea front are decorated in muted tropical style, and all have private balconies.
[i] 174 [P] 40 ⬌ [S] [≈] All major cards

RIHGA COLONIAL CLUB RESORT CAIRNS
$$$
18–26 CANNON ST., MANUNDA
TEL (07) 4053 5111
FAX (07) 4053 7072
Set in lush tropical gardens just out of town, this colonial-style complex of self-contained apartments and spacious modern rooms is built around two swimming pools.
[i] 248 + 79 studios [P] 30 [S] Some [S] [≈] [W] All major cards

BREEZES BRASSERIE
$$
HILTON INTERNATIONAL HOTEL, WHARF ST.
TEL (07) 4052 1599

Seafood is the specialty, but just about anything is available here, from a quick snack to a leisurely dinner.
[≈] 160 [P] 100 ⊖ Closed L [S] [S] All major cards

ROMA ROULETTE
$
48A ALPIN ST.
TEL (07) 4051 1076
Excellent Italian and seafood dishes dominate the menu in this personable restaurant.
[≈] 55 ⊖ Closed L & Mon.–Tues. D [S] [S] All major cards

PORT DOUGLAS & CAPE TRIBULATION

SHERATON MIRAGE
$$$$$
PORT DOUGLAS RD., PORT DOUGLAS
TEL (07) 4099 5888
FAX (07) 4099 5398
This opulent resort has every luxury, including butler service to each of the elegant guest rooms. There are acres of blue lagoons and pools and the grounds reach down to Four Mile Beach. The refined Macrossans restaurant is part of the hotel.
[i] 294 + 105 villas [P] ⬌ [S] [S] [≈] [W] All major cards

REEF HOUSE
$$$–$$$$$
99 WILLIAMS ESPLANADE, PALM COVE
TEL (07) 4055 3633
FAX (07) 4055 3305
A Queensland Tourism Award winner, this delightful tropical beachfront resort is set behind a grove of paperbark trees. Spacious veranda rooms have cane furniture, while Brigadier rooms have a nostalgic military ambience.
[i] 70 [P] ⬌ [S] [≈] All major cards

CATALINA
WHARF ST., PORT DOUGLAS
TEL (07) 4099 5287
This is a great place to head

for a sophisticated dinner after a day on the reef. It is justly famed for its seafood, and the setting is delightful. A real treat.
🍴 40 🕐 Closed L & Mon. 🚭 ❄ 💳 All major cards

FAR NORTH QUEENSLAND RAIN FOREST RESORTS

🏨 BLOOMFIELD WILDERNESS LODGE
$$$$$
PO BOX 966, CAIRNS
TEL (07) 4035 9166
FAX (07) 4035 9180
Accommodations at this isolated resort consist of fan-cooled wooden cabins set in the remote and beautiful World Heritage-listed rain forest along the Bloomfield River. No children under 14. Two-night minimum stay. Packages start at $A900 (U.S.$450) for a single and $A1,500 (U.S. $750) a double.
🛏 17 ❄ 💳 All major cards

🏨 SILKY OAKS LODGE 🍴 & RESTAURANT
Air-conditioned colonial-style cabins sit on stilts looking out onto the rain forest or the lodge's natural rock swimming pool. The lodge has an excellent Treetop Restaurant and a good selection of Australian wine.
$$$$$
FINLAY VALE RD.,
MOSSMAN GORGE
TEL (07) 4098 1666
FAX (07) 4098 1983
🛏 60 🅿 50 🚭 ❄ ❄ 💳 All major cards

🏨 DAINTREE ECO LODGE
$$$$–$$$$$
DAINTREE RD., DAINTREE
TEL (07) 4098 6100 OR
1-800 808 010 (TOLL FREE)
FAX (07) 4098 6200
The lodge has tree-house chalets set above the rain

forest canopy near the Daintree River.
🛏 30 🅿 30 🚭 ❄ 💪 💳 All major cards

🏨 PAJINKA WILDERNESS LODGE
Private cabins on land owned by Aborigines, on the northern tip of Australia. Resident naturalist and Aboriginal guides.
$$$$
CAPE YORK
TEL (07) 4069 2100 OR
1-800 802 968 (TOLL FREE)
FAX (07) 4069 2110
🛏 24 cabins 🅿 20 ❄ 💳 All major cards

🏨 COCONUT BEACH RAINFOREST RESORT
$$$–$$$$
BOX 6903, CAIRNS
TEL (07) 4098 0033 OR
1-800 816 525 (TOLL FREE)
FAX (07) 4098 0047
The resort villas are built of native woods and have lovely views. There is a very pretty beach and easy access to both the Great Barrier Reef and the rain forest of Cape Tribulation.
🛏 40 villas + 27 units 🅿 30 🚭 ❄ 💳 All major cards

🏨 DAINTREE-CAPE TRIBULATION HERITAGE LODGE
$$
TURPENTINE RD., COOPER CREEK, DAINTREE
TEL (07) 4098 9138
FAX (07) 4098 9004
Cabin resort surrounded by rain forest adjoining Cape Tribulation National Park.
🛏 20 🅿 20 🚭 ❄ 💳 All major cards

🏨 RED MILL HOUSE
$
DAINTREE VILLAGE
TEL (07) 4098 6233
There are excellent bird-watching opportunities at this

enjoyable B&B in an old Queenslander house.
🛏 8 🅿 6 ❄ 💳 MC, V

DARWIN

🏨 RYDGE'S PLAZA
$$$$
32 MITCHELL ST.
TEL (08) 8982 0000
FAX (08) 8981 1765
A pleasant hotel close to the harbor with an excellent restaurant, the Iguana.
🛏 233 🅿 10 🚭 🚭 ❄ 💳 All major cards

🏨 NOVOTEL ATRIUM DARWIN
$$–$$$
CORNER OF PEEL ST. & THE ESPLANADE
TEL (08) 8941 0755
FAX (08) 8981 9025
Very pretty hotel set in tropical gardens right on the Esplanade. Each of the spacious guest rooms has its own small kitchen.
🛏 138 🅿 80 🚭 🚭 ❄ ❄ 💳 All major cards

🏨 CARLTON HOTEL
$$
THE ESPLANADE
TEL (08) 8980 0800 OR
1-800 891 119 (TOLL FREE)
FAX (08) 8980 0888
Striking five-floor, waterfront hotel, set on tropical parkland.
🛏 190 🅿 100 🚭 🚭 ❄ ❄ 💪 💳 All major cards

🍴 TWILIGHTS ON LINDSAY
$$
2 LINDSAY ST.
TEL (08) 8981 8631
A courtyard café with a mosaic floor, in a pretty garden setting. The tasty modern Australian and Mediterranean menu has a tropical slant.
🍴 60 🅿 5 🕐 Closed Sat.–Tues. L & all Sun. ❄ 💳 All major cards

HOTELS & RESTAURANTS

KAKADU NATIONAL PARK

SOMETHING SPECIAL

GAGUDJU CROCODILE

This famous deluxe hotel is shaped like a giant crocodile. Rooms follow the curve of the croc's body and have French windows that overlook the swimming pool in its stomach. The reception is through its mouth.
$$$
FLINDERS ST., JABIRU
TEL (08) 8979 2800
FAX (08) 8979 2707
110 60 All major cards

KATHERINE

KNOTTS CROSSING RESORT
$$
CAMERON & GILES STS.
TEL (08) 8972 2511
FAX (08) 8972 2628
Comfortable cabin rooms with pool, outside bar, and in-house bistro.
127 40 All major cards

ALICE SPRINGS

RYDGE'S PLAZA HOTEL ALICE SPRINGS
$$$$-$$$$$
BARRETT DR.
TEL (08) 8950 8000
FAX (08) 8952 3822
Set on landscaped lawns beside the Todd River, with the McDonnell Ranges as a backdrop, this is the best hotel in Alice Springs. Balloons restaurant has a French-influenced menu and does a champagne Sunday brunch.
235 100 All major cards

LASSETERS HOTEL CASINO
$$$
BARRETT DR.,
TEL (08) 8950 7777 OR

1-800 808 975 (TOLL FREE)
A sleek modern hotel just out of town that houses a casino.
76 20 All major cards

MERCURE INN DIPLOMAT
$$
CORNER OF GREGORY TERRACE.& HARTLEY ST.
TEL (08) 8952 8977
FAX (08) 8953 0225
A central location, friendly staff, and comfortable rooms.
81 80 All major cards

OVERLANDER STEAKHOUSE
$$
72 HARTLEY ST.
TEL (08) 8952 2159
This popular restaurant is a carnivore's delight and is strong on native meats, including crocodile, kangaroo, and camel.
170 15 Closed L All major cards

YULARA (AYERS ROCK RESORT)

SAILS IN THE DESERT & KUNIY RESTAURANT
$$$$-$$$$$
YULARA DR.
TEL (08) 8956 2200
FAX (08) 8956 2018
The giant sails shade this airy three-story hotel. Luxurious rooms have balconies or verandas overlooking the garden. A tower offers views of Uluru. There are also six deluxe rooms and two suites.
228 20 Some All major cards

DESERT GARDENS
$$$
YULARA DR.
TEL (08) 8957 7888
FAX (08) 8956 2156
Set among extensive gardens with ghost gums and flower-ing native shrubs, this quality small hotel has friendly service and secluded modern rooms. Both the Whitegums and the

PRICES

HOTELS
An indication of the cost of a double room without breakfast is given by **$** signs.
$$$$$ Over $280
$$$$ $200-$280
$$$ $120-$200
$$ $80-$120
$ Under $80

RESTAURANTS
An indication of the cost of a three-course dinner without drinks is given by $ signs.
$$$$$ Over $80
$$$$ $50-$80
$$$ $35-$50
$$ $20-$35
$ Under $20

smaller Bunya Bar restaurants serve fresh, healthy fare in a relaxed atmosphere.
160 Some All major cards

WATARRKA NATIONAL PARK

KINGS CANYON RESORT
$$$$
ERNEST GILES RD.
TEL (08) 8956 7442
FAX (08) 8956 7410
The only accommodations within the national park: The hotel has well-equipped, air-conditioned rooms looking over the desert. There are also dormitories and a campsite. The resort offers a choice of buffet, à la carte, and barbecue meals.
96 100 All major cards

WESTERN AUSTRALIA

PERTH

BURSWOOD RESORT & CASINO
$$$$$
PB 456, GREAT EASTERN HWY., VICTORIA PARK, BENTLEY

TEL (08) 9362 7777
FAX (08) 9470 2553
This resort exudes luxury at
every turn. The guest rooms
are opulent, the golf course is
well groomed, and the house
casino is open 24 hours.
🛏 414 🅿 1000 🔁 🚭
🅰 🏊 🏊 🏋 🅰 All
major cards

🏨 HYATT REGENCY PERTH
$$$$
99 ADELAIDE TERRACE
TEL (08) 9225 1234
FAX (08) 9325 8899
All you would expect from a
luxury hotel, and in a
delightful river setting. Two
floors are dedicated to the
Regency Club. Basic rate
includes continental breakfast.
🛏 367 🅿 🔁 🚭 🅰
🏊 🏋 🅰 All major cards

🏨 SEBEL OF PERTH
$$$$
37 PIER ST.
TEL (08) 9325 7655 OR
1-800 999 004 (TOLL FREE)
FAX (08) 9325 7383
Near the center, in pleasant
surroundings, with well-
appointed rooms and suites.
🛏 118 🅿 380 🔁
🚭 Some 🅰 🏊 🏋 Off-
site 🅰 All major cards

🏨 NEW ESPLANADE
$$
18 THE ESPLANADE
TEL (08) 9325 2000
FAX (08) 8221 2190
Comfortable rooms in a great
location. Outstanding views of
the Swan River.
🛏 66 🅿 151 🔁 🚭 🅰
🅰 All major cards

🍴 FRASER'S
$$$
FRASER AVE., KINGS PARK
TEL (08) 9481 7100
The menu changes daily in
this popular Australian eatery,
but there are always good
preparations of native meats
and seafood. Reservations
essential.
🍽 160 🅿 🚭 🅰 🅰 All

major cards

🍴 MEAD'S FISH GALLERY
$$
15 JOHNSON PARADE,
MOSMAN PARK
TEL (08) 9383 3388
This impressive seafood
restaurant on the Swan River
has impeccable service and
excellent wines.
🍽 120 🅿 🕐 Closed
Mon.–Thurs. L 🚭 🅰
🅰 All major cards

🍴 PERUGINO
$$
77 OUTRAM ST., WEST PERTH
TEL (08) 9321 5420
Italian restaurant with a
deserved reputation for fine
food and exemplary service.
The imaginative menu takes
advantage of fresh seasonal
produce. Reservations
essential.
🍽 110 🅿 25 🕐 Closed
Sat. L & all Sun. 🚭 🅰
🅰 All major cards

🍴 EMPEROR'S COURT
$
66 LAKE ST., NORTHBRIDGE
TEL (08) 9328 1628
Popular Asian restaurant
serving sizzling provincial
Chinese dishes.
🍽 200 🚭 🅰 🅰 All
major cards

OUTSIDE PERTH

🏨 ROTTNEST ISLAND AUTHORITY
$$$
TEL (08) 9432 9315
The Rottnest Island Authority
has more than 200 houses
and cottages to rent at Fays,
Geordie, Longreach, and
Thomson Bays.
🛏 200 🅰 MC, V

🏨 FOTHERGILLS
$$
20–22 ORD ST., FREMANTLE
TEL (08) 9335 6784
FAX (08) 9438 7789
This 19th-century house is a
delightful B&B with wonderful
views of the harbor.

🛏 6 🅿 4 🚭 🅰 🅰 All
major cards

🍴 ROMA
$
13 HIGH ST., FREMANTLE
TEL (08) 9335 3664
Bustling, friendly Italian eatery.
🍽 150 🕐 Closed Sun. 🚭
🅰 🅰 Credit cards not
accepted

BROOME

🏨 INTERNATIONAL RESORT AT CABLE BEACH
$$$$$
BOX 1544, CABLE BEACH RD.
TEL/FAX (08) 9192 0400 OR
1-800 199 099 (TOLL FREE)
Asian-themed luxury hotel
set in landscaped oriental
gardens, with rooms,
bungalows, and suites, plus an
elegant restaurant. Stunning
views over Cable Beach. One
of Australia's best resorts.
🛏 263 🅿 🚭 On request
🅰 🏊 🅰 All major cards

KALGOORLIE

🏨 OLD AUSTRALIA
$
CORNER OF HANNAN &
MARITANA STS.
TEL (08) 9021 1320
Pleasantly old-fashioned hotel
with a large shady veranda
and comfortable rooms.
🛏 24 🚭 🅰 🅰 All major
cards

🍴 BASIL'S ON HANNAN
$
168 HANNAN ST.
TEL 08 9021 7832
Popular informal eatery with a
range of tasty seafood, pasta,
and other Italian dishes.
🍽 60 🕐 Closed Fri.–Wed. D
🚭 🅰 🅰 All major cards

THE KIMBERLEY

KIMBERLEY COURT
$$
BOX 384, ERYTHRINA ST., KUNUNURRA
TEL (08) 9168 1411
FAX (08) 9168 1055
Every room in this small and friendly hotel opens out onto a veranda.
31 P 24 AE, MC, V

SOUTHWEST

CAPE LODGE
$$$-$$$$
CAVES RD., YALLINGUP, MARGARET RIVER
TEL (08) 9755 6311
FAX (08) 9755 6322
Country retreat in the heart of a protea plantation. Overlooking a private lake, this mansion house has 18 luxurious guest rooms. The basic rate includes a wonderful breakfast. Children discouraged.
18 P 20 All major cards

ESPLANADE HOTEL
$$-$$$
ADELAIDE CR. (CORNER OF FLINDERS PARADE), ALBANY
TEL (08) 9842 1711
FAX (08) 9841 7527
A colonial-style hotel with pretty views over Middleton Beach and a welcoming atmosphere.
63 P 50 All major cards

KOOKA'S
$$
204 STIRLING TERRACE, ALBANY
TEL (08) 9841 5889
Local meats and fresh seafood make for a tasty menu.
60 P 30 Closed Sun.–Mon. & Sat. L All major cards

SOUTH AUSTRALIA

ADELAIDE

HYATT REGENCY
$$$$-$$$$$
NORTH TERRACE
TEL (08) 8231 1234
FAX (08) 8231 1120
Luxury hotel in the heart of town, beside the Adelaide Festival Centre.
367 P All major cards

STAMFORD GRAND
$$$$
MOSELEY SQ., GLENELG
TEL (08) 8376 1222
FAX (08) 8376 1111
A high-rise resort on Glenelg Beach with superb sea views.
240 All major cards

CHIFLEY ON SOUTH TERRACE
$$$
226 SOUTH TERRACE
TEL (08) 8223 4355
FAX (08) 8232 5997
The South Parklands are opposite, and the city center is a 15-minute walk away.
94 P 150 All major cards

HILTON INTERNATIONAL
$$$
BOX 1871, 233 VICTORIA SQ.
TEL (08) 8217 2000
FAX (08) 8217 2001
Luxury hotel with many facilities, in the city center. Excellent restaurant, the Grange (see below).
380 P 30 All major cards

NORTH ADELAIDE HERITAGE APARTMENTS
$$-$$$
109 GLEN OSMOND RD., EASTWOOD 5601
TEL (08) 8272 1355
FAX (08) 8272 6261
These cottages and apartments are furnished in late-Victorian style. Each has a kitchen, bathroom, lounge, and one to three bedrooms.
18 P Some All major cards

PRICES

HOTELS
An indication of the cost of a double room without breakfast is given by **$** signs.

$$$$$	Over $280
$$$$	$200–$280
$$$	$120–$200
$$	$80–$120
$	Under $80

RESTAURANTS
An indication of the cost of a three-course dinner without drinks is given by $ signs.

$$$$$	Over $80
$$$$	$50–$80
$$$	$35–$50
$$	$20–$35
$	Under $20

SOMETHING SPECIAL

AYERS HOUSE
A bluestone mid-Victorian mansion built for South Australia's premier, Sir Henry Ayers, and now a museum. Dine in the opulent Henry Ayers Restaurant or visit the elegant café-style Conservatory for lunch or dinner.
$$$$$
288 NORTH TERRACE
TEL (08) 8224 0666
P All major cards

GRANGE RESTAURANT
$$$
HILTON INTERNATIONAL
233 VICTORIA SQ.
TEL (08) 8217 0711
This lively brasserie at the Hilton International serves innovative Mediterranean and Asian-style cooking by one of the best-known chefs in Australia, Cheong Liew.
70 Closed L &

Sun.–Mon. D 🚭 ❄️
🏋️ All major cards

BLAKE'S
$$
HYATT REGENCY
NORTH TERRACE
TEL (08) 8238 2381
The Hyatt Regency's restaurant serves first-class international cuisine in a relaxed, intimate atmosphere. Impressive wine list. Reservations essential.
🪑 80 🅿️ 🕐 Closed L & Sun.–Tues. D 🚭 ❄️ 🏋️ All major cards

BOLTZ CAFÉ
$$
286 RUNDLE ST.
TEL (08) 8232 5234
This is a fashionable, young, and vibrant café, serving good quality basic food. No reservations.
🪑 100 🚭 ❄️ 🏋️ All major cards

CAFFÉ PAESANO
$$
100 O'CONNELL ST., NORTH ADELAIDE
TEL (08) 8239 0655
Smart café cuisine at very reasonable prices.
🪑 180 🚭 ❄️ 🏋️ All major cards

CHLOE'S
$$
36 COLLEGE RD., KENT TOWN
TEL (08) 8362 2574
A glamorous restaurant with a modern French menu and a 20,000-bottle wine cellar housing some of Australia's finest wines.
🪑 100 🅿️ 40 🕐 Closed Sat. L & all Sun. 🚭 ❄️ 🏋️ All major cards

UNIVERSAL WINE BAR
$$
285 RUNDLE ST.
TEL (08) 8232 5000
A longtime favorite with Adelaide's café society, the Universal always has some imaginative tasty treats on the menu and an interesting

wine list.
🪑 80 🕐 Closed Sun. 🚭 ❄️ 🏋️ All major cards

CASUARINA
$-$$
SHOP 2052 LEVEL 2, WESTFIELD SHOPPING TOWN, MARION
TEL (08) 8298 7522
FAX (08) 8298 7611
Excellent Malay cuisine, with a wine list that complements the spicy Asian flavors of your meal, in this restaurant below the massive 30-screen cinema complex. Curried fish and chili crabs are the specialties.
🪑 250 🕐 Closed L Sun. 🚭 ❄️ 🏋️ All major cards

FELLINI CAFÉ
$-$$
102 O'CONNELL ST., NORTH ADELAIDE
TEL (08) 8239 2235
Justly renowned for its wood-fired pizzas, this pleasant café in the heart of north Adelaide's restaurant row serves up excellent full dinners and hearty snacks, such as spicy potato wedges.
🪑 300 🚭 ❄️ 🏋️ All major cards

OUTSIDE ADELAIDE

ADELAIDE HILLS

THORNGROVE MANOR
$$$$–$$$$$
GLENSIDE LANE, STIRLING
TEL (08) 8339 6748
FAX (08) 8370 9950
The manor has gothic turrets and gables outside, and an interior to match, with comfortable, well-appointed rooms. Adelaide is 20 minutes away by car.
🛏️7 🅿️12 🚭 ❄️ 🏋️ All major cards

GRAND MERCURE, MOUNT LOFTY COUNTRY ESTATE
$$$
74 SUMMIT RD., CRAFERS, MOUNT LOFTY
TEL (08) 8339 6777
FAX (08) 8339 5656

Sumptuous and elegant country house in a gorgeous setting. **Hardy's Restaurant** ($$) has a stylish modern menu, served with some of Australia's finest wines. Reservations and business attire essential.
🛏️29 🅿️50 🚭 ❄️ 🏊 🏋️ All major cards

APPLE TREE & GUM TREE COTTAGES
$$
BOX 100, OAKBANK
TEL (08) 8388 4193
Attractive cottages with antique furnishings, in rolling countryside. Adelaide is a 40-minute drive away.
🛏️3 🅿️ 🚭 ❄️ 🏋️ MC, V

SOMETHING SPECIAL

BRIDGEWATER MILL RESTAURANT
This converted mill houses a stylish lunchtime restaurant that is said to be one of the best in the state. Contemporary Australian menu.
$$
MOUNT BARKER RD., BRIDGEWATER
TEL (08) 8339 3422
🪑 80 🅿️30 🕐 Closed D & Sun.–Wed. 🚭 🏋️ All major cards

BAROSSA VALLEY

COLLINGROVE HOMESTEAD
$$-$$$
EDEN VALLEY RD., ANGASTON
TEL/FAX (08) 8564 2061
Peaceful retreat in a beautiful English-style garden setting.
🛏️5 🅿️6 🚭 ❄️ 🏋️ All major cards

MINERS COTTAGE
$$
GOLDFIELDS RD., BOX 28, COCKATOO VALLEY
TEL (08) 8524 6213
FAX (08) 8524 6650
A century-old stone cottage, set among giant gum trees on

HOTELS & RESTAURANTS

a 66-acre farm.
🛈 I 🅿 🚭 📵 📶 All major cards

🍴 **1918 BISTRO & GRILL**
$$
94 MURRAY ST., TANUNDA
TEL (08) 8563 0405
Housed in a restored villa, this delightful restaurant uses regional produce and has an outstanding wine list.
🍴 80 📵 📶 All major cards

🍴 **BAROSSA PICNIC BASKETS**
$$
GNADENFREI ESTATE
TEL (08) 8562 2522
Each basket includes meat, cheese, pâté, salad, fruit, a bottle of wine, and a map showing the best picnic spots. Vegetarian baskets are also available.
📶 AE, MC, V

🍴 **THE VINTNERS BAR & GRILL**
$$
NURIOOTPA RD., ANGASTON
TEL (08) 8564 2488
Contemporary restaurant in a beautiful vineyard setting, with exquisite service, imaginative fare, and an excellent wine list. One of the best in the valley.
🍴 85 🅿 200 🕐 Closed Sun. D 📵 📶 All major cards

CLARE VALLEY

🏨 **THORN PARK COUNTRY HOUSE**
$$$$
COLLEGE RD.
TEL (08) 8843 4304
FAX (08) 8843 4296
This beautifully restored 135-year-old house lies across from the historic Seven Hills Winery and is one of Australia's finest B&Bs. House guests enjoy excellent dining and great breakfasts. Two nights minimum stay.
🛈 6 🅿 100 📵 📶 All major cards

FLEURIEU PENINSULA

🏨 **CAPE JERVIS TAVERN**
$$
CAPE JERVIS
TEL. (08) 8598 0276
Simple but adequate rooms. Counter meals are available.
🛈 7 🅿 7 📵 📶 AE, MC, V

🏨 **NARNU PIONEER HOLIDAY FARM**
$
HINDMARSH ISLAND
TEL (08) 8555 2002
Farm cottages where guests are encouraged to take part in farm activities.
🛈 7 🅿 📵 📶 MC, V

COOBER PEDY

🏨 **DESERT CAVE**
$$$
HUTCHISON ST.
TEL (08) 8672 5688
FAX (08) 8672 5198
A quality hotel—with some of the rooms underground, a feature of this opal-mining community.
🛈 50 🅿 50 📵 📵 🚆 📶 All major cards

FLINDERS RANGES

🏨 **PRAIRIE HOTEL**
$$
PARACHILNA
TEL (08) 8648 4895
Single, twin, double, and family rooms. Good food available.
🛈 12 📵 📵 🚆 📶 All major cards

🏨 **WILPENA MOTEL**
$$
WILPENA POUND
TEL (08) 8648 0004
FAX (08) 8648 0028
Part of the beautiful Wilpena Pound Resort. The basic rate is for room only, but a wide range of activities is available at the resort.
🛈 60 🅿 60 📵 📵 🚆 📶 All major cards

KANGAROO ISLAND

🏨 **HANNAFORD'S**
$$-$$$
MIDDLE RIVER, N. COAST RD., VIA KINGSCOTE
TEL (08) 8559 2237
Cottages close to one of the finest beaches on the island. Minimum two nights stay.
🛈 3 cottages 🅿 📶 No credit cards

🏨 **SORRENTO RESORT MOTEL**
$
BOX 352, NORTH TERRACE, PENNESHAW
TEL (08) 8553 1028
FAX (08) 8553 1024
The resort overlooks a beach that has a colony of fairy penguins. Accommodations are in motel rooms or separate units and apartments.
🛈 27 🅿 60 📵 🚆 📶 All major cards

MURRAY RIVER

🏨🍴 **LOXTON HOTEL/MOTEL**
$
EAST TERRACE, LOXTON
TEL (08) 8584 7266
Basic rooms in the pub plus motel units. The bistro ($$) is very good.
🛈 55 🅿 30 📵 📵 🚆 📶 All major cards

🏨 **RENMARK HOTEL/MOTEL**
$
MURRAY AVE., RENMARK
TEL (08) 8586 6755
Carefully renovated three-story art deco hotel on the Murray River. There are counter meals, a good bistro ($$), and a dining room.
🛈 68 🅿 50 📧 📵 📵 🚆 📶 All major cards

KEY 🏨 Hotel 🍴 Restaurant 🛈 No. of bedrooms 🛏 No. of seats 🚆 Train/bus 🅿 Parking 🕐 Closed 📧 Elevator

VICTORIA

MELBOURNE:

DOWNTOWN

GRAND HYATT
$$$$$
123 COLLINS ST.
TEL (03) 9657 1234 OR
1-800 339 494 (TOLL FREE)
FAX (03) 9650 3491
Luxury hotel fitted out in
flamboyant style. Four floors
form the even more opulent
Regency Club. All rooms have
marble bathrooms and king-
size beds. Excellent service.
554 P ⬛ ⬛ ⬛ ⬛
⬛ ⬛ All major cards

THE ADELPHI
$$$$–$$$$$
187 FLINDERS LANE
TEL (03) 9650 7555
FAX (03) 9650 2710
This central hotel has a cool,
almost clinical style but is
nonetheless very comfortable.
The top floor has an unusual
jutting pool.
34 P ⬛ ⬛ ⬛ ⬛
⬛ All major cards

ROCKMAN'S REGENCY
$$$$–$$$$$
CORNER OF EXHIBITION &
LONSDALE STS.
TEL (03) 9662 3900 OR
1-800 331 118 (TOLL FREE)
FAX (03) 9663 4297
Luxury boutique hotel in the
heart of Melbourne. Spacious
rooms and suites, and lots of
pampering for guests.
180 P ⬛ ⬛ ⬛
⬛ ⬛ All major cards

SOMETHING SPECIAL

THE WINDSOR
Built in 1883, this elegant
National Trust property is an
Australian landmark. The
nation's Constitution was drafted
in one of its upstairs suites.
Stylishly restored, the hotel has
exemplary Old-World service

with modern charm. Afternoon
tea here is a special treat.
$$$$
103 SPRING ST.
TEL (03) 9633 6002
FAX (03) 9633 6001
180 P ⬛ ⬛ ⬛
⬛ All major cards

MARCHETTI'S LATIN
$$$$
55 LONSDALE ST.
TEL (03) 9662 1985
Very much a Melbourne
institution, this classy Italian
restaurant serves outstanding
food. Reservations essential.
150 P ⬛ Closed Sat. L
⬛ ⬛ ⬛ All major cards

FLOWER DRUM
$$$
17 MARKET LANE
TEL (03) 9662 3655
Elegant surroundings,
wonderful Cantonese food,
and a well-selected wine list.
Reservations essential.
175 ⬛ Closed Sun. L
⬛ ⬛ ⬛ All major cards

FLORENTINO
$$–$$$
80 BOURKE ST.
TEL (03)9662 1811
This is a Melbourne
institution, established for over
100 years, and serves
wonderful Italian cuisine for
any budget. The downstairs
grill dishes up homemade
pastas and good Italian coffee,
while those seeking more
elaborate fare can head
upstairs to the formal
restaurant.
260 ⬛ Closed Sun. & L
Sat. ⬛ ⬛ All major cards

MELBOURNE SUBURBS

**CHISLEY ON
FLEMINGTON**
$$$
5–17 FLEMINGTON RD.,
CARLTON
TEL (03) 9329 9344
FAX (03) 9328 4870
Friendly and just a few
minutes out of the central

business district, with well-
appointed Victorian-style
guest rooms.
225 P ⬛ ⬛ ⬛
⬛ All major cards

**ROBINSON'S BY
THE SEA**
$$–$$$
335 BEACONSFIELD PARADE,
ST. KILDA WEST
TEL/FAX (03) 9534 2683
A delightful house, one of the
best B&Bs in the area. Five
rooms share three
bathrooms.
5 P 1 ⬛ ⬛ All major
cards

THE TILBA
$$–$$$
30 TOORAK RD. W.,
SOUTH YARRA
TEL (03) 9867 8844
FAX (03) 9867 6567
Charming and filled with
antiques, the Tilba has a small
number of comfortable rooms.
Overlooks Fawkner Park.
15 ⬛ On request
⬛ Some ⬛ All major cards

CAFFÉ E CUCINA
$$$
581 CHAPEL ST., SOUTH YARRA
TEL (03) 9827 4139
It can be hard to get a table at
this split-level Italian café,
which is renowned for its
food. Reservations essential
upstairs.
45 ⬛ Closed Sun. ⬛
⬛ All major cards

GUERNICA
$$$
257 BRUNSWICK ST., FITZROY
TEL (03) 9416 0969
Dapper modern Australian
restaurant, with an imaginative
contemporary menu and
excellent wine list.
55 ⬛ Closed Sat. L ⬛
⬛ ⬛ All major cards

**O'CONNELL
CENTENARY**
$$$
MONTAGUE & COVENTRY
STS., SOUTH MELBOURNE
TEL. (03) 9699 9600

⬛ Non-smoking ⬛ Air-conditioning ⬛ Indoor/⬛ Outdoor swimming pool ⬛ Health club ⬛ Credit cards **KEY**

HOTELS & RESTAURANTS

French, Mediterranean, and Lebanese influences make for an interesting and very tasty menu. Reservations essential.
🛏 40 🅿 26 🕐 Closed Sat.–Sun. L & Sun.–Mon. D 🆂 🆂 All major cards

🍴 CHINTA RIA JAZZ
$$
176 COMMERCIAL RD., PRAHRAN
TEL (03) 9510 6520
This is a lively blend of Malaysian cuisine and jazz, in the heart of Prahran's restaurant district. It's very reasonably priced, too.
🛏 45 🆂 🆂 All major cards

OUTSIDE MELBOURNE:

MORNINGTON PENINSULA

🏨 ROTHSAYE ON LOVERS' WALK
$$
2 ROY COURT, COWES, PHILLIP ISLAND
TEL (03) 5952 2057
Romantic seaside cottage. No children.
🛏 2 suites + 1 cottage 🅿 🆂 AE, MC, V

WARRNAMBOOL

🏨 QUAMBY HOMESTEAD
$$
CARAMUT RD., WOOLSTHORPE
TEL (03) 5569 2395
The old homestead's staff quarters have been converted to guest rooms, set apart from the main building and country dining room (open to non-guests on weekends.) The basic rate includes breakfast. No children under 12.
🛏 6 🅿 🆂 🆂 All major cards

BALLARAT

🏨🍴 ANSONIA BOUTIQUE HOTEL
$$
32 LYDIARD ST., SOUTH BALLARAT
TEL (03) 5332 4678
FAX (03) 5332 4698
Delightful two-room apartments and studios. The restaurant serves tasty meals and snacks all day.
🛏 20 🅿 🆂 🆂 All major cards

ECHUCA

🏨 RIVER GALLERY INN
$$
578 HIGH ST.
TEL (03) 5480 6902
This renovated 19th-century building has spacious, comfortable rooms that have been decorated with considerable flair.
🛏 8 🅿 8 🆂 🆂 🆂 MC, V

🍴 OSCAR W'S
$–$$
OLD ECHUCA WHARF, ECHUCA
TEL (03) 5482 5133
This elegant restaurant is wonderfully situated on the town's historic wharf, overlooking a majestic gum-lined bend of the River Murray. The food is marvelous, the wine list superb, and, for a bit of fun, in the afternoons the kookaburras come down from their trees to be fed.
🛏 100 🆂 🆂 🆂 All major cards

MILDURA

🍴 STEFANO'S
🏨 **$$$$**
GRAND HOTEL RESORT, 7TH ST.
TEL (03) 5023 0511
Superb Italian cuisine and a fantastic wine list are offered up in the century-old hotel's wine cellar. The set menu

makes the very best of fresh, local produce.
🛏 60 🕐 Closed L, & Sun. 🆂 🆂 All major cards

TASMANIA

HOBART

🏨 GRAND CHANCELLOR HOTEL
$$$$–$$$$$
BOX 1601, 1 DAVEY ST.
TEL (03) 6235 4535 or 1-800 625 138 (TOLL FREE)
FAX (03) 6223 8175
Luxury hotel on the wharf, with well-appointed, spacious guest rooms.
🛏 234 🅿 150 🆂 🆂 🆂 🆂 All major cards

🏨 ISLINGTON ELEGANT PRIVATE HOTEL
$$$
321 DAVEY ST.
TEL (03) 6223 3900
FAX (03) 6234 9053
There are just suites at this converted 19th-century mansion. Beautiful gardens compete with a fine view of Mount Wellington. Breakfast included.

KEY   🏨 Hotel   🍴 Restaurant   ① No. of bedrooms   🛏 No. of seats   🚂 Train/bus   🅿 Parking   🕐 Closed   🛗 Elevator

[f]8 [P]8 [S] [pool] [All]
major cards

LENNA OF HOBART
$$$
20 RUNNYMEDE ST.,
BATTERY POINT
TEL (03) 6232 3900
FAX (03) 6224 0112
A 19th-century building with
old-world charm, and a
reputation for excellent
cuisine at **Alexander's**
restaurant (see below).
[f]50 [P]50 [bed] [S]
[All] major cards

COLVILLE COTTAGE
$$
32 MONA ST.
TEL (03) 6223 6968
FAX (03) 6224 0500
This pretty cottage with a
white-picket fence has six
comfortable private rooms.
[f]6 [P]3 [S] [S]
[MC, V]

ALEXANDER'S
$$
LENNA OF HOBART HOTEL,
20 RUNNYMEDE ST.,
BATTERY POINT
TEL (03) 6232 3900
Beautifully presented dishes,
perhaps the best cooking
on the island, from an
international menu. Business
attire. Reservations essential.
[f]35 [P] [clock] Closed L [S]
[All] major cards

MURES UPPER DECK RESTAURANT
$$
VICTORIA DOCK
TEL (03) 6231 1999
Excellent seafood in a great
waterfront location.
[f]150 [P]40 [S] [All]
major cards

RIVIERA RISTORANTE
$$
15 HUNTER ST.,
SULLIVAN'S COVE
TEL (03) 6234 3230
A popular restaurant where
you can expect to wait for a
table. Mainly pizza and pasta

dishes, and very tasty too.
[f]100 [P]100 [clock] Closed
Sat.–Wed. L & Sun. D [S]
[All] major cards

LAUNCESTON

COUNTRY CLUB CASINO
$$$$
COUNTRY CLUB AVE.,
PROSPECT VALE
TEL (03) 6335 5777 OR
1-800 030 211 (TOLL FREE)
FAX (03) 6343 1880
Set in manicured gardens, this
luxury club and casino has
lots of amenities, including
one of the best golf courses
in Australia. The club is home
to the formal Terrace
Restaurant.
[f]104 [P] [bed] [S] [S]
[pool] [health] [All] major cards

PRINCE ALBERT INN
$$–$$$
TAMAR & WILLIAM STS.
TEL (03) 6331 1931
The comfortable guest rooms
have furnishings to match the
inn's opulent Victorian style.
[f]22 [P]18 [S] [S] Some
[All] major cards

FEE & ME
$$
190 CHARLES ST.
TEL (03) 6331 3195
Good Tasmanian wines
accompany an imaginative
Asian and Mediterranean
influenced menu, in 19th-
century surroundings.
Business attire.
[f]65 [clock] Closed L & Sun. D
[S] [All] major cards

OLD BAKERY INN
$
YORK & MARGARET STS.
TEL (03) 6331 7900 OR
1-800 641 264 (TOLL FREE)
FAX (03) 6331 7756
Nicely decorated rooms
occupy the converted bakery,
the baker's cottage, and the
stable block.
[f]24 [P]24 [All] major
cards

REST OF TASMANIA:

CRADLE MOUNTAIN

CRADLE MOUNTAIN LODGE
$$$
BOX 153, SHEFFIELD
TEL (03) 6492 1303
FAX (03) 6492 1309
Simple cabins, each with
woodburning heater and small
kitchen. The basic rate is for
room only—though you can
dine here at extra cost.
[f]96 [P]60 [S] [All]
major cards

FREYCINET NATIONAL PARK

FREYCINET LODGE
$$$
COLES BAY
TEL (03) 6257 0101
FAX (03) 6257 0278
Environmentally sensitive
resort of private cabins (with
one or two bedrooms)
overlooking Great Oyster Bay.
The basic rate is for room
only. You can dine on the
premises at the Freycinet
Restaurant, with fine views
and seafood.
[f]60 [P]60 [S] [All]
major cards

[S] Non-smoking [S] Air-conditioning [pool] Indoor/[pool] Outdoor swimming pool [health] Health club [cards] Credit cards   **KEY**

SHOPPING IN AUSTRALIA

There is never any shortage of kitsch offerings for tourists in Australia. Everything from stuffed koalas, made-in-Taiwan boomerangs, insulated beer-can holders (usually adorned with off-color blokey jokes), plastic kangaroos, coasters, and tacky T-shirts can be found in garish little shops from coast to coast. Most Aussie souvenirs—even the little Australian flags waved on Anzac Day—tend to be made somewhere in Asia. Happily, finding something a bit more tasteful, memorable, and authentic to take back home is fairly easy.

ABORIGINAL ART

Powerful and unique, Aboriginal art has become a highly prized commodity in the art world with prices for significant works by top artists stretching into the tens of thousands of dollars. Sadly, big money and the fact that few laymen have a good understanding of Aboriginal art have drawn a lot of hucksters into the business. Consequently, buying Aboriginal art can be tricky. Your best bet is to stick to Aboriginal-owned and operated galleries or, if you are actually visiting remote communities, to buy directly from the artists themselves.

The kinds of pieces offered vary from bark paintings to boomerangs, wood carvings, textiles, pottery, and didgeridoos. Good pieces will not be cheap, but then fine art never is. Expect to pay in the neighborhood of $A200 (U.S.$100) (and up!) for a nice didgeridoo, for example. Some Aboriginal-owned galleries include:

Darwin
Raintree Aboriginal Art Gallery
18 Knuckey St.
Tel (08) 8981 2732

Uluru
Maruku Arts and Crafts
Uluru-Kata Tjuta Cultural Centre
Tel (08) 8956 2153

Kakadu
Injalak Arts and Crafts
Oenpelli
Tel (08) 8979 0190
Alice Springs

DESART
Suite 1, Heenan Building
Gregory Terrace
Tel (08) 8953 4736
Represents a number of other Aboriginal-owned galleries in central Australia and can put you in contact with reputable dealers.

If you are not going into the Outback and still want to purchase Aboriginal art, try:

Sydney
Aboriginal and Tribal Art Centre
Level 1, 117 George St.
The Rocks
Tel (02) 9247 9625

Melbourne
Aboriginal Gallery of Dreamings
73–77 Bourke St.
Tel (03) 9650 7291
There are other reputable dealers, of course, as well. It is worth asking around.

ARTS & CRAFTS

Australia is rich in talent and visitors can find interesting galleries and craft shops across the continent, from Byron Bay in the east to Margaret River in Western Australia to Salamanca Place in Hobart.

One of Australia's most commercially successful artists is Ken Done, who has marketed his bright, color-splashed paintings into a very popular line of merchandise with a chain of galleries in Sydney and along the Queensland coast. Disdained by Australia's serious art com-

munity, Done is revered abroad, particularly in Japan where exhibitions of his work draws huge crowds. Some of his galleries are:

Sydney
The Ken Done Gallery
1–5 Hickson Rd.
The Rocks
Tel (02) 9247 2740

Gold Coast
The Ken Done Gallery
34 Orchid Ave.
Surfers Paradise
Tel (07) 5592 1282

Cairns
Done Art & Design
4 Spence St.
Tel (07) 4031 5592

In Adelaide the Jam Factory offers exceptionally fine glass, ceramics, wood, textile, and jewelry made by some of Australia's finest artisans.

Jam Factory Contemporary Art & Design
19 Morphett St., tel (08) 8231 0005; and 94 Gawler Place, tel (08) 8223 6809.

CLOTHING

Australia has some stylish Outback clothing outfitters and, although they are starting to make their mark overseas, their roots are still firmly in the Outback, making reliable gear for stockmen, farmers, and stationhands as they have for generations. If you want authenticity, and to get some excellent clothes in the bargain, start from the ground up with a pair of R.M. Williams boots or the Tasmanian-made Blundstone boots.

The South Australian-based **R.M. Williams** has been making boots and saddlery equipment for Outback stockmen and riders since the 1930s. Their kangaroo leather boots are incredibly soft and fit like a glove. The company is also justly famous for its tough moleskin trousers and fashionable outdoor clothing. Its gear is readily available in all cities.

In Sydney the main store is
R.M. Williams
389 George St.
Tel (02) 9262 2228

In Melbourne
R.M. Williams
The Shot Tower, Shop 229
Melbourne Central
300 Lonsdale St.
Tel (03) 9663 7126

Or visit the company's website (www.rmwilliams.com.au) for further details on outlets around Australia (and overseas).

Blundstone boots have been a working class icon since they were first produced in 1870 but lately have been getting a worldwide cachet, popping up as fashion musts on the streets of London and New York. For information on stores contact the company's Hobart office, tel (03) 6272 3000.

Although Australia is reckoned the world's driest inhabited continent, some of the world's best wet-weather gear is produced here. Both R.M. Williams and **Thomas Cook,** another long-established outfitter, make excellent oilskins, but the old classic stockman's oilskin is made by the Queensland-based **Driza-bone,** which has been making them for more than a century. They are widely available around Australia. Information on retailers can be reached at tel 1-800 773 800 (toll free) or by e-mail at: drizagpo@drizabone.com.au.

To round off the *Man from Snowy River* look and to ward off the fierce Australian sun, slap on an **Akubra** hat. Ruggedly made out of rabbit fur felt, these hats are beloved by generations of bushmen who use them for everything from carrying water

to picking up a hot billy out of a campfire. They even wear them on their heads. These too are widely available. Consult the company's website at: www.akubra.com.au

Other quintessentially Australian labels are Explorer socks, Stubby shorts, Holeproof underwear, and Chesty Bonds T-shirts and singlets. These can be found in most department stores.

OPALS

Australia has 95 percent of the world's supplies of opal. Most of it is found in Outback South Australia, near the town of Coober Pedy, with the New South Wales town of Lightning Ridge and the South Australian town of Andamooka accounting for much of the rest.

Almost every jeweler and souvenir shop in Australia seems to offer opals in one form or another, with special tax free prices for tourists.

As with any precious stone, there are a number of factors that go into determining the value of an opal, such as clarity, color, and pattern. The first criteria is the base color of the stone. A black opal is the most valuable, followed by a crystal (or almost transparent) opal, with milky opals bringing up the rear. The next thing to look for is the dominant color. Red-fire opal is the most valuable, followed by green, then blue. The pattern of colors on the stone is also important in determining its value. Harlequin opal, in which the colors are in large defined patches, is the most sought after. Pinfire opal, with its thousands of tiny specks of color, is generally less valuable.

The stones themselves come in three grades. The most valuable is solid opal, followed by doublets (a two-part stone consisting of precious opal glued to another, less valuable opal),

then triplets (a three-part stone with a core of precious opal, a backing of a less valuable stone and a transparent top piece). Accurately assessing opal is a job for experts. Stick to reputable jewelers, shop around, and compare prices.

In Sydney the following shops offer more than most:

Gemtec
51 Pitt St. (corner of Dalley St.)
Tel (02) 9251 1599
Stocks opal jewelry and loose opals. They are unusual in mining and cutting their own stones, and have a shop front cutting and polishing room where visitors may watch the progress from raw opal to opal ring.

Opal Fields
155 George St., The Rocks
Tel (02) 9264 6660
Australian opal stones and jewelry featuring the collections of seven designers. Also a museum of opal fossils and specimens.

WINE

Australia is justifiably famous for its bold, fruity, and well-crafted wines but with approximately 1,000 different winemakers around the country—even one in the desert near Alice Springs! —navigating so many unknown labels can be a little confusing for visitors. A number of useful guides are on the market, one of the best being the Penguin *Good Australian Wine Guide* which is available in most bookstores.

The major wine districts have helpful visitor centers:
Hunter Valley (see pp. 110–11)
Margaret River (see pp. 226–27)
Barossa Valley (see pp. 266–67)
McClaren Vale, Clare Valley, and Coonawarra (see pp. 264–65)

ACTIVITIES IN AUSTRALIA

Australia's sunny climate and open-air lifestyle lend themselves to a huge range of activities for visitors. Plan your holiday carefully and book ahead if you are specific about what you want to do. Otherwise, find help at a visitor information center. They will be able to tell you of the local possibilities, and probably book you a suitable option on the spot.

CAMEL TREKKING
Experience Outback Australia as the original explorers did: from the back of a dromedary. Noel Fullerton's **Camel Outback Safaris** in Alice Springs (Tel (08) 8553 9119) is one of the best established operators and offers single day treks to the ancient gorges of Rainbow Valley in the Northern Territory.

In South Australia's Flinders Ranges, the **Outback Camel Company** (Tel (08) 9543 2280) offers anything from hour-long treks to three-week expeditions in the Simpson Desert.

CRUISING
Queensland's idyllic Whitsunday Islands are one of the world's most beautiful places for yachts and cruising. For those who like to do-it-themselves, charter boats can be arranged through an information center called **Destination Whitsunday,** in Airlie Beach, tel 1-800 644 563.

Tour operators offer day-long and multi-day sailing cruises, some on well-known racing yachts of the past. Among them are:

Gretel, veteran America's Cup campaigner
Tel (07) 4946 7529
Maxi Ragamuffin
Tel (07) 4946 7777
Apollo of Sydney–Hobart Yacht Race fame
Tel 1-800 635 334

DIVING
Exploring the Great Barrier Reef is a highlight of a visit to tropical Queensland, and if you do not know how to dive there are numerous diving schools all along the Queensland coast eager to teach you, and some of the world's finest coral reefs in which to learn. As with anything, it is wise to shop around and be wary of cut-rate operators. Expect to pay in the neighbor-hood of $A400 (U.S.$200) for a five-day open-water certification course.

Cairns has a reputation for being the reef's diving capital, as well as typically being the first port-of-call for Great Barrier Reef visitors. A list of a few long-standing operators includes:
Deep Sea Divers Den
Tel (07) 4031 2223
Pro Dive Tel (07) 4031 5255
Tusa Dive Tel (07) 4031 1248
Airlie Beach and Townsville are other popular dive-school locations.

If you are already a certified diver, or simply want to do some snorkeling on the reef, finding a boat to take out to the reef is about as difficult as finding a casino in Las Vegas. They come in all shapes and sizes, from gleaming catamarans to yachts to powerboats, and cater to all budgets. Trips last from a day to several days.
Falla, tel (07) 4031 3488, and the above-mentioned **Tusa Dive** are two well-established operators in Cairns, but there are many others.

Good diving can be found in other locations, of course, from Ningaloo Reef in Western Australia to the wrecks scattered around Tasmania's King Island. Consult local tourist authorities for advice and recommendations.

FOUR-WHEEL-DRIVE SAFARIS
The Cape York Peninsula, the Northern Territory, and Western Australia's rugged and remote Kimberley offer some of Australia's best Outback adventuring. Four-wheel-drive vehicles are necessary to get into the wildest and most interesting regions and if you don't care to risk the driving yourself, numerous outfitters from Cairns to Darwin, Alice Springs, and Broome, will take you. Standards vary, so shop around and consult local tourist authorities. One well-established outfitter is Cairns-based **Wilderness Challenge** (Tel (07) 4055 6504 or e-mail: info@wilderness-challenge .com.au), which leads treks to the Tip of Cape York and through the heart of the Kimberley.

SURFING
Right from the moment Hawaiian surfer Duke Kahanomoku brought surfing to Australia (at Sydney's Freshwater Beach) in 1915, riding the breakers that roll into the island continent's 24,000 miles of coastline has been an Australian passion.

If you do not know how to surf, but would like to learn, there are plenty of surfing schools to teach you. Enquire at the local tourist information office or at surf and dive shops.

New South Wales: One of the best known beaches is Bondi (see pp. 96–97), but Manly and Sydney's other northern beaches offer good surf too. South of Sydney probably the best is at Cronulla. Byron Bay, on the NSW north coast, is another very popular surfing hangout.

Southern Queensland: A string of surfing beaches stretches along the Gold Coast. As well as Surfers Paradise, try Burleigh Heads or Kirra. The Sunshine Coast also has good surfing right up to Noosa Heads.

Western Australia: You'll find some great surf around Margaret River, about 140 miles (224 km) south of Perth.

South Australia: The best known surfing beach in South Australia is far-flung Cactus Beach, west of Ceduna. There are more convenient places on both the east and west sides of the Fleurieu Peninsula.

Victoria: The Bells Easter Classic competition is held on Bells Beach, near Torquay on the spectacular Great Ocean Road, about 100 miles southwest of Melbourne. Wilsons Promontory and the ocean side of the Mornington Peninsula also offer good surfing.

Tasmania: There is good surf around Marrawah on the west coast and the beaches near St Helens are just some of the surfing locations on the east coast, but the water round the island is cold.

WHITE-WATER RAFTING

Australia may be the world's driest inhabited continent, but when the rivers run here they really run, with Tasmania, the Snowy Mountains, and the jungle-clad mountains near Cairns offering exhilarating wild water. Two of the better known wilderness operators are:

World Expeditions
441 Kent St., Sydney
Tel 1-800 803 688

Peregrine Tours
38 York St., Sydney
Tel (02) 9290 2770

By far the most remote and wildest rafting option is on Tasmania's Franklin River, a challenging two-week-long trek through some of the most remote wilderness on the planet. Both of the above operators run expeditions on the Franklin.

FURTHER INFORMATION

Below is a list of organizations to contact for information about specific activities.

Bird-watching
Royal Australasian Ornithologists Union
415 Riversdale Rd.
Hawthorn East, Vic.
Tel (03) 9882 2622

Canoeing
Australian Canoeing Inc.
Room 308
Wentworth Park GC, Wattle St.
Ultimo, NSW 2007
Tel (02) 9552 4500
Fax (02) 9552 4457

Cycling
Australian Cycling Federation Inc., 14 Telopea Ave.
Homebush, NSW 2140
Tel (02) 9764 2555
Fax (02) 9764 2888

Diving
Australian Diving Association
Corner of Tilley & Old Cleveland Rds.
Chandler, Qld. 4155
Tel (07) 3823 1444
Fax (07) 3823 1363

Ecotourism
For information on nature-based holidays:
Ecotourism Association of Australia
P.O. Box 26
Red Hill, Qld 4059
Tel (07) 3352 7220

Fishing
Australian Recreational & Sport Fishing Industry Confederation,
ACT Sports House
100 Maitland St.
Hackett, ACT 2602
Tel (02) 6257 1997
Fax (02) 6247 9314

Golf
Australian Golf Union
153–155 Cecil St.
South Melbourne, Vic. 3205
Tel (03) 9699 7944
Fax (03) 9690 8510

Sailing
Australian Yachting Federation
33 Peel St.
Kirribilli, NSW 2061
Tel (02) 9922 4333

Skiing
Skiing Australia Ltd., Level 2
Alpine House, 120 Collins St.
Melbourne, Vic. 3000
Tel (03) 9650 8666
Fax (03) 9650 8737

Surfing
Surfing Australia Inc., Level 2
Old Burleigh Theatre Arcade
Goodwin Terrace
Burleigh, Qld. 4220
Tel (07) 5520 1501
Fax (07) 5520 1288

Tennis
National Tennis Centre
Melbourne Park
Batman Ave.
Melbourne, Vic. 3000
Tel (03) 9286 1177
Fax (03) 9650 2743

Trout fishing
Tasmania is known for its trout fishing (see pp. 352–53). For a trout-fishing package, contact the London Lakes Fly Fishing Lodge:
Fly Fishers Lodge
P.O. Bronte Park
Tasmania 7040
Tel (03) 6289 1159
Fax (03) 6289 1122
U.S. tel 800/528-6129 or 800/245-1950

ILLUSTRATIONS CREDITS

Cover: (tl,tr) Tony Stone Images; (bl) James Davis Travel Photography; (br) PowerStock/Zefa Photo Library. 1, Corbis/Burstein Collection. 2/3, Corbis/Roger Ressmeyer. 4, Corbis/Dave G. Houser. 9, John Kleczkowski/Lochman Transparencies. 11, Jean-Paul Ferrero/Auscape. 12/13 PowerStock/Zefa Photo Library. 14, Jean-Paul Ferrero/Auscape. 16/17, Jeff Carter Films Pty Ltd. 18, Medford Taylor/National Geographic Society. 18/19, Sorrel Wilby/ Australian Geographic. 20, Carolyn Johns/Wildlight. 23, R. Ian Lloyd. 24/25, Thad Samuels Abell/National Geographic Society. 27, Jiri Lochman/ Lochman Transparencies. 28/29, Jiri Lochman/Lochman Transparencies. 30, Corbis/Penny Tweedie. 32 (l), Hulton Getty Picture Collection Ltd. 32 (r), Hulton Getty Picture Collection Ltd. 34, Coo-ee Picture Library. 36/37, Michael Jensen/Auscape. 38, Image Library, State Library of New South Wales. 38/39, National Library of Australia, Canberra/ Bridgeman Art Library. 40, Mary Evans Picture Library. 41(t), Hulton Getty Picture Collection Ltd. 41(b), Mary Evans Picture Library. 42, Coo-ee Picture Library. 44/45, National Library of Australia, Canberra/ Bridgeman Art Library. 47, Hulton Getty Picture Collection Ltd. 49, David Moore/Wildlight. 50/51, Jean-Paul Ferrero/Auscape. 52/53, Medford Taylor/National Geographic Society. 55, Lorrie Graham/Wildlight. 56, Carolyn Johns/Coo-ee Picture Library. 57, Corbis/Paul A. Souders. 58, Australian Tourist Commission. 60, AA Photo Library/A. Baker. 62, Courbally Stourton Contemporary Art, London/ Bridgeman Art Library. 63, Charles Meere "Australian beach pattern," 1940 oil on canvas, 90.1x120.7cm The Art Gallery of New South Wales. 64, Parer & Parer-Cook/Ardea. 66, Jean-Paul Ferrero/ Auscape. 67, L. Hugh Newman/NHPA. 68, Medford Taylor/National Geographic Society. 69, Jiri Lochman/ Lochman Transparencies. 70, Kevin Deacon/Auscape. 71, Corbis/Paul A. Souders. 73, AA Photo Library/Steve Day. 75, Ron Ryan/Coo-ee Picture Library. 76/77, AA Photo Library/ Steve Day. 78/79, Jean-Paul Ferrero/ Auscape. 82 Phillip Quirk/Wildlight. 84/85, AA Photo Library/P. Kenward. 86, AA Photo Library/Steve Day. 87(t), Opera Australia. 87(b), Grenville Turner/Wildlight. 88, AA Photo Library/Steve Day. 89, Ron Ryan/ Coo-ee Picture Library. 90, Ben

Radford/Allsport (UK) Ltd. 91, Dave Cannon/Allsport (UK) Ltd. 92, Greg Hard/Wildlight. 93, AA Photo Library/ Steve Day. 95, Tom Keating/Wildlight. 96/97, Jean-Paul Ferrero/Auscape. 97, Jean-Paul Ferrero/Auscape. 98, Jamie Squire/Allsport (UK) Ltd. 99t Adam Pretty/Allsport (UK) Ltd. 99b Mark Dadswell/Allsport (UK) Ltd. 100, AA Photo Library/Steve Day. 101, David W. Harding/Auscape. 103, AA Photo Library/Paul Kennard. 105, Brett Gregory/Auscape. 106/7, Jean-Paul Ferrero/Auscape. 107, AFP/Popperfoto. 108, Brett Gregory/ Auscape. 109, Tom Keating/ Wildlight. 110/111, Mike Langford/ Auscape.111, Australian Tourist Commission. 112/13, Brett Gregory/ Auscape. 114/15, Nolen Oayda/Wildlight. 117, Spectrum Colour Library. 118, Marie Lochman/Lochman Transparencies. 119(t), Ron Ryan/ Coo-ee Picture Library. 119(c), Nature Photographers. 119(b), Hunter Valley Wine Country Tourism. 120/21 Jean-Paul Ferrero/ Auscape. 123, Mike Langford/Auscape. 124/25, Mike Langford/Auscape. 127, Australian Tourist Commission. 128, Steve Nebauer/Auscape. 130/31, Michael Jensen/Auscape. 132, Tim Acker/ Auscape. 133, Jean-Paul Ferrero/ Auscape. 134/35, Matt Jones/Auscape. 135, Ron Ryan/Coo-ee Picture Library. 136, C. Andrew Henley/Auscape. 137, Tony Stone Images. 139, AA Photo Library/A. Baker. 140, Australian Tourist Commission. 142/43, Power-Stock/Zefa Photo Library. 144, Jean-Marc La Roque/Auscape. 145, Brett Dennis/ Lochman Transparencies. 146/47, Jean-Paul Ferrero/Auscape. 148/49, Mark Lang/Wildlight. 150(t), Australian Tourist Commission. 150(b), Coo-ee Picture Library. 151, AA Photo Library/A. Baker. 152,Coo-ee Picture Library. 152/53, Jean-Paul Ferrero/ Auscape. 154, Corbis/Paul A. Souders. 155 (t), Mark Spencer/Auscape. 155 (b) Corbis/Stuart Westmorland. 158, Becca Saunders/Auscape. 159, David Parer & Elizabeth Parer-Cook/Auscape. 160/61, Peter & Margy Nicholas/ Lochman Transparencies. 163, Greg Hard/Wildlight. 164/65, Jean-Paul Ferrero/Auscape 166, Tim Acker/ Auscape. 167, Robert Harding Picture Library. 168/69, Jaime Plaza Van Roon/Auscape. 170, Thad Samuels Abell/National Geographic Society. 171, Thad Samuels Abell/National Geographic Society. 173, Michael Jensen/Auscape. 174, Ron Ryan/Coo-ee Picture Library. 175, Jean-Paul Ferrero/Auscape. 176/77, Peter Jarver/ Wildscape Aust-ralia. 177, Thad Samuels Abell/Nat-ional Geographic Society. 178, Ian Courtney Australian Butterfly Sanctuary. 179, S. Wilby &

C. Ciantar/ Auscape. 182, Peter Jarver/ Wildscape Australia. 184, Peter Jarver/ Wildscape Australia. 185, Peter Jarver/Wildscape Australia. 186/87, Jean-Paul Ferrero/ Auscape. 187, Dennis Sarson/Lochman Transparencies. 188, Dennis Sarson/Lochman Tran-sparencies. 190, Frank Woerle/Auscape. 191, Dennis Sarson/Lochman Transparencies. 192, Dennis Sarson/ Lochman Transparencies. 192/93, S. Wilby & C. Ciantar/Auscape. 195, Col Roberts/ Lochman Transparencies. 196/97, Philip Quirk/Wildlight. 199, James Davis Travel Photography. 201(t), Michael Jensen/Auscape. 201(bl), Dennis Sarson/Lochman Transparen-cies. 201(br), Mike Gillam/Auscape. 202/203, John Shaw/Auscape. 204, Corbis/Paul A. Souders. 205, S. Wilby & C. Ciantar/Auscape. 207, Jean-Paul Ferrero/Auscape. 208, Dennis Sarson/ Lochman Transparencies. 209, Jiri Lochman/Lochman Transparencies. 214, PowerStock/Zefa Photo Library. 215, Coo-ee Picture Library. 216, Dennis Sarson/Lochman Transpar-encies. 217, Western Australia Tourism Commission. 218, Jean-Paul Ferrero/ Auscape. 219, Jean-Paul Ferrero/ Auscape. 220, Marie Lochman/ Lochman Transparencies. 220, Jiri Lochman/Lochman Transparencies. 221, Marie Lochman/Lochman Transparencies. 222(t) Debi Wagner Stock Pics Garden & Wildlife Matters Photographic Library. 222(b) Debi Wagner Stock Pics Garden & Wildlife Matters Photographic Library. 222/223, Dennis Sarson/Lochman Transparencies. 224/25, Jiri Lochman/ Lochman Transparencies. 225, Dennis Sarson/Lochman Transparencies. 226/227 Tom Keating/Wildlight. 228/29, Bill Belsen/Lochman Trans-parencies. 230/31, G. Saueracker/ Auscape. 233, Mike Langford/Auscape. 234/35, Jean-Paul Ferrero/Auscape. 236, 237, Australian Tourist Commission. 238/39, PowerStock/ Zefa Photo Library. 240, Milton Wordley/ Wildlight. 241, Jiri Lochman/ Lochman Transparencies. 242/43, Image Library, State Library of New South Wales. 244/45, Ron Ryan/Coo-ee Picture Library. 246,Western Australia Tourism Commission. 247, Jean-Paul Ferrero/Auscape. 249, Milton Wordley/ Wildlight. 254, Jean-Marc La Roque/ Auscape. 257, South Australia Tour-pism Commission. 259, Ron Ryan/ Coo-ee Picture Library. 260/61, Jean-Paul Ferrero/ Auscape. 263(tl), H. Brooks Walker/ National Geographic Society. 263(tr), Image Library, State Library of New South Wales. 263(b), Philip Quirk /Wildlight. 264/65, Milton Wordley/ Wildlight. 266, Jean-Paul Ferrero/ Auscape. 267, Jean-Paul

Published by the National Geographic Society

John M. Fahey, Jr., *President and Chief Executive Officer*
Gilbert M. Grosvenor, *Chairman of the Board*
Nina D. Hoffman, *Executive Vice President,*
President, Books and School Publishing
William R. Gray, *Vice President and Director, Book Division*
David Griffin, *Design Director*
Elizabeth L. Newhouse, *Director of Travel Publishing*
Barbara A. Noe, *Senior Editor and Project Manager*
Caroline Hickey, *Senior Researcher*
Carl Mehler, *Director of Maps*
Victoria Garrett Jones, *Editorial Consultant*
Gary Colbert, *Production Director*
Ric Wain, *Production Project Manager*
DeShelle Downey, *Contributor*

Edited and designed by AA Publishing (a trading name of Automobile Association Developments Limited, whose registered office is Norfolk House, Priestley Road, Basingstoke, Hampshire, England RG24 9NY. Registered number: 1878835).

Betty Sheldrick, *Project Manager*
David Austin, *Senior Art Editor*
Josephine Perry, *Editor*
Jo Tapper, *Designer*
Simon Mumford, *Senior Cartographic Editor*
Nicky Barker-Dix, Helen Beever, *Cartographers*
Richard Firth, *Production Director*
Picture Research by Zooid Pictures Ltd.
Drive maps drawn by Chris Orr Associates, Southampton, England
Cutaway illustrations drawn by Maltings Partnership, Derby, England
Great Barrier Reef illustrations drawn by Ann Winterbotham

Reprinted with revisions 2001.

Library of Congress Cataloging-in- Publication Data

Smith, Ross Martin
    National Geographic Traveler. Australia
          p   cm
      Includes index.
      ISBN 0-7922-7431-8 (alk. paper)
      1. Australia—Guidebooks. 1. National Geographic Society (U.S.)
11. Title: Australia
DC16.N37 1999
914.404'839—dc21   98-54974
                             CIP

Printed and bound by R.R. Donnelley & Sons, Willard, Ohio.
Color separations by Leo Reprographic Ltd, Hong Kong
Cover separations by L.C. Repro, Aldermaston, U.K.
Cover printed by Miken Inc., Cheektowaga, New York.

Visit the society's Web site at www.nationalgeographic.com

NATIONAL GEOGRAPHIC
TRAVELER

A Century of Travel Expertise in Every Guide

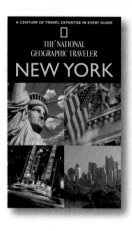
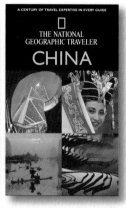
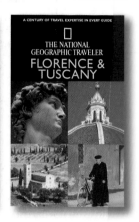